Here's what people are sayi
Beyond Trauma: Conversations on Traur
2nd Edition

"Beyond Trauma: Conversations on Traumatic Incident l   ....ent resource
to begin one's mastery in this area of practice."
> —Michael G. Tancyus, LCSW, DCSW, Augusta Behavioral Health

"I have found Beyond Trauma to be *exceptionally helpful* in understanding and practicing TIR in broad and diverse areas of practice, not just in traditional trauma work. The information from various points of view is really priceless."
> —Gerry Bock, Registered Clinical Counselor, B.C. Canada

"Beyond Trauma offers PTSD sufferers a glimpse at a light at the end of the tunnel, while providing mental health workers with a revolutionary technique that could increase their success rate with traumatized clients." —Jeni Mayer, Body Mind Spirit Magazine

"Having read the book, I feel that I have already become better at working with distressed clients."   —Bob Rich, Ph.D., author and therapist

"When I read this book, I found myself thinking of numerous people who might be helped by the therapy and strongly recommend this book to anyone involved in helping those suffering from PTSD, phobias or other trauma related problems."
> —Susan M. Phillips, Spiralthreads Reviews, UK

"My kudos go to Editor Victor Volkman, who took on the task of reaching more than 25 people to contribute to the book, including interviews with many of them."
> —Edith Henderson Grotberg, Ph.D. for *International Psychologist*

"Beyond Trauma outlines the elements with clarity and insight as to how TIR will resolve wrestling with dilemmas, understanding your demons, and climbing out of a whirlwind of emptiness."   —Sherry Russell, Grief Management Specialist and author

"Our staff therapist is finding Beyond Trauma very helpful."
> —Joan M. Renner, Director, Sexual Assault Program, Clark County YWCA

"Beyond Trauma is a recommended book for the professional or for the lay reader who wants to know about this technique before possibly seeking out a practitioner."
> —Harold McFarland, Readers Preference Reviews

Beyond Trauma offers insight and positive suggestions for mental health professionals working with children, veterans, crime victims and the family members supporting them.
> — Carolyn Harris, school psychologist

Explorations in Metapsychology Series:

- *Beyond Trauma: Conversations on Traumatic Incident Reduction, 2nd Edition* Ed. by Victor R. Volkman

- *Life Skills: Improve the Quality of Your Life with Metapsychology* by Marian K. Volkman

- *AMI/TIRA Newsletter Vols. 1-2: Selected Reprints 2004-2005* Edited by Victor R. Volkman

- *TIR and Metapsychology Lecture Series (MP3 CD)* with Frank A. Gerbode, M.D. et. al.

- *Traumatic Incident Reduction, 2nd Edition* by Gerald French and Chrys Harris

Series Editor: Robert Rich, Ph.D.

"To be what we are,
and to become what we are capable of becoming,
is the only end in life"

—Robert Louis Stevenson (June 1880)

Loving Healing Press is dedicated to producing books about innovative and rapid therapies which redefine what is possible for healing the mind and spirit.

Loving Healing Press

BEYOND

CONVERSATIONS ON TRAUMATIC INCIDENT REDUCTION

TRAUMA

EDITED BY VICTOR R. VOLKMAN

Loving Healing Press

Beyond Trauma: Conversations on Traumatic Incident Reduction

First Edition: January 2004 (ISBN-10 193269000X)
Second Edition: March 2005 (ISBN-10 1932690042)   2nd Printing: August 2005

Library of Congress Cataloging-in-Publication Data

Volkman, Victor R.
    Beyond trauma : conversations on traumatic incident reduction / edited by Victor R. Volkman.
    p. cm.
    Includes index.
    ISBN 1932690042

1. Post traumatic stress disorder--Treatment. 2. Post-traumatic stress disorder--Treatment--Anecdotes. 3. Psychic trauma--Treatment--Anecdotes. I. Title

RC552.P67 V656 2004
616.8521--dd22   2004098548

Distributed by:
Baker & Taylor, Ingram Book Group

Published by:
Loving Healing Press
5145 Pontiac Trail
Ann Arbor, MI 48105
USA

http://www.LovingHealing.com or
info@LovingHealing.com
Fax +1 734 663 6861

Loving Healing Press

This book is dedicated to the professional trainers of the Traumatic Incident Reduction Association (TIRA) for showing the world what is possible.

"If I have seen further,
it is by standing on the shoulders of giants"

— Sir Isaac Newton (Feb. 5th, 1676)

About our Series Editor, Robert Rich, Ph.D.

Loving Healing Press is pleased to announce Robert Rich, Ph.D. as Series Editor for the *Explorations in Metapsychology Series*. This exciting new series plans to bring you the best of Metapsychology in practical application, theory, and self-help formats.

Robert Rich, M.Sc., Ph.D., M.A.P.S., A.A.S.H. is a highly experienced counseling psychologist. His web site www.anxietyanddepression-help.com is a storehouse of helpful information for people suffering from almost any way we can make ourselves and each other unhappy.

Bob is also a multiple award-winning writer of both fiction and non-fiction, and a professional editor. His writing is displayed at www.bobswriting.com. You are advised not to visit him there unless you have the time to get lost for a while.

Two of his books are tools for psychological self-help: *Anger and Anxiety: Be in charge of your emotions and control phobias* and *Personally Speaking: Single session email therapy with Dr Bob Rich*. However, his philosophy and psychological knowledge come through in all his writing, which is perhaps why three of his books have won international awards, and he has won many minor prizes. Dr. Rich currently resides in Wombat Hollow in Australia.

Acknowledgments

My first and primary debt is to Frank A. Gerbode, M.D. Much of the background source material comes from his work as the former Director of the Institute for Research in Metapsychology. His work in establishing Applied Metapsychology has been a beacon to many of the contributors to this book as well as to me.

Much of the book is also a direct contribution from the many Metapsychology facilitators around the world. They have been generous in sharing their time and stories about their experiences. In alphabetical order, Rev. Gerald Bongard, Janet Buell, Eduardo Cazabat, Kathryn McCormack-Chen, Gerald French, Patricia Furze, Alex Frater, Brian Grimes, Michael Hanau, Jane Kennedy, Wendy Kruger, Ragnhild Malnati, John Nielsen, Robert H. Moore, Sharie Ann Peacock, David Rourke, Irene Schoenfeld-Szabo, Karen Trotter, Rev. Karl Ullrich, Henry Whitfield.

Interviews with Anna B. Baranowsky, Joyce Carbonell, Windy Dryden, Charles Figley, and Harriet Mall were helpful in showing the relationship of TIR to other remedies. TIR researchers Pamela V. Valentine, Wendy Coughlin, and Lori Beth Bisbey graciously allowed me to reprint their notes in the Research chapter. The following people have generously contributed a major part of a chapter or stories in more than one chapter: Teresa Descilo, Alex Frater, Tom Joyce, Robert H. Moore, and Marian Volkman. Tom Joyce also executed the front and back cover designs as well.

Posthumously contributing valuable material were Lt. Col. Chris Christensen (ret.) and David B. Cheek, M.D. I can thank them only in spirit. I must thank anonymously the dozens of clients who were asked to share their stories of how their work with TIR changed their lives.

Jennifer MacLean, Marian Volkman, and Bob Rich contributed to proofreading. This book would not have been possible without the unconditional love and support from Marian Volkman, my wife. As both technical and editing advisor, her services have been invaluable.

This book was made possible in part by my participation in the *Self Expression and Leadership Program* from Landmark Education. In particular, I thank Nitzana York from the Detroit center for training me in how to make what's possible into reality. At least half a dozen articles were produced for the book as specific measurable results from that program.

Contents

> *I have changed. I got back to my self and to be the person that I was before the incident. I got to see and deal with things that happened to me and sort my feelings out so I can deal with it. I learned a lot about myself and other people. Also I learned to not be responsible for things that others do to us, but for ones that we do to others. I also feel strongly that if I need it, help is out there, it is my responsibility to find it and live life the way I want to.*
>
> **— Domestic Violence survivor after TIR (VSC Miami)**

Foreword by the Editor

Who Should Read this Book

This book defies some of the conventional pigeonholes for trauma and therapy books because it is targeted towards two distinct audiences: people with a history of trauma who are looking for resolution of their past and mental health professionals who are interested in a powerful and proven technique to resolve the effects of past traumas. It is also my fervent hope that TIR practitioners will recommend this book to their clients as a means of educating them in the process of discovery they are about to embark upon.

How to Read This Book

The structure of the book is encyclopedic in that each chapter is self-contained and requires no prior experience. Even so, I would recommend completing Trauma and TIR (Ch. 1) first for a basic grounding in the material. Then you may wish to jump to one of the application chapters (2-5, 7, 9, 11-13) which show specifically how Traumatic Incident Reduction (TIR) has been successfully applied to various experiences (veterans, crime victims, terrorism, etc.). Mental health practitioners with backgrounds in other brief trauma techniques might want to read about Traumatology (Ch. 6), Research Projects (Ch. 8), or Integrating Therapies (Ch. 9) early on. In either case, the underpinning philosophy of Metapsychology (Ch. 14) will add to your understanding of why TIR works as it does.

The Nature of Conversations

Since this book consists primarily of conversations with people of many different backgrounds and experiences, the viewpoints each person expresses are their own and don't necessarily represent the viewpoint of any other individual or group. You may read opinions of various treatment methods with which the developers of those methods might disagree. The intent of the book is to share this broad range of viewpoints and you are encouraged to draw your own conclusions.

The Terminology of Trauma

Traumatic stress, like any other area of scholarly study, has developed its own language to describe symptoms and treatments. I have taken care to make the book as accessible to lay people as it is to professionals. Please use the index at the back of the book to find definitions of unfamiliar terms. Generally, a term is defined in the text the first time it is used.

Certified Trauma Specialist (CTS)

You may notice that quite a number of the contributors to this book have the CTS designation after their names. The Association for Traumatic Stress Specialists was formed in the 1980's to provide organization, continuing education and recognition to people working to alleviate the effects of traumatic stress. ATSS offers three kinds of certification depending on the education and experience of the applicant. The CTS designation was created for counselors, clinicians, and treatment specialists who provide individual, group, and/or family counseling and/or intervention. Among other criteria, CTS requires 240 hours of trauma treatment training and 2,000 hours of trauma counseling and intervention.

We highly recommend ATSS for their excellent annual conferences and their unique certification program. Learn more at: www.atss-hq.com.

About the Book

It has been my very great pleasure to collect and edit stories of how Traumatic Incident Reduction (TIR) has made a difference in people's lives. In the 20 years since Frank A. Gerbode began developing the technique known as TIR, it has spread as far as Australia and Russia and from Alaska to Brazil. TIR has been successfully applied by not only psychologists and social workers but also by ministers and even lay trauma survivors, such as Vietnam veterans. Furthermore, it has proven its usefulness in the full spectrum of human woes: from birth to bereavement, war veterans to widows, children to car crash victims. TIR is used every day in a variety of locales beyond the therapist's couch including domestic violence centers, jails, and even the frontlines of disasters.

I believe the multiplicity of voices and experiences that you find in this book makes the case for the broad workability of TIR. At the time of this writing, this is the first book to embrace the experiences of dozens of practitioners and clients in varied milieu and weave them into an argument for efficacy. If this book had been merely the work or experience of a single author, its voice would have been considerably weaker.

TIR allows practitioners to address trauma more deeply while simultaneously resolving trauma quickly. This allows practitioners to be more effective and able to handle more clients.

Anecdotally speaking, compassion fatigue is virtually unknown among TIR practitioners. The following quote from Alex Frater will testify the power of this:

> "In the early 90's, my practice involved 70 hours/week of face-to-face therapy in which the number of my clients/patients with trauma related matters was growing alarmingly. Through increasing medical referrals, my practice was progressively becoming unmanageable, and I began to seek more efficient ways of dealing with trauma. By chance, I came across an article written by Dr. Robert Moore of Florida, extolling the virtues of a new approach to resolving trauma known as Traumatic Incident Reduction (TIR). I went to Menlo Park in 1994 to train at Moore's recommendation with Gerald French and Frank A. Gerbode, MD.

> The results I have obtained since returning to Australia with this innovative therapy are nothing short of miraculous. TIR has done nothing to reduce my workload, but it has increased my efficiency enormously. My trauma-related patients now number something like 45/week, up from the 20 or so that I was seeing at the time I went to California, and at the same time TIR has, in fact, enabled me to produce better, faster, and much more thorough results in dealing with trauma and related matters than have any other techniques at my disposal. Quite fantastic, really. More than worth every bit of time and expense of traveling to America for the training."

> Alex D. Frater, CTS
> Campbelltown, Australia

If TIR existed whole and independent of everything else, it would still be the marvelous tool that you'll learn about in this book. In fact, TIR is part of Applied Metapsychology, a larger area of study developed simultaneously by Dr. Gerbode. Along the way, I'll be introducing a few other of the key procedures available in Metapsychology (most often, that of Unblocking). The philosophy of Metapsychology is developed further in the final chapter of this book as well as Dr. Gerbode's own book *Beyond Psychology: Introduction to Metapsychology, 3rd Ed.* (1994).

One of the challenges of editing lies in the classification and categorization of the stories presented herein. Keep in mind that these divisions are arbitrary, and though a practitioner may be highlighted in a particular area of trauma, it doesn't imply that such a practitioner is limited to that area, in general practice or specifically with using TIR. For example, John Nielsen has had great success in working with jail inmates, but their traumas are not unique to prisoners. In one case, the root trauma of an inmate related back to experiences as a civilian in the Bosnian conflicts.

It's also important for you to understand what this book is not about. Specifically, it's not a "how to" manual or instructional guide of any sort. Although you can learn the complete theory from the textbooks of Frank A. Gerbode, M.D., Gerald French, and Bisbey and Bisbey, the only way to fully achieve the potential results of TIR is to attend a TIR Workshop (see Appendix B).

At this point, you may be wondering why I personally decided to write this book given that a perfectly fine technical and training environment already exists. In the past 20 years the good word about TIR has not spread outside certain small circles of Traumatology and into wide-spread public knowledge. Prior to 2003, my primary efforts to promulgate TIR consisted of creating the Traumatic Incident Reduction Association (www.TIR.org) website in 1996 and supporting my wife's practice.

In early 2003, I heard a call-in program on National Public Radio about Vietnam veterans and their families suffering the effects of post-traumatic stress disorder (PTSD). They discussed the full gamut of flashbacks, panic attacks, unaccountable rage, depression, substance abuse, and other aspects of PTSD. The expert's consensus was basically "Well, you just try to be patient and understand what they're going through and maybe over time they'll get better."

This sort of scarred-for-life mentality is touted on the six o'clock news after each and every disaster. As such, the public at large is left with the impression that really nothing can be done about the effects of trauma. I believe what's missing, the presence of which would make a difference, is a book presenting the possibility for healing that TIR offers.

The Conversation Continues

I'm still actively seeking stories from clients who have been healed through their use of TIR and how it's made a difference in their lives. Please contact me via email to info@LovingHealing.com and <u>be sure</u> to put "TIR" in the subject line.

Foreword to the 2nd Edition

It seems that an editor's work is never finished. After the first printing, several opportunities arose to improve the content and index. Among these are a dozen new articles which update existing chapters as well as creating two new chapters ("TIR Research Projects" and "TIR in the Workplace"):

- Additional material from the files of Lt. Col. Chris Christensen (Ret.)

- An Open Letter to Members of the TIR Association by David W. Powell

- "Simple Therapy Eases Complex Past Pains of Life" by Margaret Leonard

- Anecdote about relieving stuttering by Dr. Eduardo H. Cazabat

- "Trauma and Personal Growth", by Frank A. Gerbode, M.D.

- "Thematic TIR in Application: Test Anxiety", by Robert H. Moore, Ph.D.

- "No Longer a Victim: Crime Victims with PTSD" by Lori Beth Bisbey, Ph.D.

- "Brief Treatment of Trauma-Related Symptoms in Incarcerated Females with TIR" by Pamela V. Valentine, Ph.D.

- "TIR and Anxiety Symptomatology" by Wendy Coughlin, Ph.D.

- "TIR in the Workplace: A Conversation with Wendy Kruger"

- "Trauma Resolution in an At-Risk Youth Program" by Teresa Descilo

- "TIR in a Mental Health Clinic Setting" with Patricia Furze

Conspicuously missing from this edition is the "Meet the Trainers" section. It was omitted due both to the difficulty in keeping up with the ever-expanding base of trainers worldwide and to make way for the expansion of this edition. Biographical interviews of all participating trainers can still be found on the www.TIR.org website.

I also acknowledge Bob Rich, Ph.D. for his contribution to the success of this edition and his new role as series editor for Explorations in Metapsychology.

Victor R. Volkman, Editor
January 1st, 2005

1 Trauma and TIR

Critical Issues in Trauma Resolution
by Frank A. Gerbode, M.D.

Originally presented as lecture notes from the seminar of the same name.

About Frank A. Gerbode, M.D.

Dr. Gerbode is an Honors graduate of Stanford University who later pursued graduate studies in philosophy at Cambridge University in England. He received his medical degree from Yale University, and completed a psychiatric residency at Stanford University Medical Center in the early 1970s. Gerbode is the author of numerous papers and articles, which have been published in the *Journal of Neurochemistry*, the *International Journal of Neuropharmacology*, the *Journal of Rational Emotive and Cognitive Behavioral Therapy* and elsewhere. He teaches and lectures internationally, and is the author of *Beyond Psychology: An Introduction to Metapsychology*, now in its 3rd edition.

Traumatic Incident Reduction: A Simple Trauma Resolution Technique

Most common approaches to post-traumatic stress reduction fall into two categories: coping techniques and cathartic techniques. Some therapists give their clients specific in vivo (literally "in life") methods for counteracting or coping with the symptoms of PTSD—tools to permit their clients to learn to adapt to, to learn to live with, their PTSD condition. Others encourage their clients to release their feelings, to have a catharsis. The idea is that past traumas generate a certain amount of negative energy or "emotional charge", and the therapist's task is to work with the client to release this charge so that it does not manifest itself as aberrant behavior, negative feelings and attitudes, or psychosomatic conditions.

Coping methods and cathartic techniques may help a person to feel better temporarily, but they don't *resolve* trauma so that it can no longer exert a negative effect on the client. Clients feel better temporarily after coping or having a catharsis, but the basic charge remains in place, and shortly thereafter they need more therapy.

The Need for Anamnesis (recovery of repressed memories)

Traumatic Incident Reduction (TIR) operates on the principle that a permanent resolution of a case requires anamnesis (recovery of repressed memories), rather than mere catharsis or coping. To understand why clients have to achieve an anamnesis in order to resolve past trauma, we must take a person-centered viewpoint, i.e., the client's viewpoint and, from that viewpoint, explain what makes trauma traumatic.

Time and Intention

Let us start by taking a person-centered look at the subject of time (see Fig. 1). Objectively, we view time as a "never-ending stream", an undifferentiated continuum in which events are embedded. But subjectively, we actually *experience* time differently. Subjectively, time is broken up into "chunks" which we shall call "periods" of time. "A time", for me, is a period during which something was happening or, more specifically, during which I was doing something, engaging in some activity. Some periods of time are in the past; some are in the present. Those periods defined by completed activities are in the past; those defined by ongoing (and therefore incomplete) activities are in the present.

The Contents of Present Time

For that reason, we don't experience present time as a dimensionless point. It has breadth corresponding to the width of the activities in which we are currently engaged. For example, I am still in the period of time when I was a father, when I was attending this conference, when I was delivering this workshop, when I was uttering this sentence, when I was saying this word. These are all activities in which I am engaged, and each defines a period of time with a definite width. In fact, I inhabit a host of periods of time simultaneously.

Activity Cycles

A period of time has a simple but definite anatomy, determined by the activity in which you are engaged, which we call an "activity cycle" or just a "cycle" (See Fig. 2). The period of time (and the cycle) starts when the activity starts, continues as long as the activity continues, and ends when the activity ends. The activity in question may be related or unrelated to trauma. It could be trying to get away from a sniper, or it could be vacationing. For instance, the period of time "when I was going from Paris to Rome" starts when I begin the process of getting from Paris to Rome, continues while I get the train tickets, get on the train, and eat in

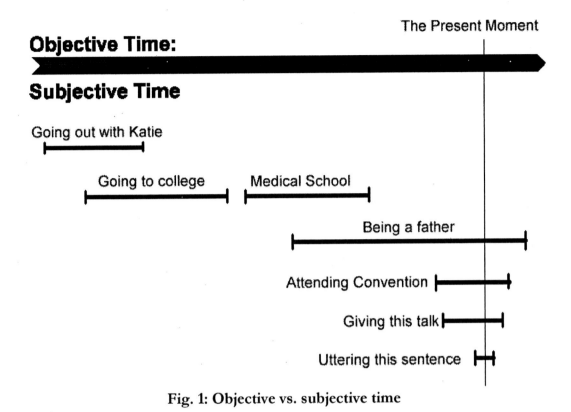

Fig. 1: Objective vs. subjective time

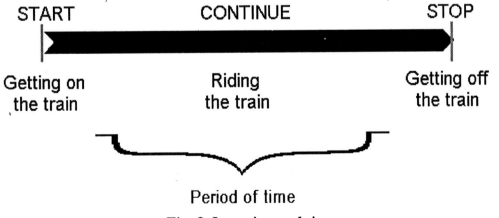

Fig. 2: Intention and time

the dining car, and ends when I arrive in Paris. If an activity has started but not ended for me, that period of time is still ongoing and is part of my present time.

The Ruling Intention

Moreover, each of the activities in which I engage is ruled by a governing intention. In the example I just gave, the intention was to get from Paris to Rome but, in the case of a combat veteran, it could be an intention "to get revenge". In effect, therefore, an activity cycle starts when I formulate an intention, continues so long as that intention continues to exist, and only ends when the intention is ended. Therefore, there is an intimate relation between time and intention.

Each of the activities in Fig. 1 is coextensive with the existence of a corresponding intention. Each continues until the intention is fulfilled or unmade. Present time consists of periods of time that are determined by my current intentions.

Ending an Intention

In fact, there are only two ways to end an intention and thus to send a period of time into the past:

Fulfill it:	An intention ends more or less automatically when it is fulfilled; because you don't keep intending to do things that you know you have already finished doing.
Discontinue it:	Even if an intention is not fulfilled, you can deliberately and consciously decide to *unmake* the intention. Unmaking it, however, requires that you be *aware* of it and of your reasons for making it. You cannot unmake an intention of which you are unaware.

In other words, you can't stop doing something you don't know you are doing.

The Effects of Repression

Repressing an incomplete cycle makes it destructive and, at the same time, much more difficult to complete. As mentioned above, to complete a cycle, I must be aware of the intention that rules it. But if, because of the trauma it contains, I have repressed the incident in which I created the intention, I am not aware that I *have* that intention or why I have it, so I cannot unmake it! That period of time continues up into the present, and some energy remains tied up in it. In fact, it makes sense to define charge as "repressed, unfulfilled intention". Getting rid of charge, then, consists of un-repressing intentions and then unmaking them.

Now it becomes obvious why we need anamnesis in order to resolve the effects of past traumas. To reduce the charge contained in past traumas, the client must come fully into contact with them, so that he can find the unfulfilled intentions that he has repressed and why he formulates them, and unmake them.

To Repress or Not to Repress?

Whenever something painful and difficult to confront shows up in life, one has a choice.

1. Allowing oneself to experience it fully.

   a. Thus being fully aware of one's intentions in the incident, and why one formed those intentions.
   b. Thus having a choice whether or not to unmake the intentions.
   c. At which point, the incident is discharged, by the above definition of "charge", and becomes a *past* incident.

   or

2. Repressing it, wholly or partially.

   a. Thus not being aware of the intentions one made in the incident, or why one made them.
   b. Thus not being able to unmake those intentions.
   c. So that the incident remains charged and continues on as part of present time.

Paradoxically, by trying to get rid of the incident by repression, one causes it to remain present indefinitely.

Effects of Charge

Charge represents a drain on a person's energy or vitality, because energy remains tied up in the incomplete cycle connected with the intention in the trauma, and more is tied up in the effort to repress the incident. Hence a person with unresolved past traumas tends to be rather listless or goalless in life. A second effect of past traumas compounds the difficulty: similar conditions in the environment can trigger or "restimulate" past, repressed traumas, just as the sound of a bell could cause Pavlov's dog to salivate. When one is reminded of a past trauma, one has, again, the choice given above: one can either allow oneself to become fully aware of what happened in the original incident or one can repress the incident of being *reminded*. Repression causes the "reminder" incident to become a secondary trauma in itself. Later, similar occurrences can then restimulate the secondary traumatic incident as well as the original one.

A Sequence of Traumatic Incidents

For example (See Fig. 3), consider a Vietnam combat veteran who has a past traumatic incident of being in a combat situation in which a close friend was killed. Contained in this incident are, say, the sound of a helicopter, a loud noise, the taste of chewing gum (assuming he was chewing gum at the time), and, perhaps, children (if he was in a Vietnamese village). Also, a tree line. Since this incident is extremely traumatic, the soldier represses it, at least partially. He "doesn't want to think about it." Later, some years after leaving Vietnam, he goes to a barbeque in the park. There, he is, say, chewing gum and sees some children. He also sees a tree line. He starts to be reminded of the original incident and feels the rage contained in it. This becomes uncomfortable, so he represses the incident in the park, wholly or partly. Contained in it were also a barbeque smell and a dog barking.

In a later incident, he is talking with his wife and chewing gum, and they are barbequing on the back porch with the kids, the dog barks, and the veteran suddenly experiences a feeling of rage, because the earlier incident, the one in the park, is restimulated by the common elements: the dog barking, the barbeque smell, and the chewing gum. This is uncomfortable, so he represses this one also, and it becomes another secondary trauma. This incident also contains some additional elements: the sound of traffic, and the person's wife.

Later, he is drinking beer on the back porch with his baby and his wife and smoking a cigarette, and he is trying to talk to his wife but there is also traffic noise. Again, he flies into a rage because of the reminders, although, because the past trauma is repressed, he will attribute the rage to something else, e.g., to the fact that his wife forgot the salt shaker for the *third* time. This incident contains a sensation of being intoxicated, the taste of beer, the smell of cigarette smoke, and his baby. It, too, is repressed.

Later still, he is smoking, drinking beer, and watching TV. The sensation of intoxication and of smoking reminds him of the earlier incident and he feels rage. Now whenever he gets drunk or watches television, he is prone to fly into a rage. Random dream elements restimulate the same sequence of traumas, resulting in recurrent nightmares. Finally, he goes to a therapist and is found to be a full-blown PTSD case.

This is a sequence of traumatic incidents, starting with a "root" incident and encompassing, probably, a large number of subsequent incidents in which the root incident or one of its sequents got restimulated. The only thing in common to all these incidents is the feeling of rage that he experiences each time. He attributes this rage to something in present time, but it actually stems from the original rage he felt in the root incident.

External Restimulators	Icons of Stimuli	Theme (Response)
. Helicopter Sound 2. Children 3. Taste of Chewing Gum 4. Loud Noise 5. Tree Line		Blinding rage
. Sound of Barking Dog 2. Children 3. Taste of Chewing Gum 4. Barbeque Scent 5. Tree Line		Blinding rage
. Sound of Barking Dog 2. Children 3. Traffic Sight/Sound 4. Wife 5. Scent of Cigarette Smoke		Blinding rage
1. Sensation of Intoxication 2. Children 3. Taste of Beer 4. Loud Noise 5. Scent of Cigarette Smoke		Blinding rage
1. Sensation of Intoxication 2. Bottles 3. Taste of Beer 4. Television 5. Scent of Cigarette Smoke		Blinding rage

Fig. 3. A sequence of traumatic incidents

The Traumatic Incident Network

Although we have only shown a few incidents, in real life a sequence may contain hundreds or even thousands of incidents. Furthermore, the average person usually has a fairly large number of these sequences, with different themes in common. These sequences overlap each other to form a network of traumatic incidents which we call the traumatic incident network or "Net" (See Fig. 4). The object of TIR is to reduce the amount of charge the Net contains so that the person is not subject to the restimulating effects described above, and also so that he can reclaim the intention units that are tied up in the Net.

What we have shown, here, is not just the situation of a Vietnam combat vet or a rape survivor. It is the human condition. Every one of us has had at least some past traumas that cause us to be dysfunctional in certain areas of life—the ones that contain restimulators.

The Solution to the Net

Stating the solution is easy, but accomplishing it is somewhat trickier. Traumas contain very intense, repressed, unfulfilled intentions, such as the intention to get revenge, to escape—and, of course, the intention to repress the incident. The client needs to find the root incident for each sequence and bring it to full awareness. Traumatic Incident Reduction accomplishes this result. When that occurs, the person becomes aware of the intentions in them and, since these intentions are generally no longer relevant to the here and now, she unmakes them. At that

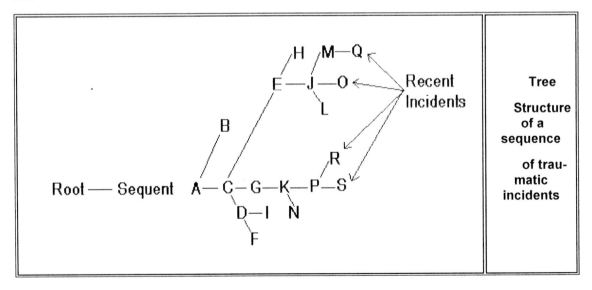

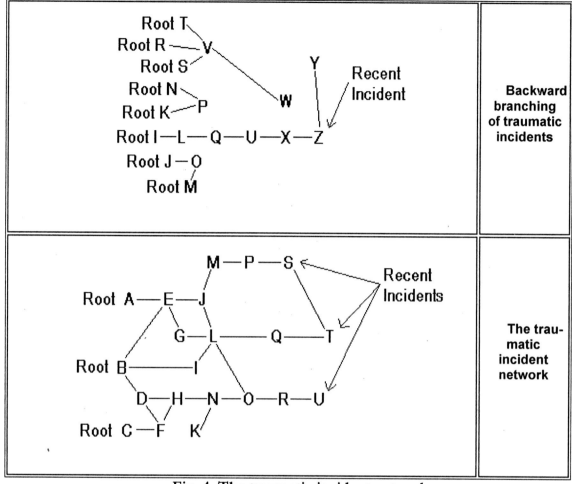

Fig. 4. The traumatic incident network

point, the cycles contained in the incidents are completed; they become part of the past, and they can no longer be restimulated.

Undoing Amnesia

What is required, then, to obtain the necessary anamnesis? An incident has four dimensions, not just three. In order to be aware of an incident, it is necessary to start at the beginning and go through to the end, like viewing a motion picture, not like looking at a snapshot. Hence, we call the procedure "viewing", the client a "viewer", and we call the one who helps the client to do the viewing the "facilitator". [For more explanation of these terms, please see the FAQ on p. 311]

You can't just glance at a part of an incident and expect thereby to have fully completed the process of anamnesis, because you will miss other parts of it—probably the most important ones, the ones that are most difficult to confront. In order to achieve a full anamnesis, you must be allowed to go through the entire incident without interruptions, without reassurances—in short without *any* distractions. Furthermore, it does not suffice to go through the incident only once. If you want to become fully familiar with a movie, you must see it a number of times, and each time you will notice new things about it. The same thing happens during Traumatic Incident Reduction, except that the client is viewing a past traumatic incident instead of a movie, and that's somewhat harder to do.

Basic vs. Thematic TIR

If, as is often the case with combat vets and rape victims—survivors of single or discrete incidents—the viewer already knows which trauma needs to be looked at, you can use a relatively simple form of TIR called "Basic TIR". You simply have the viewer go through the single, known incident enough times to resolve it. But in most cases, the viewer starts out being entirely unaware of what the root trauma underlying his difficulties is. So how can he find it? For that, we use a technique called "Thematic TIR", in which we can trace back an unwanted feeling, emotion, sensation, attitude, or pain to the root trauma from which it originates.

End Points

When the viewer finds and discharges the root incident, a very specific and often quite dramatic series of phenomena appear, showing that the viewer has achieved a thorough discharge. Then we say the viewer has reached an "end point". These phenomena usually appear in the following order:

1. *Positive indicators:* The viewer appears happy, relieved, or serene. She is not sitting in the middle of something heavy. Sometimes she will laugh or say something cheerful. In the absence of good indicators, a full end point has not occurred.

2. *Realization:* Then the viewer will usually voice some kind of realization or insight, a reflection of the fact that he is becoming more aware.

3. *Extroversion:* Finally, the viewer will open her eyes or otherwise indicate that her attention is now back in present times. She will usually look at the facilitator or at the room, or make some comment about something in the here and now.

4. *Intention expressed:* Often, the viewer will explicitly tell the facilitator what intention was present in the incident. If he doesn't, the facilitator has the option of asking him to tell of any decisions he may have made at the time of the incident.

When you see an end point, the most important thing to do is to stop. If you continue past the point when the root incident has been discharged and continue to ask the viewer to look for incidents, she will start to wander around more or less randomly in the Net, and will often end up triggering a lot of things that you may not be able to resolve with TIR. This is defined as an *overrun*.

Flows

A person can have charge, not only on what has been done to him but also on what he has done to others, what others have done to others, and what he has done to himself. These are actually four principal directions in which causation can flow:

Inflow: From something or someone in the world outside.

Outflow: From the viewer to others. These are things the viewer has done, inadvertently or on purpose, that have affected others. Handling this flow tends to alleviate guilt.

Crossflow: To others, but not from the viewer, i.e., from something in the world outside or from other people to others. The viewer is "only a spectator" here; nevertheless, such incidents can be very heavily charged, as in the case of a mother witnessing her child being threatened or hurt.

Reflexive flow: From self to self.

When a viewer has a charged incident that contains one of these flows, it is quite possible— even likely—that he will also have similar incidents on other flows that are also charged. After a viewer addresses an incident in which he was betrayed, the facilitator may ask if there were any incidents in which he betrayed another, and also whether there is charge on one or more incidents in which he observed others being betrayed. There may even be incidents in which—as he perceives it—he betrayed himself.

As a person comes up in awareness, he tends first to be aware of what others have done to him, then of what he has done to others, then of what others have done to others, and finally, what he has done to himself. Both Basic and Thematic TIR instructions can and should consider flows.

Results

We have found that TIR works well with most clients who fit the criteria for PTSD. An exception is that TIR does *not* work well with people who are currently abusing drugs or alcohol. When the viewer was drinking heavily or abusing other substances between sessions, it would fail virtually every time. Another contraindication is if the client is diagnosable with some type of psychosis.

Although the TIR procedure is not complicated or difficult to learn, it can only work in a session environment that is structured in such a way that it is safe. Much of the TIR training involves teaching certain Rules of Facilitation (see Appendix A) and communication skills specific to the TIR style of working with a client.

A complete 4-hour recording of this lecture is available on

The TIR and Metapsychology Lecture Series:
Vol 2: Critical Issues in Trauma Resolution.

(A compilation of MP3 audio files playable on all computers)

Loving Healing Press
www.LovingHealing.com

A Brief Description of Unblocking

Unblocking uses the method called *unlayering* to allow a client to look at a particular area of life repetitively, thus peeling off layers of thoughts, considerations, emotions, decisions, and opinions. Each time the question is asked, the viewer gets a new look at the subject until there are no more answers to that question. Unblocking consists of numerous questions that have been tested and proven to be most useful in helping a client uncover and remove charge from a significant issue. This is a thorough enough technique that we don't want to use it on a very minor issue, but rather something central to the person's life.

Some (real life) examples:
- your self-esteem
- your self confidence
- managing money
- your career
- your relationship with (charged person such as "your mother" or "your spouse")
- your sexuality
- marriage
- being a parent

Unblocking has the advantage of being less challenging for the client and so is often used to prepare a client for being able to use TIR, but it should not be relegated to a category of TIR preparation alone. It has great value in allowing us to address issues that may not have traumatic incidents connected to them, but are still worrisome and absorbing to the client.

TIR is what we call a "checklist technique" because it consists of a series of steps the client is asked to do in order, each of which build upon the ones that went before. Repetition comes into it in that the client is allowed to go through the incident in question as many times as needed to either bring about resolution or to allow an earlier related incident to come into view. Because the viewer is being asked to go back and re-experience a traumatic incident in TIR, it is fairly demanding on the client (though well worth the effort).

Unblocking allows the client to look at whatever comes up in response to the question, in whatever order it comes up. End points reported by clients on Unblocking include such things as greater clarity and understanding of that area of life and a greater certainty.

[Lay readers may wish to skip ahead to Chapter 2]

Psychological Foundations of TIR
By Robert H. Moore, Ph.D.

About the Author

Dr. Moore is a licensed marriage and family therapist, school psychologist and mental health counselor with graduate degrees in counseling psychology from Lehigh (1965) and Walden (1977) Universities. He is a Fellow and Diplomate of the American Board of Medical Psychotherapists; a Diplomate of the International Academy of Behavioral Medicine, Counseling and Psychotherapy.

With over thirty years of practice, seventeen as Director of the Institute for Rational Living in Florida, he has co-edited or contributed to six popular books by Albert Ellis; authored chapters on various applications of Cognitive Behavior Therapy and Traumatic Incident Reduction for professional texts by Windy Dryden, Larry Hill and Janet Wolfe; hosted his own nationally syndicated daily talk radio program; and produced over three hundred psychologically-topical news and public service segments for radio and television. He most recently operated a Domestic Violence Intervention Program in Clearwater under contract to Florida's Department of Corrections.

Introduction

Developed by Frank A. Gerbode, M.D. TIR is a regressive desensitization procedure for reducing or eliminating the negative residual impact of traumatic experience. As such it finds major application in cases of post-traumatic stress disorder (PTSD). A one-on-one guided imagery process, TIR is also useful in remediation of specific unwanted stress responses, such as panic attacks, that occur without significant provocation. "Thematic TIR" traces such conditioned responses back through the history of their occurrence in a client's life to the stressful incidents primarily responsible for their acquisition. The resolution of the primary incidents then reduces or eliminates the target stress response.

As an intervention technique, TIR is both directive and client-centered. It is directive in that the therapist who is called a "facilitator" guides the client who is called a "viewer" repetitively through an imaginal replay of a specific trauma. It is client—or, as Dr. Gerbode prefers, "person-" - centered, in that a TIR facilitator doesn't interpret or critique the viewer's experience or tell him how he should feel or what to think about it. A methodical and systematic anamnesis, TIR unsuppresses the trauma being addressed to provide the viewer the opportunity to review and revise his perspective on it. TIR's uniqueness lies, in part, in the fact that a session continues until the viewer is completely relieved of whatever stress the target trauma originally provoked and any cognitive distortions (e.g., observations, decisions, conclusions) embedded within the incident have been restructured. (Gerbode, 1989)

TIR's Philosophic Roots

TIR and virtually every other contemporary regressive and imaginal desensitization procedure used in the remediation of trauma—including "sequential analysis" (Blundell and Cade), "direct therapeutic exposure" (Boudewyns), "prolonged imaginal exposure" (Foa and Olasov), "gradual dosing" (Horowitz), "dianetics" (Hubbard), "flooding" (Keane and Kaloupek), "repetitive review" (Raimy), and "implosion" (Stampfl and Lewis)—derive directly from principles clearly articulated in the earliest writings of Freud and Pavlov. Although the latter, Pavlov, is properly credited with the identification of the "conditional reflex" and its chain-linked "secondary signaling system" (the model most commonly referenced in connection with PTSD acquisition), Freud earlier had made the equivalent observation about the development of the traumatic neuroses. He wrote:

> What left the symptom behind was not always a single experience. On the contrary, the result was usually brought about by the convergence of several traumas, and often by the repetition of a great number of similar ones. Thus it was necessary to reproduce the whole chain of pathogenic memories in chronologic order, or rather in reversed order, the latest ones first and the earliest ones last. (1984, p. 37)

The essential congruity of the Pavlovian and Freudian observations, in this connection, prompted Astrup (1965) to note that:

> From a conditional reflex point of view, psychoanalytic therapy represents a continuous association experiment with subtle analysis of second signaling system connections. (p. 126)

As TIR draws heavily on these same well-established principles, Dr. Gerbode, who was originally schooled in psychoanalysis, and Dr. Robert H. Moore—a cognitive-behaviorist colleague, and author of these notes—routinely reference this intersection of the Freudian and Pavlovian constructs in presentations of TIR to the mental health professions.

PTSD And Imaginal Procedures

Whether favoring the remedial logic of "abreaction" or of "extinction," dedicated trauma workers display a strong and growing philosophic and clinical consensus regarding the importance of addressing traumatic experience with a guided imagery procedure like that employed by TIR.

In their review of theoretical and empirical issues in the treatment of PTSD, Fairbank and Nicholson (1987) conclude that, of all the approaches in use, only those involving some form of direct imaginal exposure to the trauma have been successful.

Roth and Newman (1991) describe the ideal resolution process as one involving "a re-experiencing of the affect associated with the trauma in the context of painful memories." Such a process, the authors point out, brings the individual "to both an emotional and cognitive understanding of the meaning of the trauma and the impact it has had...and would lead to a reduction in symptoms and to successful integration of the trauma experience" (p. 281).

Grossberg and Wilson (1968) have shown that repeated visualization of a fearful situation produces a significant drop in the physiological response (GSR) to the threatening image.

Folkins, Lawson, Opton, and Lazarus (1968) have demonstrated the efficacy of rehearsal in fantasy in reducing the physiological response (GSR) to a frightening movie.

Blundell and Cade (1980) independently confirm that repeated visualization of an anxiety-provoking situation produces a significant reduction in the physiological (GSR) response to the threatening image. Frederick (1986) used a very TIR-like desensitization procedure with trauma victims:

He contended that such incident-specific treatment is essential to overcoming PTSD. Using mental images, the client reviews, frame by frame, the entire sequence of the traumatic experience. During the process, the client is able to recall and disclose significant thoughts and feelings related to the trauma and, consequently, anxiety associated with the trauma dissipates. (Hayman, Sommers-Flanagan, and Parsons, 1987)

R. D. Laing concurs:

> You can look at it with such narcissistic bonding as to bring tears to your eyes, or grimaces of distaste at what you see. After each paroxysm of self-pity or self-disgust or self-adulation, look at it again and again, and again until those tears are dry, the laughter has subsided, the sobs have ceased. Then look at it, quite dispassionately ...until you've got nothing to do with it at all. (Russell and Laing, 1992)

Some trauma therapists employ hypnosis as an accessing tool. Although this is not the case in TIR, it is interesting to note the similarity of the hypnotic and non-hypnotic approaches to resolution, once the client has contacted and begun to unsuppress a traumatic incident.

The Ericksonian procedure for addressing the content of a traumatic incident employs a trance state. Following hypnotic induction, his retrospective "jigsaw" technique guides the client in recovery of the cognitive and emotive components of a painful memory in whatever order the client can most easily confront:

> Various bits of the incident recovered in this jigsaw fashion allow you
> to eventually recover an entire, forgotten traumatic experience of childhood
> that had been governing this person's behavior...and handicapping his life
> very seriously. (Erickson, 1955/80)

MacHovec (1985) confirms that hypnotic regression can be used to help clients recall and revivify a traumatic incident, vent emotions, and gradually reintegrate the experience with improved coping skills.

PTSD And Cognitive Restructuring

Like other effective trauma resolution processes, TIR is not primarily a cathartic technique. Gerbode (1986) affirms the professional consensus that cognitive restructuring is prerequisite for thorough trauma resolution. Raimy (1975) concurs:

> Many current therapies attempt primarily to relieve the client or patient of
> his pent-up emotion, either in cathartic episodes or over longer periods of time
> in which emotional release takes place less dramatically. If we examine catharsis
> more closely, however, we can readily discover several cognitive events which
> have significant influence on the experience. If these cognitive events do not
> occur, no amount of "emotional expression" is likely to be helpful. (p. 81).

Speaking specifically to the use of imaginal exposure in the rational-emotive treatment of PTSD, Warren and Zgourides (1991) report that:

> Keane et al's (1989) implosive therapy, Horowitz's (1986) gradual dosing,
> and Foa and Olasov's (1987) prolonged imaginal exposure are methods that
> help clients work through their traumatic event, discover and revise mean-
> ings, and develop more adaptive responses to the traumatic event. In RET
> [Rational Emotive Behavioral Therapy], we incorporate imaginal exposure to
> the traumatic event.. (and).. While conducting the imaginal exposure and in
> reviewing imagined and behavioral exposure homework assignments, we are
> on the lookout for clients' cognitive and emotional reprocessing of the
> trauma that may relate to the issues of meaning of the event, shattered as-
> sumptions, irrational beliefs, and so on. (p. 161)

Beck (1970) lends additional support to the importance of cognitive restructuring during what he calls "rehearsals in fantasy" in his observation that:

> When a patient has an unpleasant affect associated with a particular
> situation, the unpleasant affect may sometimes be eliminated or reduced
> with repeated imagining of the situation even though the content of the

fantasy does not change. The unpleasant affect may be shame, sadness, anxiety, or disgust.

The data collected from patients and these experimental studies suggest that the rehearsals in fantasy produce a cognitive restructuring. With each voluntary repetition of the fantasy, the patient is enabled to discriminate more sharply between real dangers and purely imaginary or remote dangers. As he is able to appraise the fantasy more realistically, the threat and the accompanying anxiety are reduced.

Through fantasy induction (the client) is able to recognize the specific details of his conception of the situation, to reality-test this conception, and to correct the distortions. The standard techniques of free association or direct discussion of the problem may fail to illuminate the conceptualization, whereas the fantasy expression brings it into sharp focus. Once the distorted picture has been corrected, the patient feels better and can handle the situation more efficiently.

Training

Successful clinical application of TIR requires a minimum of four days of intensive training (see Appendix B)—which includes skill development exercises, live and videotaped demonstration sessions, and both giving and receiving TIR sessions under the supervision of a trainer certified by the Association (see www.TIR.org)—followed by an optional practicum with consultation.

References

Astrup, C. (1965). *Pavlovian psychiatry: a new synthesis.* Springfield, IL: Charles C. Thomas.

Beck, A. T. (1970). "Role of fantasies in psychotherapy and psychopathology". *The Journal of Nervous and Mental Disease*, 150, 3-17.

Blundell, G. G., and Cade, C. M. (1980). *Self awareness and E.S.R.* London: Audio Ltd.

Boudewyns, P. A., Hyer, L., Woods, M. G., Harrison, W. R., and McCranie, E. (1990). "PTSD among Vietnam veterans: An early look at treatment outcome using direct therapeutic exposure." *Journal of Traumatic Stress*, 3, 359-368.

Erickson, M. (1955/80). Self-exploration in the hypnotic state. In E. Rossi (Ed.), The collected papers of Milton H. Erickson on Hypnosis. Vol IV. *Innovative Hypnotherapy* (427-436). New York: Irvington.

Fairbank, J. A., and Nicholson, R. A. (1987). Theoretical and empirical issues in the treatment of post-traumatic stress disorder in Vietnam veterans. *Journal of Clinical Psychology*, 43, 44-55.

Foa, E. B., and Olasov, B. (1989). "Treatment of post-traumatic stress disorder." Workshop conducted at *Advances in Theory and Treatment of Anxiety Disorders*, Philadelphia, PA.

Folkins, C. H., Lawson, K. D., Opton, E. M., and Lazarus, R.S. (1968). "Desensitization and the experimental reduction of threat." *Journal of Abnormal Psychology*, 73, 100-113.

Frederick, C. J. (1986, August) *Psychic trauma and terrorism.* Paper presented at the annual meeting of the American Psychological Association, Washington, D.C.

French, G. D. (1991). *Traumatic Incident Reduction Workshop Manual.* Menlo Park, CA: IRM.

Freud, S. (1984). Two short accounts of psychoanalysis. In J. Strachey (Tr.), *Five lectures on psychoanalysis* (p. 37). Singapore: Penguin Books.

Gerbode, F. A. (1986). Indicators and end points. *The Journal of Metapsychology*, 1, 51-56.

Gerbode, F. A. (1989). *Beyond Psychology: an Introduction to Metapsychology.* Menlo Park, CA: IRM.

Grossberg, J. M., and Wilson, H. K. (1968). Physiological changes accompanying the visualization of fearful and neutral situations. *Journal of Personality and Social Psychology*, 10, 124-133.

Hayman, P. M., Sommers-Flanagan, R., and Parsons, J. P. (1987). Aftermath of violence: posttraumatic stress disorder among Vietnam veterans. *Journal of Counseling and Development*, 65, 365.

Horowitz, M. (1986). *Stress Response Syndromes (2nd ed.).* Northvale, NJ: Jason Aronson.

Hubbard, L. R. (1968). *Dianetics: the Modern Science of Mental Health.* Los Angeles, CA: Publications Organization.

Keane, T. M., Fairbank, J. A., Caddell, J. M., and Zimering, R. T. (1989). Implosive (flooding) therapy reduces symptoms of PTSD in Vietnam combat veterans. *Behavior Therapy*, 20, 245-260.

Keane, T. M., and Kaloupek, D. G. (1982). Imaginal flooding in the treatment of a posttraumatic stress disorder. *Journal of Consulting and Clinical Psychology*, 50, 138-140.

Lyons, J. A., and Keane, T. M. (1989). Implosive therapy for the treatment of combat-related PTSD. *Journal of Traumatic Stress*, 2, 137-152.

MacHovec, F. J. (1985). Treatment variables and the use of hypnosis in the brief therapy of post traumatic stress disorders. *International Journal of Clinical & Experimental Hypnosis*, 33, 6-14.

Manton, M., and Talbot, A. (1990). Crisis intervention after an armed hold-up: Guidelines for counselors. *Journal of Traumatic Stress*, 3, 507-22.

Moore, R. H. (1993). Traumatic incident reduction: a cognitive-emotive treatment of post-traumatic stress disorder. In W. Dryden and L. Hill (Eds.) *Innovations in Rational Emotive Therapy.* Newbury Park, CA: Sage.

Pavlov, I. P. (1927). *Conditioned reflexes.* New York: Oxford Univ. Press.

Raimy, V. (1975). *Misunderstandings of the self.* San Francisco: Jossey-Bass Publishers.

Roth, S., and Newman, E. (1991). The process of coping with sexual trauma. *Journal of Traumatic Stress*, 4, 279-297.

Russell, R., and Laing R. D. (1992). *R.D. Laing & me: Lessons in love*. Lake Placid, NY: Hillgarth Press.

Stampfl, T. G., and Lewis, D. J. (1967). Essentials of implosive therapy: A learning-theory-based psychodynamic behavioral therapy. *Journal of Abnormal Psychology*, 72, 496-503.

Turner, S. M. (1979). Systematic desensitization of fears and anxiety in rape victims. Paper presented at the annual meeting of the Assoc. for the Advancement of Behavior Therapy, San Francisco, CA.

Warren, R., and Zgourides, G. D. (1991). *Anxiety disorders: A rational emotive perspective*. Elmsford, NY: Pergamon.

2 TIR and the Soldier's Experience

I found the following stories of veterans, post-traumatic stress disorder, and TIR inspiring on several levels. As you'll read in the chapter ahead, the Vietnam veterans had several new and significant factors contributing to their malaise that generations of prior returning veterans did not.

According to the National Vietnam Veterans Readjustment Study in 1988:

> The estimated lifetime prevalence of PTSD among American Vietnam theater veterans is 30.9% for men and 26.9% for women. An additional 22.5% of men and 21.2% of women have had partial PTSD at some point in their lives. Thus more than half of all male Vietnam veterans and almost half of all female Vietnam veterans—About 1,700,000 Vietnam veterans in all—have experienced "clinically serious stress reaction symptoms."

Although veterans have suffered for many years and in many ways, the possibility for healing and returning to normal life is now available. In some cases, veterans such as Lt. Colonel Chris Christensen (ret.) took up the torch themselves and have brought TIR into their own communities.

Naturally, the effects of war are limited not only to the combatants. This chapter begins with a brief letter from a civilian participant in Vietnam. In Chapter 4 (Crime and Punishment), you'll learn about a Bosnian war refugee who fled to Canada and abused alcohol to quell endless nightmares of atrocities that he personally witnessed.

As I write this introduction, tens of thousands of men and women are in Iraq serving their country again in a foreign land with unfamiliar terrain, languages, customs, and means of warfare. According to a 2004 study overseen by the Walter Reed Institute of Military Research and published in the *New England Journal of Medicine* (Vol. 351:13-22), about in 1 in 6 returning soldiers from Iraq show signs of major depression, generalized anxiety, or PTSD. My most fervent hope is that upon returning home, those men and women will be able to find and use TIR to relieve the trauma of experiences that those who stayed home can only imagine.

Letter from a Civilian
Formerly Stationed in Vietnam

The following is an unsolicited letter sent in by a client who came in for a viewing session to handle severe symptoms of post traumatic stress:

"I worked for 13 months in Vietnam as a civilian in 1970-71. Just being in this battle-filled, sometimes hot and dusty, sometimes cold and wet, country created pressures, anxiety, and frustrations along with a desperate feeling of despair as anyone else who was there, but went on with the everyday 'churn' of life experienced by so many who returned from this war zone can attest.

I never imagined, however, I would experience an uncontrollable startle reaction (PTSD) 30 years following my return. I sought help from the Veterans Association, and because of their experience in these events, I was recommended for Traumatic Incident Reduction.

Thanks to my TIR facilitator, I am beginning to get re-established in the everyday routine of life two months following this therapy. Without this therapy, I feel I would have faced complete chaos and unable to regain my normal life style."

VIETNAM CIVILIAN

[Ed. Note: Case reports suggest that retirement-induced stress may worsen PTSD or even lead to PTSD in asymptomatic combat veterans (Pomerantz, 1991). There are no time limits to the effects of past trauma.]

Back into the Heart of Darkness
By Tom Joyce

First published by the Institute for Research in Metapsychology in 1989

Foreword by Gerald French

In 1989, Dr. Gerbode, Gerald French, and others were using Traumatic Incident Reduction (TIR) with a number of Vietnam combat vets who had been diagnosed as having PTSD. Tom Joyce, a freelance writer and (former) member of the IRM Board of Directors, was a guest at that year's IRM conference where he heard an address by one of those vets "Jack", in the accompanying essay. Subsequently he sought Jack out, and the two spoke at length. As a result of that meeting, Joyce researched and wrote a penetrating article on traumatized Vietnam veterans and the attempts that the U.S Government and others have made to help them. A somewhat abridged version of it appeared in the Institute's newsletter and even reprints sold out. As the topic he addressed continues to be one that is most popular on TIR.ORG, I asked Tom if he would produce an updated version of it for re-publication

Tom Joyce

Warning: the following article contains strong language and graphic violence. Readers who wish to avoid this should skip ahead to "A Combat Vet's Perspective on TIR" beginning on p. 49

For a glossary of Vietnam era terminology used in this article, please see p. 42

It was endless nights, trying to stay awake, stay alive, counting the hours until dawn, the days, the months, utterly alone, trusting nobody. It was waiting in rain-soaked, mud-caked fatigues for Victor Charlie, an enemy who seldom showed his face and killed mercilessly when he did, who used his school children as lethal weapons, and brutally tortured his prisoners. It was a litany of unspeakable atrocities: the grunt watching his buddy's legs blown off by a land mine, the nose gunner smoking black tar to numb the mental imagery of his gruesome handi-work on a village, the FNG [f—ing new guy] fumbling a grenade and dismembering one of his own platoon, the short-timer fragging his field commander for ordering a suicidal assault on a worthless patch of jungle. It was the freckle-faced kid so transformed by fear and rage and frustration that the sights of unspeakable violence against women and children or castrating a prisoner during interrogation were all met with indifference. It was laughing at a joke called the Geneva Convention, and wondering in suppressed horror just how far you could push that envelope of sanity before shit got out of hand.

It was walking point and dodging sniper fire along the DMZ one morning, then stepping off an airplane at SFO (San Francisco Airport) forty-eight hours later, dumped back into America's lap, expected to act civilized. It was literally being spat upon by other Americans who could no longer distinguish between vandals and victims. It was never knowing if your friends made it back alive and living with the slow-burning fuse of survivor's guilt, muted by the magnitude of your experience, the onslaught of ineffable emotion, the dumbfounded expressions of those who hadn't been there and couldn't possibly understand what you'd seen—what you'd found it necessary to do. It was separation, and divorce, and dulling the anguish with drugs and alcohol, subsequent years of sleepless nights, embarrassing startle reactions, unrelenting Technicolor memories, and uncontrollable tears.

It was a war without glory, a peace without honor, an epic with no heroes.

Vietnam: A Different Kind of War

My companion—call him Pete—lights another Marlboro and continues his measured ac-count of watching his entire platoon wiped out by an NVA [North Vietnamese Army] ambush during the first frantic days of the Tet Offensive, in January 1968. It is a graphic description of sodden fear, bleeding men, and a single, scared boy left alone too long, pushed over the edge by taunts and sniper fire from an enemy hidden in a green hell. For thirty-six hours following the ambush, Pete lived through an inferno of napalm, artillery shelling and friends dying in pieces a few yards beyond his ability to reach them, before being medevaced out of the bush with malaria. Pete was eighteen years old at the time.

His story is visceral, so much so I can feel the knot tightening in my own gut. As he speaks, the September wind outside causes the louvered glass windows in the room to slip shut with a loud crack. Pete's creased face contorts instantaneously; his arms snap out in automatic defense; his lean body tenses like a steel spring. When he notices my alarmed expression, Pete relaxes and laughs in embarrassment. "There was a time," he says, "when a noise like that would have ruined my whole f—ing day."

UH-1 Huey helicopter in Quang Tri
US Army File Photo

And he's not the only one.

Nearly a million individuals serving in the United States Armed Forces engaged in combat or were exposed to life-threatening situations in Vietnam during the years between 1964 and 1973.[1] According to a four-year study conducted by the Research Triangle Institute for the Veterans' Administration, an estimated 480,000 of those suffer from a phenomenon known as post-traumatic stress disorder. Formerly accorded less clinical terms like "shell shock" and "battle fatigue," PTSD is hardly peculiar to the Vietnam War, but the circumstances of those who lived through combat in that particular cataclysm are unique in American history.

During World War II, even though the pre-induction psychiatric rejection rate was nearly four times higher than that of World War I, psychiatric casualties were three hundred percent higher.[2] At one point in the early 1940s, more men were being discharged for "war neurosis" than were being drafted.[3] Twenty-three percent of the men who suffered from battlefield psychological breakdowns never returned to combat. Owing to immediate on-site treatment provided during the Korean War, psychiatric evacuations dropped to six percent of total casualties. But in Vietnam, psychological breakdowns were at an all-time low—twelve per one thousand.[4]

Several factors contributed to this apparent improvement. The DEROS [Date of Expected Return from Over Seas] system was employed for the first time in Vietnam. A soldier's tour of duty lasted twelve months—thirteen if he was a Marine. They served their time, tried to stay in one piece, and rotated back to the States. In the meantime, the "Fertile Triangle" along the borders of Laos, Burma and Cambodia supplied some of the finest substances in the world for numbing trauma. Soldiers caught "self-medicating" or manifesting other character disorders, by any superior who gave a damn, were given administrative discharges. And thus the whole question of psychological trauma was neatly—and deceptively—avoided. As a consequence of DEROS, drugs, and discharges, the "official" neuropsychiatric casualty rate in Vietnam was significantly lower than in either Korea or World War II.[5] It looked like the Pentagon finally had a handle on the embarrassing problem of battle fatigue.

Quite apart from the debilitating effects of drug and alcohol addiction, DEROS, like every apparent solution, created a new generation of problems. After the first few years of the war, soldiers who had trained together were rarely sent to Vietnam as a whole unit. Consequently, *esprit de corps* was almost nonexistent. A regular soldier would arrive in isolation as an FNG, ignorant of combat's horrifying reality. Considered a liability by the hardened short timer—who knew the best way to stay alive was to stay aloof—the new guy learned quickly to trust no one but himself, and f—- the rest. His private war began the day he set foot in country, and ended the moment he was airlifted out.

Before his tour was up, a grunt was introduced to the grisly nuances of guerrilla warfare, where booby traps and incessant sniper fire accounted for an astonishing number of casualties, where the VC [Viet Cong] and NVA regulars were rarely even seen, where the enemy included women and children, where the average age of his fellow combatants was under twenty, and where the ideological justification for the war he was fighting was slippery, if not impossible to grasp. A soldier's only consolation was the knowledge that if he survived his solitary year in hell, he'd eventually return with honor to his homeland.

Or so he thought.

But coming home usually proved a barren source of relief. In contrast to World War II—where men spent weeks, sometimes months, returning from the battlefield aboard ships, decompressing, sharing their experiences with understanding peers, and were honored as heroes with local parades and national acknowledgment when they arrived back home—the Vietnam veteran endured a solitary plane trip with strangers and a cool, if not downright hostile greeting from his fellow Americans. It is not surprising that many of these degraded warriors had difficulty readjusting to their previous environments.

And while the sheer joy of survival suppressed early symptoms of PTSD in most Vietnam veterans, for too many, an unsettling change began to manifest, anywhere from a few months to several years later, as they attempted to readjust to their former lives. It usually began with restlessness, feelings of mistrust, and cynicism evolving into depression, insomnia, a flaring temper, and a morbid obsession with memories of combat. Some experienced grave anxiety over the seemingly innocuous sight of a green tree line, an open field, a helicopter flying overhead, or the sound of popping corn. Perhaps worst of all was the free-floating anxiety, and feelings of guilt for having survived what so many others hadn't.

The VA: No Man Left Behind

The Veterans' Administration's policy was to refuse recognition as "service-related" any neuropsychiatric problems appearing more than one year after a soldier's discharge. Consequently, treatment from the VA was difficult to obtain and disability compensation largely unavailable.[6]

It was not until the mid-1970s that the Disabled American Veterans (DAV) funded the Forgotten Warrior Project, a groundbreaking study of the long-term social consequences of combat exposures conducted by John P. Wilson, PhD. As a result, the DAV opened storefront Vietnam Veteran Outreach Programs in more than seventy cities across the United States, staffed by volunteer counselors. The program's success prompted Congress to establish the Veterans' Administration "Vet Centers" throughout the country.[7]

But post-traumatic stress disorder was not formally recognized by the American Psychiatric Association [APA] until 1980, and its etiology is still passionately debated. Dr. Michael Cohen, an Army 1st Cavalry infantryman who served in Vietnam, became a clinical psychologist and team leader at the San Francisco Vet Center. As a member of the advisory board for the PTSD Team at the Fort Miley Veterans' Affairs Medical Center, Dr. Cohen admitted that, even among the professionals who acknowledge the existence of PTSD, there are opposing theoretical camps. He called them "residualists" and "predispositionists."

Cohen thought there was validity in both points of view. "The extent or duration of combat has a great deal of influence on the readjustment problems of the veteran," he said, "but I also think that pre-military experience and development sets someone up to react to the chaos and horror of the war around him. We do know that the problem continues with time. It does *not* go away by itself and we have to deal with both the developmental and war issues in order to treat it."

The APA's official criterion for rendering a diagnosis of PTSD is that an individual has developed "characteristic symptoms following a psychologically traumatic event generally outside the range of usual human experience."[8] While one might reasonably assume this could be applied to all combat veterans, only those who can *prove* service connection for delayed psychological disabilities are eligible for treatment and compensation. And that's not so easy to do. According to a number of vets, the VA claim forms demand the veteran's ability to succinctly describe what is wrong with him, and someone who cannot articulate his distress stands a slim chance of being compensated. One who communicates well, and understands the rules of the game, fares much better.

"I have run into psychiatrists who don't *believe* in PTSD," said Gary, a decorated veteran of Korea and two tours in Vietnam. "They're used to shell-shock victims—comatose, catatonic— and anything else is bullshit. Everybody's reading different books." Gary entered the VA Hospital in Helena, Montana in 1986 and subsequently the PTSD Treatment Unit in Menlo Park, California, where he spent nine months as an inpatient and another four in an outpatient self-help program. Gary claimed the VA took an adversarial stance toward vets applying for treatment. "If they can show some guy is a slow learner, a bit dyslexic, or came from a screwed-up environment *before* he was in the Army, then the government's off the hook. [It] has nothing to do with what happened in Vietnam. It has to do with *now*. You hold the same job for eighteen years and you're married to the same chick, you ain't got PTSD. These guys don't work for you, they work for the government."

Club Fed: The VA's Solution to PTSD

By the late 1980s, the National Center for Post-Traumatic Stress Disorder at the Menlo Park Veterans' Administration Hospital was regarded by our capricious government as *the* Clinical Laboratory and Educational Center for organizations involved in the treatment of PTSD. This state-of-the-art facility and model program—nicknamed "Club Fed" by its intimates—was directed by Fred Gusman, an MSW in clinical and administrative social work with "a lot of on-the-job training." Although a veteran of the Air Force, Gusman never served in Vietnam.

"The treatment here is to take a look at the person's total life and understand how the trauma interacts with both pre- and post-trauma experiences," Gusman explained. "There was 'another person' prior to the trauma and in order to understand *who* was affected by the trauma, you have to know who that other person was." Gusman went on to point out that "nobody ever gets what they think they should get, or even knows *what* they should get. What we do know is that if a person does not follow up with outpatient treatment, and if they do not have a supportive environment, they fail. And that's true wherever you go in the country, no matter what program you talk to."

"They put you in a controlled environment and attempt to stabilize you," Gary told me in reference to his own treatment at Club Fed. "But what they don't do is follow through. A lot of vets go back to the same inappropriate behavior when they leave because they haven't gotten rid of the feelings of guilt and trauma, and they're back trying to stay alive on the street. When the program people hear that they say, 'Well, he just didn't learn anything here. He's just not working his program.'"

Dr. Michael Cohen, who often referred veterans to the National Center for PTSD, reported that their reviews of Gusman's treatment were mixed. "There are people who really feel that it's turned their whole life around, and then there are those who feel it's a total waste of time."

Gestalting: Confrontational Therapy Redefined

Pete settles down, lights his next cigarette from the glowing butt of the last, and continues to tell me the story of his military career and subsequent downward spiral. It is like listening to the sound of a dam slowly breaking apart. A veteran of the I-Corp Combined Action Program in 1968, Pete was no stranger to unfavorable odds and extreme measures. Of the 5000 Marines who served in the backcountry CAP units, fewer than half survived. The other half had to live with the memory of what they had done to stay alive. To fend off his personal demons, Pete chose the needle.

In 1987, recovering from heroin addiction at a VA Hospital in Phoenix, Pete applied to the Menlo Park program. Shortly after being admitted, he was interviewed by a nurse who assured him the answers to her probing questions would be held in strict confidence. The following morning, Pete was introduced to Gusman's second in command, a social worker with first-hand experience in The Family, a Synanon-style "attack-therapy" drug rehab group, and his weapon of choice—a technique he called "gestalting."

Cleaning the 40mm "Duster"
US Army File Photo

Fritz Perls' Gestalt Therapy became popular in the United States during the 1960s. Defined as "a non-interpretative psychotherapy, which emphasizes awareness and personal responsibility,"[9] it has its underpinnings in German *gestalt* psychology, developed in the early 1900s by Max Wertheimer. Irma Lee Shepherd, one of Gestalts' leading proponents, pointed out the dangers involved when inexperienced therapists use its powerfully confrontational techniques to "open up" unstable people with vulnerable personalities. Such people need time, support, and long-term commitment from their therapists, she insists.[10]

"When we started the program in '78," Gusman explained, "we did a number of things that were derived from a treatment modality called "Creative Gestalt." Basically, what we do is similar to any drug and alcohol program. When a new patient comes in, the whole community has a chance to meet this person. The actual technique of Gestalt is using a creative, animated, experiential way of getting people to do self-disclosure. It's sort of a confrontation process. We review a person's chart, what the people who interviewed them wrote; we have a lot of data. There are some people that you have to handle differently based on who they are."

"We had to sit on this red park bench," Pete tells me, "and all the way around in a big 'U' are the other guys who've already had this done to them. When you got in, to take away your identity, any facial hair had to come off. You wore green pajamas for the first three to six weeks and then you had to have your big brother sponsor you to come out of pajamas. So here you are sitting on this bench, a hundred guys all around, giving you the look. [The second in command] then starts the questioning and he's got on his clipboard the 'confidential' interview you did with the nurse."

Pete pauses and stares at the glowing ember at the end of his cigarette, at a memory that still burns in his mind. "There were men who had come in there severely f—ed up, who'd molested children and gone through a treatment program, and he'd get them up there and force them to tell the entire community. I saw people faint, black out, run out the door, or somehow manage to hold it together, and as soon as they were allowed to go to their rooms, pack and run that night. Anything you've said to *anybody,* they stand up and tell in Gestalt."

"Everybody's ratting on everybody else," Gary recalled. "You couldn't really trust anybody and part of that therapy is to *learn* to trust people again."

Dr. Kraig Strapko, an Army Special Forces Medic during the "Vietnamization" period of the early 1970s, ended his Creative Gestalt session with Gusman's henchman ordering him to "sit down, you piece of shit." Strapko reported that this particular social worker "treated everyone like he had a personal vendetta with them. I found it to have no therapeutic value."

Dr. Paul Koller, team leader at the San Jose Vet Center, worked as a clinical psychologist with the Menlo Park Unit between 1982 and 1988. He agreed that gestalting "is probably the most confrontive part of the program. It's *not* my style of therapy and my initial reaction was negative, but after being there six years I really have come to appreciate the need for it as a test of motivation. If they can't do it there, it's relatively certain that they won't be able to complete the program, and it's better to find it out early."

Other clinicians agreed with Koller on this point. "I think the basic strategy of the program was to get guys, when they were new, ready for therapy," said Ron Kurtz, Head Nurse at the Menlo Park PTSD Unit for nine years. "I thought it was an effective tool. I'm sure that guys would disagree and were probably made to feel uncomfortable at times, but it served a purpose."

Hank Stamm, First Marines Force Recon in 1965, wonders what that purpose was. A police officer with a Masters degree in Marriage, Family, and Child Counseling, Hank completed a year-long internship in 1988 at the PTSD Unit in Menlo Park. His experience included process groups, depression groups, focus groups, and psychological testing. He sat in on the majority of the Gestalt groups that year but never participated, except to clarify a question for a vet under fire. "I thought the person who was usually doing [the confrontation] was going through his own shit. I found later that he made it a personal vendetta. I got embarrassed sometimes, the way he went at them."

Dr. Cohen observed that, "the treatment in this field is so new, and has so little precedent, that you have to begin looking at radical ways of treating the problem. Gestalt seems particularly applicable to the PTSD issue and although it may seem brutal from the outside, it's effective. We're talking about a population so well-defended, and so heavily into denial, that indeed it does take a bucket of cold water to get their attention. People that wind up at the PTSD Unit at Menlo Park are one stop away from killing themselves. If indeed the condition is chronic, then the best we can hope for is to help the individual get his feelings under control and wait for the next episode. We're still struggling with that issue."

And Dr. Koller conceded that recidivism was high. "About one-third of the people accomplish very little, one-third really get what they came for, and one-third are somewhere in the middle. There are some folks who simply become dependent on the unit. Every time life gets hard, they hide out there. We try to discourage those."

Gary admitted some vets abuse the system. "Working your claim" in order to profit by bureaucratic snafus is not uncommon. "The VA is paying you to be *sick*. If you're service-connected and you go to the hospital, you get one hundred percent when you're there—$1,461 a month—so, these guys get a lump sum of $10,000 for being in the hospital all this time, and they abuse themselves and use up all the money. And when it gets cold under the bridge, they have a 'relapse,' and go back and do it again. The longer you're into this behavior pattern, the harder it is to break out of it. You have this invisible umbilical cord attaching you to the VA for the rest of your life."

"This is a chronic illness," Fred Gusman concluded, "and that means that somebody being re-hospitalized after two years might be acceptable."

Imaginal Flooding: How to Make a Grown Man Cry

Fred Gusman's concept of "understanding who you *really* are" was the operating principle behind "focus," a technique considered by the vets to be the most solemn ritual of the entire program. In Vivio or Imaginal Flooding[11] is an exposure technique used in Cognitive Behavioral Therapy (CBT), and other forms of treatment since the 1960s, but at Club Fed the process seems to have been shrouded in the mystery of a Masonic ritual.

"The focus groups are this hallowed thing," Pete tells me. "They're encouraged to eat together, talk together, stay together. The psychologists rarely *ran* the focus groups; they just sat and looked at you." Members of a focus group were encouraged to try their hand at gestalting individuals in the hot seat, probing for denial and dissimulation. After relating a few of his gruesome experiences to the group, Pete had been upbraided by his "peers" and told how things really were. "I thought I was going in with combat veterans and it turned out that of my group of twelve, only three of us were. I just knew the rest could *not* understand."

Assault on Hill 875
US Army File Photo

Pete was subsequently taken into private session and "flooded" by one of the program's clinical psychologists. "This guy sat me down and told me that he wanted me to relax. 'Now, Pete, what I want you to recall is that incident you mentioned [in the focus group].'"

Pete's unit had been part of Operation Zippo, in which US troops were ordered to burn villages and force-march the inhabitants to refugee camps in Da Nang. On the banks of a raging river, during a mass-evacuation, pregnant women were miscarrying, wailing, frightened to death, so a human chain of Marines was formed to expedite the crossing. Some of them, according to Pete, had been "in country too long, seen too much death, gotten too numb." They apparently found sport in holding small children underwater beneath their boots, then watching the corpses float down river, away from sight of their CO. Women were molested in mid-stream, and no baby ever made it across, even though Pete says he helped deliver one on the riverbank. [Ed. Note: no official record of this operation has been uncovered.]

"So the psychologist tells me, 'Okay, Pete, you know—and I know—that *you* were the one drowning them.' And I thought, oh, my God! He must know something I didn't. He told me to feel those hands scratching at my legs." Pete chokes and turns away so I won't see the tears in his eyes. "Well, Christ, I was out of it, bumping into walls, crying, and he says to me, 'Now, we have to end off here. You come back and see me on Tuesday'—it was Friday afternoon — 'and I want you to *stay with that feeling*. It's important that you stay with it.'" Pete shakes his head in disbelief. "This dogshit shrink actually *convinced* me that I had drowned children. That, I *know* I didn't do."

"What I'm really trying to do is to help the patient, for the very first time, to get some insight into how they think," Gusman claimed. "And we want to dispel the myth that everybody is a steely-eyed killer."

"I learned soon enough that you can't really get into anything because you only have an hour," Gary told me. "You're in the middle of stuff and the therapist would say, 'Hey man, hold that thought, I'll see you next Monday.' So I just ended up saying, 'Look, I'm really sorry, but I haven't got years and years to spend here doing this.'"

"Staying with the feeling" and the "fifty-minute hour"—around which so many therapists construct their practice—is of scant therapeutic value for most veterans suffering from PTSD. Once revivified in a session, the horrors of war can't wait until the following week to be addressed. These guys have been staying with the feeling for years—and that, precisely, *is* their problem.

Grassroots Alternatives: Outreach and Outsource

According to Vietnam veteran and author, Larry Heinemann, "the Veterans' Administration —now kicked up to the Cabinet level—has never been regarded by Vietnam veterans as an advocate of their health and well-being."[12] Luckily, there are grassroots organizations, founded by Vietnam veterans, which provide alternatives to the VA's idea of treatment.

"The Vet Center system is based on getting out into the community and reaching the vets," explained Dr. Michael Cohen. "Where we can't, we subcontract with a clinician who is well-versed in the area of PTSD. For many of us, this is a mission. We're helping each other." But he went on to explain that outreach programs—such as Vietnam Veterans of America and Swords to Plowshares—while focusing extremely well on social services—"dabble in treatment. Essentially they hire someone who is a clinician. That person becomes the clinical coordinator and maybe starts a group, sees one or two clients for counseling, but it's not extensive and by no means is it the primary focus of the agency."

In 1987, a grassroots movement began to grow around a technique called Traumatic Incident Reduction [TIR], developed some years earlier as means of inspecting psychic trauma. A synthesis of several classic disciplines, TIR, according to those vets who have worked with it, provided a new model for the treatment of post-traumatic stress, and one unencumbered by government bureaucracy or political agendas.[13]

Traumatic Incident Reduction: Back to the Future

Dave stares down, eyes focused on a point past infinity. His eyes are narrowed, his face ruddy, like a man who is exerting an enormous amount of effort to escape from something dark and terrifying that lives in the outback of his mind.

"Have another look," says the facilitator, a big man with a silver beard sitting across the table.

Dave recounts his story for the third time and there is a perceptible edge to his voice, as if his boredom is curdling into frustration. "The district manager and I had this verbal agreement concerning the percentage of sales I would receive. But he decided to rearrange the commission structure before I was paid. We're talking about nearly seven thousand dollars here. Damn it, I earned that money." Dave breathes deeply and closes his eyes. His square jaw clenches tightly, and when he continues there is a slight trembling in his voice. "I know that I have to confront him. But every time I even think about doing it my stomach just knots up." His face flushes with rage and humiliation. "Here I am, this bad-ass, black belt Marine, scared shitless over the thought of asking for money that's actually owed me. I don't understand why people always take advantage of me. Hell, I don't know why I *let* them."

Dave stops and swallows hard. He looks up, angst radiating from watery blue eyes, and shrugs resignedly, signifying that he's once again reached "the wall"—a barrier beyond which his memory cannot penetrate.

The bearded man nods in genuine empathy. "Okay," the facilitator acknowledges. "Now, take a look and tell me if there is an earlier, similar incident?"

Dave pulls a deep breath into his lungs, closes his eyes and attempts to pierce that tenebrous cloud of the past, where unspeakable phantasms lurk and disturb the sanctity of his sleep. "Yeah, *there*," his facilitator says, "What do you see right there?"

Suddenly, Dave is a twenty-five-year-old Lance Corporal, 0351 [Infantry, Anti-tank Assault], walking through the bush near Chu Lai. It is January of 1967, and he's on his second tour of duty, his ninety-second patrol in Vietnam. There is the smell of rain-soaked foliage and warm, redolent earth. It is dusk and the mosquitoes are beginning to swarm at the saline smell of human sweat. There are the sounds of jungle life signaling the ingress of night and, above them all, there is the sound of his own heart pumping adrenaline into his veins. It is not like a recollection, not some vague, distant memory. He is *there*, in the grip of a fear that has possessed him from the moment his boots touched Vietnamese soil. He has nearly eleven more months of hell to live through before they will lift his feet out of this fetid nightmare.

When the sniper fire begins, Dave drops to one knee and wields his three-point-five rocket launcher, instinctively aiming toward the outcropping of trees he believes to be the enemy position. He calls for his first gunner to stand by for loading, but the eighteen-year-old balks and runs for the nearest cover. Dave, livid with anger, rises up and in that moment is hit in the shoulder by AK-47 fire. Pain excoriates reason; rage obliterates the pain. As soon as Dave can reach the tree line he fully intends to beat the living shit out of the callow grunt who has left him with his ass in the breeze.

It's all in slow motion now: the loping run toward the trees, the sound of "popcorn" and the rush of wind as thirty-caliber projectiles rip past his ears, the blood drenching his flack jacket, the numbing in his arm, and the overwhelming fury rising in him with the pressure of an erupting geyser. Now he spots the gunner, a solid grey silhouetted against the variegated grey of the bush, barely human in appearance, his hands shaking with spastic intensity. And in those hands is an M-16 automatic assault rifle, safety thrown, aimed directly at Dave's chest.

Looking for snipers on Hill 822.
US Army File Photo

Dave exhales a slow expletive, and only then realizes he's been holding his breath a good fifteen seconds. "Shit! I just backed off, real easy. Only a flesh wound, man. No problem. I just knew if I even looked cross-eyed at this kid he would blow me away."

The bearded man nods, signifying understanding. "I got that," he says. Dave knows he has. "Let's go back to the beginning and run through it again."

Dave does so, three more times. At first it is painful, then boring, and then, on the fourth recounting, Dave chuckles to himself. It is a small escape of air accompanying a great explosion of clarity. The facilitator nods and queries, "So, how are you doing?"

Dave looks up and his eyes sparkle with amusement. "I'm doing fine." His face has relaxed, as if some emotional pillory has been lifted from his neck. "It's a stupid thing, really. It just occurred to me that not all the people I have to confront in life are armed and dangerous. I guess its okay to be pissed off if you've got a good reason to be."

The bearded man returns Dave's broad smile; it's hard to judge which of them feels a greater sense of accomplishment in this moment. "That's great, Dave. We'll end right here."

Dave's TIR session lasted one hour and twenty-two minutes. But for him, its brief duration opened a window of resolution in a world of despair.

By 1986, twenty years after his tour of duty in Vietnam, Dave had sunk into self-imposed isolation. His marriage had failed, several business deals had fallen through, his latest girlfriend had left, and he was drinking heavily. Dave called the VA Hospital in Menlo Park and was connected to a counselor from a local veterans' outreach program. He determined that Dave was probably suffering from PTSD, and suggested he join a ninety-minute Thursday evening discussion group for combat veterans.

"It was not as advertised," Dave told me in disgust. "I think that the program was compensated by head count. Of the eleven there, only three were combat veterans. There was never any therapy given or suggested or directed. It was evaluative; they would encourage the other people in the group to give their observations, corrections, and opinions to you directly. The deeper you dug your traumatic hole, the better it was. That's working your program. I got into drinking heavily again and finally quit going."

Shortly thereafter, Pete met Dave at a Club Fed graduate function and told him about TIR, a therapy Pete credited with changing the direction of his life. And although untrained in the procedure, Pete ran Dave through a rudimentary session, enough to convince Dave of TIR's potential.

Traumatic Incident Reduction was developed by Dr. Frank A. Gerbode, along with several colleagues, as an alternative to psychotherapy. An Honors graduate from Stanford in Philosophy, Dr. Gerbode received an MD from Yale Medical School and completed his psychiatric residency at Stanford Medical Center in the early 1970s. "I also worked at the VA on a psychiatric ward. They were completely eclectic," he laughs. "They were honestly searching and groping and trying to find an answer, and they sorely needed to find a fast, effective, and systematic approach to PTSD. That, I feel, is what TIR has to offer."

According to Dr. Gerbode, "The purpose of TIR is to trace back sequences of traumatic incidents to their roots and thereby to reduce or eliminate the charge [repressed, unfulfilled intention] contained therein by completing the activity cycles that were interrupted by acts of repression. Each sequence of incidents depends for its force on the root incident from which it stems...In most cases, however, it is not possible to proceed directly to the root incident of a sequence. So much charge is usually contained in later incidents that memory of the root incident is partially or totally blocked. It is therefore necessary to proceed backward from present time, addressing later incidents first and discharging them somewhat before looking for earlier ones."[14]

Although Dr. Gerbode labels it "retrospection" rather than "regression," TIR nevertheless has its roots in the precursor to psychoanalysis. In the late 1800s, Josef Breuer, a Viennese physician used an abreaction procedure he called the "talking cure—a recalling or re-experiencing of stressful or disturbing situations or events which appear to have precipitated a neurosis."[15] His young colleague, Sigmund Freud, used the technique as his working model for psychoanalysis, noting that the key to a recent disturbance lay in an earlier, similar trauma, sometimes an entire chain of incidents.[16]

Far from exclusively Freudian in his approach, Dr. Gerbode incorporated the repetitive and gradient aspects of Behavior Therapy's "desensitization" process, developed by Joseph Wolpe and Arnold Lazarus, wrapped in the "person-centered" rubric of Carl Rogers, wherein a therapist refrains from offering any interpretation of his client's personal experiences.

In the practice of Traumatic Incident Reduction, the client is called a "viewer" and the therapist a "facilitator," nomenclature strategically designed to obviate the "patient/therapist" model. "I do not refer to people as *patients,* nor to people who render help to other people as *therapists,*" says Gerbode. "I concur fully with Thomas Szasz, who has brilliantly shown that the concept of 'mental illness' is a mere metaphor, and a useless and destructive one at that."[17]

Critical to the technique's successful application are the concepts of a safe environment and end points. "TIR requires a great deal of attention and concentration, and so the environment in which it occurs must be very safe...Flexible session lengths are essential to the creation of a safe environment. It is vital for the facilitator to be able to end a session at an 'end point,' where the viewer feels good because something has been resolved. If the viewer feels confident that he will have time to resolve anything he encounters during a session, he will allow himself to get into highly charged areas."[18]

Dr. Robert Moore, a clinical psychologist in Rational Emotive Behavioral Therapy from Clearwater Florida, has used the technique, with impressive results, with his own clients. "I went to San Francisco and took an opportunity to get acquainted with it because it sounded good, and found out that it didn't just *sound* good. There isn't anything going on in the professional community among my colleagues in psychology, or psychiatry, or counseling, or psychotherapy that equals it. My experience is that if somebody is willing to persist with the procedure, it is inevitable that he gets relief. I'm quite convinced that Traumatic Incident Reduction is the state-of-the-art handling for post-traumatic stress disorder."

> *"There isn't anything going on in the professional community among my colleagues in psychology, or psychiatry, or counseling, or psychotherapy that equals it."*
> —Dr. Robert Moore

Both Drs. Moore and Gerbode presented case studies on their work with TIR and conducted workshops at the annual conference of the International Society for Traumatic Stress Studies, held in New Orleans during October of 1990, impressing a number of clinical practitioners in the field with the technological simplicity and logic of their approach.

"Most of the people I have worked with don't have *any* trouble locating key incidents. They're sitting in them when they walk in the door," observes Gerald French, co-author of the definitive text on TIR,[19] Dave's facilitator, and a non-veteran. "All the literature you read on PTSD says it's *got* to be a vet that works with another vet. I think what we've done proves it doesn't have to be. It isn't a problem for the facilitator as long as the viewer trusts you."

Gary's facilitator is a forty-five-year-old mother of three who has never been anywhere near a boot camp, let alone a battlefield. Yet Gary feels comfortable telling her things he could not even admit to other vets. "I probably feel a lot better now than even *before* I went into the service," Gary admits, adding a note of cynicism, "Many vets will hesitate to use TIR because it might interfere with their disability claim."

Bruce, a veteran of the 864th Army Engineers at Cam Rahn Bay in 1965, spent eight months at the Menlo Park PTSD Unit. Although he felt that he got something out of the program, he soon found himself back in the Palo Alto VA Hospital with a lot of unresolved issues, a broken relationship, and flashbacks. In June of 1989, Bruce began working with TIR. "I had almost two years of straight hospital time and I have done more in two weeks with TIR. It's the first time I truly feel like I've got some direction back in my life."

Gun crew on 175mm howitzer takes a break
US Army File Photo

Dr. Gerbode believed the beauty of TIR facilitation is that it could be taught to veterans without any specialized backgrounds, enabling them to effectively co-facilitate. He developed a basic training course that teaches the rudimentary skills in about six weeks.

Lori Beth Bisbey, a former volunteer at the Vet Centers and counselor with the Federal prison system, conducted the first technically scientific study of TIR in the early 1990s. Utilizing fifty-seven crime victims, Bisbey compared the efficacy of TIR with that of a direct therapeutic exposure [DTE] and an untreated control group. Her results proved both treatment modalities to be effective, but determined that the TIR group showed significantly greater improvement in their condition.[20]

Acutely aware of the credence accorded double-blind studies by members of his profession; Dr. Gerbode was the first to express caution in his evaluation of the data. "We want to be fairly modest in our claims at this point. It seems that the one thing we can be sure of is that the specific symptoms of PTSD—the nightmares, free-floating anxiety, flashbacks, severe emotional distress—are basically handled. Usually, these people have other things that are upsetting them that don't necessarily have anything to do with PTSD. I think those *could* be handled, but it would take a more extensive program."

Lieutenant Colonel Chris Christensen was not very interested in the "scientific" imprimatur of double-blind studies. When the combat veteran and undercover sniper in Vietnam learned that his son had been murdered in Texas, Christensen loaded enough armament into the trunk of his car to take out half of San Antonio. But on his way through California, he had the good sense to call Pete—who he'd serendipitously heard interviewed on a radio program—instead of continuing south to seek revenge. After an emergency session, administered without ceremony in Pete's driveway, Christensen underwent a full course in TIR with Gerbode and French before returning to Idaho, where 110,000 vets compose more than ten percent of the state's population. Trained as a social worker, Christensen immediately began applying what he called "Wildcat TIR" to his comrades in PTSD.

"When I arrived at Job Services in Lewiston, Idaho, there were in excess of 150 disabled veterans on the rolls seeking employment. With the skills learned through TIR training—I'm talking the one week, forty-hour intensive course—I would estimate that I have worked with sixty of those people, anywhere from two hours to twenty hours, max—the average probably running closer to fourteen or fifteen hours. And out of those sixty people that I worked with, I had two—that's one, *two*—left on the rolls, seeking employment, when I left Idaho [in 1991]."

Christensen took no credit for his extraordinary work. "*They* did it," he insisted. "What a wonderful gift, to walk into a VA hospital, to be able to take one of their 'rejects' that they haven't been able to help in twelve, fourteen, eighteen months, and in a period of two or three weeks, give them a tool they can use the rest of their lives, and see a marked improvement. I don't know *what* this stuff is, but by God, it works!"

Recalling his intervention with Chris, Pete leans into his words with evangelistic zeal, a fierce desire to drive home his point. "I can't even describe what I went through for twenty years, but I know very much what it's like when I see another guy sitting in it." Pete momentarily appraises the louvered window that slammed shut in the wind as we talked several hours ago. He remembers just how far he's come since those months at Club Fed when he could not imagine passing a single hour in peace. "Look, I'm not saying TIR is a panacea," he concludes with characteristic understatement, "But I think fifty hours would handle the shit out of most people."

Last Exit: The Cynical Reality

There were no winners in Vietnam, only survivors who found themselves, in the twilight of the slaughter, desperately searching for a way to make some sense out of the insanity they had witnessed. Many never found it. "66,000 Vietnam veterans—particularly combat veterans—committed suicide within the first year of returning home from service," said Joe Fegan, Public Information Officer for Chapter 464 of the Vietnam Veterans of America. "It exceeded the total number of deaths in the war. The cause was the trauma suffered."

The survivors—every one of them—carry forever the mental image pictures of what they have seen and done. Like all soldiers, they harden themselves to those disturbing mementos; store them in the armored lock-box of their dignity. But sooner or later, all warriors must confront that darkness within their own hearts. For them it is the ultimate, inescapable battle—and regrettably one in which they lack many compassionate allies.

In 1990, I discussed these unsettling suicide statistics with an old friend, a Freudian psychoanalyst of international renown. Fascinated by the implications of PTSD, he eagerly read the above manuscript, based on my interviews with twenty combat veterans and therapists. His written response elegantly encapsulated the cynicism these veterans constantly face:

Vietnam Veterans Memorial

"Certainly, one can applaud any effort to help the guys you introduce us to; but your enthusiasm for the creativity and the idealism of the therapists—and the contrast to the distant establishment that you implicitly portray—strikes me as naïve. What comes across to me is that the psychologists, *et al* are glamorizing themselves and their results in order to make a living and feel effective—they're working their counter-claims just as the vets are working their claims. It's a tragedy—humanly and understandably corrupt. One can be sympathetic without sentimentalizing it. I'd rather see you work it into a short story that captures the painful, relatively hopeless reality. Something in the spirit of *Last Exit to Brooklyn*."

Chris Christensen died in Germany of natural causes in October 1992, while arranging airlifts of humanitarian aid to the desperate inhabitants of the former Yugoslavia. And I'm glad I never showed him the psychiatrist's letter, because the big-hearted grizzly bear of a man would probably have stalked into my friend's neatly appointed Victorian office, slapped him in the face with a long list of the vets Chris had naïvely helped—*pro bono*—leveled his steely gray eyes at the analyst, and growled: "You tell *these* folks it's hopeless, doc!"

Vietnam Era Glossary

Glossary items from Wikipedia (http://en.wikipedia.org/) unless otherwise noted

CAP: The Combined Action Program (CAP) placed a squad of Marines and one Navy Corpsman in villages from Chu Lai to the DMZ in South Vietnam from 1965 to 1971. A total of 5,000 troops were deployed in CAP (source: Tim Duffy, CAPMarine.com)

DMZ (Demilitarized Zone): In military terms, a demilitarized zone (DMZ) is an area, usually the frontier or boundary between two or more groups, where military activity is not permitted, usually by treaty or other agreement. Often the demilitarized zone lies upon a line of control and forms a de-facto international border.

Fragging: "Frag incidents" or "fragging" was soldier slang in Vietnam for the killing of strict, unpopular and aggressive officers and NCO's [Non-Commissioned Officers]. The word apparently originated from enlisted men using fragmentation grenades to kill commanders. Congressional hearings on fraggings held in 1973 estimated that roughly 3% of officer and non-com deaths in Vietnam between 1961 and 1972 were a result of fraggings. But these figures were only for killings committed with grenades, and didn't include officer deaths from automatic weapons fire, handguns and knifings (!). The Army's Judge Advocate General's Corps estimated that only 10% of fragging attempts resulted in anyone going to trial. (source: Kevin Keating)

Grunt: The US Marines divide themselves into two camps. Those who do the fighting are "grunts." Those who do not are POGs, "persons other than grunts". POGs are the support element of the Marine Corps. To a grunt, a POG is anyone with access to a hot meal and a shower and at night beds down in a cot. They resupply the grunts with food, fuel and water. They make repairs. They perform the thousands of jobs that make fighting possible. It is the grunts, however, who do the fighting, the killing and, most often, the dying. They consider themselves modern-day warriors. (Source: John Murphy)

Medevac (Medical Evacuation): A MEDEVAC is a military acronym for "medical evacuation." A MEDEVAC is also a helicopter used as an ambulance. This permits the rapid transport of seriously injured persons, particularly trauma patients, from the scene of the accident to the hospital. The US military pioneered this lifesaving technique during the Korean War. Many patients transported by MEDEVAC are taken to a specialized hospital known as a trauma center.

NVA (North Vietnamese Army): The People's Army of Vietnam was the regularly trained and organized military force of the North Vietnamese government during the Vietnam War. The PAVN typically operated in regimental strength but sometimes formed elements as small as companies. Unlike the Viet Cong, the PAVN was not a guerilla force.

Point (Walking Point): A reconnaissance or patrol unit that moves ahead of an advance party or guard, or that follows a rear guard. The position occupied by such a unit or guard: "A team of Rangers were walking point at the outset of the operation." Point is one of the most dangerous positions of combat.

Short timer: Contrary to what it sounds like, a short-timer is a combat veteran very near the end of his tour of duty. Men in such a position would often rarely take any avoidable risks. Contrast with the FNG [F—ing New Guy], a new arrival who is dangerous to everyone until he learns the ropes.

Victor Charlie: military phonetic alphabetic representation of "VC", used as a radio code-word. VC is an abbreviation for Viet Cong (see below).

Viet Cong: The National Front for the Liberation of Vietnam or National Liberation Front was known to American soldiers in Vietnam as the Viet Cong—from a contraction for the Vietnamese phrase Viet Nam Cong San, or "Vietnamese Communist."

This originally derogatory phrase was used by the Republic of Vietnam (RVN) government of South Vietnam under President Ngo Dinh Diem to describe his political opponents, many of whom were Communists, starting after the partition of Vietnam between the RVN in the South and the Democratic Republic of Vietnam (DRV) in the North which took place in 1954. Later, during the Vietnam War, the RVN and the United States government used this expression to refer to the National Front for the Liberation of Vietnam (NLF) and its guerrilla army, the People's Liberation Armed Forces (PLAF). (The NLF and the PLAF themselves never used this expression to refer to themselves, and always asserted that they were a national front of all anti-RVN forces, communist or not.) It is this use of "Viet Cong" that most people in the United States and Europe are most familiar.

Notes:

---

[1] Goodwin, Jim, The Etiology of Combat-Related Post Traumatic Stress Disorder (Cincinnati: Disabled American Veterans, 1987) p.11.

[2] Figley, Charles R., Stress Disorders among Vietnam Veterans: Theory, Research and Treatment (New York: Brunner/Mazel, 1978)

[3] Tiffany, W.J. & Allerton, W.S., "Army Psychiatry in the Mid-60s" (American Journal of Psychiatry, 1967, 123: 810-821)

[4] Bourne, P.G., Men, Stress and Vietnam (Boston: Little, Brown, 1970)

[5] The President's Commission on Mental Health, 1978

[6] Ibid. See note 1.

[7] Williams, Tom, Post-Traumatic Stress Disorder: A Handbook for Clinicians (Cincinnati: Disabled American Veterans, 1987). See National Commander's address.

[8] From the Diagnostic and Statistical Manual, Third Edition (DSM-III) of the American Psychiatric Association (APA, 1980).

[9] The Oxford Companion to the Mind, (Oxford: Oxford University Press, 1987).

[10] Shepherd, I.L. "Limitations and Caution in the Gestalt Approach," Gestalt Therapy Now, (eds.) Fagan, J. and Shepherd, I. L., (New York: 1970)

[11] Keane, T,M., & Kaloupek, D.G., (1982) "Imaginal Flooding in the Treatment of Post-Traumatic Stress Disorder." Journal of Consulting & Clinical Psychology, 50, pps. 138-140.

[12] Heinemann, Larry, "The Road From Afghanistan," (Playboy, July 1989, p.163)

[13] Joyce Carbonell and Charles Figley of Florida State University identified four promising "power therapies" in a 1993-98 study of trauma victims. In addition to TIR, they included: Eye Movement Desensitization and Reprocessing [EMDR], developed by Francine Shapiro; Thought Field Therapy [TFT], originally the Roger Callahan Technique; and Visual-Kinesthetic Dissociation [V/KD], based on the Neuro-Linguistic Programing theories of Richard Bandler and John Grinder. All have proven relatively effective.

[14] Gerbode, Frank A., M.D., "Handling the Effects of Past Traumatic Incidents" (Journal of the Institute for Research in Metapsychology, 1988, Vol.1, Issue 4, p.6).

[15] Ibid. See note 9.

[16] Freud, Sigmund, Two Short Accounts of Psychoanalysis, (tr.) James Strachey (Singapore: Penguin Books,1984), p. 37.

[17] Gerbode, Frank A., Beyond Psychology, (Palo Alto: IRM Press, 1988), p.215.

[18] Ibid. See note 17.

[19] French, Gerald D., and Harris, Chrys J., Traumatic Incident Reduction [TIR], (Boca Raton: CRC Press, 1999).

[20] Bisbey, L.B., No Longer a Victim: A treatment outcome study of crime victims with posttraumatic stress disorder. (Doctoral Dissertation, California School of Professional Psychology in San Diego, 1995).

A Combat Vet's Perspective on TIR
By Lt. Col Chris Christensen, U.S. Army (Ret.)

Excerpted from the Winter 1991 issue of the Institute for Research in Metapsychology Newsletter.

First, a bit of background: at the end of 1984, I retired as a Lieutenant Colonel after 22 years of active military service, of which 13 years were spent overseas. Two of those years were spent in a combat zone in Vietnam, during which I was frequently involved in what are called "unconventional" solo operations.

When I made the decision to retire, I had little knowledge of veteran entitlements, and *none* of PTSD—the malady associated with "those crazy Vietnam vets".

In 1985, I began working for the Idaho Department of Employment. From 1986 to 1990, I was working exclusively with vets. I am called a Disabled Veterans Outreach Program (DVOP) Specialist, and my job is to assist vets to become and remain job-ready and to obtain meaningful employment.

Through my exposure to the local vet population and my efforts to understand their situations and questions, I began my owfn painful education. I found out about PTSD. I recognized that a lot of the Idaho vets suffered from it. And I discovered that I did, too, though my own disabilities had not prevented me from being employed full time.

There were no service providers or agencies that could cure the problem. Those that claimed to have the tools available required months of in-patient therapy and appeared to address symptoms rather than causes. Further, the benefits of such programs did not seem lasting; negative behavior patters quickly returned to the individuals after treatment. Finally, and worse, there was nothing that *I* could really do myself to help the vets I worked with. I could not do my job. I couldn't get them past the "hard spots" that prevented them from holding meaningful employment. And I was tired of seeing the same people and starting over with them every six to twelve months.

Early in 1990, a colleague told me about a radio program he had heard on which a Florida psychologist named Robert Moore had discussed a procedure called "Traumatic Incident Reduction" (TIR) with Pieter van Aggelen, a Vietnam Marine combat vet. Pieter, I was told, was a layman who had been trained in the use of TIR and who had claimed some rather amazing positive results in working with other vets; he'd said, among other things, that it "handled the hell" out of PTSD.

Skeptical but interested, I managed to track down Dr. Moore and he referred me to Pieter in Menlo Park, California. Following several phone conversations with Pieter, I made arrangements to go to Menlo Park for some TIR sessions. The day I left for California, I was notified that my son, who lived in Texas, had died—suddenly and unexpectedly. Before going to the funeral in Texas, I went to Menlo Park and had my first sessions of TIR. They helped me a *lot*.

After the funeral, I returned to California and got a few more sessions from Pieter. I then spent five days in a very intensive workshop with Gerald French, in which I learned the basics of TIR. Then I went home and began to use the procedure as a facilitator—for the most part with vets whom I had previously been unable to help.

In the months since my return to Idaho, I have acted as a TIR facilitator for some 27 severely traumatized people. To date, I have done this at my own expense and on my own time. The Idaho Department of Employment does not recognize TIR as a procedure that may be used by a state employee on the job.

Yet, as I write this, nearly a year after my trip to Menlo Park, my own classic PTSD symptoms and associated behavior patterns have not returned. Nor have those of most of the people I have worked with—combat vets and abused or otherwise traumatized civilians alike. The great majority of them became and have remained fully functional and able to make sane choices as a result of our sessions.

This is not to say that none of them have any problems left. Of course they do. But the quality of their lives and their ability to control their choices have shown marked and stable improvement—with this exception: I was told during my TIR training that I would find it difficult or impossible to help clients (with TIR alone) who were actively drug- or alcohol-dependent. That, I've found, is true.

I am by nature a skeptic and a non-believer. I continue to be amazed that so simple a process works so well and in such a short amount of time. However, this assessment of TIR's power and effectiveness is not unique. I have given before- and after-TIR questionnaires to each of the people I've worked with. This test permits a quantification of progress or lack of progress. The results, though impressive, do not constitute any sort of clinical or scientific "proof" of the efficacy of TIR. Despite this, I can assure you that, for the person off the street who feels better after completing TIR, something very significant has happened. I regularly get feedback in the form of comments such as: "I don't know how I would have made it through the month without this", "I haven't felt this good in twenty years", "What did you **do**?", "Why hasn't ____ been able to help me like this in all these years?", and "I haven't held a job this long since 'Nam!" As David W. Powell, a vet who has experienced it stated succinctly—"This stuff works!"

...I believe there is a need to provide a TIR capability somewhere along the medical evacuation/evaluation chain...

In brief, the frustration I felt for so long at not having a tool I could use to help people past the rough spots has been replaced by the frustration I now feel at not having enough time to help all the people that I now know I could help. Also, by the wish that more people would be trained as facilitators so that all the suffering that could be handled with TIR *will* be.

As we enter a period of returnees from the war in Iraq, I believe there is a need to provide a TIR capability somewhere along the medical evacuation/evaluation chain so as to truly help traumatized vets to remove emotional charge before life has a chance to encsyt the trauma they will have experienced—as it did with so many of us in the past.

[Ed. Note: Christensen refers above to the first Gulf War, codenamed "Desert Storm", that ran from Aug. 6th, 1990 to March 8, 1991]

Needless to say, TIR has my personal recommendation. It worked on me, and I have seen it relieve the suffering of many others as well. I greatly regret that such a procedure was not available earlier. Much suffering and resource waste could have been avoided.

To the TIR Association and the members who support its work, I say thank you for pausing long enough to hear me, for taking the time to help me personally, and for having trained me to be able to help others—and for being there whenever I've needed support.

I *still* can't believe it works as well as I'm forced to admit that it does.

Lt. Col Chris Christensen (Ret.)
Chris Christensen, Lewiston, Idaho

January 1991

The "Wildcat": Experiences with TIR
By Lt. Col. Chris Christensen (Ret.)

Excerpted from the Fall 1992 issue of the Institute for Research in Metapsychology Newsletter

In Memoriam by Gerald French

Just two weeks before he was to join us as one of the principal speakers at the European Conference on Metapsychology in Munich, Lt. Col. Chris Christensen (Ret.) died suddenly and unexpectedly. Chris trained with us in Traumatic Incident Reduction (TIR) in 1989, subsequently devoting hundreds of hours of his own time to working with fellow combat vets, their families, and other trauma survivors, to take away their pain. His body failed while he pursued the duties of his formal work, arranging for the transshipment of humanitarian aid to the desperate peoples of Eastern Europe. His death occurred in Germany on the morning of October 29th, 1992, and was of "natural" causes, if such a word can be employed to describe the loss of this kind and gifted man to whom so many grateful people surrendered so much hurt.

What follows is the transcript of a tape that Chris sent us shortly after his arrival in Germany to take up his duties there and to scout out quarters for himself and his lovely wife, Lee. He made the tape one evening, sitting on a single bed in a small hotel room by himself.

Transcribing his words was somewhat difficult for me. Hearing Chris' voice—his laughter, the occasional pauses of the tape when he permitted himself the tears of joy that facilitators experience from time to time in reflecting on the simple miracles that their skills produce—drove home to me the loss his death represents to all the ones he didn't get the chance to help.

Chris wouldn't have approved of my reaction at all. He'd have said something like, "Stop sniveling, Ger! If I could do it, so can a lot of other folks!" And he'd have been right, of course...

Gerald D. French, MA, CTS
November 1992

This is Chris Christensen. I'm making this tape on the 2nd of March, 1992, in Stuttgart, Germany.

Some months ago, Gerald French gave me a call and asked me if I would be kind enough to talk about "Wildcat" Traumatic Incident Reduction (TIR). He then went on to say that it would be very nice if I could relate some of the "cases," if you will, that I have worked with and just give some general background on the types of people that I've worked with. Well, that obviously becomes a bit more difficult. [In what follows] I do not use names. The other thing that becomes very difficult is this: it is amazing how hard it is to recall the individual, and his or her traumatic incident and how they unraveled in our sessions. It seems as though the training that I received is extremely successful in allowing my viewers to walk away without their heavy pictures "sticking" to me. As a result, I have found that it is, in some cases, difficult even to remember the names of the people that I have worked with over the last, oh, almost two years now.

> *It seems as though the training that I received is extremely successful in allowing my viewers to walk away without their heavy pictures "sticking" to me.*

Another thing that has become very evident to me in working with TIR is that I have become much more tolerant in my understanding of what a traumatic incident is. I've realized that what is traumatic to one may well not seem traumatic to another, and that what may seem insignificant to me can be a mountain of crap to another. It is amazing to see what might be, by my definition, a very insignificant thing, cause a tremendous amount of pain—real pain—and emotional discharge in another. That's been a very positive learning experience for me, one that says, "Don't mess with the system!" TIR works, as long as you don't mess with it. Good stuff!

It is amazing how relaxed and tolerant I've become, too, when observing intense emotional discharge take place in a viewer (client) during a session of TIR. While a viewer is in the bottom of the pit—groveling, snot-running, et cetera—I've come to know full well that this is [just] a process that takes place, the end result of which is going to be just ... beautiful! And when they come back up out of that crap and look at you, clear-eyed, and say, "Wow! Thanks!" ... well, it's just wonderful stuff.

Another thing I've learned is that it's impossible to assist a person through the TIR process and mentally jump ahead to a "logical" conclusion. If there is one thing that I have found, it is that if I lose concentration during a session—if my "shield" goes down—and part of my mind jumps forward to speculate, I can almost rest assured that that conclusion I imagine for the viewer will be the wrong one when it all washes out. That again says to me: be very confident in the process of TIR itself. Let the procedure run its course. I may well tend to allow things to continue longer than I normally would, or than I would normally feel comfortable in doing, but I have found that by allowing TIR to run its course—even if it is longer than where I think it might want to go—I find that the end result tends to be much more satisfying, much more clear in the viewer's mind. And as a result, the success at the end of it is just short of phenomenal.

Okay. Having said that, I will run down a few things, for what they are worth. If you care to use any of it at all, shucks ... have at it! Anything that I can do to help spread TIR ... well, I'm for it.

During my initial training in Menlo Park, I had someone in mind to start out with on my return to Idaho: a combat vet—Viet Nam — who had been in the thick of a lot of killing and mayhem; a man who suffered the classic symptoms of post-traumatic stress disorder, who "job-hopped" and who, frankly, I was tired of seeing show up in front of my desk on the average of once every four months, saying, "Lost my job again ... I need another job ... The family's getting hungry, and, oh, by the way, I've been drunk for the last three days ... and I'm broke."

Well, that guy and I started down the road. Thinking back on it, I recall my thoughts as he relived his combat experiences. I can recall very distinctly....

Hmm! That's strange! I hadn't thought of it 'til now—that I was thinking, "That's not so bad; *I* did worse than that. *I* was in deeper crap than *that*. What's *your* problem, fella?" —those kinds of thoughts. I remembered Gerald's instructions, though: "Keep your mouth shut and let the procedure work." And I did.

That session was a long one, by the way, probably one of the longer ones that I've given. I may well have had an overrun or two, and mixed two or three incidents into the same string before it was all over, but it was dramatic at the end of it. I didn't miss the final end point. It blew in my face. It ... it was wonderful! [Ed. Note: overrun occurs when the facilitator runs a procedure past the end point.]

In the course of running down after the session was over, he mentioned that he had a friend that was in a town about thirty-five miles away, another Viet Nam combat vet who was in a wheel chair. His story I related at the first Metapsychology conference, but just real generally here, a fast one time through:

This fellow had tried to commit suicide—the one in the wheel chair, that is. The first man I'd dealt with called me, and he and I went to the hospital. We talked, and the fellow was released the following day. I took him through a couple of sessions, and he went from suicidal to working full time in a coffee shop—and by the way, he's still there! He is the person who runs around in his chair and cheers everyone else up and says, "Hey! there is something about life...!" There's a guy who has now been working almost two years ... hadn't worked before that for five or six years ... had been under professional psychiatric care, medicated to the gills. Today, he is off medication and no longer under psychiatric care. My dealings with him lasted ... well ... over a period of about three months, we probably put in somewhere close to twenty hours of TIR. It was his decision to get off of the medications; it was his decision to quit psychiatric care; it was his decision to go back to work. Hey! Not too shabby, I would say offhand.

Guess we'd better take a short break.... [Tape pause.] Very interesting thing: I got a bit teary-eyed over that. It still brings joy to the heart.

The first combat vet: we took him through ... oh, about twenty five hours by the time that he felt that he was through. We found that most all of what he had hung his combat experiences on went a little bit deeper than that—many times back to ... oh ... age four or five ... in there, though he was not specific. That fellow is still working—still with the same job that he obtained within thirty days of completing TIR.

I have had failures. Every one of my failures has been exactly where Gerald told me it would occur—in a place where the mind was not available: mind-altering drugs ... alcohol. Those are the two main causes. Mind not available ... I am not capable of getting through with TIR ... and Gerald told me that I wouldn't be. Hey, that's alright. I basically ceased working with those types of people, merely telling them that it's their choice ... that once they get to the point—and they can do whatever they want to—I will be available, if I'm geographically in the area, to assist once they're clean. Those failures ... a total of four ... I had to find out for myself. So be it. I did.

Different situation: female ... professional ... a secretary with management skills ... extremely capable individual, about forty years old ... husband an extremely successful doctor ... old home-town girl ... very efficient, friendly ... just a good professional, one that you'd want in the front office, someone who'd give you a good image with people coming through the front door. No problem whatsoever. She was operating in an office that had a management style that was based upon lies and mistrust. Employees were picked on to the point that this gal went from being that extremely efficient professional to being a woman who was afraid to type a letter for fear of making a mistake. She was completely dehumanized, if you will. Her sense of security went to zero. It affected her marriage. She was no longer capable of doing anything but going home and bawling ... by the hour. The agency where she worked had an Employee Assistance Program whereby you could call a number—confidentially—and you would get eight hours of professional counseling service. This gal sought that program and went through it. She was referred to a psychiatrist, and went to that psychiatrist for about four months. At that point, she came to me one day and said, "I understand that you have something that you have learned in California that might be able to help me, and I need help." She was then still working in the same office, and had been threatened with probation—almost unheard of there.

When she came to me for help, she had also told me that her marriage was very shaky. I happened to know her husband, and the three of us agreed to meet. At that initial meeting, we set out the procedure. Her husband was completely trusting, allowing me and his wife to be in a room alone for maybe up to three hours, undisturbed, in their home. The end result of all of that was that two and a half months later, she went to her psychiatrist for her final session—

her choice—and assisted the psychiatrist through the last, fifty-minute session. At the end of it, she said, "I don't think I need to pay you your fees any more to listen to your problems, Mrs. Psychiatrist, and at this point, our relationship is done, thank you very much!"

The lady subsequently decided to quit her job, took six weeks off, was hired back in another agency, doing the same type of work. She's held that job now for close to a year. The boss is extremely satisfied with her ... says, "Hey, this is the type of professional I've been looking for in my office for years and years and years!" One of her husband's comments sticks in my mind very clearly: "Thank you for giving me back my wife! Thank you for allowing her to have her life back"" A total success.

An interesting thing occurred as a result of that. This lady was one of, oh, five or six that I had worked with at that point, all of whom, unbeknownst to me, had been clients of the same psychiatrist. All of them, also unbeknownst to me, had quit going to that psychiatrist after doing TIR. At that point, the *psychiatrist* came to me and asked what I was doing that was causing her clients to get well, and that whatever it was, she needed it. Well, the bottom line of that story was that I went to her and the senior psychiatrist in her office and we talked for a little bit over an hour. The gist of the conversation was, "We will be glad to bring you in under our insurance umbrella; you may operate with us." Their real interest, however, was, "How many clients can you bring into the business? Because we are in the process of building our client base...." It became obvious to me that their effort and thrust was not towards making people better. It was an effort to hook those people, to make 'em dependent upon that psychiatric business. Repeat business ... repeat ... repeat ... repeat. I decided that I wasn't "into" that kind of situation.

New subject: female ... about 37 years old ... a son 15 or 16 years old ... in a situation where every three or four months, the person that she was dearly in love with would physically beat the crap out of her. He was into verbal abuse on a repeating basis as well. Such incidents would culminate in his moving out, taking their personal possessions, changing the bank account, stripping the proceeds out.

This particular lady had left a job in New York, where she'd been being paid close to $30 an hour in the engineering arena, to come to Idaho, where she'd accepted employment at $8 an hour. Her husband had been in some sort of security or law enforcement work ever since he had left Viet Nam. He prided himself on looking younger than he was, a definite physical freak—a "hard body" who did a lot of weight work, never missed two ... three ... four hours a day in the gym, and enjoyed trying to intimidate others. When she came to me, his wife told me she knew that I'd been doing a lot of work with vets, and that some of them—who also worked for the police—had told her that I knew how to do something that was "pretty good". They wouldn't describe what it was, but they highly recommended that she ask me about it. She did.

Our first session was about two and a half hours long, and towards the end of it, she looked at me and said, "Now I know why I married that person! He is my father ... he acts like my father ... he treats me like my father did ... he abuses me like my father always has ...", and she went into about a thirty minute diatribe, screaming, yelling, beating on her own body, flailing her fists on her legs—at the end of which, she slowly reached a state of calm, with tears dripping and nose running. And in the space of about fifteen minutes after that, she looked up, her eyes opened, she smiled, and said, "I'm well. Thank you!" [Tape pause.] Hmm! I'm sitting here, crying like a baby ... grinnin'! It was one of the most pure, quick sessions I've ever given and, as I recall, that was the third time through the first incident that she picked to look at. She went directly to it. She'd been seeing a psychiatrist at that time for four months, three times a week, 50 minutes an hour. [laugh.] Oh ... and before she'd left New York, she'd been under psychiatric care for eighteen months there in one stretch. She looked at me and she said, "My God! All of that money, and all of that time, and I never got through to the issues." She said, "I feel like a brand new person! I feel light ... I feel like I weigh twenty pounds!"

Well, that story resulted in the abusive husband calling her and being informed by the lady that she had filed for divorce, that the divorce was going through, that it was not her fault — the divorce—and that she had not ruined his career, that he had chosen to do that all on his own, that she was not going to kowtow to him any more....

Shortly after that conversation, she came bouncing into my office, sat down at my desk, and proceeded to tell me, in a voice that was loud enough to be heard fifty feet away, that whatever it was I had, it worked and Goddamn, she was glad to be alive again!

She has accepted employment at another firm. She has tripled her salary over what she was making in Lewiston. She left on the 20th of February, and on arriving on her new job, she picked up the phone and again thanked me, made sure that I had her new address and that she had mine. She has already sent a letter to me here in Stuttgart. She reports that her life is together, her divorce in progress, and she is ... in ... charge!

[Tape pause]

Whew! I didn't realize that I had that much emotional attachment ... in terms of pure, outright pleasure! For a male like me, who went through the military, who was raised in Montana on a rock farm, very poor; who came up with somewhat of a macho image—if you were a man, you proved what you were, and you damned sure didn't cry! [laugh]—it feels kinda good to sit here ... and grin ... and let tears run ... and not feel bad about it.

Again ... thank you.

New subject: a lady ... close to sixty years old ... petite ... someone who's spent most of her life as a social worker ... rape and crisis counselor, homeless shelter operator, family abuse counselor ... a person who, herself, was sexually and verbally abused. Her mother had committed suicide, two marriages ended in divorce, and her last husband also committed suicide. He was a man who had lived a sham, lived an untrue life, assumed a lifestyle and identity and activities that were all lies. When his money ran out and he was no longer able to continue that lie, he put a shotgun in his mouth and blew his own head off.

She found him, still hanging on to the shotgun.

When I met her, she had received professional counseling for over 18 months. She had just taken a part-time job as a nursing assistant and was in the process of losing her home, having run out of all savings, down to nothing. The insurance money was spent, and she was basically being forced back out of the home and onto the street to survive or to commit suicide herself, an act she had considered.

That's when I entered the picture, again through a mutual friend, a person I'd worked with that she knew. I started working with her. At the time, she had very acute arthritis in her hands—the skin drawn very tightly over the knuckles, over the fingers, over the bones. It didn't go with the rest of her at all. She had basically no flexibility in any of her fingers. We worked through the last suicide, and in the process, I recall her agonizing over the fact that the sheriff and the people who had investigated on that morning had told her not to wash her hands, and had basically accused her of assisting her husband to commit suicide. (Obviously, they were looking at the paraffin test for residual gunpowder on her hands.) She was *not* involved, and she was fully acquitted very quickly, but ... a strange thing: at no time, through all of that process, did they ever come back to her and tell her that she *could* wash her hands now.

Within ten minutes of completing our first session, she got up, went to the kitchen sink, took a bar of soap, and started scrubbing her hands, looking at me—crying, and laughing—and said, "My God, I can wash my hands again for the first time in two years."

Quite an impact on "the Wildcat." He almost lost it! [Laugh.]

Several sessions later she had a major realization concerning her sexual abuser, and this was coupled to her having been raised as a young lady on a farm, where she had also been sexually abused. When TIR took all the way back, she had a very definite realization that it was not her fault. She ended up going back to her own counselor, helping *him* through a couple of sessions, becoming one of his case studies – to be presented during a national meeting. Yet she withheld from that counselor the fact that she had realized where her problems had been rooted, and the case presentation turned into one in which, during a seminar, her counselor's peers attempted to tell him where he had gone wrong, what he should have done, how he might have been able to get to the bottom of the issue had he used different techniques ... and they used it as a problem solving seminar. The lady's attitude, when she heard about it, was "Let them work it out. *I* did."

She, today, is very happy doing what she is doing. She is working full time and has picked up—through her use of TIR—some techniques that she has incorporated into her own case load. She is, in fact, in charge of her life and, in her words, "quite happy".

New subject: a Viet Nam combat vet, a skilled technician, within six months of being able to retire ... diagnosed with a nervous breakdown. He came to me asking, "How do I get back into the federal system now that I have bailed out of it? Is there any way I can get back in?" We went through a few alternatives ... then I gave him a short session that had an outstanding result. We then went through five or six more sessions. They started out, oh, two, two and a half hours a shot ... ended up 15 to 20 minutes a session. He finally came to realize that a set of common circumstances were involved in the work site of his last job where he'd finally just gotten to a point where he could not work, could not concentrate, could not sleep, did not eat, went back on the bottle.... All of those things had common leads back to Viet Nam and what he had done there. *He* saw. *He* drew the parallels between them. *He* had the realizations. And the last I heard from him, two months ago, he was back with his old organization ... everyone was happy to have him back ... and he was well on his way to passing his probation period. He's off and running. He did well....

Another guy: a graduate student ... male ... the son of a friend. I watched him go through most of high school and college ... some of the normal trials and tribulations as he interacted with members of the opposite sex. He's one of those people with a gift for dealing with people ... liked by everyone who knows him ... never had a problem getting dates with the girls. But then, in graduate school, he fell deeply in love with a girl whom he wanted to marry. They discussed it, planned how it would happen ... and then it all unraveled, and very unpleasantly.

Well, falling off the deep end ("That's all that I deserve"), he turned into a real wild person. He almost flunked out of school ... withdrew from several courses ... was suspended briefly ... went back to school ... and was not doing very well at all. Not interacting well with people as he always had before ... working part time ... going to the bars and raising six kinds of sand almost full time. Wasn't a whole lot of time for studies.

He'd heard about what I was doing from his dad, and one day he came to me asked if maybe I could "try that stuff" [TIR] with him.

Within two weeks time—during which, as I recall, we had four or five sessions—he crawled out of the bars, picked up his books, and went back to studying. He's now graduated, with an MBA [Masters in Business Administration], and working hard in a very good job. He has read just about everything that he can get his a hand on that has to do with TIR. He's extremely interested in learning all of the procedures, and would like to pick it up himself.... But again, here was an individual who was heading down the wrong track, *knew* he was heading down the wrong track, needed a "tour guide" to turn him around, got one ... and turned around. He's doing great!

And I suspect that's about enough rambling into this little machine, so before too long goes past, I will get the tape in the mail. One of these days, I'd like to learn more about Metapsychology. I realize that in TIR, I've got just a little piece of it.

Lt. Col Chris Christensen (Ret.)
March 2nd, 1992

A reproduction of this tape is available on the *Beyond Trauma: Companion Disc*

An Open Letter to Members of TIRA
By David W. Powell

I am a veteran of the Viet Nam conflict. Until recently, like enormous numbers of other Americans who were there, I had increasing difficulty in dealing with daily life situations from the moment I came back form that war. I have recently handled some of those difficulties, and look forward now to handling them all.

I returned from front line, real-time combat as a Marine infantryman in the latter part of 1967, shortly before the Tet Offensive. From the moment I arrived back in the U.S., up until 6 months ago, I had "successfully" functioned in the tapestries of society as a civilian, "not at all altered" by my up-close-and-personal exposure to outrageous cruelty, maiming, death, and the dying.

I have never resembled what you might envisage when you think of Viet Nam vets. I never grew my hair shoulder length, wore combat uniforms in lieu of two- and three- piece suits, protested the war, or bragged about my experiences; in fact, I denied them, to myself and many others. In this, however, I have been as hundreds of thousands of other "functioning", "acceptable" individuals are, who continue to suffer from the effects of PTSD (Post Traumatic Stress Disorder). These people are my personal "silent majority", in that they have quietly endured the pains and sufferings that others have endured less successfully.

Approximately 2 years ago, I experienced a series of back-to-back disruptions in my life. A relationship of some five years was destroyed, I learned that my children from a former marriage had been transported across the nation without my prior knowledge or consent, an important business transaction ("in the bag") went awry, and my loving sister called to encourage me to volunteer as a speaker on the subject of PTSD because she knew that my experiences as a "grunt" would be more interesting to audiences than those offered by the uninitiated. ("Grunt" is s a term of endearment bestowed upon Marine infantrymen by other Marines.)

All of this, coming at once, overwhelmed me. I began crying. About everything. I knew I needed help, but didn't know where to turn. I thought of the Veterans Administration. I was, after all, a veteran, and – *just perhaps* – my feelings of despair had something to do with my experiences in the service.

I called a Viet Nam outreach center nearby and made an appointment with a counselor for that afternoon. I spent an hour talking with him, leaving as upset as when I first came in. I didn't return, but instead sent a letter of "thanks", along with the explanation that I would retrieve my coping "tools" from before and deal with my situations as I had done in the past – alone.

After a time, I was invited to participate in a once-a-week "rap group" for Viet Nam combat veterans at a local VA mental health and rehabilitation center. I did this for nearly 18 months and came away feeling more harmed than helped by the experience.

Some 6 months ago, a fellow veteran introduced me to the practice of facilitation and Traumatic Incident Reduction. Curious, I looked into the possibility of getting help for myself.

I have been helped... a whole lot more than I had expected. I am becoming increasingly more able to cope with upsetting situations. Ordinary, everyday events seem less and less to trigger recurring thoughts of my Viet Nam experiences. I find, finally, that I can once again look forward to enjoying all that life has in store for me, without reservation.

This stuff works!

I am convinced that the TIR methods and practices developed by Dr. Gerbode are applicable and beneficial not only to people such as I have described myself to be, but also to the more visible, obvious, out-and-out victims of PTSD as well. In my opinion, TIR work is broadly applicable to the survivors of any tragedy, great or small, from the Russian veteran of the Afghan war to the millions who have "merely" suffered mental cruelty, or lost a loved one. And who has not?

I thought you might enjoy hearing what your help has meant to one person and I wanted to thank you.

David W. Powell
March 1990

[For the complete story of David Powell's tour of duty and recovery, please visit http://www.tir.org/metapsy/davidpowellstory.htm]

3 Grief and Loss

Losses, including the loss of loved ones, and the grief that comes with them, are a part of normal life, and as such cannot be prevented. Practitioners and volunteers doing work with bereavement are cautioned not to have any set idea of how long grieving "should" take, or of what form it should take. This essentially person-centered approach toward bereaved persons allows them the time and space for all of their feelings without criticism. Certainly that is a good thing and no bereaved person should be rushed into any sort of therapy before he or she is ready. That said, much can be done to facilitate healthy grieving, not to take anything away from the experience, but to empower the person to come to a place where the future engages more attention than the past.

In this chapter, Teresa Descilo takes a fascinating look at grief and loss in the context of Western culture. Marian Volkman explains how a special application of TIR called "Future TIR" can be used in cases of bereavement. Sharie Peacock brings us a very moving account of a TIR session that brought about resolution of the loss of a child. And finally, Alex Frater shares some stories from his practice.

Relieving the Traumatic Aspects of Death
by Teresa Descilo, MSW, CTS

Portions of this article originally published in C. Figley (Ed.) *The Traumatology of Grieving: Conceptual, Theoretical, and Treatment Foundations.* London: Taylor & Francis.
Reproduced by author's permission.

For background information on Teresa Descilo, see p. 78

Significance of the Stressor to the Child/Adult System

In Uganda, when someone loses a loved one, each person who knows the surviving family member spends time with him, letting him recount his experience and what he's feeling (J. Nambi, 1995). The visitor then recounts her experience with death. In their cultural wisdom, Ugandans understand that everyone is impacted by a death; that normalizing and social supports prevent post-traumatic stress, and that telling one's story over and over again brings relief. I would wager that their cultural practice prevents post-traumatic symptoms from developing from the loss of a loved one, no matter what the circumstances were surrounding the death.

James (1994), in her book regarding children and attachment trauma offers the following definition: "...trauma occurs when an actual or perceived threat of danger overwhelms a person's usual coping ability." This definition can be expanded to: trauma occurs when an actual or perceived threat of danger *or loss* overwhelms a person's usual coping ability. Although she was defining trauma for children, the definition seems to describe what we all experience. This definition serves to explain how death could produce post-traumatic stress.

In our Western culture, where we tend to view death as an option, B. Smith (personal communication, 1995), we are ill-prepared to deal with the reality of a death, no matter what the circumstance. Because of our general lack of acknowledgment and discussion about death within our families, when it occurs, our usual coping mechanisms tend to be overwhelmed.

> *In our Western culture, where we tend to view death as an option, we are ill-prepared to deal with the reality of a death, no matter what the circumstance*
>
> **—B. Smith**

For those of us who do not have the cultural practice of recounting our loss to many willing listeners, seeking a professional who will help us relieve and integrate our loss becomes the solution.

Interventions for Bereavement

It is evident from the literature that bereavement will create symptoms which would be classified as traumatic stress symptoms (Prigerson, H. G., Shear, M. K., Frank, E., Beery, L. C., Silberman, R. Pilgerson, J., & Reynolds, C. R. 1997; Figley, C.R., Bride, B., and Mazza, N., 1997 and Raphael, B. and Martinek, N., 1997). These include any of the descriptors in the DSM IV (*Diagnostic and Statistical Manual of Mental Disorders   Fourth Edition*) of post-traumatic stress disorder. For anyone who has experienced the death of a loved one, the feelings of distress at reminders of the loved one, sleeplessness, having no energy for normal activities, feeling detached from others, and lack of concentration are all familiar feelings. While these are also descriptive of normal grief reactions, any symptoms which become long-term or debilitating require intervention. Long-term or debilitating mourning is also referred to as morbid grief or complicated bereavement. Potocky described morbid grief as "characterized by high distress and high symptom levels that are present four months after a death and may persist for a year or longer."

According to Potocky, those who are prone to developing morbid grief have one or more of the following characteristics:

> (1) a low level of social support during the crisis; (2) a moderate level of social support coupled with particularly traumatic circumstances of the death; (3) a highly ambivalent relationship with the spouse; and (4) the presence of a concurrent life crisis at the time of the death. In addition, coping with sudden loss should be seen as a special high-risk group.

Most of the interventions described in the literature reviewed were group interventions. Potocky's analysis of nine experimental studies of bereavement interventions were all therapeutic group interventions. Her article revealed "...that grief intervention is effective in preventing or reducing symptoms of morbid grief among spouses who are at high risk or in high distress."

Rando (1995) defines complicated mourning as the state when normal grief steps, which require recognizing the loss, processing it, and essentially moving on with life, are compromised, distorted, or not completed, resulting in debilitating psychological, behavioral, social or physical symptoms.

Evidence of Effectiveness

There is a large body of literature which supports the efficacy of EMDR. There is a growing body of research with regards to the efficacy of TIR. The most recent work completed utilizing TIR, is an impeccable outcome study of 123 female inmates at FCI Tallahassee. Valentine (1997) utilized a single session of TIR, given after a brief intake and followed by a session for closure and post testing, compared to a waiting list control group. Her measures included those for depression, anxiety, and learned helplessness, which are primary symptoms of post-traumatic stress. The improvements in all measures following treatment were statistically significant. Further, at a three month follow-up, all measurements showed a significant improvement for the treatment group from the first post-test.

Bisbey (1995) completed the first experimental study utilizing TIR on 64 crime victims in England. She compared TIR to Direct Therapeutic Exposure (DTE) and a waiting list control group. All subjects were screened for a positive diagnosis of PTSD. Bisbey reported that:

> In this study, as hypothesized, both treatment groups experienced a significant decrease in trauma symptoms while the control group did not. In fact, most of the members of both treatment groups no longer qualified for a diagnosis of post-traumatic stress disorder at the conclusion of the study. It was hypothesized that the Traumatic Incident Reduction group would show a larger decrease in incident specific symptoms that the Direct Therapeutic Exposure group. This turned out to be correct.

Coughlin's 1995 quasi-experimental design study looked at the efficacy of TIR in treating 20 subjects diagnosed with panic and anxiety symptoms. She wrote that:

> Clinical and statistic differences post-treatment have been confirmed. Yeaton and Sechrest (1981) define "cure" as the point "when the deviation from the norm has been eliminated (p. 163)." Fourteen participants had state anxiety scores more than one standard deviation above the mean on pretest. Deviations from the norm (+ - one standard deviation) were eliminated for eleven participants at one-month follow-up and nine participants at three-month follow-up. Thirteen participants had trait anxiety scores more than one standard deviation above the mean on pretest. Deviations from the norm were eliminated for ten participants at one-month follow-up and nine participants at three-month follow-up. The data supports the effectiveness of TIR. 64% of participants with clinically significant state anxiety remained "cured" at three month follow-up and 69% of participants who had clinically elevated trait anxiety remained "cured" at three month follow-up. TIR satisfies Yeaton and Seckrest's definition of a successful treatment. (p 64-65)

Bereavement Case Example

This case was actually presented by a student who was taking my TIR workshop class. The student volunteered to address the death of her mother. I normally don't address deaths in this classroom, but after interviewing the participant, I decided that it would be appropriate to pursue. Her mother had died six months earlier in a car accident. The client, who was in her 40's, hadn't stopped crying since then.

During the second recounting, the client began crying. I had the client review the incident 37 times in total. The client recounted different aspects to the event most times. Her sadness peaked and waned. She became angry. She began to present the theme that because of what she was taught in her upbringing, it was not OK to cry and be weak. After the 15th recounting, the client gave her first smile and laugh.

However, during the next time through, she began crying again. From this point, the grief was less frequent and less and intense. When she indicated that the incident felt the same at the 19th time, I asked her if the incident was getting lighter or heavier. From her indication, I continued to cycle her through the incident. Her recounting of the incident continued to change in content and emphasis until the 33rd time through, as which point, her affect improved and the content remained the same. After the 37th recounting, I asked her if she made any decision at the time of the incident. Her reply was "That was a sad time, but that's what it was – that was then and this is now." She had successfully completed the trauma and I ended the session there. The entire session took a little more than an hour.

Selected References

Bisbey, L. B. (1995). "No longer a victim: A Treatment Outcome Study for Crime Victims with post-traumatic stress disorder" (doctoral dissertation) California School of Professional Psychology. (see p. 322 to order).

Coughlin, W. E. (1995). TIR: Efficacy in treating anxiety symptomology. (doctoral dissertation), Union Institute (see p. 322 to order).

Doka, Kenneth J., Ph.D. (1996) *Living With Grief After Sudden Loss: Suicide, Homicide, Accident, Heart Attack, Stroke.*

James, B. (1994). *Handbook for treatment of attachment trauma problems in children.* New York: Lexington Books.

Potocky, M. (1993). "Effective services for bereaved spouses: A content analysis of the empirical literature". *Health Social Work*, 18, (4), 288-301.

Valentine, P. V. (1997). "Traumatic Incident Reduction: Brief treatment of trauma-related symptoms in incarcerated females." (Doctoral dissertation) Florida State University. (see p. 322 to order)

Valentine, P. (1995). "Traumatic Incident Reduction: A review of a new intervention." *Journal of Family Psychotherapy*, 6, (2), 79-85.

Future TIR:
A Conversation with Marian Volkman

Future TIR is a technique taught in the TIR Expanded Applications course (see Appendix C)

VV: I understand there is a technique called Future TIR (FTIR) that is used to handle traumas that a client knows is going to happen but hasn't happened yet, or that could happen. How does that work?

Marian: How it works is that we have the person take a look at the worst possible scenario of what he's worried about happening. As you say, that could be something that's very likely to happen. For example if he has a parent terminally ill in the hospital then it's likely that he is going to experience the loss of that parent. It's still possible that he could get run over by a bus before his parent dies, but it's pretty likely that he will experience that loss.

Or you can have something extremely unlikely to happen. One of the ways this can manifest is a mother who is obsessively worried that something is going to happen to her children. She controls and smothers them because she is trying to protect them from really unlikely events that she can't stop picturing and worrying about. She could be worried about losing her job and she could have real reasons for worrying about that. Or she could be worried about her job when there is no apparent reason for worrying about that. It doesn't matter; we can address it either way, likely or unlikely.

We always start with the worst scenario because that's where people's attention magnetically goes. They're not worried about the little stuff; they're worried about something really terrible happening. By allowing the person to go through the dreaded future experience, likely or unlikely, as if it's a real experience, you actually are able to reduce charge and resistance from future events. That's how it works; it works pretty fast, faster than addressing an actual traumatic incident because we are addressing a possible future incident rather than one the client has already lived through.

You go through all the worst scenarios the person can imagine and you kind of work your way back to "not as bad" scenarios. As many times as he needs and wants to go through the worst scenarios, you do. Eventually, the person gets to feeling like he's ready to confront whatever happens. It's very relieving.

VV: How does this apply to bereavement?

Marian: It's certainly not the only application of FTIR, because I use it for many circumstances. I do find it to be enormously beneficial to deal with bereavement, because you can address a loss such as "death of a loved one" with TIR and definitely get some relief but often where most of the charge is in fact, in the future as the person is looking at going on through her life without this person. This could include loss of a love relationship, a pet that is very dear, a job, or what have you.

I'll give you one example. I had a woman who lost her husband and she really felt that her life was over. Her companion was gone and she had no life. What we did is we talked about it and got the parameters set up. In TIR we want quite a specific incident; we don't want big long incidents. With Future TIR, it's different. When you're dealing with a situation that hasn't happened, you can be a little freer. I said "OK, I want you to imagine the whole rest of your life going through it exactly how you feel now and it never gets any better." She went through that a couple of times and it was really real to her the first couple of times. Then it started to lighten up a little. After 4 to 5 times through it, she said "This is ridiculous, I don't have to live like that. It's going to be work; I need to get out there and make myself do things and take an interest in things and meet new people. I've got the rest of my life—probably 40 years or so." She was starting to feel excited and extroverted and like life was worth living. At the point where her attention shifted from the loss outward on to the rest of her life that was the end point.

I have to tell you, I was pretty floored by that. It was early on when I had just developed this technique. Since then, I've used it with lots of people and different types of losses. A woman had lost her dog and to her she had lost her best friend. It was extremely traumatic and we did TIR on the actual loss and everything that led up to the death of the dog and the experience of that. Sure enough though, the future looked bleak. She needed to look at her life for the next year without the dog. It took a while with her, it was a big deal. She did shift and feel like, "Yes, I'll never have this particular special being here with me." She had to face that and get through it. When she did, she really got to the point of feeling "Life is worth living even though I don't have this wonderful dog with me anymore."

VV: The dog had already died and you were doing the future without the dog?

Marian: Yes. You can address either an impending loss or the future aspect of a loss that has already happened. I think it's important to mention pets when we talk about bereavement. She was almost apologetic for feeling so much emotion about this. Many people might have difficulty understanding the magnitude of the loss of a pet. It can be devastating. I would say that in any incident of loss where the person feels that his future is compromised, that he's lost his future in a certain sense, it would be really useful to address that with FTIR.

VV: After Future TIR, how does the future occur to that person in light of the loss?

Marian: There are a lot of ideas about how bereavement has to go. Hospice training traditionally tells you: be careful, don't rush people, it takes as long as it takes, and there's no wrong way to grieve. I agree with that but at the same time if we can do something to help the person be in her own experience, be in her own life, and be OK with that, we want to do that. Why spend years getting there if we can facilitate the healing? A loss is still a loss; she's going to miss that person, but we don't have to have the client suffering for a long, long time, I strongly feel that.

At the same time, I wouldn't ever push somebody to do this if he didn't want to do it. Suppose we've addressed the loss of a loved one, I'd say "Are you interested in taking a look at the future having your life go on without this person being here?" Most of them will say "Yes!" without any hesitation. But some will say "It's OK" or "I don't want to do that" or they have an idea about how their grieving is supposed to go. I would never argue with somebody, I would never say "Oh come on, you can get over this." Nothing like that, as it would not be person-centered. Offered the chance to improve their outlook, most people say yes and are amazed at how much better they can feel.

In the case of the woman who lost her husband, you know every day she gets up and thinks "He's not here." She does something that they used to do together and thinks about that. She can think about him and maybe feel sadness, but not have that kind of debilitating grief that just ruins your life.

Another case, I worked with a woman who was very, very close to her father. She said:

> "I've told all my friends that when my father dies, I'm going to be a basket case for months. Don't even call me or expect anything of me. I'm going to be hopeless for months because it's going to be so depressing."

It was really clear in her mind that that was how it was going to be. Her father had had ill health for many years and it was obviously an impending loss. We did Future TIR with her and just a couple of months later her father did die. It was quite a sudden death even though her father had been through many ups and downs with his health in the preceding years.

The really fascinating thing is that she was the one who pulled the family together. This was one of those difficult families with the stepmother and stepchildren and the biological children, and so on. She pulled everybody together and got out his old pipe, slippers, and hat and passed them around in a circle and everybody told stories, laughed, cried, and bonded. She was the one who made that happen instead of being incapacitated. Far from being a basket case, she was not only able to handle it for herself but she had brought about a really wonderful opportunity for the rest of the family to get together and celebrate her father's life. It gave her a feeling of contentment that probably nothing else would have.

Loss of a child – Session Notes
by Sharie Ann Peacock, RN, MEd, LCPC

Foreword by the Editor

There are few losses so shattering as the loss of a child can be, especially through something as unpredictable as SIDS. Often marriages do not survive such a loss, as the case below illustrates. This is a slightly edited transcript of an actual session given by Sharie Ann Peacock. Observing this woman's progression through various layers of emotion and reaction as she repetitively views this huge loss demonstrates clearly the "magic" of TIR at work. Be sure to notice how details of the incident change and the emotional content progresses through each viewing. Names have been changed and the facilitator's precise questions removed.

SIDS (Sudden Infant Death Syndrome) is the death of an apparently healthy infant that remains unexplained after a thorough autopsy and death scene investigation. There appears to be no suffering in most cases; death occurs very rapidly, usually during sleep. SIDS is the leading killer of infants between one week and one year with an approximate rate of two per thousand live births (1 in 500). 6,000-7,000 babies die of SIDS every year in the US. The peak age is around two to four months and the majority of the deaths occur during the winter months (October to April in the Northern Hemisphere). Researchers believe that SIDS probably has more than one cause, although the final process appears to be similar in most cases. SIDS can not predicted, prevented, or reversed. (Source: Maraget Gibbs, misc.kids FAQ)

Sharie Ann Peacock completed graduate school at University of Maine and is a Registered Nurse as well as a Certified TIR Facilitator. She specializes in trauma at her private practice in Old Towne, Maine.

1st Time through the incident:

(Eyes closed.) Tom (her husband) picked our 6 month old son Jeremy up out of the crib—it was 5 AM. Jeremy wasn't breathing, blue. I called 9-1-1 (tears). I kept telling Jeremy to wake up. The ambulance got there and they couldn't do anything. I rode to the hospital in the back of the ambulance. I sat at the hospital holding him. They kept telling me he wasn't going to wake up, it was time for me to let him go. I kept thinking, it was all a dream, he was going to wake up. I did everything the doctors told me to do. I was mad at them! Jeremy was healthy, gaining weight. They finally took him from me. Did an autopsy. They said SIDS. I said, SIDS?! Then I thought, stupid a—hole Tom did coke! (Now looking at me) He killed my baby! [Ed. Note: parental drug use is considered a major risk factor] I couldn't go back to that apartment. (Head down, eyes closed). We moved to another apartment. I kept hearing Jeremy. It went on for a year and a half. Tom kept on saying "stop crying" (looking at me). I think he hated Jeremy. He loved James (his other child) but not Jeremy! I dream about Jeremy. It was so real. He's growing. Don't want to have those dreams any more. At the wake I didn't want to leave him there either. They put make-up on him. Didn't look like him. I know hate's a strong word but I HATE Tom's family! Jeremy was so beautiful, so healthy. I miss him so much. I feel guilty because I can't go to his grave—I talk to him all the time though.

2nd Time through the incident:

(Eyes closed, tears, hands on face, feels dizzy) Tom got up to get Jeremy. He was blue, wasn't breathing. I was screaming out the window for someone to call an ambulance. Kept telling him to wake up. Oh, God, I was getting mad at them. He wouldn't wake up. We went to the hospital. I remember sitting in the waiting room waiting to come and hold him. Seemed like it was taking forever. They wrapped him up. I sat in the chair rocking him, telling him to wake up. (Viewer reports feeling dizzy). They just kept telling me I had to let him go and I didn't want to. And I let them take him. Went to the wake. I remember them trying to take him away from me there too and it hurt so bad, it hurt. I remember Tom telling me to stop crying so much, like he didn't even care. I didn't care about nothing, just going to sleep at night so I could be with him. I remember screaming at Tom telling him it was his fault. He did something, the coke or pot or something.

3rd Time through the incident:

(Eyes closed, slightly less emotion) He brought him in to me like every other morning and said he wasn't breathing, he was all blue. I was screaming, screaming. I held Jeremy trying to warm him up. He was so cold, he was so cold. I remember rocking him in the chair. I know everyone was trying to help me, my friends. We stayed at Tom's mother's house. Just couldn't go back to that apartment. They baptized him, he was supposed to be baptized. Oh, God, I just wanted to pick him up, take him home. Part of me felt like he was still alive. I just couldn't let go. We moved out of the apartment. Things between Tom and I were bad. I hate drugs. All I wanted to do was sleep and not wake up so I could be with Jeremy. Eventually the dreams just stopped. I started getting hold of myself, going to school. My friends helped me.

4th Time through the incident:

(Eyes open, looking at me at times, less emotion) They woke me up, told me Jeremy wasn't breathing. Something was wrong. My neighbor Marie called an ambulance. They said he died in the middle of the night. I remember he slept through his feeding. The doctor had said that "When they start growing that they sleep longer." I blamed Tom; I blamed myself. When the dreams stopped I kept trying to make them come back. It was like I was forgetting, like I was letting go. I don't know if it was Tom's fault. I blamed myself. I should have woke him up to feed him. I just don't understand about SIDS. I think that's what bothers me the most, I just don't understand.

5th Time through the incident:

(Even less emotion, voice clearer, looking at me) Every morning Tom would wake Jeremy up for his morning feeding and I remember something was wrong, he wasn't breathing. I remember him running outside for someone to call 911. I just couldn't wake him up, didn't want to let him go. Maybe moving out of the apartment helped, maybe it didn't. That's when the dreams stopped. I want to know what causes SIDS. I want to understand. I don't want to hate Tom, I just want to understand. I said he didn't love Jeremy but I know he did. When Jeremy was born he was so proud, his whole family was proud. (smiling)

6th Time through the incident:

Tom went to get Jeremy up like he always did before. Getting ready for work. It was hot that night. It was so hot that night I slept on the couch and must have crawled into bed in the middle of the night. He went out and got him. He went outside screaming. He ran outside screaming. I was holding Jeremy at the hospital—knew he wasn't going to wake up. I was so angry at everyone, angry at myself. I was angry at God. I hated God. And I read everything, everything, I read everything about SIDS. This causes SIDS, that causes SIDS. It was just frustrating. I do remember Tom telling me he loved Jeremy and he was so sorry because he wished he could bring him back to me. I do feel guilty for blaming him. I don't know. How can you blame somebody when you don't even know? I just needed someone to blame. I blamed him, I blamed myself, I blamed the doctors. That's why it's so hard for me. I still need to know what causes SIDS. Until I know, I think I can feel better as far as what even happened. Am I a bad person for blaming everybody? He was a good Dad (smiling). A kid will get colicky. Tom would pick him up and burp him, and feed him, and change his diaper. It's just when his stupid friends would come over.

7th Time through the incident:

(Very short run-thru) Tom got him up and brought him to me. I knew by the look on his face something was wrong. He ran out first, started screaming for someone to call an ambulance. I was banging on the wall. (sighing)   I kept screaming at Tom. I hated him and told him I hated him. I wish I never said that. I didn't really hate him. I told him I didn't want to go back to the apartment and he understood. We stayed at his Mom's. They did *everything* for me just to make it comfortable. They were trying to help…. but I was pushing everyone away instead of letting them help.

8th Time through the incident:

Tom found Jeremy, not breathing. He put Jeremy in my arms, said he was gonna get help—screaming for me to call an ambulance too. They came, did what they could do. The hospital did what they could do. Let me hold him. They were really nice. I knew he wasn't coming back. Just wish I could apologize to everybody, especially Tom. Because I know he felt guilty too.

9th Time through the incident:

Like every morning, Tom got up and brought Jeremy to me. I noticed Jeremy was not breathing. Tom gave him to me, said he was going to get help, and then he tried comforting me, he tried, in his own way. He was my best friend. I remember blaming myself, blaming him. The only thing he would say was it wasn't my fault, I was a good mom, always told me my babies came first. I just don't want him to think that I blame him. I know Jeremy is up there (smiling). Tiffany (4 year-old daughter), knows about Jeremy but doesn't know the whole story yet. I want all my kids to know about their brother. Alex and Daniel (her other sons) call him their little angel in heaven (smiling), that's what I call him. I remember Alex asking me why he died and I said, well, "God gave him to us for a little while and took him back." I close my eyes and I see him up there, you know. A beautiful little baby. Just wish I had his pictures. Mike (present boyfriend) says we're taking a trip down to get everything for Alex and Daniel. Their baby pictures, their birth certificates, Jeremy's death certificate. I need that for closure.

10th Time through the incident:

I remember they were giving me Jeremy. The first thing Tom did was put him in my arms. Said he would get help and he did. He stayed right there with me by the rocking chair. Tom's family was all there for me, telling me, "Anything I needed, anything." A lot of times I do think of him and I talk to him (laughter). I wish him Merry Christmas and happy birthday (smiling). I tell him I'll see him someday, hopefully. He was so beautiful. (Voice louder, smiling, laughing. Facilitator asked, "How does it seem to you now?"). I feel like a lot of that anger is gone, the blame is gone. There's a warm feeling here (hand on chest), if that makes sense, like he's there. It used to feel empty. I feel bad sometimes because I can't remember what he looks like, but I can actually see him, he looks so much like his father. I guess it's a good thing. He's right there (hand on chest)—my angel. They always say put the baby on his side, put the baby on his back, but, there's a lot of things they don't know. I just know he's in a good place. I've always known he's in a good place. I always felt bad I couldn't go to the grave but that's just his body. Jeremy is right here, anytime I want to talk to him (smiling). That's what I tell my kids. I don't know if it's the right thing to do but that's what I tell them. It's just something I have to try to accept— not something I can keep going on. But I can talk to Jeremy anywhere I am. That's what I believe. A comforting feeling (smiling). I'm just real relaxed, almost like a lot of stuff's been lifted off my shoulders. I was starting to feel sick to my stomach going through it but it's gone. His birthday is next month (smiling). He was a perfect little baby. I wish you had met him. OK, I feel good (smiling).

Facilitator: "OK, let's leave it at that."

TIR was followed by Communication with a Departed Loved One_in which the viewer recalled pleasant memories of her lost baby and expressed very positive and loving feelings for him. [This procedure is taught in both TIR Expanded Applications and Case Planning for TIR and Life Stress Reduction workshops – see Appendix C] She left smiling and laughing after thanking me and giving me a hug.

TIR and Grief:
A Brief Conversation with Alex Frater

For an introduction to Alex Frater, please see p. 197

VV: Do you find incidents with children are mainly about grief and loss?

Alex: Yes, certainly grief is common. One situation I find too, is where their mother or father has died of cancer. They have seen their mum die slowly at home and they can't get it out of their mind. That's what I do, I address that particular incident. I've worked with a few families where mum's died, for example, one where there were three brothers aged 15, 12, and 10. The father had insisted that they see their mum when she was laid out at the funeral. I've worked with children who had trauma when they're forced to look at their mother or father deceased; it often disturbs them.

I just finished working with a lady whose mother died 10 years ago. We covered her mother dying and it was quite dramatic. In the last six months, she had become the *de facto* mother. She was only about age 12 but she sort of did everything for mum. Then mum was taken to the hospital, and she goes to the hospital, and she's not able to do anything. She wanted to do a couple little things for mum but she was told promptly, "Keep away, mum's too sick." We did TIR and she's fine now. That grief came from when she was 12 and she carried it into her 30's.

VV: If you have someone who is dying over the course of several months do you have to do that as Thematic TIR as opposed to Basic TIR?

Alex: No, I do that on Basic TIR. During those months, there's generally a time near the end that's troubling. They went in one morning and they know, my God, mum is going to die. Before that, they'd think that mum was getting a bit better from time to time. But now they'd come to the realization that she's going to die. Most of these people had nobody to talk to. That's the other thing I find.

I was seeing another client for just general stress management. He told me towards the end of that treatment that his wife was unwell, but he said, "I'm taking her to the doctor." I didn't see him for three years and then he came in and told me that his wife had died. He had remarried to a friend of his wife who he had known for many years. He said, "There's only one big problem. Whenever anyone mentions my first wife, especially if my new wife does, I cry. It's not very good. She keeps telling me, 'That's not a problem to me; she was my friend too.' Alex, I have to do something about this."

His first wife had died of cancer. He took three months off to nurse her and nursed her right up until she died at home. It took him two and half hours to run through the incident once. When he finished, looked at me and was crying, he said, "You know, you are the only person who has ever listened to me. I feel better already." He was a very good communicator; he wanted to tell the whole story. A few weeks later he rang me and said, "I'm great, all that's gone. It's incredible that stuff, isn't it?" What used to happen was when he got tearful with his present wife, she would say, "I'll go and make you a cup of tea." Then she'd come back and ask him to keep talking. He realized later that he'd skip over the really emotional parts because men didn't express that usually.

When he finished, looked at me and was crying, he said, "You know, you are the only person who has ever listened to me. I feel better already."

I've been using TIR for ten years now and I do a lot of work with it. It's very, very good for grief. There is another technique that works well when a mother (or other close person) dies and you weren't there to have closure: I use the Communication with a Departed Loved One procedure [taught in both the TIR – Expanded Applications and Case Planning for TIR and Life Stress Reduction Workshops. See Appendix C].

4 Crime and Punishment

> Since starting sessions I have been able to deal with the shooting incident. Prior to the sessions I kept thinking about the incident and asking why it had happened and feeling guilty over the whole thing. The sessions have helped me to put everything into perspective. To realize that there was nothing I could have done. The feelings of anxiety have become less. With each session they became less and less. I have been able to take control of my life again and although I was a victim, I feel less like one now. This incident will never leave me, it will always be a part of me, but I am able to live with it now and go on with my life and my family.
> —Crime Victim after TIR (VSC Miami)

In our Western culture, we are taught that there is a winner and a loser in every conflict; however, crime has no winners. It takes its toll on both victim and perpetrator. In this chapter, the conversation covers both sides of the conflict. Teresa Descilo, MSW talks about how her free crime victims' services center uses TIR and some of the challenges of working with domestic violence. John Nielsen shares his experiences with using TIR on incarcerated prisoners in Ontario and the myriad difficulties of treating clients in jails.

See also the research study "Brief Treatment of Trauma-Related Symptoms in Incarcerated Females with TIR" by Pamela V. Valentine, Ph.D. in Chapter 8.

TIR in a Victim Services Center:
A Conversation with Teresa Descilo MSW, CTS

Teresa Descilo is Executive Director of Victim Services Center (VSC) in Miami (www.vscmiami.org), which she founded in 1995. As of April 2002, the center has seen over 3000 victims of crime. I spoke with Ms. Descilo on August 4th, 2003 to find out more about how TIR works with crime victims.

VV: Tell us about your current status and professional background:

Teresa: Currently my duties at Victim Services Center include keeping us funded, looking for additional resources to serve our clients, creating relationships that supply resources and help keep us funded, and writing and editing agency grants. I also participate in community committees and boards, sponsor relevant training for the community, train my staff, and look for new ways in which to relieve stress or promote growth for my staff and clients. Finally, I manage the general operation with my work partner, who does most of the day-to-day management.

...we are unique in that we actually resolve the impact of trauma for our victims.

I did my Master's at Florida International University. I got my Bachelors from Barry University and my Associates from Miami Dade Community College. I received my CTS in 1995 from ATSS. I also took all the Metapsychology training I could find.

VV: How and why did Victim Services Center get started, and what are its goals?

Teresa: The service got started because I was looking to find out what services were available in Miami for crime victims. In that search I contacted the Florida State Attorney's office and talked to a person who had just come off of a community task force that had determined that the mental health needs of all crime victims weren't being met. I told her about what I do and described TIR to her. She was a long veteran of victim services, and people were approaching her all the time, asking, "Can we serve crime victims?" She understood immediately that this approach would be a very good thing for crime victims. Shortly after that discussion, she persuaded the state attorney to give us office space. We drew up a memorandum of understanding, and about three months after that we started serving crime victims in the State Attorney's office.

VV: That's a really quick timeline—90 days and up and running; that's great! What, if anything, makes crime-related trauma unique or difficult in comparison with, say, an accident or bereavement?

Teresa: I don't know that it does. Sometimes with sexual assault victims one has to spend a little bit more time building trust, but for the most part, it has not been difficult. People are referred here specifically to resolve the impact of trauma, so when they get to us they are usually ready to do the work. Some people simply aren't ready to do the work, and we have to set them up. Sometimes people don't realize that it requires so much work. But when somebody is ready to sit down and engage with you, the trauma seems to roll just as any other trauma does (with TIR).

VV: Are any of these people court-ordered or referred out of something other than their own initiative?

Teresa: We do have court-ordered people now. We've been treating women from Drug Dependency Court for about three years. This has been my first experience with treating mandated clients, and I'm very happy to say it's gone very well. These women have a big incentive to do the work. Most of them have lost their children and want them back. In order to get their children back, they have to have a notice from us to the judge that they have participated in this process and resolved the traumas from their past. We've had incredible success in direct Dependency Court mandated victims. The Department of Children and Families have mandated clients to us as well.

There are some clients who self-refer, but at any given time we have referrals from 75 agencies and at least 150 individuals. There are probably 15 people at the Florida State Attorney's Office that refer to us, 20 people at Department of Children and Families, 10 people from the Domestic Violence intake unit, and others from drug treatment centers. You name it—we get the referrals.

VV: How does TIR compare with conventional victim therapies. In other words, what they were doing before you were on the scene?

Teresa: There is no comparison. There was no resolution of trauma for these people before TIR. I was in a community that was astute enough to realize that the mental health needs of victims weren't being met. Nationally, we're still pretty unique in being a trauma-specific agency whose main purpose is to resolve the impact of trauma. The National Organization of Victim Assistants has just nominated us for a national award.

> *There is no comparison, there was no resolution of trauma for these people before TIR*

Charles Figley nominated us, noting that we are unique in that we actually resolve the impact of trauma for our victims. Trauma resolution is still not happening on a national basis; it's still a huge void in terms of services needing to be delivered. For a year, I was out training people in a different state almost every month, and they would love to have a comparable service to what we have here, but it just doesn't exist elsewhere.

VV: Sounds like there's an opportunity to propagate the program in other states.

Teresa: Yes, there is a great opportunity.

VV: How good are the long term results on crime victims?

Teresa: I have never had the funding to do a longitudinal study, so predicting outcomes is purely anecdotal at this point. Very seldom, however, do clients come back once they have completed services with us. Every so often a client does return because something else comes up, or somebody, like an ex-husband, gets let out of jail or comes after them in some way, so they have a whole new fear issue. The only thing I have to go on is that people generally don't come back to us once they've been completed. We pre- and post- test our clients; post-testing indicates that they no longer have the symptoms that are associated with PTSD. Our clients reach levels where they no longer have clinical anxiety or depression, and they no longer meet the diagnostic criteria for PTSD. This condition appears to be stable.

VV: You mentioned you are getting a lot of referrals from other agencies. Do many clients have the ability to pay for services, or do they get some assistance?

Teresa: No, I am happy to say our services are free. This has become a philosophic stance for me: if you're an alleged perpetrator of a crime, you're guaranteed an attorney in our country, but if you're a victim you're guaranteed absolutely nothing. So the very least a crime victim should receive is someone to help her put her life back together, at least to a level of functioning that existed before the crime. The fact that we are supported by grants is sort of a mixed blessing because it forces us to live in a state of awareness of our impermanence—we never know when funding will get yanked. We've been grant-driven now for 8 years now and for 1½ years we worked for free. We have major support from many different grants.

> *If you're an alleged perpetrator of a crime, you're guaranteed an attorney in our country, but if you're a victim you're guaranteed absolutely nothing.*

VV: Well, that sounds like success to me!

Teresa: But it could all end tomorrow; it's the nature of the non-profit game—what are you gonna do?

VV: How well does TIR fit within the realm of conventional social work practices?

Teresa: It's a total fit, because social work practice is basically a very client-centered approach with respect to the person and her environment. For me there's no dissonance at all. I started off doing my undergraduate in psychology, but I realized I couldn't stay in that field because of the philosophic difference in the way one views and treats a client. As with TIR, social work is not a medical-model practice.

We just look at the entire client—what is going on here, what does this person need, what are all the things contributing to what is going on? Social work practice does not pathologize people, either.

VV: There's often a cycle of violence of crime. Do you ever find yourself dealing with the perpetrators?

Teresa: Not as often; we really are set up for victims. Some of the women that Drug Dependency Court sends us have become perpetrators to a certain extent. We have a Department of Juvenile Justice grant for at-risk youth, and some of them have demonstrated some really borderline behaviors. For the most part, though, we are simply not treating perpetrators at this time.

VV: How has the community received Victim Services Center? Do you get support or recognition?

Teresa: Yes. Judging by all the referral sources we have, we are recognized as unique. For a while, at first, we were the weird ones on the block; we were doing something different. We still are very different. But after eight years and all the successes we've had, it doesn't matter how weird we are to many people, because obviously what we are doing is working. So there has been a great deal of acceptance, wonderful community support. In fact we were also written into a federal grant for helping victims of human trafficking, victims of modern-day slavery. That grant provides that this agency will provide Traumatic Incident Reduction as the main approach to handling trauma, along with acupuncture and massage.

VV: I saw in your mission statement that education is part of your program. What other techniques do you use in conjunction with TIR?

Teresa: We mostly use the Metapsychology model and techniques that come under that heading. We also have some excellent psychosocial groups: educational groups that teach people about domestic violence and the impact of trauma and trauma bonding, child empowerment groups, and a court-support group. But my staff clinicians are trained in EMDR which we will use on occasion; it's also very effective. We also use Thought Field Therapy (TFT) as a coping technique.

VV: Can you tell me about your intake procedure and how you handle people who clearly aren't ready for TIR?

Teresa: After we've taken a history on somebody, if we determine that they are not ready for TIR, we do things that you would associate with Life Stress Reduction (See p. 325 in Appendix D). I have developed a whole protocol for addressing trauma bonding, which is another huge problem that domestic violence victims have—being bonded to their abusers. This protocol is also very good for building ego strength, which is what people need to do when they are not quite able to face trauma. So we'll do Recalls, Unblocking—all those kinds of things to set people up. [Ed. Note: the procedures Teresa is referring to are taught in the two workshops after TIRW Level One: TIR—Expanded Applications and Case Planning for TIR and Life Stress Reduction].

VV: Please share with us some comments from your clients after completion of service.

Comments from VSC Miami Clients

"Yes, I have become more confident in my abilities to care for myself and my children. I realize that problems that would have left me paralyzed with fear before, I can face up to. I have learned to take things one day at a time. I know that I am a capable person and hope to never let someone else have such complete, utter control of my life again just because I am scared to be alone. It was difficult to go through all the painful memories: but somehow having done that has filled me with strength. I have great confidence in your program and especially in my therapist [Rose's] application of your theories. I hope I can progress to the point where someday I can help other people, victims of domestic violence, overcome the terrible fear of having to call for themselves and their loved ones. Thank you."

From a recovering addict (male):

"When I first came here, I was definitely traumatized by the sexual abuse I went through with my father. I could not talk, think, whisper, or breathe about it without feeling sad, crying, and disappointed, anxiety for my children, believing that someone might hurt them—feelings that I know now were keeping me from moving forward in life. Now I feel free, like I've never felt before in my life. I'm calm, cool and collected. I can talk about the sexual abuse without any emotional attachment and the memory is nothing more than just another time from my past. Just like when I first learned to ride a bike is a memory from my past. They are just like other memories, just points in time and space. I feel great. And I feel that nothing can hinder my progression in a positive direction except for normal obstacles we all encounter. And even those seem like nothing. I feel free. Thank you."

After 10 hours of service:

"When I first started coming to Victim Services, I was feeling very depressed and had a lot of guilt and shame, always thinking about my past, being molested and physically abused. Today I feel good about myself. Rene has really helped me a lot through this. I don't dwell or think about my past. I have motivated myself into doing a lot of things for myself and children. I've learned to love myself more. My anger has calmed down a lot along with my attitude and the way I used to see things. I thank God that I was court ordered to attend Victim Services because it's really helped me a lot. I have learned to deal with life without physical abuse and drug abuse."

TIR in a Victim Services Agency:
A Conversation with Joanna Woodd

"I spoke with Joanna Woodd, founder and director of Victim Support Lambeth (in England), in January 2005 about the impact of TIR on crime victims and the use of TIR in that agency. As of April 2005, she is now retired from VS Lambeth."

Marian: What were you doing prior to becoming involved with victim support?

Joanna: I had been to nursing training and after that went to Uganda to work in a nursing center. It was very much like returning home as I had grown up in that country. After that, I worked in St. Christopher's Hospice, in London, with bereavement. Later I went up to Birmingham University to obtain a degree in theology and psychology together, for personal furtherment. Then I went and worked out in the community doing community development projects. I started a family and shortly thereafter began working in the field of victim support. When I started working with victims, I thought it would be more with victims of police, because I had done a survey on that subject. I started doing that about 16 hours a week and it just kept slowly growing. At that point it was mainly the Brixton area and elderly people, but over the next 22 or 23 years it grew to encompass all sorts of people and circumstances.

Marian: What inspired you to start this organization?

Joanna: I was looking for work at the time, thinking I should go back and become gainfully employed. I didn't particularly want to go back to nursing as such or straight community work as I had done before. I mean it was almost sort of by default in a sense. I was asked by a nun at school would I be interested in this sort of thing. I thought it was going to be "victims of the police," but it was people who were the victims of crime and I realized that I wanted to work with these people. In hindsight, I wanted something I could develop, be creative with, and that dealt with people. I didn't know at the time anything about being a victim of crime and what that meant.

Victim Support Lambeth is committed to

• Providing victims of crime who are resident in the London Borough of Lambeth with appropriate and sufficient recognition, support, and information to assist them in dealing with the crimes and effects of crime that they have experienced.

• Ensuring the rights of the victims are acknowledged and advanced in all aspects of criminal justice.

• Ensuring that victims receive a continuing consistent level of service throughout the London Borough of Lambeth

VS Lambeth handles approximately 15,000 referrals per year from police and other local authorities

---

My previous training at St. Christopher's dealing with bereavement allowed me to build on what I had learned about loss, grieving and traumas. I know that I also built on a lot of the community work I had done. I was very much trying to make this an organization that was there for the community where I was working. Later on, bringing in the counseling side was probably also motivated from my experience at St. Christopher's, working with people and knowing what they needed, and my own medical background as well.

Marian: In an ideal world, what would you like to see happen next in victim support?

Joanna: They recently did an exit audit on victims and they found that only about 50% of the victims had reported their crimes to the police. That means there are 50% who don't report and I believe they are still entitled to some form of support or somebody to listen to them, if they want that.

A vision I had, which I would pursue if I was years younger, would be to establish a victim support person in each of the town centres or the neighborhood centres. This support person would both receive the referrals and do outreach work, going out and saying "Hey, I'm here if anyone would like to talk to me."

Marian: How extensive is the national association for victim services?

Joanna: They cover the whole of the country of course. There's an additional organization in Northern Ireland and one in Scotland. One thing that I have to make clear is that strictly speaking we're not meant to be offering counseling. We are meant to be seen as an organization that would refer people on. I've never asked them why specifically but I think the belief is that if a victim organization is seen as offering counseling then the legal defense attorney has to ask "And what counseling have you received?" That more recently is given to me as the reason. My opinion is that it ought to be a service offered without any questions asked. The other thing I have found very much with the victims who have been to court as witnesses who have received counseling is that we are thought to influence their testimony.

Marian: Have you ever heard of Victim Services of Miami?

Joanna: No, I haven't. They use TIR and aren't considered influencing the witness?

Marian: No, not at all, as I understand it.

Joanna: When I've spoken to prosecution barristers and said "I actually want feedback on this. I want to know if there is an advantage for the victim or is it a disadvantage," they've said every time that it is beneficial, which is what one would expect. Other victims who have had a more sort of general person-centered counseling have said that they know that they couldn't have testified without receiving the counseling, they finally told the story, understood it, and it did a bit of good.

Marian: How is Victim Support funded?

Joanna: We get a Home Office grant that covers all the salaries. We get a grant from the local authority that at the moment basically covers our rent. We do a certain amount of fundraising like writing to trusts and asking if we can have a certain amount of money towards volunteers' expenses. Last year we were adopted by the mayor of Lambeth as one of his charities and he gave us a contribution. Money also comes from writing letters, donations, and neighborhood watches sometimes. But the two main ones are central government and the local authority. I also get quite a lot from the Community Safety Partnership.

Marian: In terms of the counseling part, do you have any idea of how many client-hours of service are performed weekly?

Joanna: I'd have to look it up, but each of the 14 counselors probably sees two or three people each week. Only Henry Whitfield is using primarily TIR. I do a certain amount myself, about 4 to 6 people (a week). That is due to change shortly because we have gotten a grant for supervision. We are going to be able to have a number of counselors using TIR and Henry will be providing the supervision.

Marian: What are your sources of referrals?

Joanna: Most of it's from the police, then other victim support schemes, self-reporting, other agencies, general practitioners, hospitals, housing agencies, and that sort of thing.

Marian: Are any referred or ordered by the courts?

Joanna: A few, not many. We get more from London, which is a Crown Court. They will refer if they need to make claims for compensation or they find victims traumatized. We also have our own magistrate court

Marian: Is there something different about trauma in a crime victim as opposed to any other sort of trauma?

Joanna: Not really, I don't think. I've seen crime victims but not many of other types. Although the others aren't as traumatized to the same degree, the issues they need to tackle are low self-esteem and trying to work out why their life is now as it is and trying to put that right, particularly for domestic violence.

Though there are probably areas where you could use TIR, they would probably benefit from a combination of both TIR and other methods. That's my thinking and if someone tells me I've got it wrong I'm willing to be corrected. We use other methods I suppose partly because there are the other counselors and I want to use the [counselors].

VS Lambeth started off very much as a group only interested in domestic violence and it's grown since then. They have taken on a lot of people where there has been child abuse, some sexual assaults and it's just kind of gone on [from there].

We use a lot of psychometric tests to tell whether someone is traumatized or not. I use those as pre-test and then do a post-test and then show the client after. I enjoy showing them to the client and they are like "WOW! Was it really like that? I've really got better!" And although they know it, it's nice to have it confirmed on paper.

Marian: If we trained more of your volunteers to do more techniques, would you find that useful?

Joanna: Yes... I like the picture that Steven and Henry have developed where you have your outer world and your inner world. Then you finally get down to your story and find out that you are actually blocking the reception of any more information. Often when I've brought this to victims it resonates with them. I've often explained that with kids, when mum says, "Go and clean your room," the communication disappears because there's no more room in the child's mental world to receive it when there has already been way too much going on.

Marian: How do you find the incident varying between two people who experience the same thing?

Joanna: It literally depends on what has gone on before, the baggage they're carrying and whether it builds on other incidents or not. I've worked with one man who worked in a shop and had been robbed at gunpoint. I saw him a few times and he went back to work. He was back at work 2-4 months again and the same guy robbed him again! He rang me up and said, "You won't believe this but..." So we started working with him again. We did quite a lot of work and he then started work at another store. I sent him to work with [the late] Steve Bisbey and they handled all of his past traumas.

Finally, he went back to work at his old shop. He was robbed a year later by someone different and ended up with a broken cheekbone. He said, "Although I'm now physically injured, I don't feel as bad as I did the first time." That's because other traumas had been dealt with. He said he couldn't go back to the same store, but I'm not surprised. He went back and worked for the same firm but at a different location about 12 to 18 months ago. He rang me up again after another robbery and he doesn't actually want much counseling. He knows what it's about and he knows how to get better.

So often I've found, and Steve Bisbey confirmed, that people can be re-traumatized by their employers asking, "Aren't you over it?" and so on. Four times is a bit much to be robbed. Asking, "When are you coming back to work?" Can you imagine? He was smart enough to write to the director of the company and got a phone call in response.

Marian: Any differences between men and women in dealing with crime-related trauma?

Joanna: In the end, I don't think so. I think men still find it much harder to admit, "I'm actually not OK; I need some help." I think it's easier for women to think, "I need some help." Once they get into it and realize what TIR consists of, which is working with their strengths, then they engage with it. Particularly, when you ask them, "What do you want to work on?" when one's got the full list of traumas. "You tell me, you're in control." It empowers the client.

Maybe that goes back to your earlier question: what's the difference between crime victims and other victims? I've always been a firm believer that the sooner one can allow the victim to have some control the better off they are. That is one of the reasons why I have warmed to TIR, because you're handing back the control, "You're in control, not me." I think that's why some people who are practicing counselors may not like TIR because they haven't got that same control or power. You have to give it up to work in a person-centered way.

Marian: Would you recommend TIR for other victim service agencies?

Joanna: Oh yes, definitely. I think it could probably work very well with offenders as well.

Marian: Do you find yourself working with perpetrators or offenders?

Joanna: If they come in and they are a victim then we will do that as well. We don't generally hear about them otherwise. I know when I was working with victim/offender conferencing being run by NACRO [an independent voluntary organization working to prevent crime] they were looking at not mediating, but conferencing between them. I was asked to train some of their volunteers. Particularly with young people, one day you're the victim and the next day you're the offender.

Marian: Thank you so much for your time in doing this interview.

———————————

Counseling Inmates:
A Conversation with John Nielsen

VV: Tell me about your professional background

John: I have a MSW from Wilfrid Laurier University in 1984, prior to that I have an Honors BA in Psychology from York University in Toronto. I worked in child welfare for 5.5 years in the 1980s. I worked in a generic mental health agency for a year in rural central Ontario. For 11 years I worked in a medium security[1] provincial correctional facility in Ontario.

VV: How did you start working with inmates?

John: I'm a social worker; I was looking for a job while I was in child welfare, which was pretty gut wrenching work. After over five years in child welfare, I wanted to get out of the system. The clients you are working with are really the children of the people who are committing the abuse or neglect. I would go home at night from my child welfare cases and say "Oh my God, what is happening to those children overnight? What's happening when nobody is there to monitor?" When I applied to the jail jobs, it seemed like a dream job to me because what could happen to these guys? They had four walls around them, shielded from the elements with three square meals a day. They could work if they wanted to and they were safe. So I went from a client population where the children were unsafe to one where they were pretty safe because they were inside a facility.

To me at first it was a dream job. When I realized what really goes on in a prison, I realized I had escaped into a false reality. There are lots of things that can go wrong to kill the spirit of a person in a jail system. Ultimately there were some people killed in the jail that I worked at. I was in the facility and I certainly did debrief a lot of people. It seemed a safe population to work with after child welfare.

---

[1] Medium security means inmates sentenced to "two years less a day" or less; more than that means a Canadian federal facility. Such an institution has all kinds of offenses including drunk drivers with a long record, not what you would consider hard core violent criminals. Additionally, it includes those who had committed a significant number of frauds, non-violent crimes. Thirdly, it has people who had come out of the federal system after 10-20 years on manslaughter or murder convictions and were back in the provincial system on a minor charge of less than two years. So it was common to get pretty serious inmates but not for the current charges for which they were incarcerated (those were not high crimes).

VV: Were some of these people court-ordered or were they all people who requested services?

John: In the jail system, every counseling situation is a voluntary counseling situation. The truth of it is though that, of course, there are certain advantages for them when they come to counseling. For example, if they come to counseling they have a better chance of parole. When I first started working at the jail, there was even a chance that they could get an incredibly early release under a medical temporary absence pass to get to a treatment center. And of course at treatment centers there aren't as many bars on the windows. I would say only a small portion of the inmates that I actually dealt with were seriously interested in improving their lives and leaving crime behind them. The vast majority of them were using me to look good to a girlfriend, look good to a landlord, look good for parole, look good to the guards so the guards would ease up on them. There were lots of hidden agendas.

The two strongest examples of TIR I have happened for me at the jail. One was a survivor of the Bosnian war. He was a Bosnian Muslim in jail for aggravated assault, intoxication, theft, and fraud. As it turns out, he was having terrible, terrible nightmares and in fact he wasn't sleeping. He escaped as a refugee to Canada from Bosnia and couldn't shut out the memories of what had gone on there. He ended up not being able to sleep and he ended up having those kinds of psychotic behaviors you have when you are sleep deprived. He started to medicate himself with alcohol before he was incarcerated. He didn't seek psychotherapy because he believed that his language barrier and refugee status would draw attention to him. Paradoxically, he ended up drawing attention to himself because when he drank to excess he would sometimes become quite aggressive. If he ran out of money and couldn't buy more alcohol then he would go out and just take it if he could. And if he couldn't do that he would just beat up somebody and get into trouble.

That's why he ended up being incarcerated. He still didn't want therapy, although I was a social worker. He came to see me because he said, "I'm in fear for my life. In jail I can't do the drugs and alcohol as I used to and I end up crying out in my sleep. The other inmates are going to kill me, they've told me this. I have to do something to be able to sleep." I did the traditional approaches about avoiding drinking or smoking within an hour of bedtime, doing deep breathing and relaxation exercises. He was trying all of that and not really having any success. (This was before my formal training in TIR). I said, "I'm not really trained in this very much, but we can try this procedure." I did not correctly use TIR, at least not by the procedure book.

One thing that's hard to build up in a jail is trust. I did not know that when you said "What happened" at the end of the TIR cycle, he was supposed to disclose what his traumatic experience was. I just said, "What happened" in the generic sense of, "Are you feeling better?" I didn't go through having him disclose the incident verbally. I in fact renamed TIR "Secret Therapy" because all of the therapy took place between your ears and you didn't have to talk about it. There was no way you could give me any material about your past and your life with which I could then tease you, blackmail you, or otherwise abuse you. I introduced TIR with the standard "brushing your teeth" example of going through an incident. Then I said go through your traumatic incident (find an important one) run through it, at the end of it just tell me when you're done and tell me what you feel.

We did it over two sessions. The sessions were 3-4 hours long and he went through 25 repetitions of his traumatic incident. At the 25th time, he brightened up, so I said "Hey, what happened?" He said "I now know why I've been feeling so bad." He put it together that he had survivor guilt. He felt that it was somehow unfair that he had come to Canada as a coward and had not stayed back there to try to protect his countrymen and relatives that are still being persecuted. Instead, on the 25th repetition, he suddenly realized that his purpose in coming to the new world was to tell the story. Somebody had to live to escape the atrocities to tell what happened over there and ultimately inform the world.

> *All of the traumatic memories now had a useful meaning and therefore no longer scared him.*
> —John Nielsen

He now had a purpose. All of the traumatic memories now had a useful meaning and therefore no longer scared him. They weren't to be locked away in that dark secret place where they never stayed locked in. He now could actively bring up memories and say "Yes, I must remember this story in detail; I must have the facts; I must be able to relate this story, I must be able to inform the war crimes tribunal after the war. I have a purpose; I am a spokesman for those who died."

> *"I have a purpose; I am a spokesman for those who died."*
> —Bosnian War refugee <u>after TIR</u>

VV: So his memories became a source of power instead of trauma?

John: Yes, he was able to sleep at that point and that was the objective measure of success. He was able to sleep soundly without crying out at night any more. Once he was free to remember, he said "John, I want to tell you what happened." The rest of the session was pure catharsis. He was just one memory after another of how he got on the bus, and after he got on they lined up and machine-gunned the people that didn't make it. He saw his buddies die, he saw babies slaughtered in front of their mothers. He saw horrible, horrible atrocities. Now he could remember them because they were empowering as you say.

The second example where I had notable success was where somebody was involved in the cocaine trade and had gotten involved with a deal for cocaine that went bad. There were two girls at his apartment as he had invited them to his place to do the deal. He showed them the money and the next thing he knew several large males stormed into his apartment, took the money, and proceeded to kick him for several hours until he lost consciousness. He kind of faded in and out of consciousness for a 3 day period. Each time he faded into consciousness, the overwhelming pain was so unbelievable he couldn't really stay conscious and he retreated into unconsciousness. The third day he was able to muster enough energy to crawl across the floor, push over the phone, and call for help. That's how he managed to survive this incident. He felt at that time that he was unsuccessful, a chronic bad guy, and this was his lot in life. That maybe he should have died, he had no purpose in living, he was depressed, etc.

> *"My survival was significant, I wasn't meant to die, and if I was then I would have. I'm a survivor not a victim"*
>
> — *crime victim / prisoner after TIR*

I decided that TIR might be appropriate to take the potency of that episode out of his life. We repeated that event 15-20 times. At the end of it, he also brightened up and said "My survival was significant, I wasn't meant to die, and if I was then I would have. I'm a survivor not a victim." He then went on to become more successful.

The third person I used it with more recently was a couple years ago when I was just finishing up my time in the jail. I had a young Arab fellow. He was actually from Iraq where he was born but raised in Lebanon. Lebanon is quite liberal compared to most Middle-Eastern countries, a good mixture of Christian, Muslim, and Bahai. Until the last few years, they were able to be tolerated because Beirut was more European than Middle-Eastern. He felt himself to be more Lebanese than Iraqi. He came to Canada as a young adolescent and committed some minor crimes. He was with his friend when his friend stole a car, he was found in a car with alcohol, and eventually the crimes mounted up so he was incarcerated. When he was incarcerated, his father came and said "You're not my son anymore." His father had worked very hard to get from the Middle-East to Canada and had sponsored his sons one by one to get to Canada. This was the youngest son and the father said "You're a disappointment to me. I'm sorry you came here; you're not my son."

To make matters worse, in the light of September 11, 2001, Canadian immigration tightened up considerably. As he was from the Middle-East, his crimes became deportable crimes. The methods of appeal were no longer really there anymore. They were subsumed by the hysteria to get anybody of Middle-Eastern origin back to the Middle-East if possible. What horrified him more than anything was that because his birthplace was Iraq, when he was deported, they would be deporting him to Iraq. He would be killed because he was of Kurdish descent. In Lebanon, at least he had some friends and family.

I didn't know what Future TIR was at the time (see p. 66), but I did a bit of TIR around his father's rejection of him as a traumatic event. Then I used anticipatory TIR for "What's the worst that could happen there and what are some things you could do to handle it." It became ultimately problem solving, role-rehearsal. I was ready to learn Future TIR, but I was not aware of it at the time.

VV: What are the factors that lead you to decide to do TIR with an inmate?

John: When I first got into the jail system, I had started to do some research into multiple personality disorder, now called dissociative identity disorder (DID). With DID, it seems to be fairly under-represented in the male population. It's mostly women that are diagnosed that way. One of the popular theories was that DID would manifest itself differently in males. They would use violence and out of control behavior as ways of protecting themselves. But who's to say that those aren't just simply different ways of manifesting the same irrational DID behavior? If you think about it, there are lots of logical inconsistencies in jail. For example, if you're disrespectful to a woman, an inmate might want to kill you. Yet when you inspect the backgrounds of most of these guys, they're abusive with the women in their lives. They have this duality in their code, so there is some dissociative process going on in these inmates. When I was studying DID, there is a strong trend in the field to believe that this is a coping mechanism to deal with some childhood trauma.

At first when I was working in the jail system in the early 1990s and didn't know about TIR, I was really trying to uncover whether these were coping mechanisms because of childhood trauma. Later when I met Frank A. Gerbode and had a chance to understand TIR as a process, I thought it was a more elegant way of dealing with the same factors but without having to do the digging or delving. That's how I came to use it as a tool.

I'm still struggling with how to present it to people so it doesn't appear like hocus-pocus. TIR is so different than what people expect, it seems sometimes that when I say we might be able to approach traumas and have their effect eradicated from your system, people say "Well, that's very New Agey." Traditional psychotherapy says you have to be in psychotherapy for years and years and years. I still have trouble elegantly presenting TIR as a treatment option for people... but I'm getting better!

VV: Yes that can be a challenge, when I spoke to Dr. Robert Moore, he said that when people had been through 3 - 4 therapists and drugs that they would simply not believe that their problem could be fixed. You said that trust is an issue. What other special challenges are there as therapist in a jail?

John: It doesn't relate directly to TIR, but there are political challenges in a jail system. Sometimes the guards want you to dig up bad stuff on the inmates so they can be disciplined by what you uncover. In a human institution like that where security is a very important factor, of course if something was uncovered in a counseling situation that would lead to put somebody at risk, of course I would disclose that. I would want to do that in a way that would serve everybody's purposes if I could.

What I felt pressure to do a lot was to write reports that would slant the negative aspects of somebody. If I didn't do that, then I was an "inmate lover" and then it was a challenge when it came to getting cooperation from the guards for getting inmates to appointments, making sure inmates weren't on work detail during appointments, making sure that inmates weren't in solitary confinement. I had to play ball with the correctional officers and go down and tell the "testosterone stories" and say the politically right wing things that were necessary to make it seem like I wasn't another soft, spongy, marshmallow social worker. I constantly had to say things to lead them to believe I was a "man's man."

I would need to be able to do things with inmates in the counseling session that would lead to positive change, but not put the inmates at risk. Sometimes I use some fairly strong suggestions with inmates: "What could be worse for you than the drug life that you've led up to now? So if I expect you to discipline yourself in jail, toe the line, and improve your behavior, how hard is that compared to what you've lived before?" The special challenges are between working with the authority structure and meeting the needs of inmates.

VV: Does the length of the session become an issue?

John: Yes, because meals are so rigidly scheduled. The government regulations around meals are that inmates must be given meals within certain prescribed timeframes. So when the kitchen is geared up to make a mass meal, I can't be having an inmate in my office because that disrupts the order of things and throws a monkey-wrench into the smooth operation of the jail.

So if I had a TIR session that was going overtime, I would have to call in the "credibility chips" that I have with the officers and say: "This is the one in a hundred inmates that is actually going to get better. Could you bring him food in my office so that he could still be fed (by regulation) but he doesn't have to go back to the living unit, stand in line and have the session interrupted? Can you bring the food up?" Things like that required that I played ball with the officers or I'd get nothing. They'd just send a couple of lieutenants down to get the inmate and there'd be no choice about it. And again I'd be black-balled at that point. Could sessions run on indefinitely? No. But the odd time that we really were doing some serious work, I could call in a favor and I could extend it, within limits. When it came time for the "count", all inmates had to be back on their living units. There were no exceptions to that, unless it was a security issue, and I couldn't be considered a security issue.

VV: The only other thing I can think of is the need for inmates to be relatively clean of drugs and alcohol?

John: Well that's not anything that I could control in there. I just had to use the process and trust that they were honest with me. Again, that's where I used whatever rapport I could build with the inmate and say "You gotta be clean, you gotta be straight". When I used the process in jail, I wasn't as stringent about that because I hadn't been formally trained in TIR and I wasn't aware of it being such an important factor. There are times that inmates came and they might have been slightly under the influence but I couldn't tell because I might have just thought they had the flu that day.

The other thing about TIR was that it was mysterious enough to the inmates that a few of the inmates benefited from TIR because they didn't know how to resist it

VV: How does TIR compare to what was happening before you got there, the traditional social work approach?

John: Where TIR was appropriate, TIR was much more elegant than traditional social work. Traditional social work was lip service to Cognitive Behavioral Therapy, but mostly it was kind of psycho-dynamic psycho-babble: talk about your past, talk about all the bad things that happened, get it off your chest. And counseling may go on for months and months and months and not be particularly productive. The other thing about TIR was that it was mysterious enough to the inmates that a few of the inmates benefited from TIR because they didn't know how to resist it! The traditional psychotherapy was well known enough so that if you knew enough psycho-babble words you could fool your social worker for months and months. The other modes of therapy in the jail were group sessions for addictions, anger management, resocialization. Of course TIR is not comparable to them.

VV: What do you see for the future of TIR with inmates?

John: I think it could be a very useful process. The thing about it is that jails are usually about 30 years behind in terms of strategies and techniques. They tend to go for the mainstream medical model. If there's any doubt about what a social worker's doing, they'll ask a psychiatrist and he'll just give them the straight psycho-babble. There will have to be a pilot project which can envelope the entire process.

VV: How does your intake procedure work?

John: The intake was generated by inmates themselves. There was an orientation when they were first brought into the jail. They get deloused, bedding, and assigned to a living unit. Once a week we get all the new inmates and we do an orientation: this is who you contact for medical problems, mental health problems, and then we give a spiel about what social work is about. All you need to do is let your officer on your unit know and a referral will be made and we'll see you. At that point, we do our own intake screen. Each individual social worker would be assigned to a living unit and we would handle all the problems on that living unit. The inmates that came to me would be inmates who were aware of the referral process and took the steps to be referred. There was a cattle call several times a year for group therapy.

VV: When you've got someone who is in a trauma but they're just not ready to do a cognitive thing on TIR, what can you do to get them ready for TIR?

John: What I like to fall back on is rapport; the only time any counseling takes place is when there is rapport. I don't mean it in the generic dictionary sense, I mean a real true sense of multilayered communication and comfort between your client and yourself. Once there is rapport and the trust is built then I'll start to think about whether there is safety enough for the client to go through the TIR process. I have a few clients that are mentally challenged and I don't think it would be appropriate for them. My simple answer is that I just build trust until I can get them over the hurdle and actually introduce the process to them.

VV: That's basically what I've heard from the other practitioners. They all have slightly different ways of doing it, but the end result is trust.

5 TIR and Terrorism

Experiences with 9/11 Survivors

It can be easy to forget that every participant in an incident has a completely different point of view of the event. The experiences of 9/11 survivors exhibit this disparity to a great degree, especially those of security personnel and first-responders, people who remained involved for long durations. In this article, I'll present an overview of some of the unique issues culled from the TIR experiences of various populations. Although this is not a scientific study, I believe that it does anecdotally show the efficacy of TIR.

Another unique characteristic of 9/11 is that therapists and TIR facilitators who treated the victims also in some way experienced the *same* event. Especially those in the same metropolitan areas, as Kathryn McCormack-Chen points out: "I often wondered if I were next. Usually therapists and TIR facilitators are themselves viewing another person's trauma as an uninvolved third party. It was both difficult for me to hear these stories unfold and enormously fulfilling because *I as the facilitator could do something* besides donate money."

Rescue helicopter responded to attack near Washington, DC on September 11, 2001, after hijacked American Airlines Flight 77 crashed into the Pentagon, killing 189 persons, including all aboard the aircraft.

Typical first responders such as firemen, policemen, and EMTs have been trained to handle people and problems of physical trauma, whether dealing with burn victims, triage, or removing the dead. They have been through rigorous training, simulations, and real experiences in the past. Most likely all Pentagon employees and staff would have undergone and planned many disaster drills. However the sheer intensity of 9/11 could never have been predicted. This also included unforeseen threats such as working around live high-voltage transformers in proximity of water.

Duration of the Incident

In the case of 9/11, the duration of the incident contributed greatly to the onset of typical PTSD symptoms. Many security personnel and first-responders were able to keep to the narrow focus of their training for the initial duration of the incident, especially seasoned first-responders who deal with physical trauma on a regular basis.

However, the scope of the incident was much larger than just one event at a single time. For example, first responders handling the Pentagon bombing completed their work only to come home and discover the equally tragic and protracted events in Manhattan. In this sense their normal routine of being able to put the day's worst behind them was cut off. And coverage continued on every channel of television and radio non-stop for days afterwards. Many felt the need to soldier on, working a second shift with few or no breaks.

Further complicating the cases was the extended duration at each site. At the Pentagon, Secretary Rumsfield ordered people back to work as soon as possible. There would be smoke, water, debris, fuel, and bodies being removed for days and weeks later. Imagine that being your working environment, literally down the hall from you. Similarly, first-responders would toil on in Manhattan for weeks and months, unveiling a steady stream of destruction.

Feeling Personal Safety

Another complicating factor was the basic issue of personal safety. This represented a completely new phenomenon on American soil. For example, a Vietnam veteran could be secure in knowing that when he returned home he was definitely not in the jungle even though he might still have issues of hyperarousal, for example, in reaction to secondary stimuli such as loud noises.

After 9/11, people in New York and D.C. continued to feel as if they were in the target sights, because there's physically no way out of that "jungle" if you live or work there. In that case, an exaggerated startle reaction upon hearing a jet plane engine would in some sense reward you for surviving that potential threat. In many other types of incidents, such as witnessing a drowning, the chances of actually experiencing the same phenomenon again are small. However, intrinsic to the threat of terrorism incidents is the possible recurrence of the phenomenon at any time or place.

On 9/11, many first responders in D.C. heard that there were two more airplanes on the way. This meant that while they might feel some success in dealing with the first incident, they felt as if another incident was on the verge of occurring. At that point, the first responders had to continue with their jobs under the added pressure of being under fire by potential further bombings.

Another important factor for some of these people is that the officials decided to rebuild the Pentagon again the same way, with no allowance for any of the windows to open. The original design was to prevent suicide truck bombers, such as in Beirut, but of course that design did not allow for an object to penetrate the entire structure. The element of *safety* in alleviating past traumas is a relative term here, because these people are just waiting for the next hit to come, with full knowledge that many people could be again be trapped behind inoperable windows in an future incident.

Earlier Similar

Another result determined from examining these case histories is that even in dealing with an incident as large as this, the weight of earlier traumas must be reconciled. The pain and loss that many people felt was in fact linked to earlier incidents involving totally unrelated areas of life. Some came from dysfunctional families where their parents suffered from mental illness, substance abuse, or both. Other histories contain incidents such as a man having had a gun held to his head, a woman having experienced a car accident, or early sexual abuse.

The difficulty of returning to normal life was exacerbated in those who also had unresolved childhood traumas. This, of course, was on top of going to work with a plane still stuck in the building or the scene of devastation in Manhattan that would last for months. Many first responders would have had plenty of incidents prior to 9/11 that went unresolved; it's the nature of the job. A typical decision made under such duress might be phrased as "I will never let myself be in a vulnerable position again." The impetus is towards survival but this solution raises more problems while positing an impossible task. TIR helps viewers unmask and release such intentions when the root incident is successfully addressed.

Treating Pentagon 9/11 Survivors:
Case Notes from Kathryn-McCormack Chen, MSW

Biographical notes

Kathryn McCormack-Chen is a registered nurse, licensed clinical social worker, and licensed substance abuse treatment practitioner. She received her Master's degree in Clinical Social Work from Virginia Commonwealth University in 1984. She became licensed as a clinical social worker in 1991. Special areas of expertise are incest and other domestic violence, PTSD, and addiction related problems. She is a Certified TIR Facilitator with a private practice in McLean, VA. She is currently an Adjunct Assistant Professor at the Northern Virginia Community College.

Introduction

I've been doing TIR since 2000 and it has revitalized my practice. I'm in the last 10 years of my working life and I will use it until I retire. I want to thank all of the people who have been on the ground since the beginning, especially Ragnhild Malnati, who has taken me by the hand and guided, helped, trained, and consoled me. In this article, I'm going to talk briefly about three cases of people I worked with who were at the Pentagon on 9/11. To protect these clients' confidentiality I have altered some details and combined their experiences into one overall narrative. All three of these clients were referred to me by a Certified Trauma Specialist who works as an Employee Assistance Counselor at the Pentagon. [Ed. Note: client gender has also been obscured]

Collectively, the Pentagon clients I worked with have had many years of government service. Two of these clients stated that prior to 9/11 they were experiencing no unusual amounts of stress in their lives. The third client reported that he had a mild depression, but was "struggling along, having some difficulty meeting job-related deadlines." He had been very reluctant to report his deteriorating condition because of the pervasive attitude and atmosphere to "tough it out." None of the Pentagon clients were under any psychiatric care just prior to 9/11. All of the clients reported that they managed to get through the events of 9/11 by doing their jobs to the best of their ability, not allowing themselves to "fall apart."

A summary of their general symptoms after 9/11 included: panic attacks, both spontaneous, as well as cued by known stimuli; anticipatory anxiety concerning when the next attack on the Pentagon would occur, constant reminders in the workplace, such as the smell of diesel fuel and falling debris and soot, fear of flying, and claustrophobia. They also reported hyper-vigilance, especially when hearing the sound of aircraft overhead, insomnia, numbing, nightmares, intense preoccupation with the events both in Washington and New York, difficulty concentrating, sadness over loss of friends and colleagues, flashbacks, and situational agitation.

One of these Pentagon clients said to me: "Kathryn, how many times have you had to go back to work THE NEXT DAY, with an airplane stuck in your building?" (You might recall that Secretary of Defense Rumsfeld said "We're going back to work tomorrow, everyone's going to be here as usual.") All of the clients reported just kind of going through the motions during the year after the attack, but all also reported that one of the triggering events that precipitated their seeking help was the commemorative ceremony held on 09/11/02. It seems that at that point they all realized that they just weren't going to return to normal without some therapeutic assistance in addition to that provided by the Pentagon EAP staff.

One client required a year of supportive psychotherapy and medication management because of her decreased ability to function in all areas of her life. We began her TIR work in July of 2003. It was always, "When we're ready we'll know" up until then. One day she came in, sat down and said "Kathryn, I'm ready to start now."

The intake interviews were a fairly straightforward summary of 9/11 itself and the Feelings, Emotions, Sensations, Attitudes, and Pains (FESAPs) associated with it in the ensuing year. All of the clients wanted to get rid of their irrational fears, phobias, and feelings, especially crying a lot. They all wanted to "just get over this and get back to real life."

How Traumatic Incident Reduction and Life Stress Reduction Helped These Clients

1. My experience has shown that TIR and related procedures seem to be most helpful when clients can zero in on specifics of their unwanted feelings, or can tell me of specific incidents that they feel troubled by. Two of the clients I worked with had experienced at least one other event that could have contributed to the intensity of their post-traumatic stress responses. One of them had many, many previous traumas that created numerous layers of unresolved, complex post-traumatic stress disorder.

2. The first client I worked with benefited greatly by one Basic TIR session on the events surrounding 9/11 alone. During that session another helpful technique employed was Unblocking, as she was "stuck" on one specific detail of her 9/11 experience. She said she would like to return to do Basic TIR on one other traumatic event which occurred earlier in her life.

3. One client's case was complicated by a medical problem that had similar symptomatology of panic disorder; however, we did several sessions of Thematic TIR, which gave him great relief and much more mastery over his unwanted feelings.

4. The client mentioned above who just began her TIR work in July says she wants to continue, as she is able, to resolve several other previous traumatic experiences.

I believe that without the techniques employed in TIR and Life Stress Reduction that these clients would still be suffering from the events of 9/11/01.

Impact of the Media
by Victor R. Volkman

Though we who were not there cannot compare our experience to that of the people who were on the scene during the events of 9/11 and their aftermath, many people suffered a negative impact that day. Trauma counselors I have talked to since then from various areas of the country report clients coming in with new fears and anxieties related to those events even if they didn't personally know anyone who was injured or killed on that day. Like survivors of the events themselves, these clients often have earlier incidents triggered by the events of 9/11 as well as fears about possible future events. America's "loss of innocence" comes up frequently as a theme when 9/11 is discussed. The real loss may be loss of the feeling of security and certainly most Americans took for granted before the attacks.

Thematic TIR addresses painful feelings, follows them down to the incident at the root of that feeling and allows the client to let them go. Case histories show that many clients have benefited from Thematic TIR to release the sometimes crippling feelings and fears they had post 9/11. Alertness to potential danger can aid our survival. Crippling fear does not. No matter how reasonable the fear may seem to a person going into a Thematic TIR session, completely viewing it so as to reduce the charge and resistance to is results in a viewer who is free from the negative influences of the past incidents so viewed and able to be more alert, comfortable and effective in his or her environment.

Alertness to potential danger can aid our survival... Crippling fear does not.

Marian Volkman, my wife, has found that fears for the future are best addressed with Future TIR (see p. 66). She reports having used more Future TIR than anything else in addressing post 9/11 symptoms. As an example, one client was plagued by both vague and specific fears for the future especially concerning the well-being of her children. After one session of Future TIR of slightly more than one hour in which the client addressed every negative scenario she could imagine, she was able to live without these worries hounding her and able to enjoy life again.

6 Traumatology

I asked Dr. Anna Baranowsky, a Toronto-based psychologist and executive director of the Traumatology Institute of Canada, to describe the newly emerging field of traumatology:

> The word *traumatologist* was traditionally used to describe a surgical branch of medicine dealing with physical wounds and disability. It has only recently been used to describe working with the emotional aspects of trauma survivors. A trained traumatologist may include a wide range of professionals from the police officer who is investigating a sexual assault to the nurse on the oncology ward at the local hospital to the psychologist aiding a plane crash survivor. They all deal with people who have suffered the worst kinds of trauma and need specialized training so they can offer the best services.

In this chapter, we'll hear from several people involved in the ongoing development of Traumatology in addition to how well it's being put into practice on the front lines of trauma. This chapter is primarily oriented towards mental health professionals and clinicians. Lay readers may prefer to skip ahead to Chapter 7 (Accident Victims).

Traumatology on the Front Lines
with Karen Trotter

To learn more about the Green Cross Project and what it does, please skip ahead to p. 111

VV: Tell me about your professional background.

Karen: I went to school at the University of Tennessee in Knoxville and received a BA in Academic Psychology. A few years later I went on to Oklahoma and worked for People Inc., a community-based social service organization that provides services for Developmentally Disabled individuals. During my employment there I was appointed coordinator of a program called the Oklahoma Children's Initiative. It was a program of several services including in-home counseling for at-risk youth or those reunifying with their families after being in State's custody. The program incorporated three additional service agencies in seven counties in eastern Oklahoma. Because the job required me to supervise Master's level people, which I felt increasingly unqualified to do; in 1996 I returned to Tennessee and earned a Masters in Social Work. I'm now certified and working towards licensure.

VV: How did you become involved with the Green Cross Project?

Karen: I was in Oklahoma at the time of the bombing and was supposed to be in the building on the day after it happened. The CEO of the organization I worked for then was at that time affiliated with the Oklahoma Association of Youth Services. OAYS sponsored the Green Cross to provide training in Oklahoma City for [traumatologist] responders and people who are interested in becoming responders. [Ed. Note: responders are the first people on the scene to help.] These responders would deal with situations like the Oklahoma City bombing, natural or man-made traumatic incidents. He contacted Dr. Figley and they brought Green Cross to Oklahoma City and did a series of trainings.

VV: So the Green Cross Project got started right after the Oklahoma City bombing?

Karen: Yes.

VV: I've got kind of a fragmented view of the organization. Is the major outcome of GCP the yearly conferences?

Karen: After 9/11 GCP progressed into redevelopment mode to incorporate lessons learned during the New York deployment. The mission hasn't changed; it is to provide consultation, information and education and to be able to provide trained traumatologists to respond to communities in need.

VV: Is the focus on critical incident debriefing?

Karen: To a certain extent, yes. The focus of the GCP is on making traumatologists and their specialized tools readily available in communities where they are needed.

VV: For people who are not familiar with debriefing, how would it look to an observer?

Karen: It looks like a support group where everyone gets to talk about what they experienced and what they think and feel about it. First of all you give group members some information about the process of the group, setting ground rules for confidentiality and providing information about the stress reaction, symptoms they might encounter, and possible coping 'skills. It is important to normalize common reactions. Then you facilitate a group discussion by asking a series of questions designed to provoke emotional and cognitive responses to help people stabilize their reactions. Finally, you encourage group members to utilize private and community resources to meet additional treatment needs as appropriate.

VV: Do you think TIR fits in well with the critical incident debriefing model?

Karen: Yes, I do. Yet the techniques are designed to be utilized at different stages in the assimilation of the traumatic incident.

In the initial response during the acute phase of the trauma, it is inappropriate to begin treating the trauma so soon after the incident. Debriefing is designed to help people through the initial stages of the trauma. Debriefing works well, if not to prevent the development of PTSD, to assist in the assimilation process during the acute phase. Unlike Debriefing, TIR is designed as a treatment methodology.

VV: What was the impact of Green Cross on the community in Manhattan after 9/11?

Karen: The first team arrived on 9/16. Response teams of approximately 14 traumatologists and compassion fatigue specialists were arranged in weekly rotations for 4 weeks. Several of us stayed behind to provide continuity. I think there were about 39 people altogether in weeklong shifts. I was there for almost 3 weeks of the 4 weeks total.

We began the first day at our worksite debriefing groups of up to 20 people. That was only the first day or two and the groups got smaller as we went along. I'm unsure of the total number of people we saw. I think we each talked to close to 100 people in the first three days.

After about three weeks, we began to notice obvious signs of healing. There were more conversations being held in the halls and the elevators, more smiles, more people returning to work on a daily basis. As far as impact for those we served, only they can attest to that.

VV: That's a remarkable commitment for people to drop everything and go out there!

Karen: Yes, the response was awesome. I was ready to go on 9/11. It doesn't happen that fast, you have to have the logistical arrangements worked out.

It was really interesting to see the outpouring of assistance. Most team members got to New York on donated private planes. Pilots with Air LifeLine also donated flights to get some team members home after their rotation was finished.

VV: So you had relationships set up in advance?

Karen: And some just seemed to happen as we needed them.

VV: Were the people you saw emergency responders or survivors of 9/11?

Karen: Mainly we worked with witnesses, survivors, and families, friends, or co-workers of those who were lost. Some team members did report working with responders when off-duty at our designated work site. That's a different process altogether because when they're coming off the site, for example firefighters, they'd come off a shift and then a few hours later they're going right back. They can't afford to get caught up in the emotion that will interfere with the job they have to do. They don't usually have the luxury of doing any sort of debriefing until they're finished and they're not going back into the site again.

VV: Were there unique challenges such as confusion over whether people were missing or dead?

Karen: By 9/16 there were still a lot questions. There was a lot of dissonance about the loss with people going through the grieving process starting with disbelief or denial. We found a lot of people being stuck at various stages; there seemed to be no way of understanding and preparing for the suddenness of the loss.

VV: Did you have an opportunity to use TIR when you were there?

Karen: Not really. We did do some debriefings, and utilized some other techniques that help during the acute phase. I utilized some of the TIR training, many of the Rules of Facilitation (see Appendix A) and ideas about communication. We did do debriefing and some work borrowing significant aspects of TIR. That was during the later part of my time there. The process was more modified than going through actual steps because we didn't have that kind of time. As time went on, it became more difficult to work with individuals for any length of time due to reinstatement of their job duties and expectations.

VV: Is there kind of a triage aspect to it where you refer people?

Karen: Absolutely, that was a very large part of it. When you're dealing with trauma in the acute phase you don't try to fix it. You assess, and let them know what's out there. You do what you can so that if someone is going to have continued problems with it, they'll know to get additional help.

We were actually assigned to one organization, a union in New York that did have an Employee Assistance Program (EAP) set up. So we got the people that needed additional counseling or treatment in touch with their EAP.

VV: Is the idea with debriefing and the initial stages to get as many people exposed as possible to understanding the effects of trauma?

Karen: Yes, that was our initial aim. We also did debriefing training for potential responders in the area. We set up a Green Cross Project chapter in the area and trained local counselors and therapists in response and compassion fatigue.

VV: I was thinking compassion fatigue would be an important component there.

Karen: Especially, yes. During a Green Cross response to any emergency or disaster situation, we take compassion fatigue specialists with us or make communication to have compassion fatigue specialists readily available. I see that as a very big component of what GCP is about.

[Ed. Note: Although compassion fatigue is certainly a factor for first responders on the scene of a disaster, whether natural or man-made, it is virtually unknown to practitioners of TIR for two reasons. One is that the traumatic event is over by the time you are employing TIR. The other is that the entire protocol supporting use of TIR allows both client and practitioner to attain closure on each piece of work as they proceed. This is supported by the principle that each session is taken to an end point,]

VV: In our terms, you'd say that you can't really do TIR until the incident is over. Many of the firefighters eventually stayed at ground zero for weeks and weeks.

Karen: The firefighters didn't want to leave the site. And yes, TIR is designed for use with past trauma, not necessarily the acute trauma reaction where most people have difficulty with concentration or distraction.

I was able to use some of the concepts of the TIR process with some people; some of the ideas from Unblocking and flow questions. [Ed note: She is referring here to looking at the various directions or "flows" of action: another causing something to self; self to another; another to another; self to self. See p. 11 for definition] It wasn't running a full session and we didn't have a complete end point. They were still in the middle of it; they hadn't begun to completely process it.

VV: I remember that was very poignant, the firefighters refusing to go off duty.

Karen: Yes, and it was not just the firefighters. We would see the rescue dogs coming back to the hotels to rest and then return for their next shift. We also saw new members of the Coast Guard taking their oath in the hotel lobby preparing to join the search and rescue mission.

VV: That kind of answers my question of how do you handle clients who aren't ready for TIR.

Karen: If they're really not ready to get into it, then you don't do TIR. You start where the client is, and you don't do anything that they are not willing and ready to do. At some point, you have to make a therapeutic judgment too: Is it going to do more harm to get into this? If you're not going to have time to fully address the incident, then don't start the TIR. Using some of the key questions in TIR is what I mean by using a modified session.

VV: What were some of the lessons learned from 9/11 responding—did you modify how GCP would respond next time?

Karen: We learned a whole lot about organization and logistics. We have actual written protocols now on how to logistically handle a deployment. We actually use an incident command structure, patterned after what an emergency response team would be using.

VV: Have you used any of the other Metapsychology techniques such as Unblocking?

Karen: I use Unblocking more often than TIR because I find it's easily adapted into a conventional counseling session. I especially use it with clients with whom I have an established therapeutic relationship who are having difficulty addressing an issue that they have identified for treatment. I also use the repetitive question theme with paradoxical questions sometimes with positive results. I think the key is using the techniques with appropriate clients at the appropriate times.

VV: One thing that's been fascinating to me talking to all the different people using TIR is how they create a zone of safety for the client. Do you have any specific approaches?

Karen: It all goes back to therapeutic alliance, and the question of how do you build a therapeutic alliance? I think basically it's just being real with the client, being a real person. Letting them start from their comfort zone and not saying "OK, this is what we're going to do today." I avoid having a set start kind of approach.

VV: Really stepping into the client centered approach there?

Karen: Exactly.

The Green Cross Projects: Who, What, and How

Information below has been excerpted from the Green Cross Projects website.

Who Are We?

The Green Cross Projects (GCP) was initially organized to serve a need in Oklahoma City following the April 19, 1995 bombing of the Alfred P. Murrah Federal Building. We are an international, membership-based, humanitarian assistance organization, non-profit corporation. The web address is http://gcprojects.org/. All members are certified traumatologists, most are licensed mental health professionals. All are oriented to helping people in crisis following traumatic events.

What Do We Do?

The GCP responds to requests from individuals, organizations, and other entities following a traumatic event. The requests can include any or all of the following:

1. Crisis assistance and counseling: helping those in shock get back on their feet and access their natural coping methods and resources.

2. Assessment and referral services: identifying who is recovering properly from the traumatic event, who is not, why they are not recovering and what additional or other services are needed when and by whom.

3. Orientation and Consultation to Management: educating management about the immediate, week-to-week, and long term consequences of traumatic events for individuals, work groups, families, and larger systems.

4. Training, Education, and Certification: preparing management, human resources, employee assistance professionals, and service providers with sufficient guidance and competence to first do no harm to the traumatized and help them recover.

5. Family Resource Management: designing and implementing programs for strengthening and promoting family wellness in the wake of traumatic events, with special attention to young children.

6. Long-term trauma counseling: helping those unable to recover quickly from the trauma by providing individual and group trauma and grief counseling.

These services are provided over varying periods of time and performed initially by members of a deployment team. They are transported into the impacted area within hours after the request is made. They stay from between 3-6 weeks or until local Green Cross Project members can relieve them.

How Do We Help?

The Mission of any deployment is to transform "victims" into "survivors." Immediately following a traumatic event victims attempt to address five fundamental questions:

1. What happened to me?

2. Why did it happen to me (us)?

3. Why did I (we) do what I did during and right after this disaster?

4. Why have I (we) acted as I have (we have) since the disaster?

5. Will I (we) be able to cope if this disaster happens again?

Service Provision: Organized Assistance

Prior to and throughout the deployment, the GCP works with the host or client to clarify the mission of the deployment and specify measurable and attainable goals. Typically the services provided are provided in waves:

- Wave I (Days 1-10 following the disaster): Crisis stabilization, contacting local GCP members to establish a chapter for continuity of care.

- Wave II (Days 5-15): Stress management, social support, orientation of management.

- Wave III (Days 10-20): All of the above plus training, assessment and referral, and family resource development.

- Wave IV (Days 15-40): All of the above reactions plus grief and loss consultation and counseling.

In addition to providing services through the host the GCP works with local providers for the purpose of continuity of care. By Wave IV the local providers outnumber of outside providers.

Dr. Anna B. Baranowsky and the Traumatology Institute of Canada

Dr. Anna B. Baranowsy is the Executive Director and Founder of the Traumatology Institute (Canada), offering training and consultation in the field of Traumatology. Dr. Baranowsky received her doctorate in Clinical Psychology at the University of Ottawa. She is a Green Cross Scholar, Registered Traumatologist and Trainer. She serves on the board of directors of the Canadian Traumatic Stress Network and the Canadian Centre for Psycho-Oncology. I talked with Dr. Baranowsky on August 4th, 2003 and asked her about Traumatology, TIR, and her practice in general:

VV: What is your involvement with the Green Cross Project?

Anna: The Green Cross Projects (www.gcprojects.org) started in 1995 after the Oklahoma City Bombing [see p. 111]. I came in 1997 to Florida State University and I worked with Dr. Charles Figley. At that time the Green Cross Projects were preparing for their first annual Green Cross Projects Conference. I gave a couple of brief presentations at that conference and then the following year.

Dr. Anna B. Baranowsky, Executive Director and Founder of the Traumatology Institute (Canada)

My involvement is less with the Green Cross and more with the Traumatology Institute, which Dr. Charles Figley first established in 1996. In 1998, I was asked to bring the Traumatology Institute to Canada and founded the Traumatology Institute (Canada) at that time. Currently I am the Executive Director offering training across Canada. I've been doing training and helping people to bring their skills to a certain level. I think what we need in the field is really a set of standardized training programs so that people can have the opportunity to build strong competency skills in the field of post-trauma responding.

VV: And that's the mission of the Traumatology Institute of Canada?

Anna: Yes, it's a training institute to increase the standards of practice in the field, whether you're an emergency service worker, clinical psychologist, social worker, or grief counselor. I do a lot of training, and all of the information about the institute is at http://www.psychink.com.

At this point we're in the stage of retooling, and we're hoping that the training becomes standardized right across Canada. That's the dream vision. Within the training there are two streams. There is a community and workplace stream for people who don't have a counseling background and won't do clinical work. The other is a clinical stream for people who will do more in-depth individual work with trauma survivors. Both streams have their own target groups.

For the community and workplace stream you might have human resource people, emergency medical techs, and nurses. In the clinical stream you might have psychologists, social workers, psychiatrists, people who are working clinically. Both streams have comprehensive training that allows people to understand what kinds of tools would be best used in various situations: whether it is for onsite responding or in the office where you are doing more intensive counseling work. We also have a program for people who have become overwhelmed as a direct result of their caring work. For this, we have our Accelerated Recovery Program for Compassion Fatigue.

Although we don't teach TIR in training, we certainly let people know it's one of the approaches that we endorse and use. I've actually had a really good time with TIR and I've found it to be a very useful approach. It is one of the many interventions I use because I believe in using the approach that fits the individual and the circumstances so I want a lot of tools at my fingertips.

> *I do use TIR in my own practice, yes, and I find it to be a really effective tool.*

VV: Do you use TIR in your own practice?

Anna: I do use TIR in my own practice, yes, and I find it to be a really effective tool. I'm actually really fortunate because I have a very busy private practice. Although I do perform some field work, right now I focus most of my clinical services doing work in my office.

VV: Exactly what kind of private practice do you have?

Anna: I'm a registered clinical psychologist; I work with all sorts of people in the community. Because my area of specialization is trauma, I get a lot of referrals for all sorts of different cases. When you do do work within a certain field, your name gets known for that work after a while. I do get a lot of referrals for many different kinds of traumas. That's where you get to see the effectiveness of any given approach.

VV: How do you handle clients who are not yet ready for TIR?

Anna: I tend to use a resolution approach such as TIR only after the individual has been grounded in safety and shown proficiency at self-soothing and containment, which is stage one in a multi-phase approach to trauma therapy that I endorse.

By starting with safety first we create a strong foundation from which to begin therapeutic interventions. We provide instruction, and practice all sorts of approaches for lowering body reactivity. We understand that in order for us to move into the core of a resolution technique like TIR, the person has to have a certain amount of hardiness or ability to tolerate the discomfort..

VV: As a practical consideration, do you find that the length of the session can be an issue?

Anna: It is an issue when money is an issue. What I try to do is to help people understand that this is an investment in themselves. The investment obviously means that if you're not using your energy to deal with the emotional overload that the traumatic memory can bring to you, then you have a much better chance of coping well and using your energy in productive ways in the present.

What I try to do is to help people understand that this is an investment in themselves

In general, I do work with people who either have insurance money or who are being referred through their company or who are able to understand that this is a good investment for them. When working an hour and half or two hour sessions, I book that in advance and tell them what's coming. We'll already have worked probably for a couple of sessions before I've moved into TIR sessions. [Ed. Note: Approaches vary among practitioners on when to start TIR, depending of course upon the readiness of the client]. We do this preparation work around safety first. Then once we've got that safety woven in, we can move into TIR, and they've already understood that they're progressively moving toward resolution. TIR would be one piece of it.

Active Ingredient Study:
Preliminary Findings
by Joyce Carbonell, Ph.D

The following transcript is excerpted from the plenary session of Joyce Carbonell, Ph.D at the 9th Annual Conference of what was then the Institute for Research in Metapsychology in 1995

In 1994, TIR, V/KD, EMDR, and TFT were investigated through a systematic clinical demonstration (SCD) methodology at Florida State University. This methodology guides the examination but does not test the effectiveness of clinical approaches. Each approach was demonstrated by nationally recognized practitioners following a similar protocol, though their methods of treatment varied. A total of 39 research participants were treated, and results showed that all four approaches had some immediate impact on clients and appear to also have some lasting impact. The paper also discusses the theoretical, clinical, and methodological implications of the study.

Introduction

I'll start this presentation with some background about the project, and I'll tell you why I got involved. I run the University Crisis Management Unit and I work with the Critical Incident Stress Debriefing Team. I also work with some of my fellow mental health workers in town and together we formed the Community Crisis Response Team. I've worked with Vietnam vets, people on death row, and rape victims. I've never had a traditional sort of clients in any sense of the word. My clientele were almost always in some sort of trauma, crisis, or involved in a very ongoing trauma. That is, they were sentenced to death, they had a warrant signed, they were on trial, they were in an abusive relationship, or they were raped and their rapist was at large. I also work with people who have more traditional traumas such as Vietnam veterans and law enforcement officers.

For years, Charles Figley and I have both been very interested in stress and trauma in very different ways. Charles is particularly interested in compassion fatigue, Vietnam veterans and some traumatized groups. Since we both taught at the same university, we eventually got together. As a result of leading the trauma study group, we developed this project. When you look through the literature and you get some idea of how frequent and how common trauma is, it's really appalling. The lifetime prevalence rates of PTSD are incredibly high; more for some groups than others (Christensen & Jacobsen, 1994). For example, 25% of those exposed to any stressor and 35% to 92% of those who were raped have traumatic stress. Clearly not everyone gets traumatic stress. Some people can go through numerous experiences and not develop symptoms and yet others will develop them.

Prevalence Rates

Prevalence rates became part of our curiosity also. Could we not only find a way to treat it, but could we find a model for finding out how traumatic stress gets induced? Why do some people seem to be more likely to have it happen while some people don't seem to have it happen? It happens in traumatic bereavement, in people molested as children, and in 65% of those who experience some kind of non-sexual assault. We tend to forget people like your average mugging or burglary victim.

For example, my in-laws' house was recently burglarized. They had lived out in the country for years in a rural area. They loved it and felt incredibly safe. They finally sold their small business so they could go on vacations. After their first vacation, they came home and found it ransacked. They did not leave the house empty since then. Someone is always there now, and it has made a terrible dent in their lives. And you may say "It was just things that got stolen," but what really got stolen from them was what happens to a lot of traumatized people: any sense of safety, trust, and belief in other people. There are tons of traumatized people out there who will probably never be officially diagnosed as having PTSD and never seek help for the simple reasons that they don't want to, they don't know how, they don't know the process, and they don't want to be labeled. Vietnam veterans can obviously fit into this category. A much forgotten group is prisoners-of-war from World War II and veterans of that war. Some veterans interviewed recently about the battle of Iwo Jima (50 years ago from that time) were clearly suffering badly at the slightest mention of what they had seen or done. Studying the data confirmed the importance of searching for the model of how traumatic stress gets induced.

Incidence Rates

Charles and I were just so amazed at the amount and tenacity of trauma that people suffered, that we decided this was something that we would continue to pursue. For example, burn patients have a very high rate of trauma as nurses and physicians know. The article from the aforementioned cited statistics points out that "We have done a very good job in recent years of documenting that people suffer." We document it quite well. Yet what happens is that we tend to do very little about it. There are all kinds of literature documenting who suffers and how they suffer.

The *Journal of the American Medical Association* published a review of 150 studies on PTSD and the highest success rate was 20% with an average of 30 hours of treatment. Even then, they weren't claiming to completely eliminate the symptoms of PTSD. Of course the other impetus behind this was that we realized that most treatments are slow and somewhat ineffective. "ED-75" is the Effective Dosage for which 75% of the people get relief. There are charts for drugs and all kinds of treatments with an ED-75 level. This is rather frightening both in terms of time and cost.

In Kopta's study (1994), they reviewed charts where clients had filled out questionnaires for having the presence of symptoms after therapy sessions. Then they charted out how many therapy sessions it took per symptom to resolve. Assuming a basis of $75/hour, they charted how it cost per symptom. "Crying easily," the cheapest for example, required an average of 22 fifty-minute sessions before clients felt relief. On the other hand, "Worrying too much" costs approximately $9000. There is some older research that indicates that your degree doesn't particularly make you a more effective therapist. Para-professionals do just as well in therapy, and yet certainly doctoral-level psychologists charge a lot more.

There is some older research that indicates that your degree doesn't particularly make you a more effective therapist.

Brief Treatments

Contrary to the frightening costs mentioned above, we found lots of clinical claims of being able to treat PTSD in short periods of time. These came from people like Milton Erickson, Neurolinguistic Programming people with Visual Kinesthetic Disassociation (V/KD), and then TIR practitioners. The other approach which came to the forefront recently [in the early 1990s] was EMDR. According to some sources, EMDR has become the most widely researched among current treatments. Another treatment which is probably the least known and least well accepted method is Thought Field Therapy (formerly known as the Callahan Technique). We ended up with these four approaches to PTSD, some of which were more publicly accepted than others.

All of them were very different from each other except in the one respect that they all seemed to be able to cure. That is they seemed to make people feel better in short periods of time. They were not like the aforementioned study where it took 67 hours to make clients "feel better about the future". Can you imagine if there was truth in advertising when clients came in? You would have to say "You're feeling lonely? That will be 86 sessions". My advice would be to buy a dog; dogs are wonderful for feeling lonely. We convened a panel of experts who advised us on these different treatments. We can thank Teresa Descilo for getting us interested in TIR. She approached Charles, who was talking about compassion fatigue, and assured him that she never had any!

The Study

We had some concerns. (1) It had to be something that there were at least 500 people trained in. (2) There had to be some clinical evidence of its effectiveness. (3) An international group of trauma experts with which we consulted had to agree that this would in fact be an appropriate treatment.

We devised something we called a systematic clinical demonstration. This is not your traditional methodology. Our goal was not to compare these four treatments and say which one was best. The goal was to find the Active Ingredient: What was making these things work? Why did these things work? We hoped that if we could find that Active Ingredient that we could design a model of how traumas and phobias are induced in people and how they happen. We don't have a particularly good model for that. We have some, but we still can't explain why some people do and some people don't [have traumatic stress].

Phobias are one of the strangest manifestations of traumatic stress. The worst snake-phobic I'd ever seen had no one else in her family who was ever afraid of snakes, had never had a particularly nasty experience with snakes, couldn't remember the last time she had ever seen a snake, and couldn't remember a time when she wasn't afraid of snakes. That's not particularly uncommon with phobias. Phobias are very specific. Have you ever known anyone with a chair- or table- phobia? No. There is a certain subset of things that people develop phobias about.

Many studies fail that try to look at treatments because they take people inexperienced in the treatment, have them do the treatment, and then say, "See, it didn't work." Or they'll compare two treatments with therapists that are well-trained in one but not in the other method. We wanted to see the very best for each of these. We essentially contacted the originators of each of these particular approaches and invited them to come to Tallahassee. The originators from all four of these come from no place other than California (audience laughs).

What we wanted to do is see the very best therapists for each of these treatments.

We invited these people out. TIR was our first group of practitioners, and because they were our first group, it was a little strange. I offer our sincere apologies to Ragnhild Malnati, Teresa Descilo, and Frank A. Gerbode, for the problems. Our equipment broke down; there were problems with our research personnel, and so on. We handled these before the following groups came to work with us. For NLP, we had Ed and Maryanne Reese, who had originally studied with Richard Bandler and they were using V/KD. For EMDR we had Steve Silver and Roger Solomon. Although we invited Francine Shapiro, she could not come because she had committed months before to do a Level 2 workshop. For TFT, it was Roger and Joanne Callahan.

The Clients

We advertised in the paper that we were looking for clients that had trauma stress. We gave interviews and we had blurbs on public radio. A few clients literally drove up after hearing it. We rarely turned anyone away. The therapists were not given a choice of clients; the clients were randomly assigned. We would schedule as many as we thought we could. Most of our clients had not experienced just one highly stressful event but as many as 30 highly stressful events. 98% of these clients had prior therapy, frequently unsuccessful. Many of them had been dumped by their therapists. We excluded people who were mentally retarded, minors, blatantly psychotic, drug abusers, and those people on psychoactive medications. To be included in our study, they had to have at least one active symptom of PTSD or phobia but not necessarily a formal diagnosis. Ages ranged from 18 to 58 and averaged 40 years of age.

Clients had to agree to be treated during specific dates and times. There was a week for each treatment: TIR was done for a week in September; V/KD was done for a week in October; EMDR was done for a week in November; TFT was done for a week in December. We did not give people a particular treatment that they requested. They were just assigned to the next group to come in; they did not self-select. Our clients came into these treatments knowing nothing about them except that they were brief treatments known to be effective for traumatic stress. We left description of the technique to the therapists to avoid any bias.

These are the types of traumas from clients that we saw: abusive relationships, problems with parents, moves, loss, death, accidents, imprisonment, child abuse, rape, war veterans, divorce, and phobias. Most people had multiple problems. The phobias that we saw were very, very severe. They were phobias that impinged on people's lives.

Treatments in Action

Clients who were actually seen varied by treatment. TIR therapists saw everyone who walked in the door, for which we thank them. One V/KD client rejected the therapists because he wanted TIR instead. EMDR rejected 8 of approximately 14 clients. The EMDR therapists decided that many people were not ready for EMDR and that they needed prior preparation of therapy. Also, they were concerned about abreactions to EMDR and only having a week available for treatment. TFT saw 15 out of 15 clients. We did not invite our therapists to reject our clients. We were in fact dismayed when our therapists rejected our clients. It was not what we had in mind, but they did.

Sometimes the number of clients was partly related to the average length of treatment. The TIR people had quoted two hours as the average length of treatment, though they had to allow more variance. We eventually let the therapists schedule the clients themselves, it seemed so much safer. V/KD takes close to the same amount of time as TIR. It was hard to determine the length of treatment for EMDR, because there were so many rejected clients who were never treated. TFT asked us to schedule no more than 40 minutes per client, so we were able to schedule considerably more clients. 71% of all clients were female. This may be a function of the fact of the gender statistics on mental health problems. Women are much more likely to report depression and anxiety disorders whereas males are much more likely to be diagnosed as personality disorders and substance abuse disorders. The overall rates are the same, but the breakdown in categories are different.

All of these seemed to work; you can't ask me which one did better. For TIR, the average length of a session was 71 minutes. V/KD clients were seen for 49 minutes per session, EMDR in 53 minutes, and TFT in 32 minutes. The largest number of treatments was 4 sessions since there were only 4 days in a week.

They are all so different. One of our issues became, what is the Active Ingredient? They all worked, by the way. All of our clients who were treated felt better on the SUDS [Subjective Units of Distress] scale. Some people say, "Well those subjective ratings don't mean anything."

One of the important issues is: *me* telling you that you should feel better is not particularly relevant if *you* don't feel better. How many have you ever been to physicians or had surgery and you go back in and say "Well, but it's not working, it doesn't feel good." They say

"Well, it should." Then they sort of blame it on you; you must be doing something wrong. Then they want you to go away and not come back. I like to hear what clients have to say. All of the clients felt subjectively better after treatment.

All of the clients felt subjectively better after treatment.

Narration and interpretation

Let me tell you a little about what we're trying to theorize about these treatments. V/KD and TIR involve the client narrating the incident. EMDR and TFT truthfully require very little verbalization. EMDR in its most basic level does not require much in the way of verbalization on the part of the client. TFT requires virtually nothing, if they don't want to tell the therapist what it is, they don't even have to. On the other hand, in TIR you do no interpretation for the client. You do not say to your client: "That's probably related to something that happened in your childhood." You would not presume to know what happened; you would not in fact interpret those things for the person. TFT does the same thing; they do absolutely no interpretation. They do no interpret for you why you are afraid or why you have this chronic recurring memory.

V/KD will often interpret for the person: "Maybe what you know now, that that person [in your past] didn't know then, is that it's not your fault." In EMDR, they do what is called cognitive interweaving. They will in the course of it interweave an explanation for the person. One woman got really upset every time an ambulance came by. She was actually distressed because during the cognitive interweaving he said, "It's not your fault that your father died; he had the heart attack." She snapped back "I know that." She did know that and she didn't feel guilty.

Theories about the treatments

In some ways the interpretive and non-interpretive treatments have a striking resemblance in what they do. One of our theories is to try and figure out why all of these varied and disparate treatments work. One of the theories that we are playing with is that all of these behaviors and fears are maintained, sometimes operantly. In the case of the woman with the snake phobia who couldn't go out the front door it was operantly maintained. In part, by her husband who went out and checked for snakes everyday. It's maintained perhaps in two ways in that she's maintaining his behavior also which is protective. Many of these things are probably classically conditioned. Remember Dr. Gerbode's model of things getting associated one by one [see Chapter 1]. These things seem to be classically conditioned yet to some extent operantly maintained. They are maintained by the environment, although classically conditioned to get there. This may explain why they are hard to break into. Maybe what all these treatments do is break into that loop. I also firmly believe that anxiety also has a physiological component. Very few people feel causatively anxious without having any physical sensation of anxiety, even though they don't always label it. So you have anxiety cognitions and you have physiological symptoms and there are probably some other things. Just looking at those two, they are kind of linked to together. It seems that some of these treatments are breaking into that loop or linkage.

In TIR, they keep exposing themselves to the "conditioned stimulus". What never happens? The stimulus doesn't get reinforced or interrupted. In the beginning, some of the people are starting to get very upset and they cry and they get distressed. But then as they keep going, it extinguishes. In a normal therapy session when a person gets that upset, you interrupt it. So they never get to go and experience that condition stimulus to find out that the conditioned response is never going to happen again. In TIR, that cognition gets to keep going and going. So TIR and V/KD (to some extent) seem to break in at the cognition level. The person gets to keep experiencing that cognition. When you think about it, it makes perfect sense. In traditional therapy, when a client cries what do we do? We try to stop them because we don't like it. They never get to find out that the next thing isn't coming. The reason you see that rise in emotion because they're expecting it. And eventually what happens is that it doesn't come and it extinguishes.

EMDR and TFT seem to do something very different in that they seem to be interrupting at the physiological level. One of the things that they seem to accomplish is that the clients lose their physiological sense of anxiety.

None of these treatments destroy the memories. But the clients seem to then have it as a memory as opposed to an ongoing experience. What EMDR and TFT tend to do is interrupt it at a physiological level so the person can have a cognition but not have that funny feeling. These treatments seem to break in at very different points.

We keep referring to these things as traumatic memories for people. But I actually think that all of these things we are treating are ongoing experiences. Lots of us have memories; I had six car accidents in two years, and I can remember all of them. On the other hand, we saw a client who had only one car accident with minor injuries, and at the very thought of tires squealing or cars getting close she would have basically a full-blown panic attack. For some people, and we don't know why, those things tend to remain as an ongoing traumatic experience. [Ed. Note: see Gerbode's Traumatic Incident Network in Chapter 1 for one possible explanation.] What all of these treatments seem to be able to do is move traumatic incidents into the realm of a memory. They don't look back and say "My goodness isn't that wonderful that I was raped?" But they can look back and say "I was raped. That was sad." But it's not a constant refueling of that [sadness]. These people have these sort of chronic traumatic experiences related to those memories. These treatments seem to break into this at different points. I can't say which treatment is better. Some may be more appropriate for some people more than others.

Our client who said "I never got to talk" would probably like TIR much better. On the other hand, we had clients who didn't want to talk, who were happier with one of the other treatments for a variety of reasons. They were either not willing to tell what it was or didn't want to. But then again, we didn't give clients a choice of treatments. It seems to me that what we are doing with these treatments is taking this conditioned response and separating it from that stimulus. Some of them seem to break in on that cognitive level and some of them break in on the physiological level.

The treatments seemed to work in spite of the tremendous variations between therapists' personalities. Most of our clients had been in pain for a very long time. What they wanted was relief. They cared much less about the therapist than we did. In fact, some of them actually didn't like the therapists and would say so. On the other hand, they admitted that they felt better. Some of them a week later could not remember who their therapist was. If nothing else, it tells you that therapists are fairly unimportant; clients don't care about you.

My traditional notion of therapy has always been that you're watching people get better. You can't force the person to get better. We have a distinct advantage in that most people come to therapy because they do either want to get better, to change something or fix something that's making them uncomfortable. We can give them the tools, we can watch them, but in some ways it's not us, it's them.

For more information about the **Active Ingredient Study** see
http://www.fsu.edu/~trauma/promising.html

Selected References

Christensen, A. & Jacobson, N. (1994). Who—or what—can do psychotherapy. *Psychological Science*, 5, 156-167.

Kopta, S.M., Howard, K.I., Lowry, J.L., & Beutler, L.E. (1994). Patterns of Symptomatic Recovery in Psychotherapy. *Journal of Consulting and Clinical Psychology*, 62, 1009-1016.

Recordings of this lecture and several other conversations from this book are available on the *Beyond Trauma: Companion Disc*.

(A compilation of MP3 audio files playable on all computers)

Loving Healing Press

www.LovingHealing.com

TALLAHASSEE DEMOCRAT

Simple Therapy Eases
Complex Past Pains of Life
By Margaret Leonard, Democrat Staff Writer

September 18, 1994

Teri, traumatized by repeated sexual abuse when she was a child, had been told that she could learn to cope, but could not hope for a cure for the depression, flashbacks, nightmares, insomnia and loneliness that had been her daily life for most of her 32 years. With the help of constant exercise and other stress-management techniques, she was coping—raising a child and sustaining a marriage—but she had no hope of enjoying her life.

David, a police officer for almost 20 years, had seen too many shootings—including two of himself and one, fatal, of a best friend—and too many abused children. "It's like a ghost in the closet,'" he said. "It won't leave you alone… I couldn't sleep at night. I had nightmares."

Without much faith that it would make a difference, David and Teri volunteered for a research project on treating post-traumatic stress disorder. Psychologists Charles Figley and Joyce Carbonell of Florida State University had brought in Frank Gerbode, a Menlo Park, Calif., psychiatrist, to demonstrate "Traumatic Incident Reduction," a fast, intense and incredibly simple technique he created about four years ago. TIR is the first of four treatment methods that Figley and Carbonell will study in an attempt to find the "active ingredients" in successful trauma therapy.

Therapists who use TIR need training, but what they learn to do is simple, in theory.

"The heart of this technique lies in being a tremendously good friend, who will bear witness to another person's pain as long as it takes, and encourage them to keep talking about it," Figley said. He said all nine of the Tallahassee subjects were helped by the treatment, which lasted from one-and-a-half to nine hours.

"I went home after the first session and said, 'Guess what? There is hope,' " Teri told a group of therapists discussing the technique Friday at the Psychiatric Center of Tallahassee Memorial Regional Medical Center. "I think I can rejoin society now.'"

"I went home after the first session and said, 'Guess what? There is hope',"
— sexual abuse survivor

She and two others volunteered to discuss the treatments for FSU researchers and Talla-hassee therapists. In this story, only first names of trauma victims are used, and some of those are changed. Each of the three said the treatment made it possible to "move on with my life."

"I was at the point in my situation that I was willing to try anything," said Curtis, who found the relief he wanted in one session of an hour and a half. "I don't know how many times we went through it," he said. "It felt like 50 times. It was probably 12 or 15."

In the videotapes of the therapy sessions, which took place last week, Gerbode and two other therapists—Ragnhild Malnati of Washington, D.C., and Teresa Descilo of Miami (Florida) – spoke very little.

Each time, Teri remembered, "more feeling came out—like when you see a movie three or four times and keep seeing new things." Finally, she said, "it becomes so familiar to you, and you get comfortable with it, and you resolve all your issues, and you just want to leave it; you've really seen all there is to see."

A session can occasionally go four hours or more. The session isn't over until the patient reaches an "end point," signaled by relaxation, lightheartedness, and often laughing and joking.

"It really clicked for me the first session," Curtis said. "I went back and it was gone… It's wonderful."

It took longer for David, who spent nine hours in four or five sessions. He and Teri, though they felt immediately relieved, plan to go back for more, as soon as there are Tallahas-see therapists trained in the technique.

The treatment goes on until the trauma is resolved and loses its power. Often, one trauma story leads to another, and the patient goes through each one. The trauma victims did not believe they could have done it alone.

"It's necessary to have somebody else to share it, and the only way to share it is to talk about it," Gerbode said.

Why not just tell it to a trusted friend?

After the first or second telling, Gerbode said, "peoples' eyes glaze over."

Sometimes it's not just boring, but painful.

"Friends and family tend to shut people down," said Figley, who has written about the "compassion fatigue" that can drive social workers and therapists out of their jobs. "I think as therapists we do the same thing. There are tricky ways therapists have of sort of moving them on to something that will be easier to tolerate."

"Friends and family tend to shut people down, I think as therapists we do the same thing."

—Charles R. Figley, Ph.D.

Figley and Carbonell plan to present three other treatment methods in the next three months, follow up on each to see if the successes are permanent and study them all carefully.

7 Accident Victims

A Day in the Life of a Trauma Counselor
by Irene Schoenfeld-Szabo, CTS, CMF

Originally published in the Association for Traumatic Stress Studies (ATSS) Journal. Reprinted with permission of author

Irene Schoenfeld-Szabo, C.T.S. (Certified Trauma Specialist), is a Trauma Counselor who works with survivors of traumatic events, enabling them to resolve trauma and eliminate post-traumatic stress. Ms. Schoenfeld-Szabo currently specializes in working with survivors of motor vehicle accidents (MVA).

Session notes: July 6, 1995

It's Thursday morning and I have arrived at the rehabilitation clinic early to review my clients' files.

"Cindy" is my first client for the day. In our last session, we had worked on a car accident she had 4 years ago. She had been driving at a slow speed and when she couldn't stop her car on the ice, she hit a light standard. She received some soft tissue injuries, for which she had been treated, but had become anxious about driving. I had her repetitively re-experience this car accident till her anxiety had been relieved (Basic TIR is used when the client has awareness of a specific trauma). After the session she no longer felt anxious about the incident. When she returned for the next session, she reported that her anxiety as a driver had lessened dramatically but she was still anxious as a passenger. I asked Cindy how she felt when she was in a car and she gave me a list of the three symptoms. I systematically used Thematic TIR (which traces back the negative feeling through a number of earlier incidents to the root incident) on all three negative feelings and then we went back to address the first car accident again.

It's interesting to note this was the first car accident in a series of four accidents that Cindy had in the last five years. She was sent to me because she was suffering from post-traumatic stress disorder. In the previous session—our fourth—we had spent a full two hours having her repetitively re-experiencing the first car accident. She became very agitated during the re-living of this incident but was willing to continue even when she became "freaked out" by the intensity of the emotion that this incident was bringing up. This was the turning point and from then on the affect continually lessened till it was no longer there. [Ed. Note: affect is defined as the conscious subjective aspect of an emotion considered apart from bodily changes]

Cindy arrives for today's session. I ask her if she has eaten breakfast and is well rested. She replies affirmatively on both points. For TIR to be effective clients need to be well rested and well nourished. We start the session and I ask her how she has been since last session. She reports that she has had no nervousness, body clenching or anxiety while she is a passenger or driver. She is very excited about this because she hasn't felt this calm around cars in five years. After a ten-minute session she leaves and I close her file. I notice that I have seen her for a total of 13 hours including a history-taking session. (Note: Cindy still goes to the clinic for physical therapy and reports that her nervousness has not returned. It has been three months since I last saw her).

My next file is "Joe", who had a minor car accident five months before he came to see me. He was suffering from post-traumatic stress disorder but his flashbacks went back to an incident earlier than the car accident. Three years previously, Joe had been working on a farm and had been trampled by a horse. His injuries were quite serious and he had lost most of his pre-accident memory. He had also become much quieter and enjoyed life less after the accident. He felt he had been getting over the horse accident quite well and hadn't had any flashbacks in a long time. The car accident had triggered his current flashbacks to the horse accident. We had completed the intake/history taking last session and today we were ready to tackle the horse accident. We chose to work on this before the car accident because it was what interested Joe the most. Traumatic Incident Reduction is a client-centered method; whatever the client is most interested in, we work on in the session.

At this point, Joe comes in and we settle down to do the session. I inquire whether Joe is hungry or tired and he replies no. All traumatic incident reduction sessions are structured the same way so that there is stability and the client always knows what to expect. We start the session. The first few times through the incident, using Basic TIR, go quickly because Joe is still dissociated from the incident. For the next few times through I ask him to pay attention to specific details such as "What did you hear during the incident?" This helps connect him with the incident and now it takes him longer to go through the incident. He is beginning to remember things about it that he had never remembered before. It is a vital feature of TIR that it facilitates cognitive restructuring. As he is re-experiencing the incident, he is sitting with his head in his hands, becoming extremely agitated by the memory. He reviews the event a total of eight times and at the end he is able to reconstruct the entire incident; something he had never been able to do before.

At the end of the session, he is relaxed in his chair with his arm casually draped over the back of the chair talking about the incident in a very animated way. This is an indicator that the session has reached its conclusion. It has been three and one-half hours and I end the session. I write up my notes and put the file away ready for our next session. (After six hours of Traumatic Incident Reduction, Joe reports that he no longer suffers from flashbacks or any other symptoms from the car and the horse accidents. He is socializing again and is celebrating life with his friends. He also says that slowly and spontaneously he is regaining his pre-horse-accident memory.)

As I come out of the session with Joe, the Clinic Director stops me and asks if I have time to see "Susan" who had an accident on Monday and was already developing symptoms of post-traumatic stress. She shows Susan into my office and we start as I always do. Susan is well-fed and moderately well-rested. She was not sleeping well because the car accident gave her nightmares. I choose to go ahead with the session because if the trauma is not resolved she might not sleep any better in the future.

Susan had been driving home at night during a snow storm and lost control of the car when she entered an exit ramp. She remembered most of the accident but was missing what happened between when the car started to spin out of control and when it stopped. She went through the accident a few of times and she still couldn't recover that part. I asked her to go through it again, this time moving her body, in her mind, the way she imagined it would have moved during the spinning part. The first time she did this, it didn't match the way the car was moving in the incident. She realized that the car had actually only spun around once. She had originally thought it had spun several times. As we continued to run it she got her body position to match the way the car had spun and the all the missing details of the accident started to fill in. She recalled that she had thought during the accident, "I'm going to die." Then she realized that although this was a normal reaction during the incident, it was not a true representation of what really happened. When we finished running the accident she was bright and very impressed with the process she had just experienced.

I checked my watch; our session had taken 42 minutes.

Motor Vehicle Accident: In-Depth Client Interview

I spoke with "Mary", a MVA victim who lost her only child "Joey" in a horrific vehicle crash which injured everyone in the family. She experienced severe PTSD symptoms in the months following the accident until she addressed the incident with TIR.

VV: Tell me about the incident and its aftermath:

Mary: We were in a car accident 3 years ago and my son Joey was killed when we were hit by a drunk driver. That was what brought me to Irene. I was driving the car when we were hit and my husband Karl was in the front seat and Joey (age 11), my only child was in the back. We were hit head on at 160Km/hr (100 MPH) by a driver who had more than three times the legal limit of blood alcohol. It was a second offence for her. I was in teacher's college at the time, just a month and half into the school year and after taking six weeks off I decided to back to school. It meant that I kind of had to put my healing on hold except that I was still going for physical healing with chiropractic. I was hurt in the accident and I was looking after the physical needs but not the emotional stuff. That sort of got put on hold until I got through teacher's college in May.

VV: How did you hear about TIR?

Mary: I had heard through a friend of mine who had told me about TIR. I was feeling like I was still dealing with the trauma from the accident. I was quite anxious about getting in the car and driving. I was anxious even about going downtown on my own. It felt like everything that was part of me and that I comfortable with had been ripped away from me. I felt quite exposed and raw and vulnerable to anything. It felt like I was starting over with regards to trusting again and finding my self-confidence again. That's why I started my TIR work.

VV: You mentioned that anxiety was part of your symptoms, were there other things like nightmares or panic attacks?

Mary: There were definitely feelings of panic and I would get flashbacks when I was driving. I had a hard time just being able to breathe regularly. I felt like I needed to take lots of really, really deep breaths to stay calm.

VV: Any obsessive thoughts about the incident?

Mary: I was certainly haunted by the accident. There was a lot that I didn't remember about the accident. TIR helped with that in trying to piece it all together. Also, I was driving by the [scene of the] accident twice a day on the way to the university. It was a big deal going past the accident site every day because I was driving with people who didn't want to know where the accident happened. It was people from the university who I was carpooling with, a somewhat supportive but not completely supportive group. Usually the tears would be going behind my sunglasses or my foot would be clamped against the floor (as a passenger). I was quite anxious about going past that site. TIR also helped me a great deal in preparing for trial because we had to travel to give our Victim Impact Statement.

VV: Did you experience any survivor guilt?

Mary: Of course, obviously. I felt sick. I was driving the car and even though it was this other woman's fault completely and she was charged and imprisoned, I'm still the one who has to live with the fact that I was driving the car and Joey was the passenger. You try so hard to protect your children and keep them safe. I couldn't do it in that moment. You put all that effort into making sure that they're getting to school safely, and choosing good friends, and you keep them so protected. In so many ways you trust because there are lots of things where you can't watch over their shoulder (like being at school). Here I was the one who was caring for Joey and I was the one who was driving the car.

VV: What kind of results did you get out of doing TIR?

Mary: It helped me in going over the accident and feeling clearer and calmer about it. It was hard to get through in the beginning but as we went over the story and pieced it together, it became less traumatic in terms of remembering it and going through it in detail.

VV: And you recovered some previously missing details around the incident?

Mary: There was some stuff that I did piece together. I still don't have any memory of the actual impact, but I just have a memory of when I opened my eyes. Karl and I are both a little bit confused about that. He had a concussion; he was in the front passenger seat and was able to get out of the car. I wasn't able to get out of the car; I had hit my head and was slipping in and out of consciousness. What I remember from TIR was that I looked in the back seat and had seen Joey moaning. Joey had been sleeping in the back with the safety belt on. I thought he was just waking up; it didn't even come into my consciousness that he was hurt.

At the court hearing, I was told by a police officer that Karl and I were outside the car. I don't know if my memory of looking back and seeing Joey actually happened or that's just something that I created in my mind. I'm not sure. It was something that I wanted to hold on to because it was my connection to him and gave me a sense that I was looking out for him. I'm not sure how much I was able to recall and what was real.

VV: Did you find any decisions or intentions in the incident?

Mary: We don't choose to drink and drive, but we don't control other people. There's so much that is out of our hands. I don't know what I would have or could have done differently.

VV: Are you driving well nowadays?

Mary: Yes, I'm driving every day to work and dealing with that. Not to say that I don't still get upset with aggressive drivers, who make dangerous moves and jeopardize other people's lives. I'm handling driving alright.

VV: Anything else you'd like to add?

Mary: When you have trauma in your life, it's a big hurdle to get over. It needs to be dealt with and you can't hide from it. You need to figure out how to do the healing and how to work with it and how to get past it. Karl and I still have the sadness of Joey being gone and that won't sort of ever disappear, but it's good to be past the initial trauma and anxiety that came with the loss of Joey in the accident. Doing TIR with Irene certainly helped a lot.

VV: Did your past experience with TIR help you with any recent losses?

Mary: Last week a dear friend of mine died unexpectedly. I think that when you go through the trauma of losing a child, it prepares you for dealing with death and coming to terms with it. When an older person dies, it feels like it's the order of things and I don't find it devastating. I'm not sure if it's TIR or if it's my familiarity with the loss and the process of letting go of someone.

VV: Would you recommend TIR to other people?

Mary: Yes. I think that I would certainly recommend it. It helped me get through the first six months to a year that was really quite challenging.

Accidental Death of a Spouse:
Session Notes from Jane Kennedy

Jane Kennedy is a Certified TIR Facilitator and Trainer with a background in social work and a private practice in Toronto, Ontario. One of her clients ("Sara") suffered the accidental death of a spouse in 2001. In addition to allowing the sharing of her case details, the client also agreed to present her account of TIR and the difference that it made in her life regarding PTSD symptomatology.

VV: How did she come to you?

Jane: She lives in the northern Canadian community and she was referred to me by a psychologist that I know quite well who lives there. She had had a huge trauma. On the return leg of a trip, she stopped at Toronto to change planes, and simply froze. She could not get on that next plane to go back up north. She called her psychologist in panic and said "I just can't go home." I told her psychologist to send her to me.

VV: Tell us about the incident.

Jane: Sara met a man when she was 18 and married him a year later. Then a year after that they discovered he had multiple sclerosis. Now 20 years later he was blind and disabled in a wheelchair. She did all the care for him. He was a smoker and she left his cigarettes, lighter, and lunch set up for him on the table all in a row every day in the same way. They would be on the phone several times during the day.

This one morning he called and said, "I can't find my lighter."

She said, "It's there, just feel for it. It's where I always put it."

He said, "No, I can't find it. I'm going to light my cigarette on the stove."

She said, "Don't do that. That's dangerous; don't do it."

He said, "Well, I can't find it."

She said, "Well, just look." She was quite annoyed with him. So she hung up. Some time later, she got a phone call saying "You better come home, there's been a fire." So she got a friend to go with her expecting it to be the kind of fire there was in the past when he burned the tablecloth. She was ready to give him hell for lighting his cigarette that way and causing trouble.

When she got there, the first shock she got had was that was that there were fire trucks, an ambulance, police, and a yellow ribbon all around. She tried to break through the line of the police. One neighbor finally came and took her to the neighbor's house. Sara had some experience with emergency procedures and knew there was serious trouble. The next shocking thing that happened was the police came to tell her that her husband had died. What had happened was that he had in fact lit the cigarette from the stove. She had a can of cooking oil stored on the back of the stove and he knocked it over with the wheelchair. That ignited on top of the stove and then he tried to put it out with water (they found the faucet dripping). Trying to put out an oil fire with water only made it worse.

Everything in the house was ruined, he was burned in his chair; the dog was killed by the fire. She had only the clothing on her back plus later some china that a friend rescued for her from the ruins. She refused to listen when the police told her about it, of course. It wasn't until later when a lot of people had come to her house that she understood that her husband had been burned alive and it wasn't smoke inhalation that was the cause of death.

People often become secondarily traumatized in the aftermath of a significant trauma. She asked for his wedding band back and the police said OK and gave it to her the next day. They gave it to her in the condition they found it: blackened and with skin attached. They just handed it to her like that, which absolutely freaked her out. Her brother-in-law was standing there and had the presence of mind to take it away from her and get it cleaned properly.

Another secondary traumatization concerned Sara's mother-in-law. This woman was calling Sara several times daily to cry and would not seek her own help although Sara encouraged her to do so. She found it hard enough to deal with her own grief and didn't want to deal with her mother-in-law's problems too. One day her mother-in-law called and said "I have to tell you a story." After arguing, her mother-in-law finally put her foot down and told the story despite Sara's protests. She said: "I had a dream in which your husband (my son) was sitting in his wheelchair and he was burning and reaching out for me and yelling 'Help me, help me!'" This vision became another horror for Sara to deal with.. The last piece she needed to address was when she had to leave her husband and the dog in the graveyard.

She stayed in Toronto and we did 19 hours of TIR sessions. This is very little time to resolve a trauma of that magnitude. Afterwards, she went back home and had to go through all the first things like driving past the house for the first time, deciding to sell the house, and so on. She sold the house and moved in with a friend and decided to go back to work.

She is now in a new relationship and is very happy. The second anniversary of the fire is coming up and she says she'll be OK. She says she's going to have a hard day on that anniversary but that she'll be able to handle it alright. It's quite a miraculous recovery. She has an extensive support system; she is a well-liked person and has a lot friends.

She is now in a new relationship and is very happy. It's quite a miraculous recovery.

Before TIR, Sara exhibited the standard symptoms for post-traumatic stress disorder: real or actual threat to life of self or others; intense fear or helplessness, persistent flashbacks re-experiencing the event; avoidance of any stimulus associated with the trauma [she couldn't get on the plane to go home] and persistent symptoms of arousal. Sara couldn't be in the dark, couldn't be alone, couldn't be in a store, [agoraphobia] and couldn't walk anywhere alone. She couldn't get in a car unless it was with somebody she trusted and couldn't go out at night. She had frequent nightmares and flashbacks which were added to by the incidents mentioned above. She was good with close friends but not with other people who would say, "I'm so sorry to hear about your tragedy." She wasn't eating or sleeping. She couldn't bring herself to see the house for several months. She knew that when she left me and went home that she was ready to complete her grieving for her husband.

VV: Did she have any survivor guilt?

Jane: Yes, she did. She thought she should have died. She was angry with him for being so stubborn as to light a cigarette that way. She was angry with herself for not being a lot stronger about dissuading him. They had had that conversation many times and he did it anyhow. She definitely thought she should have died. She had to grieve for the dog as well so there was a lot going on for her.

VV: What were some of the decisions she made during the incident?

Jane: She thought she would never meet anyone else or never want to be with anybody. This husband of hers was the love of her life for 20 years. [

[Next, you'll hear the client's side of the symptoms and about her journey to recovery.]

VV: Sara, what brought you to seek help on the trauma?

Sara: It was probably prompting from friends because I just wasn't coping at all. I was kind of vegetative; I couldn't go out in public; I was afraid of everything, and I was just scared of everything. I didn't want to live and didn't want to continue on. Having great friends, they saw this and prompted me to get help.

VV: Had you heard of TIR before your facilitator mentioned it?

Sara: No, nothing. In the first couple of sessions, I was completely out of it. I was like "What is she doing?" I had no idea what was going on.

VV: Can you tell me about the sort of symptoms that you had (obsessive thoughts or nightmares)?

Sara: Yes, obsessive thoughts, unexplained fear like I've never felt before, and total panic. I couldn't go out in public or in the dark. All I would see would be images of what could have happened or what did happen. Not knowing what did happen, I was constantly imagining things.

VV: What kind of results did you get from TIR?

Sara: I think the results were not that I accepted it, but that I understood what happened.
I understood that there was nothing I could have done to change it. Whatever I believe happened, I will never really know. So I've just come to accept that I can't change it and there's nothing I can do. I see a life ahead of myself where I couldn't before. All I could focus on was the incident and that day when my world was ended.

Now with the therapy and everything I worked through, it was gradual. I couldn't see beyond this wall. Then it got further where there was a wall in front of me. Then I got to the point where I could see over the wall, but I couldn't get there. Then I finally got over that and I'm trying to get on with my life. Basically I think if I wouldn't have had TIR, I wouldn't even be here. I'm serious, I was staying down south and I knew what I was going to do—nothing. I would get up every day and I would just wait until 11 pm [to go to bed] because I couldn't wait for my life to be over.

> *Basically I think if I wouldn't have had TIR, I wouldn't even be here.*

VV: Would you recommend TIR to others?

Sara: Absolutely. I would recommend Jane!

VV: Anything else you'd like to say about the whole experience of TIR and clearing up the past traumas?

Sara: It's been a long healing and I'm still healing. A lot of it was that Jane got me past the accident itself and she let me to do my grieving in my own way. She got me through that fear when it happened and not being able to sleep, not being able to cope, and not able think of anything but that.

VV: You couldn't even get started on the grieving?

Sara: No, because I couldn't even accept that it happened. I had the idea that I was going back to the town and everything was going to fine, everything's going to be there—my home and my husband. I wouldn't accept that it wasn't that way. The conscious part of me knew it, but there was another part of me that couldn't accept that. I couldn't accept that because that meant accepting the fear of what he had gone through and everything.

VV: It was kind of protecting you from seeing that?

Sara: That was very interesting because I was with Jane and the first two or three sessions required 90 minutes of travel. I went because my friends and the counselor recommended her to me. I thought, "Why is she doing this to me?" [asking me to revisit the incident] I wasn't really listening at first, I did this because I had to, because I was prompted to do it. Basically in my mind, it didn't matter because nothing was going to help. I would do this because I was being pushed to do it. I wasn't listening at first because I didn't know and I didn't want to deal with it.

I thought, "Why is she making me go through this over and over again?" It took me a while to get it, but I finally got it. As painful as it was, after about three weeks of seeing her once or twice a week, I told her I dreamt of my husband the night before. I said "He was OK in the dream." I think it was because my mind had allowed me to see him and before it wouldn't let me. I couldn't even put a picture of him in my head. You know when you close your eyes and want to picture someone? I couldn't even picture him. All I could focus on was that half-hour of that day. The 20 years before I had had with my husband were missing. All my mind could take in was the half-hour of that day. There are fewer scars on me for sure. Now there is nothing that will prevent me with going on with my life.

8 TIR Research Projects

In this chapter, I present brief overviews of doctoral research from three pioneering TIR researchers. It can be difficult to bridge the gap between an abstract of a thesis and the hundreds of pages of detail that they provide. I hope to have reached a compromise that allows you to learn about the structure, methods, and conclusions without becoming bogged down in details.

The first presentation in this chapter, by Lori Beth Bisbey, Ph.D., was delivered at the 1994 IRM conference and is an edited transcription of her actual speech. The next presentation by Pamela Valentine, Ph.D. was adapted from the *Proceedings of the Tenth National Symposium on Doctoral Research in Social Work* (1998). Last, Wendy Coughlin, Ph.D., provides an overview of her 1992 study of TIR and panic / anxiety disorder symptomatlogy.

Some additional outcome results from a pilot project can be found in "Trauma Resolution in an At-Risk Youth Program" by Teresa Descilo in Chapter 9.

Please see Appendix C for information on how to obtain reprints of dissertation materials.

No Longer a Victim: A Treatment Outcome Study for Crime Victims with PTSD
By Lori Beth Bisbey, Ph.D.

Transcript of the plenary address at the 1994 Metapsychology Conference.

As of 1994, the published research on PTSD primarily supported the use of relaxation and exposure-based techniques. One of the issues that has been raised by practitioners in connection with using these kinds of techniques, such as flooding, is the possibility that current trauma might be connected with earlier trauma. Does flooding address this issue? The implication is that any treatment which has both an exposure element and an element that deals with earlier trauma should be more successful in treating PTSD.

My study had three conditions.

One was Direct Therapeutic Exposure (DTE), which combined imaginal flooding and progressive relaxation. DTE protocol starts and ends with progressive muscle relaxation with flooding in-between. There is research indicating that this is a good way of doing it. For most people, flooding involves visual imagery, but not necessarily so, because some people are not visually based. Relaxation may improve the ability to visualize.

The second experimental condition was Traumatic Incident Reduction, the third a control group. We wanted to see which one (if either) treatment would be the more successful in treating crime victims who had PTSD. Before this study, there had been a lack of controlled outcome research with a sufficiently large population in this area. The first objective of this study was to provide a sound, sufficiently large treatment outcome experiment comparing a method that has been researched previously (DTE) to an upcoming method (TIR). These are the limitations of the previous research: small sample sizes, poor measures or instrumentation, multiple concurrent treatments, poor reporting and analysis of the demographic data, and poor inclusion and exclusion criteria. These are the issues that we tried to address when the study was constructed.

The second objective was to provide further data on the efficacy of DTE in treating a complex syndrome and to compare it with TIR. The third objective was to improve on these methodological flaws of the past. My study had 57 subjects, which is quite large in treatment outcome research, although it might sound small to you. It's the third largest study done on PTSD before 1995. In addition, what we did (myself and my committee), was to base our sample size on statistical power. I wanted to be sure that I would detect a difference between TIR and DTE if there was one. Also, earlier research often had poor inclusion and exclusion criteria. This meant that it wasn't clearly defined who were eligible for the research and therefore what population were you looking at. In my study, people were excluded on the basis of a diagnosis of active substance abuse, or if they did not qualify for a diagnosis of PTSD. We did not try to diagnose any other psychological or psychiatric disorder. This proved to be quite interesting.

We gathered detailed demographic data including subjects' previous experience in treatment. Another frequent issue is that a proportion of victims of crime and a proportion of people who suffer PTSD after an event get better on their own in three months, no matter what you do with them. I wanted to make sure that whatever results we got, it wasn't going to be able to be said that "Well, it was because that all of them were less than three months from the trauma." I'm not going to provide detailed demographics in this presentation, but people who are interested can obtain a reprint of my thesis from Dissertation Express [See Appendix C].

Hypotheses

There were ten hypotheses for this study. The first three predicted that the treatment groups would show a significant decrease in PTSD-related symptom measures. The next two predicted that both treatment groups would show a larger decrease on two of the measures than the control group. Another hypothesis predicted that the treatment groups would show a decrease on an individual trauma checklist. There was one hypothesis that predicted that the TIR group would show a larger decrease in symptoms on that checklist. That was the only hypothesis that specifically compared the two treatments. The last group of hypotheses had to do with job and relationship satisfaction.

All the subjects were victims of crime. We didn't set out to choose people who were victims of just one crime or many crimes. As it turned out, 82.2% of the subjects were victims of violent crimes and 71.9% of the subjects were victims of more than one crime; that was from a random sample. Analysis using a lot of statistics showed up no demographic differences between the three groups. One factor showed up a difference that approached significance. I'll describe this later.

Concurrent treatment is one of the things that is frequently mentioned as a confounding problem in a research study of this type. It's not unusual to have someone referred for specific PTSD treatment who is already in therapy with somebody else, or to be on one or two different medications, or to be an inpatient. That's one of the areas that I looked at. There was one subject in the TIR group and two subjects in the DTE group who were on anti-depressant medication. They had all been on medication for more than three months prior to the study. None of my subjects were in any other type of treatment during the study and all of them had stopped other treatments at least three months prior.

There were four therapists, two men and two women (including myself). All were trained in both treatment methods, regardless of their previous training or experience. The purpose of this was to standardize their training. We did not look at gender differences between therapists. Whenever possible, subjects were pre- and post-tested by someone other than the primary therapist. Treatment subjects were randomly assigned to groups and given a maximum of twenty hours of treatment. First we looked at whether or not they were in relationships. We wanted to maximize the number of people across the groups who were in relationships so we could get relationship satisfaction data. Then they were randomly assigned. Treatment lasted approximately five weeks; we then post-tested two weeks later (at seven weeks).

The reason I say "approximately" in places is because, as you may know, TIR doesn't have a fixed session time. The DTE session groups were two hours each twice a week. For TIR, it didn't necessarily work out that way. Statistical analysis after the fact showed that this did not have a discriminating impact. The average total treatment times weren't significantly different. I found that people who had fewer treatment hours were actually doing better, which sounds strange. But, in fact when you look at, it does really make sense. People who had fewer treatment hours were possibly doing better to begin with. However, the difference was not statistically significant. The variation was very small, the typical subject having from 12 to 20 hours (average 17.9 hours) treatment.

I used a number of measures: the Penn Inventory (Hammerberg 1982), and the Impact of Events Scale (Horowitz, Wilner, & Alvarez, 1979) for PTSD. I used the Symptom Checklist (1990 revised) which has an embedded scale within it called the Crime-Related PTSD Scale. I used individual trauma checklists in which I took each trauma that the person reported and had them rate level of distress on a scale of 0 to 5. I used the work and co-worker scale from the Job Descriptive Index (JDI) to measure job satisfaction and the Dyadic Adjustment Scale for relationship satisfaction. I also used the Therapy Gain Scale because the therapists were doing a portion of each group and I needed to see if they were perceived differently depending on the treatment they were administering. No difference was shown there.

Results

The TIR group performed better than DTE on the Impact of Events Scale (Fig. 1). This turned out in statistical tests to be quite significant. I used multivariate analysis of variance and followed that with extremely stringent criteria to make sure that if there was a difference between the groups that it wouldn't be an artifact. In this case, the TIR group was significantly different from DTE and both groups were significantly different from the control group. The Crime-Related PTSD Scale (Fig. 2) has a clear delineation between PTSD diagnosis and no diagnosis. What ended up happening was that more than 50% of all the treatment subjects no longer had PTSD. The TIR group was significantly different from the DTE group. The Penn Inventory also has a cutoff score and also showed TIR significantly different from DTE and the control groups.

What does all this mean? One of the things that didn't happen was differences in the relationship variables, which was somewhat surprising. However, we didn't really have enough subjects to see significant differences. Although we had 57 subjects, not all were in relationships that could be measured by this scale. The Dyadic Adjustment Scale measures relationships that are "serious" meaning that they are living together or married. We had many other people involved in relationships that were not that long-standing. Additionally, some of the subjects actually were in what they perceived to be negative relationships at the beginning of treatment. They saw that as a very positive change, but on the Dyadic Adjustment Scale it doesn't come out that way.

The same was true with job satisfaction. First, my choice of a measure was not very good, because people had difficulty understanding it. There were adjectives that they had to mark as "yes" or "no" about their job and co-workers. I chose this instrument because it had some standardization and I wanted to make sure it would relate to other areas. However, many people complained about it. Additionally we had the problem of not enough people again. Some people were unemployed at the start, some people quit their jobs during treatment, and still others found new jobs during the course of the study.

In hindsight, if I were to do this again, I would try to find different ways of measuring relationships and job satisfaction. One of the things said about TIR is that it affects more than just PTSD. This was the reason I wanted to look at other areas quantitatively and ask the question, "What other areas of life would successful TIR affect?" Unfortunately, I wasn't able to get this information. However, some very tentative supplementary analyses were done on a few of the nine sub-scales of the Symptom Checklist (1990 revised). The depression sub-scale was examined because it's one of the most common co-diagnoses that go along with PTSD. Interestingly enough, there was a significant difference between DTE and TIR vs. the control group.

However, there was not a significance difference between the two treatment conditions. We weren't using the best measure of depression because it wasn't a central concern of the study and we didn't diagnose for it. I think the Beck scale would have given us a better pre/post measure. These were just reported depression symptoms and it's possible that if we diagnosed we might have found out that in some cases the depression was secondary to the PTSD and in other cases the depression preceded the PTSD. Those groups might look differently in terms of treatment effect (if they could have been isolated that way).

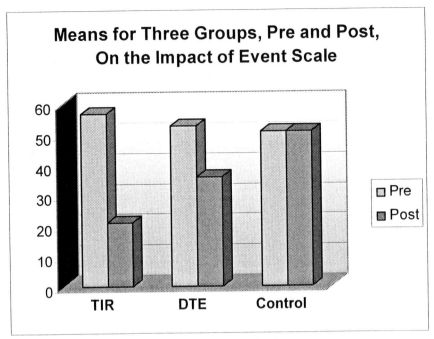

Impact of Events Scale (Fig. 1)

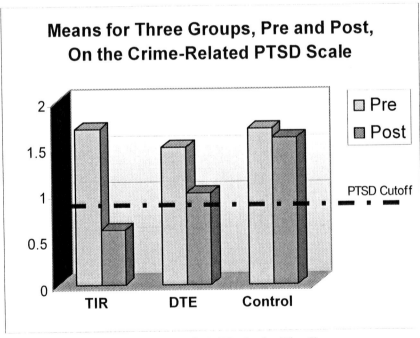

Crime-Related PTSD Scale (Fig. 2)

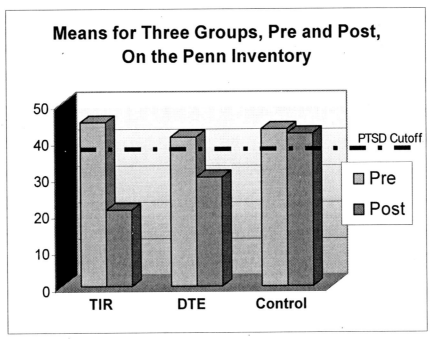

Penn Inventory (Fig. 3)

I wasn't actually looking at curing depression, but I was interested in the fact that depression results changed. Differences were maintained at six and twelve months' follow-up for people who had large differences. The TIR group is looking brilliant for the 6 months and 12 months results that we have. Nobody has gotten worse and nobody has relapsed. There are some people where things stayed the same and some people where things have gotten better.

A crucial issue to me is whether the person was already depressed and then traumatized or whether they were traumatized and the depression was a result of the trauma. It is possible that the treatments for PTSD affected depression for people who were not depressed before suffering trauma. We actually had a mixed bag; some people would have already had a diagnosis of depression before the trauma. Those people were probably the ones who didn't change. The implications of this are pretty important to patients in the UK. If you complain of PTSD and depression and you go to your family doctor, then you are prescribed anti-depressants. However, if they could actually distinguish which came first, the depression or the trauma, and then made an appropriate referral they would have a better resolution without having to medicate.

The Penn Inventory (Fig. 3) showed that after TIR, 89.47% no longer qualified for a diagnosis of PTSD. The corresponding figure for DTE was a pretty healthy 57.89%. In the control group, 31.58% had actually changed without intervention.

The other thing that changed was obsessive-compulsive symptoms. There is some suggestion that there is actually a relationship between some of these symptoms and PTSD.

The only other changes I noted on Symptom Checklist 90 was that the paranoid scale showed changes for both treatment groups; and the psychoticism scale changed for TIR but not for DTE. I didn't look at these specifically enough to give an adequate explanation. I propose that the next study looks for more than PTSD, and explores what other co-diagnoses might be present (using something other than the Symptom Checklist-90). I would suggest the Minnesota Multiphasic Personality Inventory-2 because I think that's a better measure of general psychopathology. My study was unable to answer the question of whether TIR is affecting things other than PTSD.

The study provides further evidence that exposure-based treatments or treatments that require repetitive contact with the trauma are very effective in treating PTSD. In previous research and theoretical articles, two factors have been hypothesized to be necessary for successful treatment: (1) exposure to the traumatic material (which both treatments obviously have) and (2) some sort of cognitive shift where the traumatized individual doesn't see the importance of the event in the same way. One of the criticisms frequently made about DTE-based treatments is that a cognitive shift occurs by luck rather than by design, if at all. In contrast, in TIR, specific questions may be used to actually provoke that cognitive shift. Personally, I think this is one explanation why the TIR group did better than the DTE group. I think the second explanation would be the issue of looking at earlier connected incidents, which DTE doesn't do and TIR does. There was some anecdotal evidence to support this. A couple of subjects completed DTE, and after post-testing were changed to TIR. These individuals had many, many traumas that were connected and knew that they were connected. They did much better with TIR than with DTE.

It is always possible that therapist bias and experience could have been responsible for the difference. Two of the four therapists were more experienced in TIR than in DTE; two of us had about equal experience in each. We tried to control for bias in this study by first of all standardizing the training of therapists before they participated in this study. Second, we added the Therapy Gain Scale to look at whether the therapists were perceived differently in treatments when they were doing DTE or TIR. No significant difference was found. We also had some external supervision on random samples of sessions to look at whether the sessions were being conducted properly. But even with all that, I think you can't completely control whether there was a bias in the research. After the issue was raised at my thesis defense, I went back and did further statistical analyses to see whether or not this was an issue. I believe the only way that this question will be answered is by replication (of the study).

What we do know is that both treatments work and that is an important message. For me, the highest significance is that DTE is the most researched treatment with PTSD to date. What we've learned as a result of this research is that TIR is at least as effective as DTE, and maybe more effective than DTE with this population. Our results show TIR to be significantly more effective, but we need to wait for replication because there hasn't been enough research on TIR. Still, my study is a good starting point; it's a good way to compare the results with what's already been done. We are gathering six-month, twelve-month, and two-year data and hopefully I'll report on that when it's finally collated. So far, both groups look like they are OK. So far, a few DTE subject have suffered partial relapses, but not one TIR subject has done so. We have collected more data on TIR subjects.

I have five definite one-year follow-ups on TIR subjects right now and I should say that these were complex cases. One of the interesting things was that it didn't matter how complex the case was in terms of hours. Some of the more complex cases took fewer hours to handle and that's quite strange. These were spectacular cases in that they had no symptoms left afterwards. After one year they were still at the same level, but there was intervening trauma. The comments I got back on the follow-up were:

> "This [crime] happened to me and it was amazing to see that I didn't react. I had a response to what was going on in the *present* and not what was triggered in the past."

That's been repeated and that's what's so exciting for me. That's why I want to keep collecting data as time goes on. What they're saying is: "I had a similar trauma, and I *did* react to it like any human being would react to it, but what didn't happen was that it didn't trigger earlier stuff and therefore it was resolvable quite easily on my own without needing intervention." To me that's not remission, although I do dislike the terms remission/non-remission in that model. That would actually be cure if they're not actually triggering into earlier stuff.

Brief Treatment of Trauma-Related Symptoms in Incarcerated Females with TIR
By Pamela Vest Valentine, Ph.D.

Pamela V. Valentine is an Assistant Professor in the Social Work Program at the School of Social and Behavioral Sciences at the University of Alabama. Dr. Valentine obtained her Ph.D. from Florida State University in 1997. The following article is based on materials presented at the *Proceedings of the Tenth National Symposium on Doctoral Research in Social Work* (1998).

Statement of the Research Problem

Conducted in the Tallahassee Federal Correction Institute (FCI) in Florida, this experimental outcome study examined the effectiveness of Traumatic Incident Reduction (TIR) (Gerbode, 1989) in treating trauma-related symptoms of female inmates who were victims of interpersonal violence. TIR is a brief (in this case, one session), straightforward, memory-based, therapeutic intervention most similar to imaginal flooding. A memory-based intervention implies that the symptoms currently experienced by a client are related to a past event and that lasting resolution of those symptoms involves focusing on the memory rather than focusing on symptom management. TIR is straightforward in that the roles of both the client and therapist are very clearly defined and strictly followed.

TIR is both a client-respectful and therapist-directed intervention. It is client-respectful in that the client's perception of the traumatic incident takes precedence over the therapist's perception of the incident. For example, should the client have multiple traumatic events in her past, she would choose the event to focus on during the one-session TIR intervention, and her version of the event would be undisputed by the therapist. Additionally, an event is considered traumatic if the client so deems it. In other words, the client, not the therapist, is considered the expert regarding the client's life and the impact of the traumatic event on her life. TIR is a therapist-directed technique in that the therapist acts as a guide, not an interpreter, evaluator or problem solver. Both the non-intrusive stance of the therapist and the client's work of confronting the painful incident combine to empower the client (Valentine & Smith, 1996).

The study specifically examined the effectiveness of TIR on symptoms of posttraumatic stress disorder (PTSD), depression, anxiety, and low expectancy of success (i.e., low self-efficacy). Symptoms of PTSD include intrusion, avoidance, and arousal (American Psychological Association, 1994; Waldinger, 1990). Intrusion involves nightmares, recurring thoughts and flashbacks. Avoidance speaks of numbing of feelings, avoiding places associated with the event, and attempts to refrain from thinking about the event. Arousal, among other things, pertains to an exaggerated startle response and hypervigilance. The diagnosis of PTSD means that the symptoms are more present after the traumatic event than they were before the event, and that the symptoms have existed for at least four weeks. Other symptoms associated with trauma are low self-esteem and a reduced sense of being in control.

The theoretical underpinnings of TIR are considerable and are closely related to the etiology of trauma-related symptoms. Psychodynamic theorists explain the effects of trauma as consequences of unresolved emotional processing that occurred during a traumatic episode (Gerbode, 1989). Behaviorists write of classical conditioning and seek treatment that reveals the stimuli associated with a particular traumatic event (Resnick, Kilpatrick, & Lipovsky, 1991). Cognitive theorists speculate that one's basic beliefs about the world were shattered during the traumatic event and that the shattered beliefs cry out to be restored (Janoff-Bulman, 1992). Cathartic theory, on which TIR is primarily based, agrees with each of the above conceptualizations. It also asserts that a heightened physiological state (much like the state experienced in the original incident) must be recreated to finish the emotional processing and to reveal the associated stimuli and/or the distorted cognitive schema (Straton, 1990). TIR is structured so that the incident is viewed repetitively, non-intrusively, and in an open-ended time frame. The activity is designed to elicit a heightened physiological state so that the client can process the event to its completion (Gerbode, 1989). The open-ended time frame is crucial in allowing the client to emotionally engage in the memory without fear of being cut off.

There are several reasons for studying the influence of TIR on previously traumatized female inmates. Since 1980, the rate of family homicide has increased fivefold (Joffe, Wilson, & Wolfe, 1986). Women are the target of much violence, as illustrated by the following: 75% of adult women have been victims of at least one sexual assault, robbery, or burglary (Resnick, et al., 1991); and 53.7% are victims of more than one crime. Abundant data suggest that PTSD can result from having been a victim of crime or having witnessed a violent crime (Astin, Lawrence, & Foy, 1993; Breslau, Davis, Andreski & Peterson, 1991; Resnick, et al., 1991). Therefore, the number of women affected by PTSD is growing as violence and sexual abuse increase in society as a whole (Ursano & Fullerton, 1990). There is a lack of empirical research on the traumatic effects of interpersonal violence (e.g. robbery, rape, incest, physical assault). Since inmates are typically victims of interpersonal violence (Gabel, Johnston, Baker, & Cannon, 1993), the inmate population studied was particularly suitable for TIR.

Another reason for studying the influence of TIR on previously traumatized female inmates is the increased number of female prisoners in the last decade (Gabel, et al., 1993; "As Inmates Pay, so do Kids," 1995). This increase is due to a boost in drug-related arrests and sentencing. Between 1980 and 1989, 25% of women in police custody were arrested for buying drugs; whereas among men, drug purchases accounted for only 10% of the arrests. More arrested females regularly use drugs than do their male counterparts.

Among women incarcerated for violent crimes, a 1991 study (US Department of Justice, 1991) found that 61% of female inmates had victimized a male and that 36% had close relationships with their victims (Gabel, et al., 1993). Violent offenders with a history of physical or sexual abuse are more likely to have killed relatives or intimates than strangers. In contrast, female inmates with no prior history of abuse were more likely to have victimized a stranger while committing a robbery. These statistics suggest a connection between female victimization and women who victimize. The impact of unresolved trauma needs to be explored.

The traditional treatment of inmates seldom incorporates the influence of prior traumatic events on current behavior (A. McNeece, personal communication, 4/18/1995). Furthermore, most trauma treatment is lengthy and nonspecific, making it difficult to reach conclusions about treatment efficacy. The above reasons mandated the need for this study.

Finally, while both clients and therapists throughout the United States report that TIR alleviates trauma-related symptoms (Valentine & Smith, 1996), little experimental research has been conducted to substantiate such claims (see next section). By conducting an experimental outcome study on the effects of TIR on traumatized, female inmates, knowledge is built pertaining to (1) the effectiveness of TIR, and to (2) the treatment of victims of interpersonal violence.

Prior Research on TIR

Although advocates of TIR suggest that it is a highly effective and cost-efficient brief treatment modality, there is little research to justify such claims. Most of what is written about TIR is anecdotal. A case study (Valentine, 1995), a multisite clinical debriefing study (Valentine & Smith, 1998), a dissertation based on a quasi-experimental design (Coughlin, 1995), and another dissertation, a true experimental study based on victims of crime in England (Bisbey, 1995), comprise the body of TIR studies.

The studies by Valentine (1995) and Valentine and Smith (1998) used ethnographic methods and were qualitative and discovery oriented. The client perspectives gathered in these studies expanded and clarified the existing theory base of TIR. The former study provided a vivid case study of the application of TIR in an outpatient setting. The latter study employed extensive phone interviews of the experiences of four clients living in three states who were treated by three certified TIR practitioners. Although the research designers did not allow conclusions about the efficacy of the intervention protocol, clients' and clinicians' enthusiasm about their experiences led the authors to conduct a controlled clinical trial of TIR.

The current study employed a credible design with a three-month follow-up and relied on multiple published measures of anxiety, depression, PTSD and general satisfaction. Furthermore, the sample consisted of female inmates who represented different ethnic groups and diverse socioeconomic classes. Finally, it used an analytic strategy that allowed conclusions about whether the treatment and control conditions differed after treatment and at a follow-up interval. Although the study was not intended to be a definitive test of TIR, it provides a rigorous examination of its efficacy with women of color from varied socioeconomic classes.

Research Questions

This study addressed the following research questions:

1. How does TIR influence PTSD-related symptoms in incarcerated females?

2. How does TIR influence intrusion?

3. How does TIR influence avoidance?

4. How does TIR influence arousal?

5. How does TIR influence anxiety?

6. How does TIR influence depression?

7. How does TIR influence sense of control?

Methodology—Clients

Subjects in the study were recruited from the Federal Correction institute (FCI), Tallahassee, Florida. The sample was drawn from the total number of inmates at the facility (N = 730). The population (N = 730) filled out a Participation Questionnaire to indicate interest in the study. This questionnaire was used to determine eligibility based on whether inmates (1) had experienced a prior trauma in their lives, and if so, the nature of the trauma; (2) had experienced one or more of the trauma-related symptoms; and (3) were willing to further discuss their traumatic experience with a mental health professional. 248 inmates met the initial criteria. The inmates were brought together, in groups of approximately 12, to have the study explained to them and to have them sign consent forms when they chose to participate. 148 agreed to take part and were randomly assigned to either treatment or control conditions. 25 subsequently withdrew from the study, leaving 123 subjects. The reasons for withdrawal varied and included work-assignment constraints, disinterest, self-reevaluation of their level of traumatization, and/or a change of heart.

Average age of inmates in the treatment condition was 32.8 years (SD = 9.1), and the average age of those in the control condition was 34.9 (SD = 9.8). The majority of the participants were Black (50%), 38.5% were White, and 24% identified themselves as Hispanic. 32% of participants had never been married, and the treatment and control conditions did not differ significantly on marital status. 35% of the participants had no high school diploma whereas another 35% had some college or vocational training. The treatment and control conditions did not different significantly among age, racial distribution, marital status or educational level.

The following exclusion criteria were used: inmates who were on antipsychotic medication; inmates who had been hospitalized within the last three years with a diagnosis of bipolar disorder or schizophrenic disorder; inmates experiencing a severe depressive episode that required immediate psychiatric hospitalization; inmates experiencing hallucinations, delusions, or bizarre behavior; inmates with an alcohol or drug abuse disorder; or inmates who were victimized within three months prior to participation in the study. These criteria were in part modeled after the Foa study (Foa, Rothbaum, Riggs, & Murdock, 1991) and the recommendations of clinicians in the correctional facility. In general, the exclusion criteria represented acute situations that would be counterproductive to the process of TIR.

Methodology—Practitioners

All TIR practitioners were female; had graduate degrees in social work, marital and family therapy, or psychology. They had a mean age of thirty-five, with 7.2 years clinical experience on average. They were given sixteen hours of training in TIR by a certified TIR instructor. Practitioners delivered TIR using a standardized protocol in three to four hour blocks to every client in the treatment condition. A comprehensive treatment manual was created in order to control for differing practitioner skills. Random sessions were audiotaped, and an independent observer who was well versed in the TIR protocol reviewed sections of the tapes to ensure treatment integrity. Alpha was set a .05, beta was set at .20 , and the effect size was estimated at .50.

The primary hypothesis of the study follows: Those inmates receiving TIR will experience significant reduction in one or more of their self-reported PTSD-related symptoms, while those in the control conditions will not.

While all subjects completed pretest, posttest, and follow-up tests, additional steps were required of those in the experimental condition. Those steps were: (1) have a one-on-one orientation to learn the nature of TIR and the roles that the inmates and the mental health practitioners would play, (2) receiving a session of TIR, and (3) completing a debriefing session.

Results

The instruments used to determine the efficacy of TIR on trauma-related symptoms were the PTSD Symptom Scale (PSS), the Beck Depression Inventory (BDI), the Clinical Anxiety Scale (CAS) and the Generalized Expectancy of Success Scale (GESS). These instruments were administered in a pretest, posttest, and three-month follow-up format.

To analyze the data, an ANCOVA (with the pretest as the covariate) was conducted on each of the above measures, as well as on the three subscales of the PSS: intrusion, avoidance, and hyper-arousal. Analysis revealed that TIR showed significant differences at the .05 level on the PSS, the BDI, the CASE, and the GESS at both posttest and the three-month follow-up. In other words, both times, the experimental condition showed a statistically significant *decrease* in symptoms of posttraumatic stress disorder (and its related subscales) and of depression and anxiety, while those in the control condition remained approximately the same. Subjects assigned to the experimental condition *improved* on the measure of self-efficacy at a statistically significant level, while subjects assigned to the control condition did not. The null hypothesis was rejected, and the research hypothesis confirmed.

Although the results of this study were promising, care should be taken in generalizing to larger populations. For example, while we demonstrated TIR's effectiveness in treating trauma-related symptoms in female inmates, it would be a mistake to assume that TIR is effective with male inmates, or with female inmates in different institutional settings, or with persons outside a prison setting. Additional studies should be undertaken with those populations before definitive conclusions are drawn about TIR's more general efficacy. Besides testing TIR's effectiveness on different populations, TIR should be compared against other brief trauma treatments. Finally, research implications involve testing TIR's effectiveness on different ethnic groups and discovering the variables associated with training therapists to deliver TIR to a variety of ethnic groups.

Implications for Social Work Practice

The implications for social work practice are multiple. Social work's knowledge base is increased in realizing an effective trauma intervention with female inmates. The knowledge base would be increased further by researching (1) TIR's effectiveness with other populations; (2) TIR as compared with other brief trauma interventions; (3) and the implementation of TIR with various ethnic groups.

One primary practice implication pertains to the accessibility of TIR to social workers in a variety of settings. TIR is an unfranchised therapeutic intervention. While social workers should be trained to deal with clients' traumatic memories, Gerbode (1989), the originator of TIR, does not require licensure nor certification to practice TIR, making TIR more accessible to a greater number of social workers. Furthermore, TIR training usually costs a fraction of the price of other trauma-focused interventions. Social work educators continually search for effective practice modalities that can be taught to students. Because TIR follows a detailed treatment protocol, it represents a practice model that can be easily taught to students within schools of social work. [Ed. Note: TIR Workshop attendees can now receive Continuing Education units approved by the National Association of Social Workers].

From a practice perspective, it is also noteworthy that addressing only one item from the list of traumatic events still brought about statistically and clinically significant results in the inmates. This underscores that assessing for traumatic events will not necessarily embroil practitioners in very lengthy treatment procedures. Instead, the results suggest that substantive issues can be addressed in only one session. Such results define a win-win situation for both clients and practitioners.

The comments given by inmates suggest that they were highly appreciative of the client-respectful nature of TIR. For many of them, this was their first experience with a treatment provider who was both effective and respectful. Given the histories of victimization cited by inmates, this feature represents one of the most important contributions of this intervention protocol.

Another practice implication is the applicability of this technique to the population of social workers' typical clients. Many clients are oppressed and have likely been traumatized; yet, few psychosocial interview protocols exist that focus on the effects of trauma. Therefore, the demonstration of the effectiveness of TIR with previously traumatized female inmates should have several practice implications: (1) inclusion of a history of prior traumatic events in assessment of client problems; (2) inclusion of prior traumatic events in the treatment plan designed for the client; (3) encouragement of social workers to be trained to administer brief treatment to traumatized clients; and (4) practice of TIR by agency-based social workers, understanding that TIR has demonstrated effectiveness against trauma-related symptoms in incarcerated females. This study has shown TIR to be effective in the treatment of traumatized federally incarcerated females and renders TIR a promising intervention that begs further research.

References

American Psychiatric Association, (1994), *Diagnostic and Statistical Manual of Mental Disorders* (4th Ed.). Washington, DC; author.

"As Inmates Pay, so do Kids: More Mothers Jailed, Researchers Say." (1995 May). *NASW News*. 40(5), 7.

Astin, M. Lawrence, K., Foy, D. (1993) Posttraumatic Stress Disorder Among Battered Women: Risk and Resiliency Factors. *Violence and Victims*, (8), 17-28.

Bisbey, L.B. (1995). *No longer a victim: a treatment outcome study of crime victims with post traumatic stress disorder.* Doctoral dissertation for California School of Professional Psychology, San Diego. UMI publication number 9522269.

Breslau, Davis, Andreski & Peterson (1991) Traumatic events and posttraumatic stress disorder in an urban population of young adults. Arch Gen Psychiatry 48(3):216-222.

Coughlin, W.E. (1995). *Traumatic Incident Reduction: Efficacy in treating anxiety symptomatology.* UMI publication number 9537919.

Foa, Rothbaum, Riggs, & Murdock, (1991). Treatment of posttraumatic stress disorder in rape victims: A comparison between cognitive-behavioral procedures and counseling. *Journal of Consulting and Clinical Psychology, 59,* 715-723.

Gabel, K., Johnston, D., Baker, B., & Cameron, H. (1993) Female Offenders. Prepared for the *Encyclopedia of the National Association of Social Workers.*

Gerbode, F. (1989). *Beyond Psychology: An Introduction to Metapsychology.* Palo Alto: IRM Press.

Janoff-Bullman, B. (1992). *Shattered Assumptions.* New York: The Free Press.

Joffe, P., Wilson, S., & Wolfe, D. (1986). "Promoting Changes in Attitudes and Understanding of Conflict Resolution Among Child Witness of Family Violence." *Canadian Journal of Behavioural* Science, 18, 356-366.

Resnick, H.S., Kilpatrick, D.G., and Lipovsky, J.A. (1991) *Profile of Jail Inmates, 1989.* NDJ-9097. Washington, DC: Bureau of Justice Statistics.

Straton (1990). Catharsis reconsidered. Australian *and New Zealand Journal of Psychiatry,* 24, 543-551.

Ursano, R. & Fullerton, C. (1990). "Cognitive and Behavioral Responses to Trauma." Journal of Applied Psychology, 20 (21), 1766-1775.

Snell, Tracy L. and Morton, Danielle C. (1991), *Women in Prison, Survey of State Inmates,* Washington, DC: Bureau of Justice Statistics/

Valentine, P.V. (1995). "Traumatic Incident Reduction: A review of a new intervention." *Journal of Family Psychotherapy,* 6, (2), 79-85.

Valentine, P.V. & Smith, T.E. (1996, November). *Brief Treatment of Traumatized Clients: An Ethnographic Study.* Paper presented at the annual meeting of the National Association of Social Workers in Cleveland, OH.

Waldinger, R.J. (1990) *Psychiatry for Medical students.* (2nd Ed.). Washington, DC: American Psychiatric Press.

TIR and Anxiety Symptomatology
By Wendy Coughlin, Ph.D.

No outcome evaluation studies of Traumatic Incident Reduction (TIR) had yet been done in 1992. Its efficacy had not been established except through anecdotal evidence offered by proponents of the methodology. As I began doctoral study, I was intent on finding tools to remove blocks to therapeutic progress. After attending a seminar introducing TIR, it became clear that Traumatic Incident Reduction worked to resolve these barriers. It seemed logical to develop a research project to evaluate its therapeutic utility. Only one other study had begun, a comparison of TIR and DTE (Direct Therapeutic Exposure) being conducted by Lori Beth Bisbey in England.

The premise for the study of TIR included several initial assumptions. First, it was clear that therapeutic barriers often occur when an individual attempts to avoid addressing sensitive material. Second, the sensitive material frequently has a traumatic content.[1] Third, the barrier needs to be resolved so that the individual can deal with the traumatic material. This allows the person to desensitize to it, and cognitively restructure its meaning so that it is no longer aversive material. Traumatic Incident Reduction satisfied the three major known components required to address therapeutic impasses.

In 1992, I lacked the resources for mounting a full-scale study. Anyone familiar with the requirements of outcome evaluation research can attest to the complexity of conducting a fully replicable investigation. There were few mental health clinicians certified to conduct TIR. No preliminary data was available to guide further research. And, the Institute for Research in Metapsychology (IRM) was anxious to publish data to substantiate the utility of the procedure. In order to bring supporting evidence to the professional community as quickly as possible, a pilot study was developed using a quasi-experimental pre-test/post-test design. Anxiety was chosen as the most clearly measurable component of both therapeutic avoidance and traumatic response. A subgroup of individuals with panic symptoms was also assessed.

Efficacy studies measure the impact of treatment. To best measure that impact in the most realistic setting available, the research was conducted in private practice settings of established facilitators of Traumatic Incident Reduction [2]. A list of qualified facilitators was provided by The Institute for Research in Metapsychology. TIR is a standardized procedure. Therefore, delivery of service does not vary among practitioners. This feature made it possible to compare the outcomes of service provided by different individuals. All participating facilitators signed an affidavit to attest to their adherence to the official TIR protocol. Due to the simplicity of the procedure, it is not necessary to have clinical background in order to administer it. TIR also includes ground rules (See Appendix A), which generate both empathy and a safe therapeutic space. It not only does not require therapist insight, but it prohibits interference from, or customization by, the facilitator.

When taught and supervised by a certified TIR trainer, any adult with average intellect can execute the procedure. According to TIR developers Gerbode and French (1992):

> "We have found that *anyone* of good will and reasonable intelligence who wants to be able to help people who are unhappy can become a competent facilitator."

Although some of those providing data for this research did possess substantial mental health background, some did not. The initial experimental design had to be modified to accommodate facilitators who did not have a background in mental health.

Originally, we hoped to pre-select our study participants to include only those suffering from anxiety or panic disorders. This was only possible if there was an initial diagnosis, but not all participating facilitators were qualified to diagnose. Thus, we were not able to screen participants. In the end this proved more valuable than problematic. Our data indicate efficacy for a broad range of anxiety levels including those customarily experienced by normal people in normal environments. In short, because of this seeming limitation, the results are more validly applicable to a general population.

Two instruments were used to assess clients. A standardized and well validated test of anxiety, The State-Trait Anxiety Inventory (STAI) (Spielberger, 1983) was used to evaluate State and Trait Anxiety levels. State Anxiety represents immediate feelings of apprehension and tension, the anxiety a person feels "at the moment." Trait Anxiety reflects the individual's tendency to respond to the world in an anxious fashion. State Anxiety is generally amenable to short-term therapeutic interventions whereas Trait Anxiety tends to be an enduring characteristic of the individual. I specifically designed the second scale for this study. It was The Symptom Checklist, intended to elicit the symptoms of panic as defined by the diagnostic criteria set down in the DSM-IV (APA, 2000). Symptom checklists allow individuals to directly rate the presence or absence of specific symptoms. There is a high degree of reliability as they represent a direct report from the client and are free from researcher bias. Neither instrument required facilitator interpretation.

Method

Six facilitators trained in TIR provided data from their private practice. A total of twenty-five participants commenced, but five withdrew for reasons not related to this study. Each participant completed both the STAI and The Symptom Checklist on three occasions: on intake, and on one and three month follow-ups. The efficacy of Traumatic Incident Reduction as a treatment tool for managing anxiety and panic was assessed by a change in the reported symptom levels before and after treatment.

Results

There was a substantial and statistically significant reduction in State Anxiety for the entire sample. State Anxiety levels dropped by nearly one third of their original levels. Looking at the scoring on the STAI, the drop moved the group average from an anxiety level which would cause clinical concern and personal discomfort to a level that is considered normal for most people. The reduction in State Anxiety remained significant three months after treatment ended. Trait Anxiety levels also decreased by approximately twenty percent and held steady over the three month post-treatment period. These results indicate that Traumatic Incident Reduction is very effective in reducing anxiety. It is noteworthy that the reduction in anxiety levels occurred both for those in the normal pre-test range of anxiety as well as for those whose anxiety levels began at a higher, clinically significant level. This demonstrates that TIR is an effective tool for anyone. It will help those whose anxiety creates a problem in their life to bring that anxiety to tolerable levels. It will also help those who are only mildly anxious, perhaps only voicing reasonably normal concerns about their life, to reduce their discomfort and achieve a state of less worry and greater calm. Interestingly, there were no significant differences in the reduction of State or Trait Anxiety levels for individuals who also had panic disorder and those that did not suffer panic. There were, however, major differences in the level of panic symptoms. There were no additional follow-ups past three months.

Panic is defined as a discrete period of intense fear with symptoms of extreme anxiety such as pounding heart, shaking, shortness of breath, nausea, and fears of going crazy or dying [3]. Seven members of the study reported having at least one panic attack in the previous month. The average length of treatment time for the panic group was 10.3 hours with a range between 3 hours and 24 hours of treatment contact. In that relatively brief period, the mean number of panic attacks decreased from 12.1 to 1.1. That represents a 91 % reduction in the number of panic attacks. Additionally, the number and severity of the symptoms decreased substantially. There was a 64% reduction in the number of usual symptoms. The number of severe symptoms decreased by 67%. For individuals who suffer from panic disorder, this results in a marked improvement in their quality of life. It is important to note that these results occurred without the need to use sedating, often addictive, medications which are commonly prescribed to manage panic disorder.

The sample group was subdivided, based on the presence or absence of panic and the levels of State and Trait Anxiety. The general trends and results were similar across groups with one important exception. The group that suffered from panic and had low State Anxiety scores reported an approximately 25% increase in State Anxiety and a 50% increase in Trait Anxiety following treatment.

Further research needs to be done to determine the cause of this aberrant response. One possible explanation relates to the function of the panic attack for some individuals. A panic attack may serve as a psychological mechanism to "hold" or release anxiety. Once the panic symptomatology has been dispersed, related anxieties manifest as both State and Trait anxiety symptoms. While this appears to be objectively problematic, it is subjectively more manageable. An individual with State or Trait Anxiety can manage those symptoms with cognitive behavioral tools. State and Trait anxiety are more amenable to control and management than panic. Any treatment intervention which returns conscious control to the individual is usually considered beneficial.

Discussion

Traumatic Incident Reduction is an effective technique for reducing many types and symptoms of anxiety. The most debilitating presentation of anxiety is the panic attack. TIR is highly effective in reducing the number of panic attacks, the number of symptoms experienced during a panic attack and the severity of the symptoms. The procedure of viewing used in TIR allows the individual to revisit his/her panic symptoms and begin to understand why they occur. Once an understanding is present, the individual is able to take conscious control over the symptoms. The most frightening aspect of most panic attacks is that the individual does not know what is happening. Frequently, panic originates with an earlier, fearful event that has been forgotten by the individual. Because TIR does not proceed in a logical, linear fashion, it may unlock the memory and reveal the significance of panic symptoms more readily than traditional therapeutic approaches.

State Anxiety, which is nervousness about an event or situation, is highly responsive to treatment using TIR. One might normally encounter this type of anxiety prior to an important event, during public speaking or when making a major life change. Anxiety can be defined as "anticipatory fear". Based on past experience, we anticipate that the approaching event contains an element of danger. Traumatic Incident Reduction allows the individual to investigate the interconnecting cognitions which may link a past event with a current event and the belief that there is danger. In re-viewing the linked events, a clearer understanding may be achieved and, through cognitive rehearsal, the individual may come to feel less fear. In this way, TIR may facilitate the reduction in State Anxiety.

Once an individual begins to evaluate the origins of his/her anxiety, once he/she has gained control over overt symptoms, there is often an enhanced sense of competence in handling life. The reduction in Trait Anxiety may result from an overall sense of enhanced mastery that can be the outcome of using Traumatic Incident Reduction. Of those people who began with clinically significant levels of Trait Anxiety, 69% had this score reduced to within the normal range. "Cure" is often defined as eliminating the deviation from the norm. It can therefore be suggested that TIR cures pathological levels of Trait Anxiety approximately 70% of the time.

Figures and efficacy of this magnitude are seldom found in traditional psychotherapeutic modalities, given that the average length of treatment was 13 hours which would on average have occurred in only 4-5 sessions. It can be postulated that the extraordinary treatment outcome was related to practitioner expertise. However, this would not be a valid assumption. Facilitator expertise was determined only to assure adherence to the protocol. Treatment administration does not deviate from one provider to another among those fully trained to provide TIR. The language and response patterns are specifically scripted so as not to vary among presentations. Unlike most forms of psychotherapy, TIR does rely on practitioner talent to provide results. It requires only adherence to the protocol for administration.

Comparisons to Other Modalities

The parsimony in explaining why Traumatic Incident Reduction works lies in its incorporation of knowledge gleaned from the main schools of psychotherapy.

Psychodynamic theories approach symptoms as signals of unconscious material. Freud identified anxiety as originating in events that threatened the individual. Psychodynamic therapy focuses on uncovering the originating incidents and releasing the unconscious material leading to enhanced understanding which typically causes the symptoms to decrease or disappear. Traumatic Incident Reduction addresses incidents in an individual's life which were 'traumatic'. When the impact of those incidents is 'reduced' the symptoms decrease or disappear.

Behavioral theories view anxiety as a conditioned response. Behavioral treatments therefore focus on extinguishing the conditioned response through desensitization. A behavioral protocol would require the individual to repeatedly be exposed to anxiety-inducing stimuli without reinforcing (responding to) the anxiety. After repeated exposure, the individual becomes desensitized and no longer responds with anxiety. Treating anxiety with Traumatic Incident Reduction similarly requires the repeated viewing of incidents related to the symptom, releasing affect until the individual no longer responds with the symptom.

Cognitive theorists view the underlying belief systems of the individual as the foundation to healthy or unhealthy responses to the world. Foa and Kozak (1985) view pathological anxiety as originating in previously stored "fear programs" contained in the informational network of the memory. To resolve symptoms, the therapist assists the clients in uncovering their "fear programs" in order to reevaluate their validity. Typically, once the symptom producing "program" is uncovered, it is recognized as containing irrational beliefs. Once identified, the irrational beliefs can be reframed thus eliminating the symptom. Thematic TIR asks the viewer to identify "an incident that could have caused" the symptom and to chain back through events connected to the symptom. Once the salient events are re-viewed, the viewer is able to determine possibly erroneous decisions that were made at the time of the incident and re-evaluate their validity. Once that material is identified, the viewer is free to reframe the incident and resolve the symptom(s) connected to it.

The essential difference between traditional treatment modalities and Traumatic Incident Reduction lies in the role of the practitioner. Traditional treatments evolving from psychological theories rely on a therapist to conduct and interpret the treatment. TIR relies only on an individual to facilitate the procedure. The full implication of this difference is beyond the scope of this chapter. However, several benefits are clear: TIR does not require years of collegiate study to pre-qualify the provision of assistance to others. The efficacy of TIR is not contingent on the unique talents of a particular facilitator. The procedure is standardized and does not require continuous adjustments. It is universally applicable to anyone of average intellect who is able to focus sufficiently to follow the procedure. Most importantly, Traumatic Incident Reduction does not allow interference from the practitioner. I believe that it is precisely the prohibition against interpretation and discussion that frees the individual to investigate his/her cognitive content in order to uncover the specific cause of his/her specific symptoms without bias. This freedom allows for the efficient and precise resolution of symptoms using Traumatic Incident Reduction.

End Notes

[1] The term "trauma" is used herein in the broadest sense of the term. Material is traumatic when it threatens the physical or psychological life of the individual.

[2] At the time The Institute for Research in Metapsychology, headed by Frank A. Gerbode, the developer of TIR, credentialed all research facilitators.

[3] For a full definition of panic disorder consult The Diagnostic and Statistical Manual of Mental Disorders (4th edition).

References

American Psychiatric Association (2000). *Diagnostic and Statistical Manual of Mental Disorders*, 4th ed. Washington, DC: Author.

Foa, E.B. & Kozak, M.J. (1985) Treatment of anxiety disorders: Implications for psychopathology. In A.H. Tuma & J.D. Maser (Eds.) *Anxiety and Anxiety Disorders* (pp. 421-461). Hillsdale, NJ: Lawrence Erlbaum.

French, G.D. & Gerbode, F.A. (1992). *The Traumatic Incident Reduction Workshop*. Menlo Park, CA: IRM Press.

Spielberger, C. D. (1983). *Manual for the State Trait Anxiety Inventory (STAI)*. PaloAlto, CA: Consulting Psychologists Press.

9 Children and TIR

There are many theories about what can and cannot be done effectively with children in a therapeutic setting. In addition to those ideas, some therapists believe that preverbal memory cannot be addressed with TIR since TIR involves having the client recount the experience of going through a traumatic incident, each time through.

In fact, preverbal incidents resolve as readily as later incidents. We can understand this when we consider that the client goes through and re-experiences the incident silently each time and then tells what happened. Children, having a shorter time from which to drawn incidents than adults have, tend to go into preverbal incidents rather sooner than adults do. This does not present a problem.

The biggest factor in determining whether a child (or an adult) is able to make use of TIR is his or her ability to focus attention on the material being addressed. The ability to determine this takes some practice on the part of the facilitator. The use of lighter techniques first goes a long way toward establishing a child's readiness for TIR. In the interviews that follow you will see a variety of approaches. Some practitioners simplify the language and the technique to adapt it to the child's world. Another uses a creative method for making the steps of the technique clearly understandable to the child and usually uses the same set of instructions that he would with adults. The most unusual technique I've heard of is using a craft project to calm "right brain" activity.

The proof of all this lies in the results. Some intriguing results are included here. In this chapter, you'll hear conversations with a number of practitioners about their experiences with TIR and children. I begin with a report from Teresa Descilo on how TIR has been successfully deployed in an inner city school for at-risk identified youth. Brian Grimes shares an incident about a boy who had nightmares of an incident that happened before he was born. He describes another incident in which a young motorcycle accident victim recovers from psychosomatic pain.

Janet Buell speaks about a girl who lost her parents and developed a crippling fear of separation. She also talks about how TIR might be modified for use with very young clients. Karen Trotter shares stories from her private practice about how she used TIR with teenagers and younger children.

Alex Frater describes an interesting case where a child's repetition of a fantasy incident produced the same level of traumatic stress found in children who have experienced physical incidents.

Trauma Resolution in an At-Risk Youth Program
By Teresa Descilo, MSW, CTS

Since 2001, Victim Services Center of Miami has received funding from the Department of Juvenile Justice in Florida to help at-risk youth resolve the impact of trauma. At-risk youth were defined as children who had risk factors in three of four domains—school, family, substance abuse and behavior. We primarily provided services at Madison Middle School, an inner city school in the Miami area zip code with the highest juvenile crime rate. Madison hosts approximately 1300 students from grades 6 to 8. In a recent year, 20.7% of the students missed more than a month of school per year. Compared to schools nationwide, Madison ranks below the 30th percentile in math and reading skills. One out of six students qualifies as learning disabled. A typical year sees about 300 incidents of crime and violence (see distribution in Fig. 1). The most common violation of the Student Code of Conduct at Madison is fighting. As one Assistant Principal explained, sixth graders are immature, "they look at each other—they fight." (TCPR & AP, 2000)

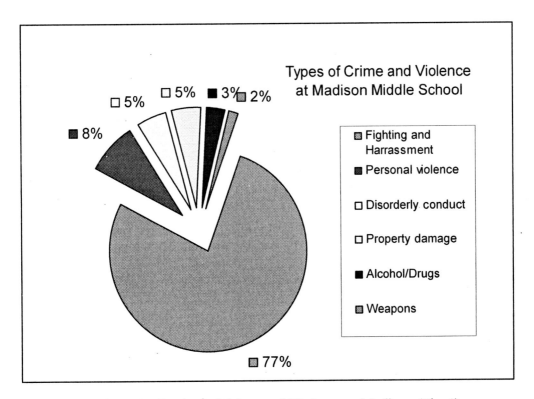

Distribution of Crime and Violence at Madison (Fig. 1)

Source: www.schools-data.com

Simply outlawing violence in schools doesn't work. In reaction to nationwide outrage at highly publicized gun incidents, many school districts instituted a Zero Tolerance policy wherein any weapon infraction could result in a compulsory lengthy suspension or expulsion. Madison's principal Thelma Davis contributed to the controversial report "Opportunities Suspended: The Devastating Consequences of Zero Tolerance and School Discipline" (TCPR & AP, 2000) which rebuts this approach. The report concludes:

> The increasing use of [zero tolerance] practices throughout the country is denying thousands of children opportunities for education, and alienating more from the educational process. Moreover, data clearly shows that minority students are frequently far more harshly disciplined than their white counterparts for similar, or less serious, offenses. Zero Tolerance is unfair, is contrary to the developmental needs of children, denies children educational opportunities, and often results in the criminalization of children.

Victim Services of Miami were originally invited into the school by the school social worker in order to provide bereavement groups because many children at the school lost caregivers to AIDS and homicide. Many of the children we served were from these bereavement groups. Others were from the severely emotionally disturbed group and many more were referred by the school social worker who had identified that they had overwhelming trauma in their lives.

Trauma and Childhood

Our understanding of trauma in children is strongly informed by the work of Ricky Greenwald, Ph.D. of Mt. Sinai Medical Center. In his book *Trauma and Juvenile Delinquency: Theory, Research, and Interventions* he documents the role of trauma in conduct disorder, antisocial behavior, and delinquency. This book also highlights the success of trauma-informed and competent services for at-risk youth.

Another influence in our thinking is Bruce Perry, M.D.'s research on child maltreatment. Perry explains how persisting fear can alter the developing child's brain. Specifically, these early traumatic events contribute to schizophrenia in patients who have a genetic predisposition. The neurodevelopmental costs of adverse childhood events can no longer be ignored. In *The Cost of Child Maltreatment: Who Pays? We All Do* (Franey, Geffner & Falconer, 2001) Perry states that children with PTSD as a primary diagnosis are often labeled with Attention Deficit Disorder with Hyperactivity (ADD/HD), major depression, oppositional defiant disorder, conduct disorder, separation anxiety or specific phobia. Underlying this is the idea that the brain forms in a use-dependent fashion. Childhood is a critical and sensitive period for brain development; disruptions at these times may lead to abnormalities or deficits in neurodevelopment. Experiences of over-activation of important neural systems during sensitive periods of development can manifest in several ways, including:

- Malorganization and compromised functioning in:
    - –humor, empathy, attachment and affect regulation
    - –being insensitive to any replacement experiences later in life, including therapy

- Being stuck in hyperarousal or dissociation:
    - –males tend to manifest hyperarousal
    - –females tend to manifest dissociation

- Fear becomes a trait:
    - –Very easily moved from mildly anxious to feeling threatened to being terrorized
    - –Maladaptive emotional behavioral and cognitive problems arise

Treatment Approach

Traumatic Incident Reduction was the primary approach that we utilized. The only difference in how it was delivered to children was that we incorporated some sort of craft activity that the children would engage in as they recounted their traumatic incidents. Beadwork turned out to be the most popular activity for both girls and boys. It seems that pairing a relaxing, right brain activity, with an initially distressing right brain activity, lowered the arousal for the children through recounting rapes, beatings and homicides.

Madison Middle School

Since we changed our measurements for the third year of the grant, the following data only represents the 2003 academic year. Two factors limited our impact on the student body to thirty-five students during year three. Funding was the primary limiting factor and secondarily that children had to have three out of four of the aforementioned domain risk factors. It should be noted that the Madison Middle School program is strictly a pilot project—whose purpose is to see what outcomes are possible—rather than a research driven project.

Measurement Scales Utilized

Our treatment approach used four different scales to pre- and post-test the children on the impacts that trauma was having on their lives.

- Child Report of Post-traumatic Symptoms (CROPS) (Greenwald and Rubin, 1999) – with a clinical cut-off of 19

- The Depression Self-Rating Scale (Birleson, 1981) – 13

- Self-Concept Scale for Children (Lipsitt, 1958)

- Youth Coping Index (McCubbin, Thomposn, and Elver) – acceptable range -91.8 to 95.4

Case Summaries

Two of the thirty-five cases are highlighted here in brief:

Case #1: A 12 year-old Hispanic female—victim and witness of abuse, in the Florida Department of Children and Families system who underwent 14 hours of individual treatment with TIR and 12 hours of group therapy over a seven month period:

Measurement	Pre test	Post test
Student Form	19	0
Depression SRS	15	0
Self Concept Scale	88	109
Youth Coping Index	53	102

After treatment, she wrote:

> "The changes I've had ever since I started sessions here is I don't think I have to be perfect any more to impress my friends. Ever since I stopped trying to be perfect, my friends said I have become a better artist and a better friend. And I have become a better person as well."

Case #2: A 15 year-old African-American female—victim of sexual abuse, drug abuser and run-away. Underwent 15 hours of individual treatment with TIR, labeled as Oppositional Defiant

Measurement	Pre test	Post test
Student Form	39	6
Depression SRS	18	2
Self Concept Scale	47	102
Youth Coping Index	71	128

After treatment, she wrote:

> "I know that my behavior changed. My attitude, my ways and also my language. And the service help me a lot because I don't do bad things any-more or don't follow people. And my grades in school has improve a lot with As, Bs, Cs in conduct."

Results

First, I need to emphasize again that this was not a research project; the statistics gathered were in the interest of practicing responsibly. Children measured in the study all had symptoms of traumatic stress. Although there was no attempt to diagnose for PTSD, many of the children were above the PTSD cutoff on the Student Form and Depression Self-Rated Scale. Both scales show children significantly below the PTSD cutoff levels following treatment, as the following charts indicate:

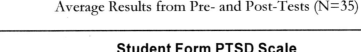

Average Results from Pre- and Post-Tests (N=35)

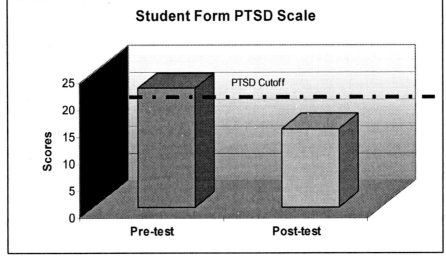

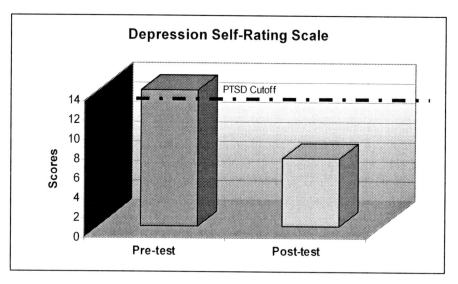

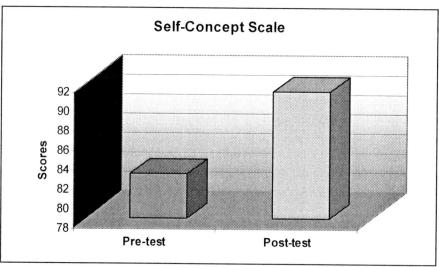

[Ed. Note: average data for YCI was not available at time of press.]

Summary

We have heard from the school social worker at Madison Middle School that our trauma focused program is the most effective service received by her students. She has reported to me that the children who went through our program are doing better academically and with behavior at school and at home. I see that this program will offer a deeper solution to stopping the cycle of violence and helping youth move out of the category of "At Risk" and into truly resilient people.

References

Depression self rating scale [DSRD] (1981). Birleson P. IN: Corcoran K & Fischer J (2000). Measures for clinical practice: A sourcebook. 3rd Ed. (2vols.) NY, Free Pr. V.1,Pg.535-536

Self concept scale for children [SC] (1958). Lipsitt LP. IN: Corcoran K & Fischer J (2000). Measures for clinical practice: A sourcebook. 3rd Ed. (2vols.) NY, Free Pr. V.1,Pg.617-618

Youth coping index [YCI] (1995). McCubbin HI; Thompson A; Elver K. IN: Corcoran K & Fischer J (2000). Measures for clinical practice: A sourcebook. 3rd Ed. (2vols.) NY, Free Pr. V.1,Pg.628-631

Franey, K., Geffner, R., and Falconer, R., Ed. (2001). The Cost of Child Maltreatment: Who Pays? We All Do. Family Violence and Sexual Assault Institute, San Diego, CA.. http://www.fvsai.org

Greenwald, R. & Rubin, A. (1999). "Brief assessment of children's post-traumatic symptoms: Development and preliminary validation of parent and child scales". *Research on Social Work Practice, 9,* 61-75.

Greenwald, R. (2002) Trauma and Juvenile Delinquency: Theory, Research, and Interventions. Haworth Maltreatment and Trauma Press.

Civil Rights Project, The & Advancement Project (2000). "Opportunities Suspended: The Devastating Consequences of Zero Tolerance and School Discipline Policies." Delivered at National Summit on Zero Tolerance (2000). The Civil Rights Project, Harvard University. http://www.civilrightsproject.harvard.edu/research/discipline/opport_suspended.php

Experiences with Children:
A Conversation with Brian Grimes

VV: Tell me a little bit about your background.

Brian: I was with Frank A. Gerbode at the former Institute for Research in Metapsychology (IRM) in the late 1980s. Gerald French and I used to do TIR Workshop training, and I became a Certified Trauma Specialist. I was at IRM from 1985 until it ended operations in the early 90s. I am the former Director of the Reading Research Council located in Burlingame, California. I was personally trained by Ronald D. Davis, author of *The Gift of Dyslexia*, and worked with dyslexics for 8 years. Later, my wife and I started our own business working with dyslexics.

VV: Do you find in general that the length of TIR sessions is different with children?

Brian: My experience has been that it's shorter. They tend to reach an end point more quickly. It seems to have something to do with the fact that they don't put a lot of added significance into the experience like adults do.

VV: It's more about "what happened" as opposed to "what it means because it happened to me."

Brian: You got it exactly. They bleed off the emotion rather quickly, and they're done with it. They don't need to dissect it from any intellectual perspective.

VV: Because they haven't built up a whole series of stories about how they were made right by being a victim?

Brian: You got it. That's exactly right. Or, "It's been serving me really well to have this locked up in my psyche," or other reasons. It's just something that they experienced. It was unfortunate or unpleasant, but that's what it was. They go through it and then they are done.

VV: Are there any special techniques that you need to use to prepare children for TIR?

Brian: Sometimes I'll do some recall work with them to heighten their awareness of what it's like when they're in their mental environment. [Ed. Note: these techniques are taught in the TIR – Expanded Applications and Case Planning for TIR and Life Stress Reduction workshops. See Appendix C] What it is that we want to look at or some of the content that they might have forgotten or might be relevant to be able to take the charge off the episode. If I get them in there and I find that they're having a difficult time contacting the incidents, sometimes what we'll do is scale back and do a little more recall work and then go back to TIR work.

VV: Do you mean, recalling pleasant experiences?

Brian: Yes. I'll check what perceptions they are able to remember in recalling an earlier time, etc. Most children I've worked with just jump right into TIR.

VV: Do you find end points to be different with children?

Brian: Yes I do; the contrast would be that children report, "It feels better" or "It's OK now." Adults will tend to be more philosophic about how they viewed it vs. how they view it in the present (after doing TIR).

VV: Karen Trotter said they often seem to lose interest in the incident or gain interest in something else. Do you find that true?

Brian: Yes, exactly. Their attention span is much, much shorter. Yeah, "That one's fine... Let's move on," or "What's next?"

VV: Do you find you have to modify the language or the procedure to be less sophisticated with children?

Brian: No. I found the nomenclature, wording, and steps to be comfortable. But I make sure that I do a "dummy run" with them before we actually get into anything. I go over the questions and directives so that they have the procedure locked in. So that I open my mouth as little as possible and they know what I'm asking for and why. I'll say:

> "I'm going to create an incident here. What I want you to do is, when I say start, that's when I want your camera rolling. Very closely watch what it is that I do, every movement, every expression of my face very closely. Then when I say stop, turn your camera off. Then what I'm going to do is walk you through exactly what happened and have you tell me what you saw."

I pick up a pencil or something from the desk, toss it in the air, catch it, and then give a puzzled look at the pencil, then I look at them, and say "stop". Then I walk them through that with the actual steps of TIR. So they have a comparative base and an understanding of what TIR is.

VV: So they say, "You caught it?"

Brian: That's right. I'll ask them, "Was there anything else you saw me do?" And they'll say, "No." I'll say, "Did you remember me looking at that pencil funny?" Then they say, "Yeah, I did!"

VV: That's interesting because it also has the effect of bringing them into the present, if they were not quite there.

Brian: Exactly, because it takes them out of their head. They tend to enjoy it because it has a little bit of gamesmanship to it, which they like.

VV: Is there some kind of minimum age or how would you decide whether or not to handle a particular child on the basis of maturity?

Brian: To be honest, I don't put an age limit on it all. What I would say is that if they are really young, I wouldn't follow the exact same series of steps. I would basically just do a very lightweight Exploration to try to get them to scan through it and just tell me: What did you notice happened? How did you feel? I keep it kind of light but the principal thing I'm trying to do is to get them to communicate. Get them to tell what is going on and what their perception is, and how they felt. If they're rather young, you really don't have them very long before they're ping-ponging all over the place wanting to do something else.

[Ed. Note: Exploration differs from other techniques in the subject in that no rote questions are used. Once you start on a checklist type of technique (such as TIR) or an unlayering type (such as Unblocking) there is usually no need to depart from the set of viewing instructions you are using. In Exploration you are constantly coming up with new questions to ask while staying on the topic and staying person-centered.]

VV: Are there any special challenges in working with children as opposed to adults?

Brian: Only the attention span. Sometimes what I've found is that if I work with a known incident [Basic TIR], where we have a known event that happened such as a bicycle accident where they were injured, I could do only what I could within the short timeframe of that session knowing full well that it hadn't been completely resolved. In other words, it still had bite to it. Then what I would have to do is come back and do it over a series of sessions. Revisit it until we had gotten it to a proper end point.

VV: Are there any particular types of incidents that are more prevalent with children as opposed to adults?

Brian: The incidents seem to be mostly about social interactions, as opposed to losses or accidents.

VV: Are there any memorable cases you can share with me?

Brian: The strangest one I ever did was in San Diego with an 8-year old boy who had nightmares. It was the son of an acquaintance whose child was having nightmares that were getting more amplified and more disruptive. He thought it might be a good idea if I would work with the boy. I told the parent, "I'm happy to do it, but what we don't know is whether this child is going to like my personality and what we're going to be able to do."

I ended up meeting with the boy and I did an interview with him. The dreams had to do with fire. In my interview, I was asking a lot of questions: Have you been playing with matches? Were you burned recently? Were you playing with magnifying glasses? Did you see anything burning lately? None of these were the stimulus at all; I could tell he was being honest. He said "It just suddenly started. I was watching Discovery Channel about the Apollo mission."

He didn't know about the Apollo 1 fire. The event that unfolded in the TIR session was what sounded like a replica of what might have happened if one had been present for that. I just let it go, but at first he was a little weirded out by it. He said "What is this?" I said "It's OK, it is whatever it is; just let it unfold and we'll keep going." He said "OK."

We just kept at it. His descriptions were rather interesting: a gloved hand reaching up and checking toggle switches, but he didn't have any basis of comparison for that. He heard chatter inside a helmet, clipped communications, checking items off, and then all hell broke loose. He was struggling to get out and couldn't. Here was a child not old enough to be alive when the event happened. It was the only session I ever gave him and the nightmares turned off. The session was just over an hour and 20 minutes and he returned to being a happy kid.

VV: I'm a little unclear. Had he seen or not seen the documentary on the Apollo 1 fire?

Brian: No, what he had seen was the initial stages going into the Apollo program. They hadn't even gotten to that segment yet.

VV: Are there any other client stories you can share?

Brian: There was a boy who had been hit by a motorcycle and there was a really severe wound that went all the way to the femur bone. What I did was I took him actually out to the accident site and walked him through it and had him show me where it happened, what his body position was, and then we actually did the session on it. [Ed. Note: this is called the Re-Enactment Remedy] The pain turned on in the femur pretty strongly in the course of the session. He was fascinated by that.

VV: How did it change through various viewings? Did it become more intense or less intense?

Brian: Yes, what happened was initially there was no pain at all when he first made contact with the incident. Then on subsequent times through, the pain intensified and actually got pretty severe. He wanted to discontinue it at that point. I let him know that that was normal and if we were to just continue then we would get it turned off. Fortunately, we stayed with it and it did [turn off]. He was pretty happy with that.

VV: Afterwards his symptoms were considerably less?

Brian: You bet, yes. I spoke with his mom and she said ever since that session the healing process just seemed to go so much faster. He just talked about what happened without emotion but more matter-of-factly, as something that just happened. He described it with no affect in his voice. I've done many, many sessions and very few come with a revivification of pain. Certainly not this intense.

[Ed. Note: Some facilitators report that pain or other sensation coming on during a session and then going away to be fairly common.]

VV: Do you find that there's any relationship with trauma and dyslexia?

Brian: Yes, on an emotional level, you bet. My theory is that we're recording everything that happens, whether we like it or not. So those memories are locked up and if there's a humiliating experience that was emotionally traumatic for a person and you get them anywhere near similar circumstances to what existed back then, they can trigger right back into it. There were a few times, not many, but there were a few times where I actually had to use TIR working with people doing the dyslexia program.

VV: Because they got restimulated?

Brian: Yes, they were right there in the memory. The counselor would just say "I have no idea what to do with this. They tell me about it but they're not getting calmer, they're getting more upset." I would just take over and do a TIR session. It would be pretty fast usually.

VV: You're working with dyslexic children and adults?

Brian: Yes, even Ph.Ds, lawyers, computer analysts and so on. Fascinating people.

Experiences with Children:
A Conversation with Janet Buell

Janet Buell has received a BA in Education and is an ordained minister. She is a member of the International Pastoral Association, an ecumenical group of pastoral counselors. She is the author of more than a dozen books including *Your Mind and Body are a Corporation and You are the CEO*. Janet has been a TIR facilitator for many years and guest speaker at former annual conferences of the Institute for Research in Metapsychology.

[Ed. Note: Conversational TIR, often used with children, is taught in the TIR Workshop – level one. The other sorts of remedies Janet refers to are taught on the TIR – Expanded Applications and Case Planning for TIR and Life Stress Reduction workshops; see Appendix C]

VV: Tell me about some of the outstanding experiences you've had working with children?

Janet: One that comes to mind is a 12-year old child I worked with. This is a female child of color who had lost both parents. I took a while assessing her to see how mature she was. First, I checked to see if she was mature enough to sit still through the procedure and secondly to find out how good her ability to recall things was to see if she was a candidate for TIR. When I first saw her, she appeared much more mature than the average kid of that age. I started the procedure as usual and she actually spent several hours on it. It was a somewhat shocking and unexpected loss for her, an automobile accident. She did very well with it.

She spotted the moment when she first heard that it occurred and some of the decisions that she made. One of the decisions she made was never to be a parent herself, because if you were never a parent then you could never cause that kind of loss for someone else. That was the decision that had the potential to impact her life most heavily. She was 12 when I worked with her and it was about 3 months after the accident occurred. She did, quite naturally, after reducing some of the charge from the incident, realize that it had also been extremely upsetting when her grandmother had passed away. The incident had been similar in the sense that it was also a shock to her. I probably would not have pursued it because she had given me a realization, but she seemed to have a lot of energy left. She seemed OK, so I sent her back and had her tell me about the loss of her grandmother.

That incident was much lighter in the sense that it didn't take nearly as much time as her parents' loss had taken. If I recall correctly, she realized that the prior loss of her grandmother had actually lightened the shock when her parents died because she had already realized that you might lose someone suddenly. She realized that she had sort of distanced herself. The reason she had seemed so old and wise for her age because she had realized with the earlier loss at age 7 or 8 that you couldn't always depend on someone to be there. She decided that you needed to not be too dependent on people because they might not always be there. Her words were, "It was almost like I started preparing to lose mommy and daddy because I already knew that something like that could happen." She did have some realizations then about the way that that had altered her behavior to have had that happen early in her life.

I remember her making some observations about other children having a little different attitude about life. She related good and bad things; that she always feared another major loss and that caused her to be more fearful in general. She also realized that it had made her more mature than other kids her age. So she felt that the earlier loss had mixed outcomes. In some ways it was a blessing because she mentioned that she had always been very certain of communicating with her parents and not being upset. I believe with her grandmother there had been a little bit of an upset with her before she passed away and she vowed not to let that happen again. She was always very careful to make sure that if they were going to be separated, that they were on very good terms. Her overall realization was that at least she had succeeded in not having any upsets between herself and her parents when they died. Also that she always made a point that if they were going to be separated for any length of time to make sure that she told them she loved them. Those are the nature of the realizations that she gave me.

VV: Did she have any classic trauma symptoms like nightmares and intrusive thoughts?

Janet: Her aunt was the person who brought her to me. The girl was being very brave about it but she was very concerned any time her aunt went anywhere. She was having nightmares and her biggest concern was much too strong a fear that she would continue to lose other people. She was very a serious girl. If her aunt was going out to get the mail, she felt she had to tell her she loved her. Her aunt was the one who took over her care after her parents died. It got to the point where her aunt felt that the girl couldn't go through her life focused on that. It was an extreme fearfulness of losing someone. That was the prime manifestation. Fortunately, she got her to me fairly soon after the accident happened. I think it came up when she didn't want to go to a school event that would have required her being away from her aunt. It seemed as though her fear of being separated was too strong for her to have fun on this trip. That was the presenting reason that her aunt saw that it could be real trouble for her in the future.

VV: You've got a really good memory for detail, thank you for that story.

Janet: She was an extraordinary child. I've probably done several thousand hours of TIR, but this one made quite an impact on me.

VV: Let's talk about how you modify things for younger children. Can you give me some specifics?

Janet: When I have a young child who has had a loss, I spent quite a bit more time doing remedy type things in terms of focusing them on the environment around them. I probably would work in shorter sessions and use more of a less formal procedure, watching more closely for signs of tiredness. I would probably also focus on having the child look at one particular portion of what occurred rather than the whole incident on the first round. I would simplify the terminology and to make it much simpler.

VV: By portion, do you mean addressing one aspect of the incident..?

Janet: It would depend a lot more on what the incident was. I would be watching much more closely for signs of fatigue and signs of their attention going off it. I would settle for them talking about one aspect of it and brightening up some. Probably I might know that there might be more work needed on it, but I would do it over several sessions so that the attention span wasn't as big a factor. A lot would depend on their engagement, if they got into it I certainly wouldn't leave them. I would stop at a point of relief even if I wasn't necessarily convinced that it was over. I might then choose to take it up again on another day.

Ordinarily, if I'm working with adults I'm going to schedule as much time as needed and I'm going to try to get them through to a full end point in one session. But with a child might not have the attention span or the stamina for that. On the other hand, I've had a few small children who were so fixated on an incident that there wasn't anything else they could pay attention to. It would probably depend on the degree of the trauma.

VV: I think I've heard that from a few different practitioners, that they spread the incident out over 3 or 4 separate sessions.

Janet: I think it depends. If the child is completely fixated on it and stuck on it then you might as well feed them well, get them well rested, and do as much as you can to prepare for a longer session. But if it's something that affects the child only sometimes and they are not totally fixated on it, then I would probably try to do some lighter remedies rather than go into TIR right away.

VV: Are there any other cases that stand out in your memory that come to mind?

Janet: I worked with a boy who was also interesting. He was 16 at the time but he seemed much younger. I believe the official diagnosis for him was "mild autism". Even though he was 16 or 17, he acted more like a child of about 9 or 10 years old. He had suffered a loss; he had been attending a residential school that had been helping him a great deal. I don't remember the exact circumstances, perhaps the school had closed but there was a reason he could no longer live there. He had quite a loss from that. The parents were trying to find alternative places for him to get the kind of care he needed. He was very fixated on the friends he didn't see and even more so on the resources which the school had provided. He was very upset and he seemed incapable of understanding that they didn't have a choice in the matter. He was upset with his parents and upset with the school.

I worked with him as though he were more like 8 or 10 years old and did more of a Conversational TIR remedy with him. It stood out in my mind because it did go well. The usual things you look for in an end point he didn't necessarily have, and I had to judge my results more by the fact that by one point his parents took him to visit another facility that might be able to keep him there and he seemed interested. It was the fifth or sixth place they looked, but it was no better or worse than those they had already seen. I did work with him over the course of several sessions.

VV: Rather than dramatic realizations, he just got to a point of acceptance?

Janet: Yes, he would talk to me a great deal about the place he'd been that was so important to him. He was very focused on counting. He was a child who could tell you the ZIP code or area code of any place in the world. So it was a loss of things that he had there that he used. It was a very unusual situation but they were very real losses, including some kind of computer program that he was interested in developing. He was apparently quite good at it and he was worried about being able to use his strengths at another school. Even though he had been to other schools that could provide that, he wasn't ready to accept that. When they took him to the last one, they felt like he was finished because he was ready to go to that school.

It was a little bizarre and flying by the seat of my pants because I had to view it the way that he viewed it and see what a big loss it had been for him. Some things might be hard for an average person to understand; such as how he would miss this one project he was working on. I heard from his parents that he did very well at the new facility. It's kind of a case where you realize that someone with a mental illness can be traumatized just like the rest of us. That end point that you're going to get is not necessarily that they are going to be cured, it's just that they have dealt with that loss. So you have to change your standards. I didn't think that it was going to cure autism, and it didn't, but it made him a happier autistic kid.

VV: I've heard the same thing with regards to dyslexia. You can develop incidents around dyslexia.

Janet: That's true actually. I've dealt with quite a few people on dyslexia in regaining their self-confidence because that was lost by the way they were treated more than the dyslexia. I've actually treated a few young people with that.

Experiences with Children:
A Conversation with Karen Trotter

VV: How have you used TIR with young people?

Karen: I first used TIR with teenagers at a school in Oklahoma after two girls had been killed in an auto accident. We (a co-worker who had also attended the Green Cross training and I) went to the school the day after the accident and talked with many of the students. I ran some modified short sessions with one girl there. She seemed to have a positive experience with the process. Because the trauma had not completely set in, we couldn't address the whole incident. Instead we did Thematic TIR on her grief and where her grief came from in that situation. She was relating the grief in this incident to a history of grief from previous similar incidents such as family deaths and so forth. We came to a pretty good end point. She seemed to gain a deeper understanding of her feelings. And she seemed to gain more insight into why she was reacting so deeply the grief and loss of these friends.

Since then, I've used TIR mainly with adults who have experienced trauma related to a history of abuse, or auto accidents. For example, a client who experienced abuse and had continuing problems with relationships seemed to gain a better understanding of the choices that she is making after TIR. I then followed up in later sessions with some more traditional counseling and skill-building to assist the client in figuring out where to go from there, setting goals and accessing additional community services.

I've also used TIR with children a time or two with various success rates. On Gerald French's suggestion, I drew out several film frames on a long roll of butcher paper. The kids stood on that and as they progressed through the story they went frame by frame, backing up and going forward as they viewed the incident. With younger kids and pre-teens the process depends on the developmental level and readiness of each child.

Experiences with Children:
A Conversation with Alex Frater

For an introduction to Alex Frater, please see p. 197

VV: Do you use TIR with children?

Alex: I do use TIR with children and they do run shorter sessions. I'm always amazed how quickly they can do it. One case that comes to mind is the case of a family where an 18 month old baby slipped under the wheel of a 4-wheel drive truck that was backing up. It was a horrific accident; the child was actually killed as the vehicle ran over his head. There were four children in the family: a girl of 10, a boy of 7, another boy 4 years old, and the baby. The eldest child couldn't go near car parks [parking lots]. She was having flashbacks. We got her trauma resolved in about 4 sessions. Incredible, absolutely incredible. I find that with kids.

Another case I had a little while ago was a 12 year-old boy who had to sleep in his parents' bedroom the past four years. He was frightened to go to into bed and that sort of thing. I said to him, "When you go to bed, what happens in your mind? What kind of pictures do you have?" He said, "I'm just scared." I said, "I want to know the picture you see." He said, "People rob the place."

When I went to do TIR with him, he remembered four years ago he heard a car stop at the front and doors banging. In his mind, he thought they were robbers. As time went on in his mind (none of this happened) he imagined those people coming into the house, breaking the door open, and shooting his mother, father, and sister. They point the gun at him and they are about to shoot him in the head. He was dreaming this too after a while. None of this was true, but he had thought about it so much that it had become reality to him. We fixed him in three visits, just by running that scenario in his mind

> *None of this was true, but he had thought about it so much that it had become reality to him.*

VV: So you ran the fantasy of the incident?

Alex: Yes. Before TIR, when he went to bed, he'd run that fantasy through his mind. He of course had all the emotions that went with it and he couldn't get it out of his mind until we used TIR on it.

VV: Do you find end points different with children?

Alex: Yes, they probably are less dramatic. Mind you, I find some adults not very dramatic either. You have to be very careful with kids because they reach the end point sometimes quite quickly. I ask them. "How did it feel?" and they say, "Oh it feels quite good." But they don't go into raptures. I modify the language to be less sophisticated and I do that with adults too sometimes. I get doctors, lawyers, businessmen and I get some people who have barely borderline IQs. I change the language a little bit, but the handouts I give them are all at an adolescent reading level. Everybody gets the same handouts. I find some of the kids are pretty bright, and they handle it alright.

VV: Any special challenges to working with children?

Alex: I find that they are a delight to work with. The sessions are generally not as long for a child as with adults. I've always booked longer hours with kids, but I've never ever needed it. I find usually 40 to 50 minutes is about as long as you want.

VV: Some facilitators have told me that in working with children they need to spread out the incident over 2 or 3 sessions, only addressing part of it in each session. Do you find that to be the case?

Alex: You've got to watch because they get bored with it. When I notice that happening, I ask, "Do you feel OK." They say, "Yeah, I feel good." So I say, "Alright if we leave it here today?" On the other hand, often I've had no trouble with them covering the whole incident in a single span of time. That young girl with her brother being killed, she was able to go through the whole thing from the word go, including up to and including the funeral she went to. The first session ran for an hour and 20 minutes.

In doing this, I find that the first time is a bit straggly. It's something that they've never seen done and they find it a bit weird I think. I don't worry unduly about the first one. It's mainly to get them going and using it. I find that the second session runs better; they don't find it strange. When I'm explaining it to them sometimes, I'll say, "It's a bit weird, isn't it?" I find that sometimes the first one tends to run a bit raggedy. After that, their second session they jump right into. Most sessions we do comfortably within an hour, quite easily. If it's too long, they lose their power of concentration.

10 Integrating Therapies

By "integrating therapies," I am not advocating some kind of melting pot of different techniques. Rather, I am speaking of the real life aspect of a professional practitioner who has a number of techniques at his disposal. It's quite common to find a social worker, for example, who is certified in TIR, EMDR, EFT, and several other disciplines. The intriguing question for me becomes: how do they reconcile the differing underlying philosophies and approaches? Also, I want to know how lessons learned in one discipline can be applied in another.

It's an often cited empirical observation that the client does not care which method is used so long as it's an effective and efficient use of time. In that light, you will see practitioner directories organized by many different keys: geographical location, professional designation or affiliation (e.g. Licensed Clinical Social Worker or Psych.), and least often by methodology. Nevertheless, it is critical to the case planning process for practitioners to weigh the pros and cons of each method against each other. In this chapter, I invite you to look at other methods that are often positioned in the same solution space as TIR.

Robert H. Moore, Ph.D who is well-versed in Rational Emotive Behavioral Therapy (REBT) provides insights on how lessons learned from TIR can influence an REBT practice. As former director of the Rational Emotive Institute of Florida for more than a decade, he is eminently qualified on the subject. I also followed up with Windy Dryden, Ph.D, one of the leading authorities on REBT. The conversation continues with Alex Frater, a psychotherapist originally trained in REBT who now has 10 years experience with TIR.

Marian Volkman, my wife, has used both TIR and EFT in her private practice. Her experience provides interesting insights on applications for these two techniques.

In this chapter, I hope you'll discover how TIR may fit with techniques and tools that you already know about.

TIR and Rational Emotive Behavioral Therapy (REBT): A Conversation with Robert H. Moore, Ph.D

Robert H. Moore, Ph.D, 17 years director of the Institute for Rational Emotive Therapy in Florida (now the Albert Ellis Institute), is also a 16 year practitioner of Traumatic Incident Reduction (TIR). I caught up with Dr. Moore on July 13th, 2003 and discussed how TIR has affected his practice and how he integrated it with his use of Rational Emotive Behavioral Therapy (www.REBT.org)

VV: Can you give me a timeline of your career and positions?

Bob: I taught for a year right out of college. I had had a mentor by the name of A.S. Neill. He was a wonderfully maverick English schoolmaster, best known for *Summerhill* and several other books that started the "free school" movement. Neill and Carl Rogers made a huge impact on me in the early years that actually turned me from teaching to counseling. Looking back on it, they gave me my first exposure to what we now call the person-centered viewpoint which, of course, is bedrock for many of us.

But I date my main career track from 1965 when I got my Master's in counseling. This was in Pennsylvania. I worked at a hospital and a couple of mental health clinics for a few years after that while I continued graduate study at Lehigh. It was during this period that that loveable scoundrel, Albert Ellis, came into focus for me, and I began making regular training trips to his Institute in New York.

A few years later, in 1973, when Al told me there was a move on to open a branch of the Institute in Clearwater, Florida and suggested I go down and "do it." I jumped at the chance, even though I hadn't quite finished my doctoral program. My wife, Erica, was about eight months pregnant at the time, but we started packing and moved practically the day after our daughter was born.

Not in 30+ years of practice have I used a more remarkably effective clinical procedure

I took a position on the Hillsborough County (Tampa) school psychology staff to get us started and worked at the Institute evenings and weekends. I managed to get my dissertation written by 1976. Those were busy years.

In the early 1980's, I met Sarge [Dr. Frank A. Gerbode] and others who were putting Metapsychology together and it knocked my socks off. It produced such a quantum leap in my continuing education that, in 1990, I turned the Institute over to one of my REBT associates, Vince Parr, and shifted my focus almost totally to trauma-related studies and TIR. And that's pretty much where my head's been ever since.

VV: For what diagnoses have you found TIR to be most effective?

Bob: Just so you know… I don't bother too much with formal multi-axial diagnosis, unless I'm working with an insurance company that requires it. [Multi-axial is a classification based on five different dimensions first published in the *Diagnostic and Statistical Manual of Mental Disorders Third Edition*] But to speak to the spirit of your question in a nutshell… TIR is applicable to anyone whose problem has some experiential "roots". It's almost an axiom, of course, that emotional or psychological problems have roots of some sort. So one could, I suppose, use it with almost anyone. In actual practice, though, it's not entirely practical to do that.

Certainly when someone presents with anxiety or panic though, which is very common, there's rarely a better approach than TIR. There are very few anxiety problems that don't have specific historic roots. In fact, there very often is a fairly clear-cut before and after, and many clients recognize the fact. Most of them understand that they weren't born with the problem. It usually came along at some point in their lives or, occasionally, snuck up on them over time. In either case, TIR sorts it out better than any other technique I know of.

Of course anybody who presents with an actual trauma, that is who walks in and says, "Hey, I've never been the same since the day I dropped a brick on my foot" (or whatever happened in his life), is announcing his candidacy for TIR right from the start. But presentations of this sort actually are in the minority of cases, because people don't typically announce the roots of their presenting problem. They more often announce the current symptoms and/or the circumstance in which those symptoms occur. It does happen occasionally, though, that they just hand the key historic events to you on a silver platter: "I've never been the same since I was divorced", "…since the accident", "…since the rape", whatever.

Chronic anger and depression also generally have accessible historic roots, sometimes multiple losses that can be addressed with TIR. I'd say most presenting complaints involve at least some unresolved prior experience worthy of a client's review. But it's really up to the clients whether addressing background of that sort is a priority. If they're interested in it, we do it. Otherwise we do something else. That's what person-centeredness is about, isn't it? But it really is remarkable how easy it is for people to observe, on their own, the connection between the problems they're having in present time and certain unresolved past personal experience. So the truth is, it's not hard to find opportunities to use TIR. The logic of it has a lot of appeal to the layman. And the results are outstanding!

VV: Are there cases for which you wouldn't use TIR?

Bob: Well, if someone is actively abusing drugs or alcohol, that needs to be the first order of business. We don't do TIR or anything else very usefully until they've cleaned up their act chemically. Then they have become eligible for TIR or other procedures.

VV: As a practical consideration, do you find that the length of the session can be an issue?

Bob: It's more of an issue for the practitioner than it is for the client. Clients don't care much about that. They don't care whether they are in session for 30 minutes, 45 minutes, or an hour and a half, unless it's a payment problem. But of course therapists themselves have to reorganize their lives a little bit so they're comfortable giving as much time as is needed to a given client when they're using a procedure like TIR. That doesn't have to mess up their schedule. It just takes a little practice. It's not unusual for therapists just starting out with TIR to schedule people late in the day so they have some elbow room. When you get fairly adroit at it, though, it's not a big issue; you just have to be a little less than compulsive about how you clock people in and out, because that's not the main consideration.

For the client, the time consideration translates into money, and they need to know that up front. They need not only to have enough time on their schedules, they need to have the resources to be able to purchase a service that could be two or three hours this week instead of the traditional one hour. That doesn't usually turn out to be difficult to justify, though. Clients quickly catch on that their problems are finite and that the sooner we address them the sooner the job gets done.

Clients quickly catch on that their problems are finite and that the sooner we address them the sooner the job gets done

It's not as though they're going to be spending more time and money in counseling because they come more often or have longer sessions. They're going to be making progress faster and getting it over with.

That's a new concept for a lot of counselors as well as clients. Especially because in our profession so much maintenance and "management" work passes for therapy. So many things are dealt with just symptomatically that counseling often tends to go on and on with no real resolution or end point in sight. When that's the case, there's quite a big difference between seeing someone one hour a week versus two or three hours a week.

TIR and related techniques are very unlike the services that the profession has traditionally provided; those are mainly coping-oriented. There's a lot of long-term, symptom "management" going around in the professional community these days.

VV: Sounds like a there's a presupposition that the symptoms aren't really fixable?

Bob: That's right… much therapy and counseling is based on the idea that, "we'll make you clever at handling your pain (anger, anxiety, or whatever), or minimizing its intrusion into your life; we'll give you a sort of mastery over it; but when all is said and done, you're still gonna have it." That's the sort of thing that makes counseling go long term. We meet a lot of clients who've been doing that sort of thing for a long time.

VV: So they must expect that actually getting to the root of it and getting rid of it is going to take a couple of years, right?

Bob: It's kind of nice when you get someone who's come right off the street and who has never been to any therapist and has no such expectation or background. They tend to believe what you tell them. When you tell them that, "It's fixable; we can wind the clock back, and you'll be your old self again and not have to be running maintenance or remedial routines on yourself", they say, "OK, great, let's do that."

But when they've had a lot of therapy and they've used a lot of medication, and you're the fourth therapist they've seen this year, and you say a thing like that, they go into disbelief. They say, "Hey, I've been struggling with this for many years. I've seen all sorts of doctors, tried all kinds of techniques, and used every drug you can imagine. If what you're saying is true, why hasn't somebody said that to me before?"

VV: They believe that they *are* their condition?

Bob: Yeah... as though it was wired in at the factory. And you couldn't possibly help them, because nobody else they've seen ever has. So you must be an oddball. I've actually been fired by clients on day one because they were so attached to the idea that they couldn't possibly be helped that they wouldn't trust anyone who said they could. Makes you wonder what they were doing in my office, doesn't it? Anyway... off they went, I suppose, to find someone who would agree they couldn't be helped.

VV: How has the entire method that supports the use of TIR affected your practice?

Bob: It has affected it enormously, particularly my professional priorities. I had been involved in the practice of cognitive psychology for almost 20 years. So it shifted my attention dramatically. I transferred certain roles and responsibilities I had had for years to colleagues, so I could give my full attention to developing the new specialty.

In that sense, it had a remarkable effect on my professional growth and direction. In consequence of that, I developed a domestic violence program... not something that everyone involved with TIR does, of course. But at that time I was looking for trauma-related things to do. I would happily take on any kind of program or role that called for addressing trauma. I'm in a different phase of my career now. It's called... approaching retirement.

TIR had a remarkable effect on my professional growth and direction

So I've just recently passed the domestic violence program to another of my colleagues. But I'm still doing corporate crisis management, another aspect of trauma work that I've been enjoying for the last several years.

VV: Tell me something about your involvement in corporate crisis management.

Bob: There are a number of companies that specialize in helping corporate clients address unusual problems of one sort or another: threats of violence, robberies, embezzlements, catastrophic accidents, massive downsizings. They use mental health professionals with training in critical incident debriefing and trauma resolution as consultants. I represent several such companies. It's like an Employee Assistance Program focused on the most dramatic and traumatic events that can disrupt the stable operation of a company.

VV: Have you had any opportunity to use TIR in that context?

Bob: It's always phase two, but yes we get to do it or refer people to it occasionally. It's not the entry level thing to do in most situations. We usually do a simpler sort of debriefing and sorting out, identify the people who need various services and, secondarily, and then refer them to whatever services they need: triage.

VV: Can you compare and contrast TIR with Rational Emotive Behavioral Therapy?

Bob: I was a very happy practitioner of REBT (whose broader category is cognitive behavior therapy). It's a very useful construct that gives all of us personal responsibility for our emotional well-being. Clients are taught how to intervene in their own disturbance-causing belief systems. What it doesn't do, of course, is look for the historic roots or acquisition of specific, disturbance-causing beliefs. It just gives people tools with which to combat them in present time. What was delightful for me, personally, as I began to get interested in TIR, Metapsychology, and other trauma-related phenomena was finding that there is no philosophic conflict between the basic principles of the cognitive psychologies and Metaspychology. It was very gratifying to me to realize that the mechanism that puts an emotional problem in place, from the Metapsychological point of view, is consistent with what I had learned as a cognitive behaviorist. My new specialty simply expanded my understanding of the disturbance acquisition process. It got me to the core of the matter and gave me additional clinical tools.

TIR and other Metapsychology protocols, of course, are person-centered. Whereas REBT and the cognitive psychologies are not—although, quite frankly, a good practitioner of REBT needs to be. I think most of my cognitively-oriented colleagues learn that over time in their practices. A therapist can't push his personal viewpoints and judgments on clients and upstage their understanding of what's going on in their lives and get very far with REBT or any other therapy. To be effective, you really do have to see things from the client's viewpoint, use his terms for his feelings, and acknowledge him as the ultimate authority on his own experience. That makes you a better therapist no matter what clinical approach you use. But if you choose to use TIR and related approaches, you often find yourself addressing the very core elements that constructed the client's problem. At that point, you're not merely combating the problem. You're actually deconstructing it.

I find that training in TIR has made even those of my colleagues who only rarely use it better therapists. They listen better. They have less of a tendency to rely on the one-size-fits-all, disturbance-causing cognition package that is so popular in the cognitive therapies. This is why, as I say, learning something about TIR makes better therapists even of those who use mainly other techniques.

> *I find that training in TIR has made even those of my colleagues who only rarely use it better therapists*

TIR quickly plunges you into the core of a problem without your having to infer the nature and quality of the client's thinking from his emotional responses to a situation. There's nothing generic about it. It's very specific, very personal and very correct in the sense that the client, not the therapist, provides the important data: "This is how I think; this is how I feel," and so forth. Whereas, in REBT, the therapist often fills these blanks in from his own (generic) understanding of the cognitive-emotive connection. It's much more satisfying, to therapist and client alike, for these key observations to come directly from the client... for him to revise his thinking to his own satisfaction on the basis of his own, newly acquired insights.

VV: Any other Metapsychology techniques, such as Unblocking, that you use in your practice?

Bob: Yes, we run into people for whom TIR is a bit much, and they need to sort things out somewhat before they can productively address specific incidents. In such cases, there may be too much of a muddle in their lives, at present, to be identifying past traumata or even to be tracing back thematically with TIR. Unblocking is especially useful when clients' present time concerns are in a sort of disarray or confusion... when current events have their attention tied in knots. You may suspect that their personal angst is based in some historic stuff, but they're riveted on the horrible conditions of their relationships today, or getting a job tomorrow, or getting out of a problem this week. When their attention is all tied up with stuff like that, then a gentler approach is more appropriate.

> *Bottom line... you have to put your attention where the client's attention is.*

Bottom line... you have to put your attention where the client's attention is. You can't just plunge everyone straight away into addressing their old baggage with TIR. You have to get with their priorities. Unblocking is very useful for sorting things out in this connection.

For any young person who is coming along into the game, I would recommend establishing a relationship with a Metapsychology technical director, for ongoing case supervision.

[Ed. Note: Technical Director is the person in charge of planning individual curricula and session agendas. She is also responsible for ensuring that the facilitators are doing their jobs correctly, and she makes sure they get help promptly if they get into difficulties].

TIR and REBT:
A Conversation with Windy Dryden, Ph.D.

Windy Dryden, Ph.D., professor of psychotherapy at Goldsmith's College of the University of London, shares his viewpoint on TIR in relation to REBT. Professor Dryden who is author, co-author, or editor of over 130 books as well as book chapters and journal articles is a recognized authority in his field. He is interviewed here by Henry Whitfield, a certified TIR facilitator and trainer in London, England.

HW: What drew you to attending a TIR training workshop?

WD: I was always very appreciative and admiring of Bob Moore's contribution to REBT. He is a very creative and deep thinker about REBT processes. I'm not sure if I recall exactly, but I am sure that the reason I became interested in TIR was that Bob got me interested in some way, and as part of a course I was arranging at the Centre for Stress Management – (I think it was an advanced diploma in REBT), a weekend course – I believe it was by Frank A. Gerbode and some guy from Holland, gave us, and I attended that course on TIR. I don't necessarily work with post-traumatic stress disorder myself. So it seemed to me that it brought together some interesting concepts. I gave Lori Beth and Stephen Bisbey an opportunity to contribute to a series that I was editing on brief therapy, and they did one on PTSD, using TIR *[Brief Therapy for Post Traumatic Stress Disorder: Traumatic Incident Reduction and Related Techniques,* ISBN 0471975672].

HW: In Bob Moore's interview by Victor Volkman [contained in this section] he mentions the importance of person-centeredness, even in REBT usage. To what extent would you agree or disagree with that?

WD: Well, I don't quite understand what he meant by that, but what I think he means is: one, understanding the person from their own frame of reference, and two endeavoring to help them to change within their frame of reference – rather than just being indifferent to that frame of reference and trying to teach them the REBT model without reference to their frame of reference.

HW: And you would agree with that?

WD: Yes, I would.

HW: In the second year of your Masters of Science program in REBT, TIR is offered as an option. Could you describe how TIR fits into the framework of REBT?

WD: The main goal of REBT is to encourage people to think rationally about events and act healthily, and emote functionally. Now that is normally done by targeting the irrational beliefs that underpin the processes pointed out by Bob Moore in the interview you mentioned. But there are more ways of skinning a cat. It seems to me that by the repetitive viewing process – that seems to me to be a key feature of TIR – that the person can actually change beliefs as a result of going through this process, and therefore I see it, in a sense as a more indirect way of helping people to think rationally, rather that directly targeting and having people to change directly and actively their irrational beliefs.

> *It seems to me that by the repetitive viewing process...*
> *that the person can actually change beliefs as a result of going through this process*

HW: In the second level of TIR training there is a method you use for targeting specific irrational beliefs. For example, if your client clearly has the irrational belief 'All men are evil', you give them a repetitive exercise that consists of getting the client to purposely imagine the reality of their actual belief, as well as its opposite (elicited from the client). So within the school of TIR you do target very specific beliefs as well. Going back to Bob Moore's article, what other impressions did you have?

WD: It was interesting, because although I knew he was moving towards TIR from REBT, I didn't realize he had given up the Institute for REBT in Florida. As I say, I have a lot of time for Bob Moore as a practitioner and a thinker, and I think that if he is pointing to something for its effectiveness, I would certainly pick up my ears and listen. Now the reality of choosing a life where one teaches, trains, sees patients and writes, one cannot pursue actively in detail, virtually anything. So although I might be interested in exploring TIR further, that would mean something else would have to give, and therefore that would kind of be quite difficult. But certainly I would be interested to learn more from you, Henry – about what opportunities there are for TIR training. If I can be helpful in actually promoting that, I'd be pleased to.

HW: I'm finding it really interesting comparing the two [TIR and REBT].

TIR in a Psychotherapy Practice:
A Conversation with Alex Frater

Alex D. Frater is psychotherapist, Certified Forensic Trauma Specialist, and clinical hypnotherapist. He has been practicing in Campbelltown, Australia since 1986. Originally schooled in Rational Emotive Behavior Therapy (REBT), he now uses Traumatic Incident Reduction (TIR) and Metapsychology techniques a great deal in his practice. He is also trained in Thought Field Therapy (TFT) and other techniques. I spoke with Alex on November 14th, 2003 about how he uses TIR in several aspects of his private practice.

VV: What was your practice like prior to learning TIR and how did it change?

Alex: By the early 1990's, my workload had consistently reached 70 hours a week (Monday/Friday, 8 am to 10 pm) and had started to encroach on my weekend. I found that some of my patients would get better using REBT, and while it helped a lot of patients, some it didn't. I started looking around the world for different ways of handling trauma. I read Robert Moore's paper [see Chapter 1] and spoke with him and that inspired me to get TIR training in the USA.

The whole idea behind learning TIR was hopefully to: (1) decrease my workload and, (2) to be more efficient with my patients. I became much more efficient with my patients, but it did nothing for my workload. Because I was being more efficient, it meant that I was getting more referrals. In the area here, probably 18-20 medical practitioners use me and 85% of my practice is medically referred. In the early stages, the local psychiatrist had used me quite extensively. I nearly always had 5 or 6 of his patients in my practice. I found TIR certainly much more efficient, but it was my fault that I wanted to reduce my workload and I did nothing about that. I think I can say that anybody that I used TIR on for various traumas was successful. It's certainly extremely valuable in making me more efficient and it keeps my practice rolling along very, very well.

One of the things I do in using TIR, because I've been trained in REBT (which is cognitive), I spend the first session doing a complete assessment. The second session, I spend an hour showing the concepts of REBT. I spend two or three sessions on that and give them handouts. When I first came back from Menlo Park, I started to do TIR straight off. I found that I would get better results if I put it off a bit and did some basic work. That's seems to help people a lot.

VV: Patient education?

Alex: Strictly an education. I give them a relaxation tape, handouts, and homework to do. You put them down that path and I don't ever attempt TIR, even if I know exactly what they came for, until we've done three or four sessions. I just find that works very well.

VV: The increase in effectiveness is basically working through traumas in a shorter period of time?

Alex: It's more efficient and shortens the time. I get a lot of motor vehicle accident (MVA) victims, policemen with PTSD, rape victims, and marriage problems.

VV: What elements, practices, or beliefs of the traditional psychotherapy model did you have to give up?

Alex: I've really given up nothing; I've just brought TIR in and it forms part of my practice.

VV: I was kind of just fishing for the 50 minute hour there, but you didn't take the bait!

Alex: With TIR you have to leave it open ended, but this is not the real world. I can't be booking out 3 to 4 hours to do TIR. I've found that only on one occasion have I actually exceeded 2 hours. When I'm doing TIR, I always book out 2 hours. I generally get them done in 90 to 105 minutes.

VV: I think 90 minutes for TIR is pretty typical from what I've heard.

Alex: There was one woman I saw who had a case of multiple rape. We did the usual 2 hours and came to an end point. She suddenly rang me later and had different stuff coming up, but I was going away for a week the next day. I said to her, "You take a nap this afternoon, if you can. Come down at 10:15 pm and we'll do it." We ran it for 3 hours; it was 1:30 am when I left my office. That's the only one who ran much further past 90 minutes.

VV: How do you prepare a client who is not yet ready for TIR?

Alex: I explain it to them what it's all about; I have some handouts and I show them what it is. They've all said, "Yes, I think that's a good idea." I explain to them why we have to go back earlier sometimes. For example I often have people that come in from an MVA with PTSD or phobias from it and you go fix that one, but you find that there is a car accident 20 years ago that still isn't resolved. But they'll assure me that it's fixed. Then I say "Yes OK, then. We'll just go in and have a look at this one." Invariably the earlier incident isn't fixed when we get to it.

A typical example was a lady who was injured at work and she was coming to me because she was having panic attacks driving to the hospital to get her pay (because she was on disability). She was having panic attacks going to the bank, the shopping centers, and so on. I was doing TIR and asked, "Is there anything previous?" She said, "No, no, it just started since I've been going to the hospital." So I started doing that incident, she improved some but didn't get completely better. I said, "What is that first thing you feel when you're driving down the road?" She explained, "There is a feeling that I have in the top of my stomach." I said "Does that feeling relate to anything earlier?" She said, "No, no." I said, "Just think about it a moment." Then she said, "When I was 17 or 18, I was involved in a car accident where it tipped upside down." She was trapped in the car until the tow truck came, but she said, "That's OK; look I don't have any problem with that." So I said. "All right then, well let's just take a look at that. It might lead somewhere else." We addressed that and she actually had a panic attack in my office. We fixed that, and no more panic attacks.

That's what I find about TIR. People come to me with anxiety or panic attacks and I say to them that it only comes from two places: burnout at work and traumas. I find that people who are burned out at work develop the anxieties and major depressions from it. Or else it comes from a trauma and we go looking for something that happened. I've found this to be true without exception. That's where I've found TIR to be very, very effective. With REBT it might take months to find that; you may never find it. That's what I found before I learned TIR. Actually, panic attacks and anxiety, I pick them up very quickly. There are a couple of doctors I work with who as soon as the patient mentions the word anxiety, they say, "You better go see Alex Frater, he'll fix you up quick."

I get some patients arriving with very, very bad panic attacks. Often they relate to incidents 15 to 20 years ago. That's not uncommon. I had a lady who basically couldn't leave the house most of the time. She said it all started when she was driving along and saw some red lights and had a massive anxiety attack. She had a feeling in her leg; that's where it started. It turned out she was listening to the radio and actually laughing at some item on the radio when she felt the feeling and went into a very severe panic attack. They had to call an ambulance because she couldn't drive at that time. Tracking that back, she was in her mid-40s when she went to school to see her son onstage at a school play. Her son made a bit of an ass of himself, everyone laughed, and she got embarrassed. She remembered that feeling then. We handled that with TIR and she's never had any more panic attacks. Up until then the panic attacks had been getting progressively worse, but they were all tied to that incident.

Using REBT you basically don't find that. Because the underlying incident hasn't been found, they change their thinking a lot, but they still get panic attacks. That's where I find TIR absolutely magic. People come in with anxiety attacks, and they're very bad by the time we get to them, but we fix them. Even with car accidents you find that there's one that happened years and years ago and they'll tell you its fixed and of course they believe it's fixed. But when you go back and do it, the emotions are there. It works very, very well there.

We handled that with TIR and she's never had any more panic attacks.

VV: What are the criteria you would use to select TIR as the method to use on with a client with anxiety, depression, or other PTSD symptoms?

Alex: Certainly if people are having flashbacks or intrusive thoughts, then I get into TIR by the 4th or 5th visit. With anxieties, I find that they are burned out at work or they are being affected by a trauma. Particularly with anxiety and depression, quite often I do REBT when they are starting to improve, but if it's not really going well then we start doing TIR.

VV: Would you recommend TIR to other mental health professionals?

Alex: I'd certainly recommend TIR to other mental health professionals, simply because it's so efficient and thorough. Just about two years ago, I brought Gerald French over and had him teach advanced TIR to me, my daughter, granddaughter, and another psychiatrist. ["Advanced TIR" refers to the second level training. See Appendix C.]

On another occasion, I had a patient come to me to deal with an MVA. We fixed her up and she said, "I have a feeling of helplessness. I've been to three psychiatrists and about five people like you and they can't fix it." I said, "OK then, do you remember a time when you first had it?" She said, "Alex, I have it everyday and I'm on medication for it." She said, "I'll tell you when I remember one anyway. I was 13 and my father had a heart attack, but believe me that's not the problem." I said "OK, well let's go back and address that and then we can go earlier." After three sessions, we reached an end point and she's never, never had those feelings again. I asked her to ring me up six months later and she said those feelings had never returned.

TIR in a Mental Health Clinic Setting:
a Conversation with Patricia Furze, MSW, RSW

VV: Tell me a little bit about your background, schooling, and work experience.

PF: I'm a social worker and received my Master's in Social Work at the University of Toronto (1986). I started off in my career with a Bachelor's of Social Work which was combined with a Sociology degree at McMaster University (1983). Most recently, I've become a Certified TIR Trainer. I had decided early on in my teenage years that I wanted to be a probation officer. I wanted to work with families of youths who were in the criminal justice system. I was fortunate enough to get a placement in the area of probation. I was an Assistant Probation Officer for a couple of summers. It was very exciting and it also made me aware that I wanted to work at strengthening families and supporting children.

After I completed my Bachelor's of Social Work, I worked for the Children's Aid Society in Ontario (Canada). I worked there for a couple years and had an amazing experience with families. It was a generalist position, so it allowed me to do a variety of interesting work. This was a child protection agency so our mandate was child protection and safety. As a generalist I was involved in protection investigations, placement of children in foster homes, group homes and residential care, adoption work and strengthening families through the provision of parenting groups, individual and family counseling. It was a resource poor area so we also had the opportunity to create new programs. I was involved in creating a play therapy program with a family therapist and a professor from a nearby University. The tragedy in the lives of those children and parents and their resilience propelled me to pursue the goal of becoming a therapist who could assist people in transforming life's challenges into meaningful lives.

I returned to school and completed my Master's degree specializing in children and families. After graduation, I stayed in Toronto, Ontario and began working for a Children's Mental Health agency for the next 10 years. I was intensively involved with street kids for about 8 years and developed a model for working with them. We provided various therapies to address their mental health needs and develop skills. The goal was to assist them to sustain employment and manage relationships. This highly traumatized population taught me that trauma is replicated in all systems that an individual engages with. As a result we intervened to create and support healthy contexts with these youths to create meaningful change. It was an amazing period of growth for me in terms of understanding trauma and the basic needs that unite us as people in general. I also did consultations with adolescents, between ages 13 to 19, with emotional and severe behavioral problems in our two residential programs.

In 1992, during the fall of communism, my reputation for reconnecting youth led me to be selected to work in Hungary with a team consulting to an orphanage. We developed community programs and assisted youth to create a sense of family beyond the orphanage.

About 8 years ago, I went to work at Markham Stouffville Hospital. They were opening a child and family clinic in mental health. They needed a team of people to actually develop the program and I was fortunate to be involved in the creation of it. It's a small community hospital that has a philosophy of empowerment for the frontline staff. Basically the unit was self-operating with the support of management. It has been a really exciting place to work and a wonderful clinic.

The team consists of a part-time psychiatrist, child psychologist, and two and half positions for social work. It's a really small clinic but it does amazing work. Over the past five years I've worked with my colleagues in creating a model that incorporated TIR. We've used TIR to assist when people were blocked by trauma, in order to get them past those blocks to support the child. We did this whether they were aware or unaware of what was blocking them.

VV: Can you describe to me the steps that a patient entering the hospital would go through and how TIR works within the total treatment plan?

PF: The clinic is an outpatient mental health clinic in a community hospital in a rapidly growing area north of the city of Toronto. The referrals are all from doctors who have a connection with the hospital. The doctors make the initial referral of the client, often with a question about severe behavioral problems or possible mental health concerns that need identification and treatment. It could be disruptive disorders, anxiety disorders, depression, or Post-Traumatic Stress Disorder. It's usually quite serious and often times with children who have been suffering for some time. The physician offers support in the ongoing care and connects with this clinic to request assessment and treatment to address the presenting problem. We serve children from toddler-hood all the way up to their 19th birthday.

The referral is by phone and usually sent to the social work staff for assessment. The social work staff connects during an office interview with the family and child and assesses what the needs are. At times, the child psychologist will also do those initial screenings. If she's running a particular depression group for example, she might screen for that particular depression group and assess needs. At that point, the person who assessed with the family would start working with the family, which allows for continuity of care. If it was determined at the time of assessment or afterwards that the child needed a psychological assessment regarding diagnosis of anxiety, PTSD, or disruptive disorder, then a referral would be made to the psychologist. The other possibility would be a need for a psychiatric assessment in order for there to be some medication or diagnosis. There is a lot of interaction between the therapists and mental health professionals in order to support the individual.

Primarily the people identifying the need for TIR are the social workers. For example, they may decide that a person could benefit from individual therapy and family therapy. They may work for some time with them trying to address the presenting issues with Cognitive Behavioral Therapy. In that work they may find that despite their best intentions and the hard work of the family, they are running into certain blocks and the individual isn't able to get past those blocks. Or they may find that they are able to resolve some things but they aren't able to maintain that level of resolution of the presenting problems over time. We would encounter parents or children who seem unable to integrate new skills despite their understanding and commitment to make changes.

In those situations, the social workers flag those particular patients and speak to me (since I provide TIR for the group). We talk about the possibility of offering TIR and presenting it to the family and the individual involved. We talk to the family about the lack of progress and try to help them identify where the "stuckness" is associated in their life and find other times where they might have felt similarly. As a result, often times the children, youth and/or parents became aware of something that may have happened in the past that was operating in the present. Through that recognition they are often interested in doing a piece of work to resolve that stuck point in order to make progress again and gain relief from the problematic behaviors. Most of the time people are very interested in feeling better and gaining relief from what's happening. As a result, they're very frustrated by their lack of progress. So, offering TIR at this time is often really supportive. Initially, they often feel ambivalent and wary because it's hard to confront difficult issues. But usually they are very much more interested in seeing what they can do support their child. This has been one way the need for TIR was identified and offered.

Alternately, during intake it will be noted that someone has had a trauma that seemed to be underlying the presenting problem. For example, someone could identify a loss and be experiencing complicated grief and therefore unable to get past the loss. Some individuals will tip you off by saying "a part of me died that day" or "I just haven't been myself since that person died" or "I haven't been able to even think about that person." Another typical scenario is a parent with a child who had a very serious childhood illness such as leukemia or another hard to diagnose illness. The child got hospitalized; the parents were really scared and didn't know what they were dealing with for a long time. It created a trauma for that family and then life carried on. The disease was identified and the child received treatment, but what lingered was the impact of that initial period of prolonged uncertainty and the fear that the child might die. These experiences could have been part of what is identified in the family's history. What currently is going on seems to replicate the fear of loss and feeling overwhelmed and anxious. We often see that in trauma, it gets replicated in all kinds of different ways. In such cases, my colleagues who were able to identify these patterns and the underlying trauma that was operating in the present refer to me to provide TIR on the unresolved trauma.

The initial therapist picks up the case after the completion of the TIR work. Many families are positively affected by the TIR work: they become interested in doing work about maintaining good and healthy boundaries, social skills, life skills, parenting skills and coping strategies. Parents and children are able to integrate new skills into their repertoire after the charge from the underlying trauma has been released. This dynamic is really important for organizations to understand, because those individuals cost programs significantly in time and resources, since the unresolved trauma can block the integration of new learning. In addition, the "stuckness" for the individual can be demoralizing, frustrating and create hopelessness. Family members can blame one another for the lack of progress leading to further relationship breakdown.

Over the years I have encountered many people who were unable to sustain growth despite being all kinds of skill building and cognitive therapies, understanding the problem, and being very motivated. They couldn't seem to maintain the growth that they were experiencing. And yet, many times, TIR would eliminate the problem. Often if someone had had a lot of work prior to TIR in terms of skill-building, TIR would bring it together in a very different way and they would be bolstered by that earlier work. So whether it came before or after, the skill-building could be integrated better after TIR had been completed. It seems that people's amnesic barriers become dissolved and it allows them more fluid access to their internal resources and as a result more stability emotionally. It's very exciting. I believe that adding the TIR approach to an existing clinic helps to shorten treatment time and costs and strengthens effectiveness and relief for individuals. It can help to address the "revolving door" that can plague mental health organizations.

VV: Part of the Metapsychology theory is that when you release the traumas you have more free attention to do the things you want to do.

PF: Yes, in fact we use that theory to educate the clients. That's one of the things I talk about with people about the benefits of pursuing TIR. One of the ways we did it was through identifying the parenting styles. Often times we were dealing with families where the parents were traumatized and the kids were traumatized or where parents were traumatized and the kids were secondarily traumatized by the parenting style used. A traumatized person can use an extreme parenting style: it can be either overly close or overly distant. That parent finds it difficult to be consistent and to be able to be close to the child while holding them accountable. They would get overly close to the child and over-identify and, therefore, not be able to hold them accountable and/or they would get so angry and distant that they would be harsh and ineffective.

Sometimes we talk about holding the children accountable in a loving way and helping parents to identify the stuck points around that experience. Other times we talk about the impact of the child's trauma on that parent's parental behaviors. For example, childhood leukemia treatment takes five years and can result in secondary trauma for the parent. So we look in both areas where the parent's history can impact the child and the child's history can impact the parent. We have also encountered situations where the child had an accident that a parent witnessed and therefore they had their own secondary trauma around it.

Trauma can compel us to act in a certain way, often unconsciously. If we make that more conscious, we find that people are more interested in doing the work. Also what excites them is the potential to do a chunk of work in a one-session format which allowed them to have resolution inside the single session. This is absolutely why people were more interested in TIR rather than pursuing a series of other interventions. They are more able to see themselves completing a chunk of work at once rather than attending sessions repetitively.

VV: Did you have to do anything special to account for the unknown length of sessions in this environment?

PF: To some extent, yes. I typically set aside a three hour block for these appointments. That would allow most people to complete the work. If it needed to go a little longer, I would set it up at the end of the day or over lunch. My commitment to the person was to complete it within that timeframe. I do get a sense of the time needed after the first TIR session. The hospital is publicly funded through the [Canadian] Medicare system. As a result we all share the responsibility of providing sound, cost effective services. TIR is an approach that is effective and can shorten treatment times. The longer sessions are offset by the effectiveness of the approach.

VV: Did you have any resistance from management about using TIR in this approach?

PF: I got support for using TIR and other approaches because of my competence and because the impact of the work was positive and people got better. I think that larger institutions tend to be more conservative. There isn't as much research on TIR as there is on some other approaches. Management was appropriately cautious but was very supportive of my work. They saw that people were being incredibly helped rather than harmed. I experienced a lot of trust from management for my work. They saw me supporting this new unit. I was fortunate that my own good reputation as an ethical client-centered therapist allowed me to do something atypical for a hospital setting. Markham Stouffville Hospital is very patient care oriented and succeeds in providing excellent care and service to their patients. They are committed to making sure that patients are not harmed and that each visit is a good one. I believe that we proved over time that our patients were pleased with their service so it didn't become an issue for management.

VV: What kind of advice would you have for someone establishing a similar program in a hospital or similar setting?

PF: I would definitely support them getting training in TIR and really understanding and practicing it before incorporating it into a unit. What happened for me was that I was able to take it and work with people in my caseload. Once I became aware and proficient about when and where to apply it, I could work with my team and introduce them to it. I could educate them into identifying underlying trauma and the best way to assess it. I explained how to approach it, how to understand the associational chain and teach it to patients and so on. My thorough understanding enabled me to communicate with my team and promoted teamwork in supporting the patients coming in. I am an approved TIR level one trainer and am also willing to consult to and support individuals and organizations seeking to establish a similar program into an existing health care practice.

VV: How does TIR change when you are working with children?

PF: With children I look at the level of their attention span. I find that the sessions tend to be shorter with children, generally speaking. There isn't a significant difference in how I do TIR. I take a lot of time in teaching them what to expect. As with adults, I talk about the process of TIR work and the feelings, thoughts, and sensations that arise. I find this helps children and adults a lot by knowing what to expect. I find it a similar process for each. I'm just more cautious about the age of the child and their ability to sustain focused attention.

VV: Do you find the end points to be similar or different between children and adults?

PF: You know it really can be similar or different. What I find is that there are very wise children who reveal incredible insights. There are some parents who never have an insight they can identify, and vice-versa. It really depends on the individual: I don't find that age is the determinant; rather each person comes with his or her own level of ability to verbalize, to release things and to be insightful. Sometimes I see differences between male and female in terms of expression. I find that people are so unique that they each bring their own abilities to the fore. One of the most exciting things about TIR is that it's like a journey that unfolds and you just don't know how it'll look at the end. The other thing that has been the most exciting is in hearing the person's process you can actually see where an anxiety disorder began or where the tendency towards depression existed. It's almost as if it gets decoded as the individual goes through the session and it's most instructive as to how mental health does and doesn't work for people.

In terms of education for the therapist, it's a phenomenal experience. I believe everyone -- all students -- should actually learn TIR so they can learn about mental health through that process because it is absolutely more instructive than anything you get at school.

TIR and EFT: A Practitioner's Perspective
A Conversation with Marian Volkman

VV: How long have you been doing TIR and EFT respectively?

Marian: I've used TIR since the very beginning of it because I was lucky enough to meet Dr. Frank A. Gerbode when he was developing it in the early 1980's. I've been using EFT since about 1993. [Ed Note: Marian is a Certified TIR Trainer, Metapsychology Facilitator, and on the board of the TIR Association]

VV: Is EFT similar to any other techniques that other people may be familiar with?

Marian: First came TFT[1] (Thought Field Therapy) developed by Roger Callahan. Then Gary H. Craig developed EFT (Emotional Freedom Technique) out of his experiences with that. These two approaches are different than other trauma treatments because they involve tapping acupuncture meridians. It's a really different approach than any of the cognitive exposure techniques where you're actually having the person look at what happened.

I prefer to use TIR when I can, rather than one of the tapping techniques, because TIR allows the person to really process the incident emotionally, cognitively, and psycho-physiologically. Then he usually comes to some sort of realization as part of the end point. Sometimes he just says "I feel better about that now and I'm done with it" and that's all there is to it. Often there is a realization, because as you mentioned earlier in this book, people tend to make decisions in time of stress. They are trying to understand what is happening or to prevent that experience from happening again. When you embed a decision in all that pain and stress, it stays there pretty unobserved because that traumatic experience is outside of normal experience.

Thought Field Therapy (TFT) is a systematic method of treating psychological distress using the energy meridians of the body. The client is asked to think about (or get in touch with) the problem (e.g, anxiety, anger, guilt, phobia, trauma, depression, panic, etc.) and then tap several times in a precise sequence on specific acupuncture points at various places on the body. Usually the client is also asked to hum a tune, count out loud, move their eyes in various directions and repeat certain affirmations while tapping and thinking about the distressing emotion

---

In TIR, as the person goes through the effort and emotion and everything to do with the trauma, sooner or later the thought or decision that's embedded in there comes to the surface and at that point often the person has a realization. That's the really exciting part of TIR; that's why I prefer to use it.

There are times though, when you don't have time to do TIR. For example, the client is going to take a big test and you don't have enough time to go looking for all the traumas which may relate to why she has test anxiety. Or she is going to have surgery soon and you might have time to do one or two TIR sessions, but you don't have enough time to do address everything that might be related to this situation. You can still give her a technique from the tapping therapies (and I use EFT just because it's very simple to teach people) that the client can use on her own anytime to reduce anxiety and self-soothe.

Another instance to consider is when the client may be unwilling to look at the traumas themselves. There are some people who simply don't want to do that, at least early in their work with a TIR facilitator. Tapping techniques can be used to relieve some of the emotional content there. Another use for tapping techniques occurs when you have one of the more global things, such as depression or anxiety—those rarely come from a single trauma. Sometimes they do come from one trauma, but most often they are a part of a big package deal. Panic attacks can be similar too. Sometimes you can get lucky and you can contact one traumatic incident, or sequence of related incidents, that causes panic attacks and clean it up with one TIR session. Often there are a great number of sequences of traumatic incidents that have added up to the point where it's the straw that breaks the camel's back and then the person starts having panic attacks. Sometimes you're going to have to do more work to get that to go away entirely. I like to give my clients EFT to use between sessions if they have something like anxiety or frequent panic attacks so they have something to calm it down between sessions until it is gone completely.

Another good instance of when I use EFT is for a major addiction or bad habit that a person has. You can certainly use TIR to help a person get rid of the traumas that contribute to why he practices an addiction. Usually an addictive behavior is a solution to something else: it's a form of self-medication, a way to make life seem tolerable; it's a solution to something else. You can use TIR to address the underlying circumstances and cause of the underlying addiction, but you really have to have the person out of an active phase of his addiction to use TIR effectively. EFT is something the person could use to bring down those addictive urges and gain control of the situation. It's just a very useful technique for clients to use on their own.

VV: Are you saying that EFT could be similar to running a thematic approach from a physiological point of view?

Marian: No, I wouldn't say that at all, because you're not actually *addressing* anything the way we do with TIR and Metapsychology techniques. Nobody really knows why these tapping techniques work. My theory of why they work is that every time we think a thought it makes an actual neural pathway in the brain. Most thoughts we can think about or not think about, as we choose. We can say "Oh, it's time to start thinking about the taxes," and then, "No, I don't want to think about that right now." We can push that aside; we are able to do that. But if you get something that is embedded somehow or it's very deeply grooved in then the person can't even get close to that thought without going right there and being stuck in it. So why electro-convulsive "therapy" works when it seems to work (and I don't advocate it at all), is that it does a pattern-interrupt of all those neural pathways. So instead of the person having to think that old thought, they can think a new thought.

The interesting thing is that tapping the acupuncture meridians seems to have a similar effect. It does a pattern-interrupt of what the person was stuck in and it just makes it go away without the violence of something like electric shock. That can be very valuable but I still do prefer TIR. When we use TIR whether it's Basic (one incident) or Thematic (a series of incidents connected by a feeling we call a *theme*), the client gets a sense of mastery from that. She's actually gone in there and faced the lions. She comes out the other side and might be tired, but she's often triumphant that she's gotten through this thing. She often has realizations, relief, mastery, knowledge, and certainty of what happened. She says, "Now I know what happened!"

Most often in a traumatic incident, too much happens too fast. There's impact and the person is not able to track with what happened. In TIR, you enable him to take the time to look at all the aspects of it. At the point where he can really see it and say "Yes, that's what happened" then a lot of confusion and uncertainty comes off. You don't get that in the tapping techniques. The client says "I have this feeling of panic" using a tapping technique can cause it to go away fairly quickly. It may stay gone or it may come back another time.

VV: Are there are any cases in which you would use EFT to prepare a client who is not ready for TIR?

Marian: Yes, if it seems as if she need a good first-aid type of thing. If she is chronically anxious or suffering in the moment and she is not ready for TIR for any of a number of reasons, I would teach EFT to that client.

VV: Almost like a locational technique (from Metapsychology)?

Marian: You could call it that, but it doesn't work the same way. In a locational technique, you're saying "Come into contact with the physical world." You're bringing the person into contact with the physical world by having him look at or touch various objects in the environment and that extroverts attention. The tapping things are a different kettle of fish. You're having him tap on various points that are acupuncture meridians on his own body.

VV: What are the major differences between TIR and EFT? You talked about cognitive vs. non-cognitive, anything else?

Marian: There are a number of TIR practitioners who also make use of EFT or TFT, but we definitely do not consider the tapping techniques to be part of TIR or Metapsychology. They don't fit within the framework of being person-centered. (Though I should note here that people trained in TIR who have come to value the person-centered model, usually tend to do other methods such as TFT, EFT. EMDR, etc., in a more person-centered way than their originators might. That's just my observation.) In Metapsychology and TIR, it's the person's experience that rules the day; that is what the session is all about. In the tapping techniques, if you came to me and said "I feel really panicky and I have only 30 minutes before a job interview, what can I do?" I'd say "I'll teach you this and you can use it to calm yourself down." But you wouldn't necessarily have any realization or be facing up to anything. It's more like the technique is doing it *to* you. With TIR, when you're the client, you are *employing* TIR in order to do this piece of work of getting through some traumatic incident (or series of incidents) in order to get resolution. You're doing the cognitive work in TIR.

VV: How long-lasting are the results of EFT vs. TIR?

Marian: In TIR, if you address something and you take it to an end point, then that piece is done. Sometimes you have a complex incident with a lot of aspects to it and sometimes a person will bring up the same incident on another sequence. Addressing "a terrible feeling of fear" for example may bring up Grandmother's death. The child knows something's wrong and nobody is telling her what's happening and she has a terrible feeling of fear. Later on you could be addressing a "sinking feeling in your stomach" and she goes through a series of incidents. At some point she says. "Oh, when I was 4 and my Grandmother was dying and I didn't know what was happening, but I knew something bad was happening, I had that sinking feeling." Then we deal with that aspect of that incident. Sooner or later, there's going to be nothing left of that incident, even if there are a number of aspects to it. Each piece of work, when you do it with TIR, when it's done, it's done. You really get completions.

With EFT, it can happen that something goes away completely from a person tapping it once or many times. I have often seen a good result occur that was not permanent. What it's really good for, in my opinion, is giving the person the ability to take a feeling down when they cannot cope with that feeling and they don't want that feeling at that time and they don't have time to deal with it in another way.

There was one client who had a horrible motion sickness and she couldn't find any incident that had any bearing on it. She could just barely stand driving a car herself, but could not stand being the passenger. The only traumatic incidents she could see were the times she had this feeling. She had used TIR successfully in dealing with other issues, but she was not interested in using TIR on this particular thing. She just wanted it to go away. I taught her the tapping and we took the feeling down to nothing. So then I said "OK, well let's go in the car." She said "Whoa!" So we did some more tapping, but it didn't take very long. She said "OK, let's try it." We got in the car and I proceeded to drive. As I pulled out of the driveway she said, "Normally I'd be on the floor by this point!" We went around the block and she said it was fine. I made sure she understood the technique and she was able to use it a number of times on her own when that came up again, but as I understand it, she didn't need to use it too many times more. That was a circumstance in which a client didn't want to use TIR, but just wanted it to go away, and it did go away.

Certainly my preference is to use TIR when possible, and most of my clients who are really familiar with TIR and have had a good success with it would prefer to use TIR also. There are times when tapping is a great fit for the client.

TIR and EMDR: Notes from the Field
By Victor R. Volkman

There seem to be nearly as many opinions as there are practitioners trained in both TIR and EMDR. Some greatly favor one technique over the other, but I looked for people who routinely use both methods in order to get a balanced view. Among these practitioners the consensus emerges that both can be excellent tools for the resolution of trauma.

While there are important differences between the two methods, they are similar in providing the client access to traumatic material and the opportunity to both observe this material and to find links between one traumatic incident and another, though they go about this in different ways. Both subjects contain safeguards for the client. In TIR they are the session protocol (as taught in the Communication Exercises in the first workshop) and the Rules of Facilitation. In EMDR they are the specific Eight Phase Protocol as well as the fact that EMDR is done within the context of therapy.

One practitioner mentioned that she prefers EMDR partly because of the fact that the physical component is included in EMDR by asking the client, "Where do you feel it in your body?" Another felt that TIR is better for more fragile clients, as Francine Shapiro in her original book on EMDR, cautions that clients doing EMDR need a support system of friends and family to, "nurture them through any between-session disturbances."

In TIR, the practitioner expects to almost always reach a definite point of resolution on the material being addressed within a single session. This is aided by the fact that the process of tracing links between traumatic incidents is more tightly contained in TIR. Both subjects, TIR and EMDR, aim for the full resolution of trauma which tends to connect the two subjects in the minds of the public, despite significant differences between them.

With practitioners who frequently use both methods, the choice often comes down to the client's preference. Some clients "hate" the repetition inherent in TIR. Other clients "hate" the eye movement or the bilateral stimulation (tapping on alternate knees) of EMDR. Even clients who do not actually hate anything in the two methods often have a decided preference for one or the other.

Interestingly enough, practitioners who feel strongly that one method is preferable to the other also tend to believe that their preferred method goes deeper, or is more thorough than the other. Practitioners who use both methods on a regular basis do not express this belief, but unanimously express appreciation in having a variety of tools to effectively address trauma with their clients.

Comparing TIR and Other Techniques

By Frank A. Gerbode, M.D.

As I explained in Chapter 1, up until recently, there have been two main approaches to PTSD:

- Coping techniques.

- Cathartic techniques

Some therapists give their clients specific *in vivo* ("in life") methods for counteracting or coping with the symptoms of PTSD. These clients learn to adapt to, to live with, their PTSD condition. They learn, for instance, how to avoid situations that trigger them, how to distract themselves when they are triggered, how to breathe into a paper bag to avoid hyperventilation. Women who have been assaulted or raped may take self-defense classes.

Others encourage their clients to release their feelings, to have a catharsis. The idea is that past traumas generate a certain amount of negative energy or "emotional charge," and the therapist's task is to work with the client to release this charge so that it does not manifest itself as aberrant behavior, negative feelings and attitudes, or psychosomatic conditions. This notion, derived from Freud's libido theory, is a "hydraulic" theory of psychopathology. Charge generated in past traumas theoretically exerts a pressure towards its expression. If not expressed in affect appropriate to the experienced trauma, it must express itself in inappropriate ways. Therapists espousing this theory use methods such as implosion therapy (flooding), psychodrama, and focus groups to help the client release the charge.

Coping methods and cathartic techniques may help a person to feel better temporarily, but they don't actually improve the client's stability. Clients feel better temporarily after coping or having a catharsis, but the basic charge remains in place, and shortly thereafter they feel a need for more therapy. In most cathartic work, the presence of an affective discharge indicates that the client has contacted a past trauma and worked it through, but not that she has eliminated it. Coping strategies don't provide a permanent solution either. A week, a day, or an hour later, some random environmental stimulus such as a loud noise or the sound of helicopters can trigger anew the same charge.

TIR is an exposure technique since the point of TIR is to help the viewer become more aware of the traumatic incident. Exposure theorists rely on a desensitization model, in contradistinction to TIR's person-centered model, but the two techniques converge on the need for repeated exposure to the trauma.

There are certain features of TIR that do not form part of the Direct Therapeutic Exposure (DTE) approach, however:

a. TIR embodies the concept of an end point, with certain particular characteristics. DTE's "end point" occurs when the client feels little or no distress as a result of confronting the incident. In TIR, we usually await the onset of positive emotion, not just the absence of negative emotion. Plus there are the other components of an end point, as described in TIR: insight, extroversion, and frequently the expression of what the intention was that the viewer made in the incident.

b. TIR is stricter about not permitting *any* input from the facilitator concerning detail or content of the incident. In DTE, the therapist reads a script to the viewer, and the viewer goes through at the therapist's pace. In TIR the viewer confronts only what she feels comfortable confronting on any particular run-through. Exposure in TIR is client-titrated, rather than therapist-titrated.

c. In TIR, we endeavor to reach an end point in a single session; in DTE, working on a given incident typically takes a few sessions.

d. TIR includes specific ways of checking for earlier and similar incidents that might be triggered when running through a later one. A sequence of incidents can be traced back to its root in a single session and resolved.

e. When the client suffers from unaccountable uncomfortable feelings, emotions, sensations, psychosomatic pains, and unwanted attitudes, but there are no obvious major traumas in evidence that could be addressed, a type of TIR called "Thematic TIR" can be used to trace these "themes" back to the incidents they came from and eliminate them, also in a single session.

Like TIR, EMDR and V/KD contain elements of exposure, but they also contain other elements, such as inducing eye movements or producing other repetitive, bilateral stimuli (as in EMDR) or creating a deliberate state of dissociation (as in V/KD). Otherwise they differ from TIR in the same ways that DTE does. TFT is utterly different from TIR, relying, as it does, on tapping acupuncture meridians.

11 Phobias and Anxiety

Although TIR is not specifically directed at phobias, it often occurs that trauma is at the root of phobias. Phobias and of course fears in general reduce the clients' ability to cope in the world because they eat away at the feeling of safety.

In *Motivation and Personality*, Abraham Maslow posited the theory of a Hierarchy of Needs. This theory is that people are motivated by unsatisfied needs and that certain lower needs must be met before higher needs can be satisfied. Above the lowest level of physiological needs, all other needs such as love, esteem, and self-actualization require the bedrock need for safety. Without safety, we fail to do more than meet basic survival needs. After addressing the full sequence of incidents surrounding a phobia, breakthroughs are possible for the client. In this chapter, we'll look at a dramatic example.

From the files of Robert H. Moore, Ph.D., there is a clearly illustrated case of how Thematic TIR solved one person's case of extreme test anxiety.

Finally, there are a pair of remarkable stories of how stuttering was alleviated by addressing the incidents that brought it about. TIR is not a substitute for medical treatment. However, as researchers slowly gain further understanding of the mind-body dichotomy, it becomes less surprising that the relief of mental trauma produces a physical outcome. I present the results reported here neither as expected nor typical, but rather as notable anecdotes demonstrating the power of trauma relief in the mind-body system.

You may also want to peruse Chapter 8, which includes a summary of research about TIR and anxiety symptomatology by Wendy Coughlin, Ph.D.

Bug Phobia—Interview with David Rourke

The following story has been excerpted from transcripts of the 2003 TIRA Technical Symposium.

This woman was referred to me by a colleague. He said, "This woman is a mess but I've been working with her for a while to kind of keep her grounded." I thought this is great; at least she's got some coping skills. She came with an absolutely intense phobia of bugs where she was a hostage in her own house.

In the summertime, she lived completely indoors. Her sole outdoor activity was to step out on a small cement patio for a few minutes so the dogs could relieve themselves. When doing this, she covered her head with a towel to keep the bugs off, and then she went quickly back inside, shaking off the towel to make sure no bugs were on it, and locked her doors. Of course she would only risk this much exposure when no one else was at home.

She came in with a purse and a shopping bag each jammed full of stuff. Items included a towel (to keep bugs off her head), washcloths, Kleenex, books, water, medications, phone (for help) pens, paper, and so on. On her first visit she also brought her daughter. She was on six Clonazepam (Klonopin: an anti-seizure medication) used as an anti-anxiety medication and 60mg of Paxil (anti-depressant) daily. Everybody in her family was held hostage because of this phobia. My first thought was to send her to somebody else.

She went through a whole box of Kleenex on her first visit. The first thing I tried was EFT, which I suspected would not work due to the medications, and it did not help. We did some Unblocking on an unrelated loss she had and it gave her some relief and whole lot of courage, because she did want to get better. This was a 53 year old woman who had been on medication for the past 5 years. Her life was getting crazier and crazier. Looking back now, she says, "I never had a life at this time."

We got into addressing an incident when she was 4-1/2 years old. I asked "What was the worst thing that ever happened in your life?" She said "I got my tonsils out when I was age 4-1/2". I said "Oh, tell me about that," and we used TIR on it.

She lived in Scotland at the time. She was woken up in the morning and her mom said "Come on, you're going to the hospital to get your tonsils out." She said "No!!" She didn't want to go and was running around the house trying to stay away from her mom. Her mom went and fetched the neighbor next door and they both struggled to get her coat on then dragged her down to the bus. They then dragged her on her feet through the hospital while she tried to resist. She hid under the chairs in the waiting room and kept throwing them in front of her when people tried to get at her. They moved the chairs, grabbed her and the nurse brought her in to get a bath. As she was getting a bath, her mom left with the neighbor. So there was an abandonment issue there.

She was then put in this crib, which she vividly described with silver bars and other details. She was crying, crying, and crying. The nurse told her to be quiet or she would move her. Eventually, the charge nurse of the ward got fed up and moved her bed way to the back where she was left all alone. In the morning, this guy in scrubs came to get her with a stretcher. He was trying to pry her fingers off the bars but she was fighting and she wasn't letting go of those bars if her life depended on it. So he just let go of her and he went and got another kid. Away they went and then this kid was gone.

The orderly returned later with someone else and he was trying to lift her out while the other guy was trying to pry her fingers off the bars. They carried her and took her from there to a gurney where there was a curtain across an alcove and there was another child in there. Both of the children were naked, but she didn't know exactly how that happened. Next thing she knew, she was grabbed and brought into this operating room with big bright lights and lots of little tiny drawers all over the wall. That was the end of the incident – as she recalled it. We ran the incident many times. At the end of it, she said "I'm so sad, what a horrible thing to happen to a little girl."

I thought, "Oh, the end point." It was about a minute later and we were both sitting in silence, then she said quietly "I know why I'm afraid of bugs." I said "Why is that?" She said, "He looked like a bug. The guy who came to get me had a green mask, green scrubs, a green hat and green boots." I figured, "Wow, this is great!"

She went away and things started getting better over time. She was coming back for other sessions on family-of-origin issues and so on. But I noticed that the shopping bag was getting smaller every week. She wasn't seeing a lot of change but I just noticed that things were clearing up. She was in this totally hypervigilant state but gradually she was letting go of things without even knowing it. She was coming for sessions on her own and not feeling the need to carry so much stuff with her all the time.

At one point, I asked, "How's the thing with the bugs?" She said, "I've got a problem with moths." I said, "Well, what's the problem?" She said she really hated them, they terrified her. She would even go on the Internet to look at them to try and get over her fear, but that only restimulated her anxiety and terror. Her daughter came home and found her paralyzed with fear and crying in front of the computer. "Do you know what one looks like up close?" she said. I said "Well, why don't we address it?" So we did a theme on fear of moths (see Thematic TIR on p. 10).

The first incident we found happened when she was alone in her house (her husband was a long-distance trucker) just a couple years ago. She was in the blackness; she would have all the lights out because lights would attract bugs. She had the TV on, which was the only light in the house. This thing flew at her and she thought it was the size of eagle. It was coming right at her and it was a moth. She says now, "At that time, I never knew it was a moth."

She freaked out and fell on to the floor and grabbed a cover. She covered herself up, crawled into her bedroom, slammed the door and just waited there until daylight, and never slept a wink. She was prepared in the house. She had cans of RAID (insect killer) everywhere in the house. She had three cans in the bedroom. She opened the door, stuck her hand out and emptied one can. Then she grabbed another can and went out spraying and she went out. Then she sprayed another whole can and then grabbed another one out of the kitchen, went back and did the bedroom in case she had missed it. More toxic stuff... We started running that and blew the charge off that. There was another similar incident we ran through once, but no charge there.

Then we found another earlier incident: "We were getting ready for bed; I shared the room with my two sisters. My little brother (age 2) would come in and we'd all get ready for bed together. He'd stay with us for a bit to settle him down, after he would go into our parents' room. I'm jumping on the bed. I looked up and saw a moth on the ceiling and screamed. I jumped under the covers with my brother and pulled the covers over my head."

We went through that incident a couple times, then we got more detail: "...then my mom came in and killed the moth."

Next time: "My mom came in and killed the moth; I heard the door close."

We ran the incident a few more times and then the detail changed dramatically: "We're jumping on the bed, I'm getting ready for bed, I take my nightie off, I look at the window and there's a man looking at me. I jump under the covers; I pull the covers over, and the last thing I see is a moth flying around the light." That was it, done! *This memory of the incident had been completely repressed up until that very moment.* End of session.

After about three months of seeing each other, she had been weaned off all her medications. She called me recently and for the first time she went out to her granddaughter's soccer game. She's out and she's free!

Post TIR Follow up

I have recently spoken to this woman again and she informed me about an incident which just happened to her in late September 2003:

She was returning to her truck after a meeting with a newsletter in her hand. She noticed from a distance her truck had changed from silver to black. As she drew closer it became apparent that her truck was covered in black and red striped beetles. [Ed. Note: these are box elder beetles which are slow moving and harmless to people, but prone to swarming in the autumn.] Backing up to assess the situation without any fear whatsoever, she noticed that her vehicle was the only one with any bugs on it. The passenger door had the least amount of beetles so she decided that was the door she was going to enter.

With the newsletter in hand ready to swat the beetles, she went between the parked vehicles and started to clean off the door by brushing the beetles away. She then unlocked the door and quickly climbed inside. She proceeded to kill about 8 beetles that had entered with her as she got into the driver's seat. Then she turned on the window wipers so as to see where she was driving and pulled out of the parking lot, hoping the beetles would be blown off. After a 10 minute drive, she was about to enter Highway 401. The truck was still carrying many of the tiny passengers. Somehow, a few more had managed to get inside her vehicle and she killed them immediately. Still she had no fear... She was not enjoying this by any means but she remained calm and in control. Not wanting to return home with these bugs, she got behind a transport truck hoping the wind current would clean her truck off. It helped somewhat.

Her husband was just leaving for work when she returned home. He could not believe that so many beetles still clung to the truck. He sprayed inside and out of the truck for her with bug killer to make sure they were all gone. He was so impressed at how calm and in control his wife remained through all of this. He said that if this had happened a few months ago, she would not have reacted in the same way. All of this and without *any* medication.

In her most recent email to me: "I'm so happy Dave. Thank you so much for all your help. I could never have accomplished this without you and I love you for that."

Thematic TIR in Application: Test Anxiety
By Robert H. Moore, Ph.D.

Excerpted from the Summer 1991 issue of the Institute for Research in Metapsychology Newsletter

The tidiest example of TIR in application to PTSD would be of a straightforward narrative procedure on a one-of-a-kind trauma to which the client had been flashing back regularly and which resolved in due course without the involvement of earlier incidents or complexities of any sort.

A more typical example, on the other hand, should illustrate the interesting and often hidden connection of a client's current complaint with some aspect of his trauma history. Given that "Tom" didn't report any flashbacks when he first appeared for therapy, his case provides such an example.

Tom was a first year law student with a whopping case of test anxiety. He'd had the problem for as long as he could remember—at least since junior high school—but it didn't really catch up with him till he got to college. There, he controlled his most disruptive thoughts with alcohol and/or a mild tranquilizer and sometimes actually did well enough in his studies to be exempt from the feared final exams. But he was clean when he sat for the LSAT [Law School Admissions Test] and he choked up and 'bombed' the test. Unable to see how he would get into (much less through) law school if he couldn't take a test without his "chemical courage", he went for help.

It didn't take more than ten or twelve sessions of biofeedback-based (EMG) relaxation training and cognitive reorientation to bring his test-related anxiety, palpitations, throat constriction, and nausea under his control. At that point, he was able to re-confront the LSAT and scored well enough the second time to get into law school. The demands of his first semester, however, put Tom into a panic he couldn't completely shake. His image of himself as a student eroded with each successive challenge. He barely survived his mid-year exams by alternating periods of study with periods of cassette-guided relaxation. By the time he came to see me, with final exams approaching, he was on academic probation and in dread of flunking out.

To give him a bit of breathing space, I first reinforced the relaxation and quieting routines he'd learned in college. Then I set about to discover just what it was (cognitively) that pushed his buttons so badly in connection with being tested. It had always felt, he said, as if his respectability hung on the outcome—as though each test were a rite of passage, and if he didn't do well he would forever be "consigned to hell." No matter that he had usually done well at whatever he tried; he was "haunted" by the cumulative evidence of his inadequacy. He approached each and every test, audition, and interview with fear and dread, throbbing nauseously throughout as though he were on trial for his life. (Not an unfamiliar presentation for a test anxiety case.)

We know that dramatic reactions in non-dangerous circumstances are frequently secondary to earlier trauma (whether the client reports actively flashing back or simply a "haunting inadequacy"), and my attention was hooked to some extent by his description of the way he *had always felt* in testing situations. So I briefed Tom on the essentials of PTSD and TIR and invited him to take a look at the problem in retrospect. He agreed. As he had no special interest in any particular historic episode, I took the thematic approach. His choice of themes: "anxiety." ("Not just any old anxiety", he made it clear but "that throat-clutching, nauseating kind of anxiety" peculiar to the threat of a testing situation.) And he had no trouble recalling the several occasions on which he'd had it most acutely.

[Ed. Note: A sufficient number of clinically insignificant details in this case illustration have been altered to ensure the anonymity of the client.]

The first incident he selected, the bombed LSAT, "turned on" (restimulated) very shortly after he got into viewing it. His pulse raced noticeably and he reported that waves of nausea punctuated the memory of this "trial by entrance exam." By his fourth time through reviewing the incident, the persistence of his discomfort made it clear we should look earlier for another incident containing anxiety.

His major comprehensive exam as a senior in college was indeed such an incident. He had passed the test, but he choked up badly doing it. Similar circumstance; similar emotional/visceral reaction. It took only two or three repetitions to give him a headache (on top of everything else) and confirm our need to look for yet an earlier incident.

It took him a while to spot the next one, because he was expecting it to be—and was at first looking for—an earlier testing situation of some sort. But the Thematic question is unequivocal: Is there an earlier incident of any sort containing anxiety? So it surprised him for a moment (though only for a moment) when he recalled suffering the same excruciating anxiety after school one day in the tenth grade. He had gotten so nervous auditioning for a part in a play that he threw up right there on stage in front of God and everybody. I thought maybe we had a primary there for a moment, but as a viewer's verbal and non-verbal indicators are always—but always—senior to a facilitator's unspoken personal speculation about what's going on in the session, I was soon convinced otherwise. After five repetitions, Tom's embarrassment (added to his earlier discomforts) was still unabated. So there must have been an earlier incident containing that kind of anxiety.

Several minutes passed during which Tom silently reviewed memories of his early years, his tightly squinting eyes reflecting the urgency of his need for relief from the cumulative discomforts of the incidents he'd been viewing for nearly an hour. Then quite abruptly his squint intensified momentarily, his head jerked back, and he dissolved into anguished and uncontrollable sobbing. The impact of whatever he had recalled was such that Tom sobbed and gagged continuously for nearly five minutes before he could so much as speak. (During those minutes, I simply waited quietly.) And when he did speak it was in the desperately rasping, tearful voice of a ten year old little league infielder who had just taken the full force of a line drive square in the face—in his first game. He'd had just a fleeting look at the ball as it leapt off the bat in his direction faster than he could bring up his glove to meet it. The next thing he knew, he was on his back and gagging painfully on what was left of his front teeth and gums. Add to that a splitting headache, nausea, embarrassment, the rigors of reconstructive surgery and with it all the certain knowledge that *by displaying such complete incompetence as he had done—jerk that he was! — he had forever lost the respect he had so yearned to win from his peers.*

It wasn't an easy incident for Tom to confront. His first several times through were nothing more than a blinding, consciousness-obliterating flash. Only gradually over the next ten to fifteen agonizing repetitions did the incident open up and reveal the brutality of its impact to his conscious inspection. And only gradually thereafter did it lighten to the point at which he could recount its traumatic detail without gasping in pain. But it did completely discharge, as primary traumata inevitably do if one is diligent and patient. "I caught it right in the teeth," Tom said dryly at the end, "and I made a big deal out of how bad it made me look. It hurt like hell, that's for sure! But I blew it out of all proportion. And that's all there is to it!" Two and a half hours into the session, thoroughly exhausted but amazed and exhilarated, he added "I thought since I'd stopped reverberating over that mess while I was still in high school, that it was history. I'd never have believed it could still affect me that way. Boy was I wrong about that! That was unbelievable!"

Tom reported in his next (and last) session that he'd "had a smile that wouldn't quit" for several days following his TIR and that although he hadn't bee put (literally) to the test, he couldn't imagine why he should ever again be shaken by any exam or interview. He was to call me without hesitation if he had the slightest recurrence of his test-related discomfort. When I hadn't heard from him by the end of the year, I put him on the list to receive our follow-up "Counseling Effectiveness Questionnaire." Felt-tipped boldly across his reply, right beneath the heading that identified his presenting problem, Tom's brief response said it all: "TEST ANXIETY? WHAT TEST ANXIETY?"

Notes:

Correct thematic TIR procedure requires the selection and running of one very specific symptom or theme at a time. In this case, although Tom describes his 'anxiety' in terms that make it sound like a symptom cluster, the facilitator was persuaded that "that kind of anxiety," in fact represented one well-defined theme. Had it turned out to be only one of several individually distinguishable and separable themes (e.g. anxiety, constricted throat, nausea, embarrassment, etc.) each potentially with a sequence and primary of its own, the appropriate procedure would have been to address and run as many of them separately as held Tom's interest.

TIR and Dissociative Identity Disorder:
A Conversation with Aerial Long, CMF, CT

Aerial is a Personal Growth Counselor and Certified Traumatologist in private practice and has been counseling since 1977. She is founder and board member for Trauma Relief Services of the Northwest (TRSN) in Beaverton, Oregon, a non-profit educational foundation providing counseling services and education in the field of trauma. Her training includes certification as a facilitator in Applied Metapsychology.

I asked Aerial to share her experiences in using TIR with clients who have been diagnosed with Dissociative Identity Disorder. See What is DID? below for more information.

VV: What should practitioners know before taking on clients with DID symptoms? Imagine that you are a Technical Director and you are setting up a case plan for a practitioner.

Aerial: They should be an advanced Metapsychology practitioner or have some prior training in DID. I wouldn't say that TIR Facilitator training is sufficient. They would need Certified Metapsychology Facilitator training. It would be better if the facilitator is a mental health professional who is already trained in DID as part of their background.

It's too complicated to do TIR on DID people as a general rule. I have only taken on clients who had quite a few years of DID therapy and wanted to handle their trauma. Even as an advanced Metapsychology practitioner, I have referred out several clients with DID symptoms because they didn't have the ego strength to do TIR and I didn't feel I could serve them.

What is Dissociative Identity Disorder?

Recently considered rare and mysterious psychiatric curiosities, Dissociative Identity Disorder (DID) (previously known as Multiple Personality Disorder-MPD) and other Dissociative Disorders are now understood to be fairly common effects of severe trauma in early childhood, most typically extreme, repeated physical, sexual, and/or emotional abuse.

In DSM-IV, Multiple Personality Disorder (MPD) was changed to Dissociative Identity Disorder (DID), reflecting changes in professional understanding of the disorder resulting from significant empirical research. "Personality" is no longer used to describe these entities. Other terms often used by therapists and survivors to describe these entities are: "alternate personalities," "alters," "parts," "states of consciousness," "ego states," and "identities." It is important to keep in mind that although these alternate states may appear to be very different, they are all manifestations of a single person. (From: The Sidran Institute www.sidran.org)

VV: What kind of results have you achieved with clients who have DID symptoms?

Aerial: I've only had three clients who told me they were diagnosed with DID. Since I don't diagnose, I cannot confirm that there were more. The results that I've had have actually been fairly positive. Two of them that I saw reached what I call "full integration". These clients had already had years of psychotherapy. They were at the point where they could stay centered and be the witness or controller of their other identities.

VV: From the DID theory I've read, a typical person has four or five identities and one of them is usually a "helper"...

Aerial: Well, there is one that they center in and that one helps handle all the others. They have to have a place to center or they get lost. Usually in prior therapy, they've already been able to ascertain which persona or identity they can center in to help them with the work. Then we just ask them from that point of view, to talk to the other identities and ask, "Who is willing and ready to step forward to handle some of their traumas?" Someone al-ways steps forward and is eager for healing. Whoever is the first identity to step forward is the one that we take (because that identity is the one most accessible). I treat that identity as I would treat the client and find the traumas that could have caused the "split".

VV: So you look specifically for the trauma which precipitated the split?

Aerial: I usually ask for traumas because it's sometimes too hard for an identity to find "the trauma". I have to work backwards just like I do with a regular client. I take incidents closer to that identity's present time and then go earlier as the client's confront comes up. We either take themes with Thematic TIR or we'll use Basic TIR and ask for a specific trauma that could have caused the split.

VV: Are there any ways in which the DID clients differ from those with typical PTSD issues.

Aerial: Yes, I've had to be very, very careful at the end of the session to make sure that everybody (meaning all the identities) is OK. Sometimes when working with one identity, it will restimulate upsets and trauma in other identities. I check with all of the parts involved to make sure that nobody else has gotten restimulated, that they are all OK. Whereas with a typical non-DID client, you know when you've finished the trauma that they go away resolved. The client gets their end point and they are fine with it. In the DID client, it's like having several people in the room. I would check with those other identities (parts) that are there to make sure nobody else has been restimulated.

VV: And how do you handle it if they are restimulated?

Aerial: I don't necessarily use TIR with them. We will do run some other kind of lighter technique to get them into present time. This insures that they all leave session feeling released and resolved from that session. When they are ready, we'll take up their trauma from their point of view.

VV: I gather that memory loss or amnesia is a big part of DID. Do you find them recovering a lot of lost memories?

Aerial: Actually yes. When an identity re-members a particular time period (for example ages 8 to 10), that time period has often been occluded from the whole. When TIR is used to help that identity resolve the charge and re-gain conscious memory of their trauma(s), then those memories are available to all the other parts. That's the beauty of the integration.

VV: What unique challenges are there for working with DID clients either with TIR or in general?

Aerial: It's like having five people in the room, not just one. You've got one person that's the leader and he or she is helping you with the others. It's a little more challenging I believe in that respect: keeping track of who is speaking and making sure that the client stays really focused. You don't want to be talking to somebody else all of a sudden. You really need to have a client who can manage this kind of work.

VV: How do you handle it when clients "switch" in the middle of an incident?

Aerial: I find out who is talking to me. I ask, "Who is speaking to me?" They know who they are and they identify themselves. I just treat it like an origination from an ordinary client. I might ask, "Is there anything you need to say?" or "Tell me what happened?" Someone might have gotten upset and I sort it out. So I would handle that and go back and finish what we were doing with the original identity I was working with prior to the upset.

One of the things that happens also using TIR with DID clients is that it promotes a tremendous amount of compassion and understanding from the other parts. They're watching this 8 to 10 year old go through their trauma and come out the other end. All of a sudden, there's more connection and that's part of the integration. It creates understanding with the other parts: "Well no wonder", they'll say, "look what happened here with little Joe". TIR raises conscious awareness and promotes integration

VV: Have your clients experienced a loss after their parts had been integrated?

Aerial: When we got to the point where all of these identities or parts were integrated, the person became whole. So there was nobody to talk to anymore. It was very strange for the client since they were used to having quite a bit of internal chatter. Their world became quiet and lonely. I handled this by Exploration and allowing them to talk about it. I also used some grounding procedures.

VV: Do you ever need to run the other parts through the same incident?

Aerial: No, because it wasn't their experience. I may have to handle their upset about it, but I don't have to run them through it. As a caution, one of the things that might happen is that some of the identities are in conflict. For example, a critical adult and another identity that has a more childlike viewpoint might be-come at odds with each other. The adult keeps trying to tell the other one what to do all the time. That creates complications. You want to handle the ability of the different identities to communicate with each other before you ever address trauma. They have to be able to at least tolerate and respect the fact that there are other parts there.

VV: Do you have some method of building up understanding between parts?

Aerial: It is very much like group counseling or relationship counseling. With the DID clients I helped, they had gone through a lot of prior counseling and their identities had re-solved much of their conflict prior to our sessions. One of the things from TIR that happens which promotes understanding is that it is a tremendously freeing thing for them too to realize why an identity was set up. When they go through the trauma, they become aware of why that identity was set up. There's some need that wasn't being met, such as safety. Behind each identity is an intention or reason why it was set up and assumed.

VV: Part of the TIR theory is that there is intention that you are trying to fulfill and you carry it around because couldn't com-plete it. Is the intention most often to be safe?

Aerial: Well of course that's a very basic thing in trauma: to be safe. It could even be to have peace. Sometimes there are chronic traumatic patterns. People go along and they reach a breaking point. Chronic traumatic pat-terns can be addressed with TIR also and I have used TIR on an entire time period using TIR or Unlayering (repetitive procedures).

Relieving Stuttering in an Adult: an Anecdote

By Eduardo H. Cazabat, CTS

Reprinted from the Summer 2002 issue of the TIRA Newsletter

I'd like to share with you an experience I had recently with a 30 year old fellow who had been stuttering for his whole life. He had tried different treatments with no result. I treated him with Traumatic Incident Reduction (TIR) which is a regressive, non-hypnotic treatment. Specifically, I used "thematic TIR," a form of the technique based on the belief that all themes— unwanted feelings, emotions, sensations, and the like (connected in this case with stuttering)—have a traumatic event at their root. Thematic TIR is aimed at reaching that root, and at resolving it and the theme related to it by "unburdening" its emotional charge. The first incident he reviewed was a relatively recent one containing the stuttering. Then he looked for and found earlier and earlier incidents, on and on, until he arrived at a traumatic event he suffered when he was 3 years old.

His grandmother had poisoned his grandfather.

He could recall the exact moment when the family realized the fact that she had committed the crime, and all of them were, of course, very shocked. When the police came to notify the family, my client was not given any explanation. He felt alone, apart, and scared. Nobody gave any support at that moment and they didn't consider it necessary to address the subject. They just told him "go to the backyard to play."

He also recalled a moment prior to his Grandfather's death, while the two were eating soup together—the poison was in the food—and he remembered his Grandfather's sad eyes, and felt guilty for not having done anything to save him. Even though he was only 3 years old, he still felt he should have been able to help. Children of that age often blame themselves for a tragedy. The topic of the murder was taboo in his family, and only eleven years after the incident, at age 14, did he find out why she was jailed. After he remembered this event, and reviewed it enough times to remove the emotional charge from the memory, he ceased stuttering.

TIR can elicit intense catharsis and quite often does. This was not the case with this client. He reviewed and recounted the incident many times, but always calmly. The only sign of the emotional discharge was that he ended the session completely soaked with sweat. He finally decided to talk to his family about the subject. After 27 years of silence, all of them were taken by surprise! Now, he and his older brother have decided to investigate the event and to write a book about it.

Prior to our work with TIR, he used to avoid contact with others as much as possible because he feared stuttering. Now he finds that he can speak calmly and doesn't feel intimidated. If he starts to feel anxious, he calms down with just a deep breath and continues to speak fluently. He still has a slight trembling in his voice, which I think could be resolved with phonoaudiologist training.

Eduardo H. Cazabat – Psicologo (Licensed Psychologist)
Certified Traumatologist
Buenos Aires-Argentina

Relieving Stuttering in a Child: An Anecdote

Facilitator/client names changed by request

[Ed. Note: The ability for children to take advantage of TIR depends on their cognitive level. In this anecdote, it should be noted that the child was gifted.]

How young can a child be and still be able to do TIR?

Our son, Charlie, was two years old, and had recently learned to talk. He loved to communicate, and practiced at every opportunity. One day he started stuttering, not badly, but noticeably. It became worse, and within a few days he literally could not talk. We took him to the doctor and asked "What is wrong?"

"Don't worry," the pediatrician replied. "It's not unusual for children to stutter at this age."

"When will it get better?" We asked.

"Maybe in six months. Sometimes it takes years."

We looked at each other. Our son was already terribly upset, terribly frustrated. We knew he would never recover from such an inhibition of his ability to communicate.

We went home; we talked; we tried to figure out what might have caused this. It had started suddenly; could something have triggered the stuttering? Then my husband remembered: a week earlier he and our son had gone out back of the day care center to look at large construction machines—tractors, backhoes, and such. Charlie had been fascinated, and father and son had a wonderful time looking at, touching, and talking about these amazing machines. The following day he had started stuttering. Could the machines have been a trigger?

Fools rush in where angels fear to tread. I didn't know that young children couldn't use techniques such as TIR. We were desperate and I was willing to try anything. After lunch, I sat down with Charlie and said, "Do you remember when you and Dad went to look at the big machines?" He said "Y-Y-yeah, b-i-ggggg m-m-m-achines".

"Tell me what happened."

He tried; he did his best to tell me. After a few minutes the terrible stuttering eased just a little.

[Ed. Note: It is vital not to push a child past any kind of end point as that will cause the child to be unwilling to participate in the future. This facilitator is particularly adept at noting end points in children – a specialized skill]

The next day I asked again. "Do you remember when you and Dad went to look at the big machines?" He nodded. "Tell me what happened." We went through the incident a few times, but there didn't seem to be much there.

What do you do when you've been through something and there's nothing more there? As far as I knew, this was the first time Charlie had seen such big machines since he had been born.

I took a deep breath and asked, "Was there an earlier time when you saw the big machines?" Charlie looked at me and his attention went "zap" onto something. He started shaking and stuttering and nodding, and then he started laughing. He laughed for three or four minutes, and I laughed with him. He finally stopped and hiccupped, and we smiled at each other.

He never stuttered again.

12 TIR in the Workplace

A Conversation with Wendy Kruger

VV: What is your educational background?

Wendy: I have a degree in psychology, education, and industrial psychology. In South Africa, one usually elects to pursue only two majors; I chose to do an extra one to keep my future career options open, and then went on to do an honors degree in psychology. Then I qualified as a psychometrist after completing an internship and sitting for the Health Professions Council South Africa (HPCSA) examination.

VV: What type of work do you do?

Wendy: In terms of full time employment, I am Organizational Development Manager for a large company based in Johannesburg, South Africa. My role encompasses performance management consulting. This in turn involves training, development and counseling. Prior to that I worked as Human Resources Development Manager in the retail industry. Concurrently, I have acted as an independent consultant for a number of different companies and lectured to some 1,500 students part time, designing their training material for the past 3 years in subjects related to Research Methodology, Human Resources, Training and Development. I also work with private clients, coaching them from a personal development perspective.

VV: How did you first happen to encounter TIR?

Wendy: I was advised to attend a TIR training course given by Gerald French as part of a master's degree I am doing in trauma. I did so, but only with great reluctance, as I had just completed another good course relating to trauma two months prior to the TIR workshop and didn't believe that I was really going to gain anything new. To be honest, I was hoping that the class would be really full and impersonal, so that I could get on with other work instead, and only participate actively when really necessary.

In fact, though, as it turned out, the knowledge and skills that I acquired in the TIR training exceeded anything I have learned in all my past studies put together. Gerald's passion for TIR was contagious, and I have found myself sharing that passion ever since the workshop.

VV: How does your work relate to TIR?

Wendy: Part of my current role in both my full time job and consulting is employee wellness. This is important because employees who have current or unresolved traumas in their lives usually battle to be fully productive. In our wellness center we therefore invite employees with personal problems to contact us. Such problems typically include depression (sometimes associated with attempted suicide), relationship problems (both work- and non-work- related), drug and alcohol abuse, assertiveness problems, stress management, burnout and anger management. Since taking the workshop, I have experienced major successes in addressing all of these areas with TIR.

How has TIR affected your approach to dealing with drug abuse?

Wendy: Drug and alcohol abuse in the workplace is expensive to deal with as it involves lost worker hours due to rehabilitation, sickness and counseling. Further costs are incurred due to the consequent need to employ and train "temps". TIR has quite radically altered my approach to dealing with drugs and alcohol—I've found its use to represent a very appealing and effective alternative to traditional methods.

In one particular recent session, an employee—"Marc", who has had a problem with cocaine for over 6 years—reached a very clear "end point" in the course of which he stated,

> "You know, I never really enjoyed using coke. I had one good experience when I first started (using drugs) and I have spent the rest of my time trying to re-create that first experience again. I don't get much pleasure out of it at all; it's not really worth it."

He has not used cocaine since that day. At the end of treatment, he reported:

> "The (TIR) process has helped me feel lighter... I feel as if I have enough energy to face life again... I feel as if I am as good as other people now and I can face them too."

In another case, I was approached by a supervisor due to his suspicions of an employee's drug use and continual absenteeism. In a detailed intake interview, the employee stated that one of his principal issues was the fact that he had feelings of "not liking himself."

His "viewing" of this with TIR unfolded in successive "runs" as follows:

- Presenting incident: "It was my 21st birthday and my parents never wished me happy birthday. I felt extremely hurt and rejected."

- "It was my 21st birthday and my parents never wished me happy birthday. They were angry as my girlfriend was pregnant."

- "It was my 21st birthday and my parents never wished me happy birthday. They were angry as my girlfriend was pregnant and they were trying to punish me."

- "It was my 21st birthday. My parents never wished me happy birthday and made me feel as if I had to choose between them on the one hand and my girlfriend and daughter on the other." (Crying softly.)

- Realization—"I have never been able to choose between the demands of my parents and my girlfriend and daughter since my twenty-first birthday." (Continues crying.) [Note: It was very tempting for me to see this realization as an end point, but I noted that the other "end point indicators" were missing.]

- "It was my 21st birthday. My parents never wished me happy birthday and started treating me as an adult even though I was the younger brother." (Still crying softly.)

- "It was my 21st birthday. My parents never wished me happy birthday. I feel that I have lost my youth since then and that I have been forced to be part of an adult world way too early. I use drugs to escape an adult world. And I don't have to do that. (Body language changed as he opened his eyes, wiped away the last of his tears and gave me a small smile.)

This employee has not used coke again for thirty weeks. Whilst I certainly don't view these results as definitive or conclusive proof of this approach, I have found them to be extremely promising when compared to his earlier results following rehabilitation.

[Ed. Note: TIR is generally contraindicated for use with clients who are *currently* abusing drugs or alcohol. In order to maintain the concentration required for viewing, they should abstain from alcohol for a period of at least 24 hours prior and longer, if possible, for street drugs.]

VV: What else have you used TIR for in the corporate environment?

Wendy: I frequently see employees who say that they are experiencing a form of depression. The TIR training has taught me the importance of clear communication, so I begin by defining the term depression to ensure that they are not using the term "DEPRESSION" as an umbrella term to describe another feeling.

I have, for example, used TIR with someone who first complained about depression, but who in defining the word we clarified and narrowed it down to feeling that she had no meaning or purpose in life.

In this instance, we employed Thematic TIR, addressing a feeling of purposelessness. Many incidents within the workplace were taken up, and then we went back to her university days. Eventually, she described how her mother tried to abort her when she (her mother) was about eight weeks pregnant. As a very new TIR facilitator I felt a little uneasy with this, as it sounded as if the incident she was discussing was her mother's incident and not her own. I needn't have worried however. The "CEs"—Communication Exercises, taught as part of the TIR training—came to my rescue, and it turned out to be her own memory/incident. [Ed. Note: see also Chapter 13 for more description of pre-birth incidents.]

She recalled sitting on the bed and listening to her mother confess that she had attempted to abort her, but that she had not been successful. The client had a sudden insight into the fact that everything in her life had started going wrong at the point her mother had "shared" that with her. Her suicide attempts had also begun shortly after she'd been told about it.

[Ed. Note: One might make one of several assumptions about what is reported here: 1. The client actually contacted and re-experienced a prenatal incident; 2. The client, having been told the content of the incident later by her mother, was actually running off that information and not really contacting a pre-birth incident; 3. There are actually two incidents here—that of the pre-birth incident itself, and that of the later incident of being told what happened. The point though is that none of this matters. In the person-centered context as long as the client contacted something that was real to her and got relief and insight from addressing it, we do not need to decide anything about it.]

Her end point came shortly after this realization, and included her stating that "I am going to take charge of my own life from here on; I won't be a puppet fulfilling the wishes of some other negative force that tried to destroy me at birth."

She had initially asked me to schedule six sessions with her, but she only came back for one more (to deal with something totally different) and sent me an email describing how much and how positively her life had been changed by the initial session.

Another employee, "Ryan," in his mid 30s, did run "depression" after we first determined that the word identified a very distinct feeling for him. He started out talking about a recent incident relating to his vehicle financing, where he failed to obtain loan approval.

Thereafter he moved to an earlier incident in which his parents were lecturing him, continually telling him he was no good. After running that incident four times he moved to an earlier incident in which he was five years old and his father was beating his mother.

As he viewed this incident, his body language changed dramatically. He had been leaning forward, resting his elbows on the round table in front of him, with his hands gently clasped together and his two index fingers pointing forward and touching. As he viewed the beating incident, however, he sat up straight, rigidly, and began wringing his hands. He had had a rather deep frown on his face all along, and this intensified during the viewing of this incident.

He remembered feeling helpless in the first time through, as he couldn't do anything to stop his father beating his mother. In the next run he moved from feeling helpless to feeling useless. After viewing the same incident three more times, Ryan opened his eyes, saying, "I've become just like my father, the person I hated most!" After one more viewing his engagement with the incident fell away, clearly no longer necessary and he moved into the present moment with me, saying, "I'm **not** useless! I was only a child then, and couldn't have done anything differently, but I can do things differently now." He visibly relaxed and smiled saying, "I'm in control of my life."

I have seen him again since then to continue working through other issues of interest to him, and he has never expressed a need to look at depression again.

Another employee, "Roland", felt depressed following a divorce. After using TIR and other life stress reduction techniques in his case plan, I have seen him change from being suicidal and introverted to someone who eagerly has set goals for his life and is actively pursuing attaining them.

Another client who comes to mind when discussing depression is "Yvette". I met Yvette, age thirty-six, in a company I was consulting in. She was told that she has suffered from depression since childhood days, but she really struggled to define depression or tell me how it made her feel. By the age of eighteen she had seen three different therapists and clearly stated that she never gained anything from any sessions with them. If anything, she said she felt irritated and exposed as a result.

With probing, she described herself as feeling dead, separate and alone, but indicated that this did not bother her as she couldn't remember ever feeling any other way, and that she imagined all people to feel this way. She further stated that she had fairly good relationships with others, a successful career and a happy marriage. This led me to ask her why she had come to see me, as it did not appear that she wanted to resolve or change anything.

Yvette replied that she wanted to discuss the fact that she had been sexually abused as a child. She had never discussed this with any therapists she had seen as she found them to be intrusive and did not want to share this information with them.

We used basic TIR, looking at the incident containing sexual abuse. Yvette initially battled to engage in the process and spoke mechanically and very much from the present perspective. By the fifth time through, however, she had become fully engaged in the process. By the eleventh run she was sobbing softly and clearly back in the past as shown by her statements such as "I'll never be the same again," "I've changed forever" and "my world is bricked in and separate to everyone else's." Yvette says that she has never cried about the incident before the TIR session, and that she also never really cries about anything. Her end point was not dramatic, but soft. She wiped her tears away, lifted her head up out of her hands, opened her eyes, looked up at me and said,

> "It's okay to cry—I don't have to pretend to be perfect any more and that's a f—ing relief. If people can't accept me as imperfect that's their problem, not mine. People who like me because of who they think I am aren't true friends anyway. I'm tired of pretending, I want to be real from now on."

VV: Have you used TIR for an issue directly related to an employee's work performance?

Wendy: Yes, for assertiveness. This is an area that people frequently want to discuss. They either feel unable to say "no," or they feel that they do not speak up sufficiently.

Traditionally, assertiveness has been treated with training in the workplace. This approach gives people the underlying theory of assertiveness and allows them to practice assertiveness skills to some degree. Whilst the theory leads to increased knowledge, very little change tends to occur with that approach. Adding some behavioral roleplaying or simulation does lead to some change, but the root of the problem is often never addressed, leading to limited successes in the immediate short term only.

Using TIR changes this dramatically, as it allows the viewer to move through various experiences in which she believes that she was not assertive enough.

Typically, I start off by defining the word, "assertiveness". It is important to define the concept of assertiveness upfront. In many instances people believe that they are not assertive due to feedback from others, but often this is incorrect—a "wrong indication" in the useful parlance of Metapsychology that I am beginning to learn.

I clearly define assertiveness in my sessions by using pre-written cards containing various dictionary definitions on them. We define assertiveness, aggression and passivity, and I use sixteen cards.

The viewer and I then move through each card and agree on whether the words used there match their own definition of assertiveness, aggression and passivity. Should they differ, we unpack the word in the definition on and clearly define it. It is thus really useful to have a dictionary nearby for this exercise.

After agreeing on the definitions, I ask the viewer whether they believe that they need to change their assertiveness levels. If the answer is yes (I have had "no" answers, especially where clients were told that they have low assertiveness levels by their managers and these were in fact wrong indications) we go directly into a session where we apply basic TIR to a known incident.

One client, "Jennifer", started her session by talking about a board meeting in which she was upset with herself as she failed to speak up when she had valuable input to give. She was the only female in the boardroom, but she assigned no significance to this factor in the first seven times through. By the eighth time, however, we encountered an incident in which she remembered being told by her mother that she was not assertive enough. This bothered her so much, she said, that she started dressing, walking, and acting like a boy in an attempt to come across as more assertive. She remembers having done this for at least a year. By the eleventh run, she remembered that her father had always wanted her to be a boy, not a girl, and that she never felt good enough—she felt inferior because she was a girl.

A clear change in body language was evident at this point and she opened her eyes, looked up in surprise, and said, "You know what? I am assertive. I'm only **not** assertive when I am with **men**! I feel so inferior when I'm with them. That's ridiculous! I can be assertive with them too!" She started becoming excited with her newfound knowledge. Two weeks later her manager indicated that she had noticed a definite improvement in her contribution and assertiveness during meetings. She confirmed this herself at her next session.

In another session, "Craig" met with me since he felt he could never say no to anyone. This was having an impact on his work performance; he could never complete his own tasks as he was often running around doing arbitrary tasks for others. He also built up a lot of resentment toward people who asked him for assistance, and he felt this was damaging his relationships. In a TIR session, he viewed parts of his adult life and then moved to his childhood. He viewed an incident in which he was punished as child for saying "no." His end point was, "I'm living out my past. I've been scared that my mother would disapprove of my saying "no" but that's ridiculous as she isn't even alive any more! And you know what, she probably would have said no to some of the things herself if she'd been asked to do them." He started laughing from deep down in his belly at that point and then said, "I can't believe that I actually wanted professional help for this," shaking his head and smiling at me.

VV: Do you deal with a lot of relationship issues in the workplace?

Wendy: Yes. In fact at least half of all sessions are due to relationship issues—either in employees' personal lives, or in the workplace. For example, "Lisa" approached me because she was disturbed by her poor relationship with her immediate manager. She felt that her manager was picking on her, over-exaggerating the bad things that she did, never acknowledging the good, and not treating her as fairly as she did other employees.

Prior to attending the TIR training, I would have listened and then dealt with the issue from a conflict management perspective. The TIR session, however, showed that she was scared of her boss not noticing her and not caring as opposed to her initial complaint of her noticing her too much. Their relationship had previously involved her boss playing a very supportive role in her life due to a bereavement she had experienced then, and when she came to see me, she was experiencing, in fact, a severe sense of *loss* due to that closeness having changed back to a normal working relationship. She interacted with me again later to say that she realized that she wanted her boss's attention, and that she had changed her behavior from passive resistance to acknowledging her feelings and reaching out to her. Their relationship improved vastly and I have seen them go out to lunch together again.

VV: How do relationships outside of the office affect employees?

Wendy: OK… an employee had a breakup with her boyfriend and was devastated. Her manager phoned me to say that she was sending her home, as she was too distraught to work. She asked if I could see her first though, as she did not believe the employee was in a fit condition to drive home. The employee, Tracey, was in fact fairly hysterical when she walked into my office. During a basic TIR session which we ran looking at the actual break up incident, I saw relief eventually coming (this took approximately forty minutes) and she stopped sobbing. She chose to return to work immediately instead of going home as initially planned.

I bumped into her in the hallway a week ago and asked how she was doing. She confirmed that the incident had been dealt with once and for all during the viewing.

Another significant relationship incident comes to mind, also due to a breakup in which the employee's husband was unfaithful. She feared having contracted AIDS and I used Marian Volkman's Future TIR [see Chapter 3] with very positive results. Luckily the result of her preliminary HIV/AIDS test was negative then. Retesting should occur in a month or two, but to date she has not needed any further viewing. This is amazing as she was clearly distressed when I initially met her.

There is a further issue that I can recall that started out as a workplace related issue, but ended up linking to an incident that occurred in the employee's childhood. "Michelle" came to me to report a case of sexual harassment.. Usually in business [in South Africa], very few people come forward to report sexual harassment cases due to fear of victimization, fear of not being believed, lack of trust in confidentiality, or embarrassment.

Whilst Michelle initially discussed the sexual harassment in the workplace, the incident kept becoming heavier. Her voice kept becoming louder and louder until she was shouting so loudly that employees in nearby offices could hear her. It had triggered the emotional charge contained in a childhood incident when she had been sexually molested as a very young child.

This was the second longest TIR session I have had to date, requiring two hours and fifteen minutes and involving viewing incidents twenty-one times. As we went through TIR, Michelle's distress became worse and worse. She started off by crying, but this turned to sobbing that was so loud that one of the employees in the next office had to turn some music on so as to avoid hearing what was being said. (The doors were already closed!) This changed to anger at a point and she pounded her fist onto the table once or twice. Towards the end, she calmed down slightly and sat holding herself protectively and rocking forwards and backwards. Four runs before the end point, she pulled up a second chair and put her legs up on the chair. Over the next runs she started slipping down until she was virtually lying down on the two chairs.

Eventually, she reached a splendid end point; Michelle states that TIR has set her free of her nightmare forever.

VV: Has it been your experience that many people carry painful baggage from their past and that TIR assists them in dealing with it?

Wendy: Oh, definitely. Often, as I've noted earlier, the person starts off by dealing with something from the present, only to end up resolving it by resolving something from the past. I recall an incident in which two employees had a disagreement regarding money. One started doing TIR with me at her manager's request. He said she had poor relationships in the workplace as she was always borrowing money from others.

She was willing to co-operate, although not overly excited, yet she showed sufficient interest in the process to commence. She started by viewing an incident in which she, "could not stop herself from spending money," but her end point was linked to the fact that her boyfriend, whom she had left six years earlier, used to beat her. Relief visibly swept over her body during the session.

Another employee, "Elizabeth", began our session by discussing her poor work performance and ended up realizing that her confidence had been destroyed during an earlier personal relationship where she had felt abandoned and during which she had internalized her boyfriend's verbal abuse, that she was useless. Her end point involved stating,

"Before David left me I was always an achiever. I was somebody. I suppose I felt so awful when he left that I made myself into a failure and turned myself into a nobody. He didn't do it to me, I did it to myself!"

VV: Are there any other contexts where that you have used TIR?

Wendy: Yes, I have used TIR in a bereavement situation where I dealt with "John", an employee who lost four family members in an accident, and I must admit that I was amazed that TIR could even assist with such a raw, open wound. The relief that I saw sweep over John was truly awesome... and I am not using that term loosely.

I do believe, however, that there is room to use Future TIR in this situation, so as to enable John to confront fears that he had earlier mentioned regarding the absence of his family.

Gerald also mentioned that it might be useful to have him converse with departed family members, thus allowing him to complete any "unfinished business" he may feel he has with any of them. I've been trained on that now and look forward to using the tool.

[Communication with a Departed Loved One is a procedure taught in both TIR Expanded Applications and Case Planning for TIR and Life Stress Reduction workshops – see Appendix C]

VV: In closing, is there anything else that you believe TIR would be useful for in the workplace?

Wendy: I would like to use TIR in cases of excessive absenteeism and I believe that I would see significant results. I am also really interested in conducting research into the effects of using TIR to enhance work performance. Once again, there is no doubt in my mind that TIR will prove to make a significant positive change.

VV: We share that belief, Ms. Kruger. Thank you for your time.

13 Spiritual Experiences

> *I am totally at peace. My laughter and silliness is back. I've learned to totally love. Strongest I've ever been spiritually; it's all good from here on. If God is with me, who can be against me?*
>
> — Domestic violence survivor (VSC Miami)

Access to trauma is of paramount importance in any cognitive technique. Since TIR is client-centered as a matter of first principles, this means that whichever handle offers the client the best grip on a trauma should be allowed by the facilitator. By access to trauma, I mean of course the part of the experience which seems most real to the client and therefore actively using her attention. On occasion, clients access trauma through spiritual experiences as metaphors.

The most important part of access to trauma is not in fact how the trauma actually occurred but how the client can address it in a way that is safe for him and releases charge effectively. In many cases, the access to trauma will be brought forth by the client as a metaphor. Whether the metaphor represents something real or not is another question. In TIR what we want to know is "Does this access to trauma result in releasing charge?" If the answer is yes, then the access is a valid one. Some common client reported experiences which fit into the spiritual realm include any of the following:

- Experiences before birth
- Experiences between lives
- Past life experiences

Additionally, there are a variety of other spiritual experiences that manifest as real to the client. In many cases, these can be more intense and integrated into the client's belief system than the list above:

- Near death experiences (NDEs)
- Experiences with non-corporeal beings
- Communication with other life forms (e.g. animals)
- Experiences outside the body (OBEs)
- Peak experiences with oneness, God, or infinity

Taken together, the complete list represents *transcendent experiences*. Do some or all of these phenomena really exist? The answer in the context of person-centered work is that it doesn't matter. If it's real for the client and it presents her with access to trauma, the facilitator is going to have to work with it. A flippant or casual invalidation can violate the safe space provided by the facilitator and will be unlikely to affect the viewer's opinion on it. Conversely, in a client-centered practice the facilitator does not go on a fishing expedition for extraordinary phenomena. A transcendent experience appears most often when elicited by the standard line of questioning, such as "Was there an earlier, similar incident?" And the client replies, "...yes, when I was in the French Revolution" (or whatever).

Metapsychology as a discipline remains firmly ecumenical. It has been successfully applied with clients of all faiths from all continents. The presumption of presence or absence of divinity is not in evidence in the curriculum. In this chapter, I invite you to set aside your convictions on transcendent experiences and really see things through the client's eyes.

In the 1960s, Dr. David Cheek pioneered the field that now goes by the term *near birth experiences*. Encompassing a range of experience from conception through birth, these Transcendent Experiences may include trauma. Although Dr. Cheek's use of ideomotor (unconscious movement) techniques is outside the realm of Metapsychology, the exploration of transcendent experience can provide access to trauma. He often used hypnotic techniques, but please remember that TIR is strictly a non-hypnotic technique. I'll also present the work of Rev. Jerry Bongard, who studied with Dr. Cheek and refined the use of TIR in near-birth experiences.

Last, I'll visit with Rev. Karl ("Doc") Ullrich who is in the unique position of being a trained clinical psychologist and an ordained Episcopalian minister. He discusses anger with God as a response to trauma. Another story where a client reconciles her anger with God can be found in the Chapter 3 (Grief and Loss) starting on p. 69.

Fetal Perception and Memory

by David B. Cheek, M.D.

Transcript of 1992 IRM Conference Plenary Address

Foreword by Gerald French

This article is a talk given by David Cheek, M.D. (1913-1996) on April 5th, 1992, to a plenary session of the Sixth Annual Conference of the Institute for Research in Metapsychology in San Francisco. In the 1950's, Cheek wrote the first academic paper ever to address the phenomenon of fetal perception *in utero*. He spent fifty years caring for pregnant women, taught clinical hypnosis to physicians, psychologists, and dentists in the United States and abroad, served as the 6th president of the American Society of Clinical Hypnosis, and published fifty papers and books that remain milestones in pre- and perinatal psychology and health. In this talk, he describes some of his experiences as a therapist in using an ideomotor technique [see description in text] that often allows his patients to realize life-transforming insights.

Though the reader will probably notice major differences in technique, it is both fascinating and validative to see so many philosophical parallels between our two approaches to the common goal of human betterment.

My subject is what goes on in the uterus, and most of what I've been learning that is really meaningful to me has come within the last five years when I began to push back the boundaries of my biases.

I used to think, as Freud did, that it was impossible for babies to know anything until they were either 3 or 4 years old. I had known about Otto Rank, who felt that babies knew a lot at birth. Rank found that psychotherapy was greatly shortened when he allowed his patients, in hypnosis, to talk about what they remembered at birth. He felt that birth was always traumatic. It isn't. It can be very wonderful for some babies, but it is rough, and it's rough enough on them, mainly because the mother puts out adrenal hormones—epinephrine—in labor. This seems to make memory permanent. The baby will pick up what is going on at that time, whether it's good or bad, and will remember that. The impact of the adrenal hormone overrides nice, left-brain, left-hemisphere type of information, like, "I love you; you're a wonderful kid," if the baby has felt that mother was not awake in the delivery room and didn't care enough to say, "hello". Because of what we obstetricians do to mothers and babies, her baby may never forgive her for having been "somewhere else" when she should have been right there, saying, "What a beautiful baby I've got!"

These are things I've been awakened to. I've found that it isn't just what goes on in the delivery room that is important. It's what's gone on for the previous nine months, and *maybe ... even ... longer!* I woke up to the possibility—suggested to me by a psychic—that we do a lot of thinking before we arrive in a physical body. When we're in a holding pattern out there, waiting to come on in for a landing, we do choose. We don't always choose the right person, but we choose them in terms of what we have known about them before.

This was kind of wild for me. I don't talk about this very often except in a nice group like this. I was telling Sarge [Dr. Gerbode] that this is the one group that I've met within the last year where I have felt as though everyone was open and receptive. Though they might not really totally believe, they were willing to listen and to think about what we talked about.

Anyhow, I was in Hamburg, Germany two years ago, and one of the psychologists in the group asked me to work with her as a demonstration. She said, "My mother and I have never gotten along, although I love her very much. She lives in Berlin. I try to avoid talking to her, but she calls me and we always get into arguments on the telephone. I'd like to know what can go on that might help in my relation to her, because she's getting old; she needs me. I would like to be helpful, but I always find myself uncomfortable around her." So I invited her to come up for a demonstration.

We set up ideomotor—thought/muscle movement—ways of signaling unconscious information. This can be as simple as asking the client to designate one finger to signal "yes" and another finger to signal "no". I simply asked her to go back to when she was just emerging out into the world.

You don't have to go through a long induction technique. That is so surprising for someone to try to conjure with: that they could remember their birth.

She didn't have to be in a trance to begin with, but she went right in, to be there at the time of her birth. Her head turned to indicate the way her back was in relation to her mother. An arm came out when I asked, "Which arm is delivering first?" This is a physiological memory that was imprinted by the adrenal hormones that were present, added to a lot because she was born in Berlin in 1943 when there were a lot of stimulating things happening—like bombs arriving.

She said, "My mother is so happy she almost screams with pleasure to see this daughter of hers, this beautiful child."

I said, "Well, that sounds pretty good. How does the child feel?"

She shrugged her shoulders and said, "Na-ah", as though it were nothing.

To me, that meant there must have been something that had gone on earlier that had set the stage for her to reject her mother's joyful acceptance of her. So I asked her to go back to the time when her mother learned she was pregnant. I have found that this is an important moment: women are happy, or they're scared, or they're mad. This emotion seems to make the memory lasting. She signaled that she'd done so.

I said, "How does your mother feel?"

She said, "Scared," and then there was a pause. I was trying to think of what else to say, and in the pause, she said, "She doesn't want me." That was her interpretation of her mother's being scared.

Being scared has to do with survival. This is a right hemisphere type of impression. It's the psychic, spiritual side. It's very important for animals to know where the danger is, and to remember how they got out of danger before. Tremendously important. So "scared" meant, "She doesn't want me."

Korzybski—the father of General Semantics, you know—said "The map is not the territory." The way you understand the territory is very different. The map only gives you colors, and maybe some lines of topography. What we hear and what we pick up in other ways, we filter out in accordance with our background of knowledge. Asking about the background of knowledge of a little spirit that has selected a mother is very helpful.... I found out that she had selected her mother. I always ask about this. It helps so much psychiatrically if someone who hates his or her mother discovers that he chose her, or she chose her, in the first place. It lets them look at the possibility that there might be something else wrong, and they might be willing to reframe their impressions of their mother. So I asked about that.

"Is there another part of your mother that does want a little baby?"

I knew it would be "Yes", because I've found, as a gynecologist/obstetrician who has been concerned with fertility for 45 years, that women do not get pregnant unless there's a biological readiness for pregnancy. Now that's at a physiological level, way down deep. At a higher level, one which has to do with the environment, they might not be ready for pregnancy. And for years, I've enthusiastically supported the right to terminate an unwanted pregnancy, because, all during pregnancy, the little baby inside is picking up the feelings of its mother as to whether she really is accepting of what she's carrying, or rejecting it. It's very hard—it's almost impossible—to change a baby's attitude towards women if it has felt unwanted all during pregnancy.

Sometimes I have wondered how many of my colleagues in obstetrics had mothers like this themselves. I talked with Frederick LeBoyer about this. I asked, "Do you get the impression in France that obstetricians do not like women?" He said, "Oh, ho, mon Dieu! That was why I gave up obstetrics!"

And that same year—1968—was when I gave up obstetrics. I just didn't feel comfortable in an environment where nobody thought the way I did. In California, it's legally dangerous to have feelings that are different from your colleagues'. I had thought I could work—sort of like the communists used to work—"from the inside". But instead, I've been working from the outside, educating women to stand up for their rights and their choice of having babies, and hoping that they're going to educate their obstetricians. It's a hard job, I warn you. Have you tried?

Anyhow, this woman discovered that the reason for her mother's being scared was not that she didn't want a baby.

I said, "Move forward to when your mother tells your dad that she's pregnant." Right away, she said, "He isn't there," in a flat tone of voice. She was seeing his absence as yet another abandonment.

"Well," I said, "What's going on that keeps him away?"

And then she used her later knowledge. People can do this. She was able to say, "He's on the Eastern front, fighting the Russians."

I said, "Well, this is a rather bad time in the world in general, and certainly for your mother. How does she know that he's ever coming back? Couldn't it be that she's afraid for the future? For what's going to happen in Germany? Isn't she possibly afraid that your father may not come back?" And she had to admit that all these things were true and that helped her to reframe her attitude towards her mother.

> Ed. Note: If a client is interested in addressing birth or some period of time before birth, it is possible to do so using TIR and keeping the fully person-centered model. We note that if hypnosis is used a client may need more guidance or than with a non-hypnotic technique such as TIR.

Then I asked her to come forward to when her mother was going into labor.

I wanted this to be a different thing. People can hallucinate—imagine—the right kind of labor and the right kind of delivery. They know all about that! That's built-in genetic learning: babies ought to be delivered in about 2-1/2 to 3 hours. Ugandan babies are, and so are the babies of all the women that I've trained who have practiced doing the thing with their power—of turning pain on and off—so that they can be relaxed and don't have reflex tension of their muscles and their pelvis. They will have 2-1/2 to 3 hour labors, just the way the Creator intended it to be. So I asked her to "walk into cold water".

It's really important to know how simply, how easily, you can recall the familiar experience of standing in cold water until you get used to the coldness. That "used-to-the-coldness" is essentially a partial analgesia. That's all you need. You can stub your toe or bark your shin in cold water and it doesn't hurt until you get out and get warm. Everybody seems to know what this is like. So you have them "go in" [mentally] up to their knees. And then when they signal that they're numb, ask them to go in further, up to their waist. With women who are going to deliver, you have them "get in" up to the lower part of their breast, which is high enough over the top of the uterus to allow them to be able to turn on that numbness anytime they want to. You have to "program" them, and it's very easy to do. We all have computers between our ears. You can ask them to squeeze their finger, or to pull an ear—or use any kind of "anchor of action," as neurolinguistic enthusiasts call it. It's really the associative process. You have them squeeze the fingers together and have a finger lift (see example p. 250) to promise that forever after this, anytime they want to become instantly numb, all they have to do is to squeeze their fingers together. You don't want to take 10 minutes to get numb when you're having contractions every 5 minutes. It has to be an instant thing.

So she did this; she played with it. She was a little old for having babies herself, but I wanted her to see what her mother could have learned, and she was able to do this. I asked her to go through the delivery with her mother squatting on the floor—as woman have done for thousands of years—instead of being on a table with her legs up in the air in a most un-physiological position. And I said, "The sheets don't have to be sterile because you've got all the immune capabilities that your mother has. Bugs don't mean a thing to you. And instead of a doctor, let's have a midwife, who's thoughtful enough to catch you and put you on your mother's abdomen, skin to skin, to feel the warmth of her body ... and right to her breast."

All mother mammals—except humans—nurse their young. They lick them and nurse them right away after birth. She was able to imagine this, and I asked her to hear what her mother would have said, She didn't have to use imagination. Her mother's welcoming joy was already there. She heard it again, only this time there was adequate preparation in her mind. She could accept her mother's acceptance of her. She went home that night, called her mother, had a wonderful conversation, and came back in the next day feeling really good about the change in the relationship.

What she did impressed me so much with what seems to me to be a fact: we have to consider all the aspects of the beginning of a pregnancy, of the beginning of an embryo on through the rest of the pregnancy, and to help that little being get a really good, and open, and fair impression of itself and of the world around it. Now it is *possible* to work with people who are very badly mangled by what's happened in their lives. This is what you folks are doing all the time. You're doing it in your way. I do it using communications that do the same thing. I don't know enough about your ways of doing it, but you're doing it.

> **Now it is *possible* to work with people who are very badly mangled by what's happened in their lives. This is what you folks are doing all the time.**

I have a terrible curiosity: I like to know exactly—at least, what seems to be exactly—what allows people to bring about the changes in their lives. I think often, with any kind of therapy, they will have some sort of idea of it, But, you know, we've been struggling for over 150 years to use techniques to help patients find out what has caused their neurosis. Neurosis used to be thought of as only "in the mind", but now neurosis also includes the body, and as Buddy Braun—a psychiatrist in Chicago—has said, the only way we were ever able to separate mind and body was with the guillotine during the French Revolution. Whatever happens with the mind can also happen with the body. There has to be a change from normal physiological and emotional development to something different. Curiously, the human mind is capable of knowing exactly when there's a change. That knowledge seems to come from the reticular activating system—the "RAS".

The RAS is a network of nerve fibers that seems to think for itself. Every axon, every cell that starts the axon off, seems to have some knowledge of what to do. It's amazing. This is the sort of thing that Candace Pert [author of *Molecules of Emotion*] and others have been working on for a long time: the messenger molecules and neuropeptides that go through the body turning keys and getting cells to do things.

This reticular activating system surrounds the whole spinal cord all the way on up into the forebrain. Around the brain stem, the most primitive part of the brain, is where it is most highly developed. This is where all of the twelve cranial nerves come in. The impact of what they bring in is then decided upon by the reticular activating system. The front part of it—the upper part, the cephalic part—will decide "What do we send up higher? and what do we suppress?" It's an amazing capability. It isn't always correct. It doesn't always do the right thing, but it tries.

In about 1956, there were three people who were working with cats to find out about their attention. (Two of them I knew previously—Raul Hernandez-Peon and Michel Jouvet, a neurophysiologist, a wonderful person from Leon, France.) They were particularly interested in hearing, and so they trefined [drilled a hole into the skull] over the same part of the brain of each of their cats—I think there were 27 of them—to have access to the cochlear nucleus, the first relay system of hearing. They put a little stainless steel filament into the cochlear nucleus—got it fixed in position with beeswax or whatever they were using at that time—and then they let the animals recover health, recover from the anesthetic. They wanted them as normal as cats can be with a piece of steel in their brain.

> *"The only way we were ever able to separate mind and body was with the guillotine during the French Revolution"*
> —Buddy Braun

Then they brought them into a room, one at a time. They were pretty careful not to let the ones that they first experimented with get back and talk to the others; they separated them after the tests were done.

They had amplifiers in the room and they had a sound-producing machine that would make beeps. They attached the steel wire to an electroencephalogram and then they made a "beep" sound. The side of the cat's brain that had the thread in the cochlear nucleus sent out an electrical potential that made the machine make a little blip, up and down, like an electro-cardiogram. This had its full impact—reached its highest level—when the cats first heard the sound. But if they kept that sound going at the same interval, the cats began to lose interest in that sound. Physiologically, they toned down the response. It didn't disappear, but it became very hard to see. On the other hand, if they made the intervals shorter or larger, the cat paid full attention again.

See: if you're an animal, it's really important that you respond with all of your energies and do whatever is needed if something new—like a lion—comes into your field. So they got the full arousal response each time they changed the interval of time.

That was important. The cats were using what we have learned to use. For instance, we struggle with anxiety to drive a car correctly when we first begin. Then, after about a year of driving, we can talk to somebody rather intelligently while we do all the right things with the car. Most of our driving has become ideomotor—at a lower level of awareness than speech.

Now we can do that. We have learned to do that only because we'd go nuts if we had to pay conscious attention to everything we do. The cats had learned to do this. They had the full impact of the sound going, and then they brought in something that they thought would be would be really meaningful to a cat. They chose to use two white mice, sealed into a jar so that there would be no noticeable odor that would say "mouse" to a cat. It was just a single stimulus. Immediately, the cat suppressed totally the beep sound. They took the mice away and brought in something else meaningful: fish oil on a piece of cotton. They put it under the nose of each cat. Again, the cat immediately suppressed the impact of the sound.

That's the reticular activating system and it is really an impressive thing. If you want to read a little bit about it, Harold Magoun wrote a book that's old but very good. Magoun was really the one who controlled this experiment. He and Moruzzi were among the first to point out the importance of the reticular activating system in controlling not just reactions to the environment but also endocrines and everything else. It has much more control than the pituitary alone has. It tells the pituitary and the hypothalamus what to do. Magoun's book is called, *The Waking Brain*, and it's a neat little book. If you ever can get a hold of it, it's a classic.

You can use thoughts and muscles to get at unconscious information. Police inspectors and FBI agents have known for a long time what to do if you want to get details about what really happened when the bank was robbed, or the person was a hit by a car in front of them, or somebody got shot. You ask the witness (a volunteer witness; you don't do this with criminals because you can't depend on what they say) to tell you what they did from the time they got up in the morning to when they went home or whatever it was they did afterwards. You do not interrupt them. I've been working with the FBI for about 15 years now, and I sit with Bob Goldman and watch the witnesses who are instructed to do this. They start off with bright-looking faces, and their voices inflect their words with quite a range of tone. As they go on talking, wondering what comes next, they begin to diminish the modulations of their voice. Their words become slower, their facial expression irons out. When they come to a blank place and they're wondering, "What next?" they may look up about 20 degrees above the horizon—just like little kids when they're telling you about a movie and they forget what came next. And they go into a beautiful trance state while they're doing this "narrative," as they call it. And then I come along and the inspector introduces me—"He's going to hypnotize you and improve your memory."—And the witnesses come right out of trance because now they're *challenged* by somebody.

An Ideomotor Technique

So I have to ask them to do the *same* sort of thing, but not try to remember a thing. I'll say, "This index finger (I'll identify the finger with them at first; later I ask them to choose) is going to lift when you're getting up in the morning. This finger"—and I identify it, touch it for them so they hook it up in their brain—"will lift every time you come to something you feel might be helpful for us in this situation, and when you're going home at the end of it, your thumb will lift." (I usually use a thumb for that.) And they sit there and do the *same* thing. They go right back into the *same* trance—only usually a little deeper—and I ask them to "keep going over it, and when you get to the end and your thumb lifts, go back to the beginning and please keep on doing that until you feel that you have given us enough worthwhile details."

This is basically what we do in psychotherapy, often without really realizing what we're doing. We're helping a person in a narrative to go into a trance while they're telling us what they think we ought to know. And we should avoid asking questions during that time. We should really let them do it. It's hard to do it when you've only got a certain length of time to see somebody. But if you are retired—as I have been, sort of—when you have a little more time to do it, it is very interesting to notice how easily people go in.

Milton Erickson was the first one, to my knowledge, to point out that whenever people recall sequences of action, they go into a hypnotic state to do it. You can also see this in the case of post-hypnotic suggestion. I have said to a person under hypnosis, "When I remove my glasses, I'd like to have you go over to the door there and open it up ... and have menstrual cramps" (I used to do this with people who had dysmenorrhea), "and when you come back and sit in the chair, you'll feel instantly comfortable. This doesn't mean that doorknobs are going to induce cramps with you; it's just that I'd like to have you know that there are all sorts of signals that we set up for ourselves to have trouble with." I then continue, "When you know you can do that—and maybe not remember what I've been talking about—your 'yes' finger will lift."

Then I'll ask her to awaken, and before she's had a chance to catch on to what I've just told her—I learned this also from Milton Erickson—I'll pick up something like this water glass and say, "This is very interesting. I wonder if it's cut glass, or just molded that way...", to get her attention onto the glass. And while I'm talking with her about the water glass, I'll notice that every once in a while she's looking at that door, even though she has amnesia for the original stimulus of what's going to do it and I haven't removed my glasses yet. But when I do remove my glasses, it's even harder for her to keep her attention on the water glass. She's going to keep *thinking* about that door, but she can't just get up and open a *door* when a doctor's talking to her, so she has to rig up *some* way of getting there. And she'll say, "It's kind of hot in here. Would you mind if I open the door?" And I ask her to do that.

But she's going to have a cramp! She *knows* that, physiologically. So she'll get to the door and ... maybe get to the *aura* of the doorknob, and I'll say, "Please, put your hand on that door knob because I don't want you to get hemorrhoids or something later on just because you haven't followed through with what you think you ought to do."

So she does it, and then she looks off into space, wondering "What next?" ... and then she looks a little uncomfortable.

I'll say, "Where do you feel them when you first get those cramps?", and then she starts talking about it, reminds herself of it, and that's enough. I ask her to come back and sit in the chair. She's already accepted suggestion, and she's comfortable.

Actually, this is basically what happens with most illnesses, whether physical or emotional: something happens that sets a memory pattern, and there's amnesia for it, and a compulsion to carry it out. Dr. Herb Spiegel wrote a paper about this many years ago.

I put down epinephrine and amnesia together on this blackboard because they seem to be vitally related to what we call imprinting, and for birds and mammals, imprinting is very important for the young ones that have to be cared for by their mother or their father. They have to pay attention, to know who their parents are, because—particularly with birds like the goslings that Conrad Lorenz was working with—if they go to the wrong mother, they'll be drowned. So knowing who their mother is has survival value for them.

This is basically what happens with most illnesses, whether physical or emotional: something happens that sets a memory pattern, and there's amnesia for it, and a compulsion to carry it out.

Now, how do you suppose they set up the communication system that tells them who their mother is? We used to think it was just the first thing that they see, or the first thing that happens to them. It isn't. It's gone on a long time before. Telepathic communication is the secret for survival among warm-blooded animals. The other ones just lay their eggs and go off and leave them, and the young have to depend on genetic learning to survive. But warm-blooded animals—birds and mammals—have to know who is in control, and who to go to when there's danger. They can't just learn this after they are hatched out or born. It's got to be in place long before then.

So if you can open up your channels of understanding and acceptance enough to realize this, then you can see why a psychologist can go back and tell me how her mother feels at the time the doctor tells her she's pregnant. This is *telepathic communication*—the hearing sense is not there yet. It takes four and a half to five months for the hearing mechanisms to develop in the nervous system of an embryo. I used to think that they couldn't see, either, but yesterday a woman told me what her father was wearing when he learned—happily—that her mother was pregnant. I asked her, "How big are you?", and slowly she brought one hand up and she put her thumb and forefinger about that far [several centimeters] apart. There's a proprioceptive knowledge of size. Usually, in the early months of pregnancy, they double the space, but you would *expect* them to say, "How the hell do I know how big I am?" But it's very definite. You argue with her and say, "I think you're bigger than *that*. Don't you think so?", and her "no" finger will lift. Try it; you'll see.

These are communications—unconscious communications—not only telepathy, but clairvoyance as well. So think about that. Think hard, because if you're dealing with somebody that you think is a kook and you're going to do the best you can but you don't really think much is going to happen, you're very much like the owners of pedigree dogs that expect them to be show dogs but don't know how to give love.

[Here, Dr. Cheek gave a demonstration of hypnotic induction and the ideomotor technique described above. Though for reasons of brevity, that activity has not been transcribed here, a number of parenthetical comments he made during the session have been. See paragraphs below, followed by ellipses.—Ed.]

Remember what I said: sequences are important. As an obstetrician, I found that most of the complications that can happen with surgery occur during the nights after surgery when there's a "reviewing" of something that was possibly misunderstood—or heard as it really was said by a surgeon who didn't know that people are listening. Most of the complications in obstetrics occur because of statements that her mother-in-law may have made to the mother ... or words said by some friend who had a terrible time having a baby....

With the use of ideomotor response, you're opening up channels of communication that, for me, have been the only way I've been able to get at the origins—the really traumatic experiences. It isn't enough to get a later one; it isn't enough to get a satellite trauma. All of the earlier hypnotists—Joseph Breuer, Freud, Jung, Ferenczi—were looking for a trauma. They thought that when they got it and somebody starting screaming, that was the whole thing. It wasn't. People didn't get better, and all of them gave up hypnosis—particularly Jung, because he found people inventing trauma that had never actually occurred. He wrote about it.

Then came all these other things—researching dreams. But dreams are worthless unless you can get what went just before the dream. Sometimes people can be asked to interpret their dreams over and over again, and can go into hypnosis deep enough to have the access to what went before. But it's so much quicker to go right to the original thing by having them learn to go over their night of sleep and to pick up whatever seems to them in some way related to why you're talking with them. It's as simple as that....

Hypnosis is a state-dependent process. We go into hypnosis when we're in danger; we go into it when we lose consciousness; we go into it when we're lulled, when we're mesmerized—as babies are mesmerized by nursing. And when you go into hypnosis—even just relaxing—you may suddenly find yourself flashing back to a tonsillectomy ... or falling out of a tree ... or just before the car hit yours, when you go into a different state.

In that state, your tolerance for pain goes way up. People who have been injured in accidents don't feel any pain until they realize what's wrong with them.

It's a curious thing: when you go into hypnosis, something else goes into action, too. It was discovered by James Esdaile, a Scottish surgeon who went to India in 1845 to work in a little prison hospital outside Calcutta. He was appalled at the mortality rate with surgeries—even superficial skin operations. People would go into shock, hemorrhage, or die of infection. There was 50% mortality with any kind of surgery ... and this was only slightly above the level everywhere else in the world where people were in better shape—in better physical condition and better nourished than these prisoners were. This was before anesthetics were available in India.

Esdaile read a newspaper article about mesmerism being used in France by several surgeons. Cloquet wrote about it. The article said that the "operator" sits in front of the person he's working with, with his knees outside of the patient's, and that he passes his hands down over the patient's face and over his arms and shoulders and down to the hands. And these patients would go into a state that allowed surgery to be done painlessly.

Esdaile thought, "What a wonderful idea!" He was really tired of having attendants hold screaming patients down while he operated on them, so he worked with it. He didn't dare do it with a surgical patient at first. He was a doctor. He got somebody that had an abscessed eye first—a retrobulbar abscess [behind the eyeball]—and he began doing this. In his wonderful little book about mesmerism in India, he describes how he kept it up for 45 minutes and nothing happened. So he sat down. His back was bothering him and that it was very hot and humid. While he was sitting there, the patient said, in a low voice, "You are my mother, my father, my sisters and brothers." The only way Esdaile could interpret that was as a compliment, and it gave him strength. So he got up again and started to mesmerize some more, and the man went into a deep state. Esdaile didn't know what it was; it looked as though the man was in a coma.

Now the newspaper article didn't say how you wake people up, and Esdaile didn't know what to do next. So, like all doctors, he went and saw the patients he did know something about—he made rounds. When he came back, he noticed a very wonderful thing: the redness around that eye had gone away, and the swelling had diminished. That gave him enthusiasm to go on further and he recognized within a very short time that when you remove pain at an unconscious level, the other three cardinal signs of inflammation—redness, swelling, and heat—will disappear.

He didn't really think in terms of "conscious", or "unconscious," but what he was really dealing with was the unconscious element of pain, which doesn't appear in our dictionaries—even our medical ones. We think that pain is only what a person says "Ouch!" to. But subconscious pain is the important kind. It can smolder for years, unrecognized, and then light up later with a back problem or shoulder problem that may have started in the delivery room with the way the baby was born.

In 1947, Hench, of the Mayo Clinic, found that when you give cortisone to people who have rheumatoid arthritis, the swelling, redness, and heat will disappear and they will get more mobility in their joints. It was a wonderful discovery—except that a few of them began dying from miliary tuberculosis. They had had the tuberculosis "walled off," and the tuberculosis spread, got into the blood stream, and they died. Cortisone had other side effects as well, like depression, and suicidal attitudes. Cortisone can remove inflammation, but it does not improve healing, and it can cause a lot of other troubles.

> *Subconscious pain is the important kind. It can smolder for years, unrecognized, and then light up later with a back problem or shoulder problem that may have started in the delivery room with the way the baby was born*

The key to hypnosis was well known to Mesmer but he didn't describe it very fully. Esdaile discovered that hypnosis stops the redness, swelling, and local heat. When you remove the pain and there is no pain, the interference with the immune system that cortisone causes doesn't occur. In fact, the system is enhanced, so he also found that his patients stopped dying of infection.

And all of his surgical patients were infected. Doctors washed their hands when they got through surgery. They never washed their instruments afterwards to get the blood off, so their hands and all their instruments were contaminated with bacteria that were greatly enhanced in their capability of causing disease, because they had passed through other patients who had died or been infected in the hospital. We know that if you pass a pathogenic organism through a person or an animal and then culture it and give it to somebody else, its potential for doing damage is increased. So all his patients were very much at risk, yet his mortality dropped from 50% to 5% in three thousand operations—some of them major ones, like leg amputations.

Nobody *listened* to this. The poor guy died depressed after he returned to England. He'd been promised that somebody would publish his papers, and nobody was interested. They all had chloroform, ether, and nitrous oxide to use, so why waste time doing this sort of thing in front of somebody? You see, the receptiveness of people has to be right. You have to have the right audience, and he didn't have it.

Well, I wanted to touch on some of those things—not to convince you, but to add, I hope, to your curiosity.

Recordings of this lecture and several other conversations from this book are available on the *Beyond Trauma: Companion Disc.*

(A compilation of MP3 audio files playable on all computers)

Loving Healing Press
www.LovingHealing.com

In Memoriam
by Victor R. Volkman: October 1996

David B. Cheek, M.D., passed away in September 1996 at the age of 84. I had the honor of hearing Dr. Cheek at two past IRM conferences. With his warm heart, friendly demeanor, and total candor, he was an immediate hit with everyone. Though not a Metapsychology practitioner by training, I feel that he embodied all of the best traits that a practitioner could have: an open mind and complete respect and empathy for his clients.

Dr. Cheek's legacy lives on through the work of his students. Rev. Jerry Bongard and his book *The Near Birth Experience* provides another intriguing look into life before birth.

From the newsletter of the *Association for Past Life Research and Therapies* (Obituaries)

David B. Cheek, M.D., a physician and surgeon in Santa Barbara, CA. Diplomate of the American Board of Obstetricians and Gynecology, he was also Fellow and Past-President of the American Society of Clinical Hypnosis. In later years his practice was limited to psychosomatic medicine and infertility. He was a noted lecturer and author of six books and 41 papers on hypnosis, clinical hypnotherapy and mind-body therapy.

The Association for Pre- and Perinatal Psychology and Health (APPPAH) created the David B. Cheek Memorial Lecture on Psychosomatic Obstetrics in 1997. David was a beloved and loyal member of APPPAH, served on the board of directors for five years, and was a popular speaker at congresses.

TIR, PTSD, and the Near Birth Experience:

A Conversation with the Reverend Jerry Bongard

In addition to being a Certified Advanced TIR Facilitator, Gerald Bongard is an ordained Lutheran minister, and he was a student of Dr. David Cheek which inspired him to author *The Near Birth Experience*. Gerald Bongard's interests and work spans a wide range from helping individuals resolve traumatic stress, including PTSD, to counseling individuals who are interested in exploring past life experiences. I spoke with Jerry Bongard on May 27th, 2003 and asked him about his experiences with TIR.

VV: I'd like to ask you a few questions to give people some more context about your work.

JB: I started out with what we called Metapsychology and TIR. That's really been a turning point in my life. That's where the impetus came for this book that I wrote. And also a lot of the counseling that I do, as well as the way that I look at life.

VV: What are some of the areas where you've applied TIR and found it really effective?

JB: The nine years I was director of the Chrysalis Counseling Center, we became known as specialists in helping people with PTSD – post-traumatic stress disorder. There were many different people that came in with trauma. And I just used straight TIR with them and found it very effective with Vietnam veterans.

TIR is the most effective technique I've ever encountered

One case that really impressed me was that of a second lieutenant just out of officer's training who had been put in charge of his own squad. He was so concerned with those folk's lives that he did something the Army wouldn't have wanted him to do. He had them retreat into part of the jungle where they set up a perimeter and just took care of themselves. They didn't go out to engage the enemy at all. He just wanted to make sure all those men would come back home alive and safe.

But they were overrun and everyone was killed but him. When he woke up he was in a bodybag and somebody said "Wait, I think this one's alive." He had suffered, you can imagine the trauma of not only his injuries and the death of his people he was responsible for but his great concern for their lives. He had done so much to protect and save them and now they were all dead. The degree of trauma was quite disabling for him. TIR was so effective for him that he was, in a matter of 4 or 5 sessions, restored to a very normal happy life. He also, even though that could have finished the counseling, became interested in the Near Birth Experience. But that's kind of typical [that number of sessions], although perhaps a little more dramatic with all these people being killed.

VV: So he had the classic symptoms of flashbacks and panic attacks?

JB: Yes, yes, and unaccountable anger that would lash out. Divorce too, because of his inability really to deal with his emotions and his marriage relationship after he returned from the war. The inability of his family really to understand how this had impacted him and what to do. He had all the classic kind of symptoms.

When Hurricane Andrew hit Miami [in August 1992], I had already begun working in TIR with Teresa Descilo. She invited me to Miami where we did workshops and dealt with not only counselors, but also the survivors of that hurricane. This was a really important thing for me because it helped me see how effective it was. Remember, this was when I had just started working with TIR. It was so effective that ever since then Metapsychology, TIR, and the Near Birth Experience that came from Dr. Cheek became very much the focus of my life.

VV: Tell me about your background in ministry and how you got started.

JB: My professional career started as a teacher at St. Olaf College in Minnesota in the Psychology department. After three years in teaching, I decided to go to seminary. A lot of the counseling that I did there got me really interested in what we call the psyche or the soul, this spiritual part of us. After three years of teaching, I went to Lutheran Seminary and became an ordained minister in the Lutheran church. I was an assistant pastor in Everett, co-pastor in West Seattle, and finally pastor in Bellevue over the course of 15 years.

And then that's when I got in touch with people from Metapsychology. I learned some of the techniques and I began to go to the Metapsychology conferences. I saw Dr. David Cheek's demonstrations at the 1994 conference where he gave the keynote address, and I became very interested in his work. He had worked with Milton Erickson and Leslie LeCron, who are so important in the field of clinical hypnotherapy. Clinical hypnotherapy can be used in dentistry, obstetrics, and psychiatry, and just so many fields. David Cheek gave such a good presentation and interested me so much, that I became a student of his for a while. We corresponded a lot and met just a few times. He gave me a lot of interesting information on the subject. When I told him I was interested in writing a book, he gave me a lot of encouragement.

Dr. Cheek said that this area of life before birth or even of life before conception was one that he was very interested in. But as a medical doctor, he had not especially published the part about "life before conception", because he thought his professional colleagues would think of him as too far out. But he thought it was time to do that kind of publication, and was very encouraging and so I did. I collaborated with him, actually, on the first edition of that manuscript. I became a counselor and director of Chrysalis Counseling Center in Bellevue

Washington. For 9 years, I stepped outside the traditional parish ministry to do that ministry, not as a religious counselor, but as a counselor.

I used TIR, Metapsychology, and the techniques that David Cheek had developed for getting in touch with the soul. This meant that a lot of people regressed back to a previous life. We found that that previous life was a very effective metaphor for the things they were struggling with in this life. And we used that it in that way. We didn't necessarily say that it either was actual fact that they were here before or it wasn't. We used that material that came out as a metaphor. But it was so emotionally charged for so many folks that they became convinced, and I did too, that this was in fact getting in touch with a previous life.

Then, I wrote this book which talked about the importance of pre-birth memories while in the womb and the importance of memories just before this life. These were memories with God and an inter- or between-life kind of a thing and earlier life reincarnation. In the book still I used them pretty much as metaphors because it was so helpful in counseling. Specifically, helpful to people to look at that material and apply it to what the issue was for their lives right now.

It became very helpful for a lot of folks and very fascinating and interesting for me. It became really the focus of my life for, not only for that time, but even yet. Nowadays, I do some counseling with TIR and I'm listed on the website as a facilitator for TIR and use that a lot and also the Near Birth technique. But I'm also retired right now as a Lutheran minister, and as a counselor, and just do this when people approach me. Many people do approach me either from the www.TIR.org website or from reading the book or from word of mouth. So I've stayed quite active but am officially retired right now.

Later, I went back into Lutheran ministry as a chaplain for people and their families who had developed Alzheimer's. I'm very interested in that dementia aspect and the grief and working with families. But then I retired from that too. Now I'm just living on an island in Washington State and just enjoying it a lot. I'm doing counseling when people approach me and, surprisingly, different speaking engagements. That's what happened when I was invited to The Learning Annex [of New York City] as a result of my book. People there were very interested in the possibility of existence before birth, whether in the womb or earlier.

Another focus of my life, spirituality, had begun already in the Lutheran ministry and that's part of the whole thing. How the spiritual impact of this kind of permanent part of us, which transcends this life, can be something we can get in touch with to be more of who we are. I give the credit to Metapsychology, to TIR, and especially to Sarge [Dr. Frank A. Gerbode] and Gerald French. For those first few years they were really mentors to me. So it's been a really exciting time ever since I got in touch with that group.

VV: Can you compare how your practice was before TIR and after and your level of effectiveness?

JB: TIR is the most effective technique I've ever encountered. Although the Near Birth Experience for some people will have some of that same impact. This is something that doesn't really apply to your question. There are people, who are very religious people, who get in touch with me (being a pastor) and I find that a lot of those people are not interested in using those techniques. And so with a lot of those folks I use kind of a traditional, supportive, pastoral role even if they aren't members of the congregation I serve.

That's helpful to people, but for those who are open to it, these techniques are so much more powerful. Because they get the results that they really want instead of getting kind of a supportive friend or a listener. They really get the tools to help themselves and much more than that. If people aren't willing to use these tools, I am still willing to work with them anyway. But, I much prefer those who are open to do this whole self-exploration with the most powerful tools that are available. This is what I believe TIR and Metapsychology have. I also believe that this Near Birth Experience for me, probably just because my interest is so high, produces very good results and very helpful things for people and it's somewhat different. But I started it from Metapsychology and Dr. Cheek's plenary address at the 1994 IRM conference.

VV: I was there and I remember a room of 100 people who were literally spellbound for 90 minutes during Dr. Cheek's address [Ed. Note: as reprinted in this chapter].

JB: I was one of those people, and I was spellbound. It opened up a whole new way to view reality, with an open mind rather than a closed one.

A Conversation with Rev. Karl Ullrich, Ph.D

Rev. Karl ("Doc") Ullrich has a wide range of experience in the helping professions. From his career in the FBI to achieving a Ph.D. in Pastoral Psychology, he has a unique perspective on human behavior and treatment programs. I caught up with Karl Ullrich on August 15th, 2003 and asked him some questions about his experiences with TIR:

VV: Tell me about your professional background.

Karl: I was ordained in 1992 as an Epsicopal minister. I served as associate minister at a church until 2002. I was head of a charity from 2001 to 2002. I'm also retired from the federal government; I was a federal agent—Supervisory Special Agent retired in 1998 from that. I received my Doctorate in ministry in 1996 and my Ph.D in Pastoral Psychology in 1998. I have had a practice under a counseling charity since 1998. For the last six months, I've been working for Orange County (California) Mental Health setting up a field program with law enforcement and mental health clinicians riding together.

Rev. Karl "Doc" Ullrich Ph.D

VV: How did you first find out about TIR?

Karl: I believe I saw it a conference back in 1997 or so. I saw a TIR booth there along with EMDR and others. I was kind of intrigued with TIR and so I took the course. I was attracted to the work of Frank A. Gerbode, M.D. and slugged my way through his book and found it fascinating.

VV: How often have you used TIR?

Karl: I've used it quite a bit. Essentially my practice is trauma, I work with PTSD cases from Vietnam, rape cases, religious abuse, dissociative disorders, satanic ritual abuse (SRA), early childhood sexual abuse, etc.

VV: Do you feel that TIR has changed your effectiveness as a counselor?

Karl: Yes, it's one of the early tools that I started to use and I think I have used it effectively. I think it certainly has increased my effectiveness and it's an important one of the skills that I have in my bag that I can employ.

VV: Have you ever found that the length of the session becomes an issue?

Karl: No, I don't because I never schedule anything less than two hours. I don't use the therapeutic hour (or the therapeutic 20 minutes as most HMOs give). If I'm going to use TIR,

I block out 3 or 4 hours and tell the client we're going to be here a while. Get a big box of Kleenex, a bottle of water, a trash can next to them and so on.

VV: Do you find clients having spiritual insights out of TIR?

Karl: Because I am a pastoral psychologist and God (by however it's defined by the patient) is always a part of what we are doing, I have Jung's phrase that was over his door: "Summoned or not summoned, God is always present." In that sense, yes, I think that people do come to spiritual insights through TIR. The big problem that always happens whenever you're dealing with trauma is, "Where is God in this picture?" "How did God let this happen to me?"

> *...Yes, I think that people do come to spiritual insights through TIR*

Anger with God is a classic response to trauma. Yes, in that sense I think once you can start to clear up the trauma itself, once the client starts to grasp what's causing her to be traumatized, then it takes the heat off of God and becomes a tool of enlightenment actually.

VV: Then you find issues of, say, responsibility, maybe someone starts off as a victim feeling that God was punishing him. He ends up realizing later on well maybe there was a decision I made that caused that.

Karl: Yes, that's exactly what I'm talking about.

VV: Any other spiritual insights that clients have typically (or uniquely) uncovered using TIR? I'm wondering if clients reach other conclusions after TIR or Unblocking.

Karl: Specifically, I had a client in her 40's who was the daughter of a Baptist minister. She was raped at age 16 (a virgin) and was thereafter molested by her brother-in-law, also a minister. Her mother blamed her for the rape in that she went out with a girlfriend when she was supposed to be just spending the night at her house. As for the brother-in-law, no one, including her sister, believed her. Her marriage thereafter was a disaster with an abusive spouse who ultimately committed suicide. We worked on the rape with TIR which had a positive outcome and used Unblocking on the molesting events and the suicide. There was also a late term miscarriage which we closed by naming the child and ultimately conducting a memorial service. The client was able to deal with the loss of the child, not as God's will but as a biological incident. She reconciled with her parents and ultimately her sister; the brother-in-law was divorced after it was learned that he had been involved with other women.

As for the "It is part of God's plan" viewpoint, I am not predestination; my God doesn't have a plan, otherwise there would be no such thing as freewill. In my theology, God is working in our plan with us; we are co-creators with God in our daily lives. My God doesn't arbitrarily and capriciously kill little babies or causes a person to suffer; that is the work of us human beings. Look far enough back in any traumatic event and you will find a human cause.

VV: Of course, we're not saying it's a substitute for faith; it can work in conjunction with your faith just fine.

Karl: Right, even though Metapsychology is sort of atheological in its concept, I felt comfortable with the TIR folks, I never felt uncomfortable with them at all. They knew who I was and my orientation. It was clear from questions that I asked that they accepted me and it was fine.

14 Philosophy of Metapsychology

One thing which sets Frank A. Gerbode, M.D. apart from other developers of traumatic stress treatment methods is his meticulous attention to detail in describing the philosophical underpinnings. This chapter includes four of the papers which I believe have best expressed the philosophy behind TIR and Metapsychology. After reading these papers, I hope you'll understand a little bit more about why these techniques work and the fundamental assertions upon which they stand.

- "Trauma and Personal Growth" (1994)

- "What is Science?" (1995)

- "Applied Metapsychology: Therapy or Personal Growth?" (1995)

- "Metapsychology: The Un-Belief System" (1990)

Trauma and Personal Growth
By Frank A. Gerbode, M.D.

The following article was excerpted from the plenary address at the 1994 conference of the Institute for Research in Metapsychology.

The term "traumatic" is generally used to describe the epitome of what is undesirable and bad in life; thus, it may seem strange to talk about trauma in a positive light. Certainly a rape survivor or other violent crime victim could be expected not to appreciate another's thinking that there could be something positive about their having been traumatized. Such thoughts would seem to trivialize the survivor's experience.

A while back, a woman I was having dinner with told me about an incident in which she had been sexually abused as a little girl. The incident clearly held great emotional charge for her. She had been bitterly angry about it all her life and still expressed a desire for revenge on the perpetrator. In an effort to be helpful, I said to her, "You know, there is a procedure called 'Traumatic Incident Reduction' that I think could help you. If you were to have a few TIR sessions, I think that incident could be entirely resolved, to the point that you wouldn't have to keep thinking about it."

She seemed curiously reserved about the idea of getting TIR, a fact which I attributed to skepticism on her part concerning its workability. Weeks later, however, she revealed to me that she had actually felt furious when I had said what I did, because she thought it showed me to have been oblivious to the depth and seriousness of the trauma she had experienced. She thought that in offering her a "quick cure", I was diminishing the significance that the incident had for her, and trivializing her pain.

I'm afraid I got a little snide with her at that point. I said that if someone came to me, having just broken his leg, I would have a choice: either to commiserate with him about the pain he was suffering, or to offer to take effective action in setting the leg—assuming, of course, that I had confidence in my ability to do so—and that it seemed to me that the latter choice would be the more helpful.

I am hoping, then, that in pointing out that there is a positive side to trauma, I am not going to step on too many toes. Yes, trauma by its very nature is painful, and often tragically so. Yet this is not a reason for adopting the viewpoint that the life of a trauma survivor is therefore going to be permanently altered for the worse, or ruined, by the trauma. In fact, we don't have to cope forever with the negative aftereffects of trauma. It is resolvable, and the best way I know of resolving it is, in fact, the procedure we call Traumatic Incident Reduction. I and others have written and spoken about TIR at length elsewhere, so I won't be going into any great detail about it here.

The fact that trauma is resolvable indicates that trauma is a state inherent to a person's mind and is not something external to it. Otherwise the person could not fully resolve it by mental means. Furthermore, at the point of resolution of a trauma, the viewer experiences something positive: an insight often a profound one and a feeling of relief, happiness, and empowerment. This is what is most curious and, on the face of it, unbelievable about TIR: psychologists often think that to "go through" a trauma multiple times would only re-traumatize the client, driving him into its painful affect even more strongly. But in fact, after numerous uninterrupted repetitions, having just perused one of the worst experiences of his life, the client is suddenly laughing and feeling wonderful about it. He feels something positive has come out of the trauma, some new piece of self-knowledge that he probably would never have learned, had it not been for the trauma. So curiously enough, the net effect of the trauma is positive: an acceleration of personal growth! The negative aspects are eliminated and the positive gain remains.

Now before proceeding, let me hasten to state that I'm not recommending that we all go out of our way to be traumatized so that our lives may thereby be enriched! There are other, less painful ways of learning what we need to learn in life. But I am saying that to experience trauma is not to be ruined for life, and that we can get something positive out of it. And as I said earlier, I don't mean to trivialize the experience of being traumatized by saying that. Trauma, by definition, is horrible, difficult, and painful. But without justifying the perpetration of any kind of trauma, we can still talk about how to derive a positive effect from it, a kind of alchemical transmutation of past trauma into present freedom, compassion, and wisdom.

What is it about the nature of trauma that allows for the positive side to come out, under the right conditions? Life is full of physically and emotionally intense experiences. What makes some of these painful and traumatic and others pleasant or even ecstatic? This may seem a strange question, but the fact is that the very same intense experience may be interpreted in one circumstance as painful and in another as pleasurable. People usually don't enjoy the experience of being bitten or having needles stuck into them. But a "love bite" at the right time may contribute to the ecstasy of the moment, and former heroin addicts can derive a "contact high" from pricking themselves with needles. The act of sexual intercourse, when desired, is among the highest forms of pleasure, but when it is forced on someone, it is considered a devastatingly traumatic intrusion on one's person. Is deep-tissue massage or childbirth painful or ecstatic? It depends.

What is the difference? When something is experienced as physically or emotionally painful, the experiencer, at that time, has an aversion to what he or she is experiencing. From this we can derive a useful definition of pain or trauma:

Definition: Pain is the presence of something to which one has an aversion.

or, alternatively:

Definition: Pain is an aversion to something that is present.

This definition is not about a physical sensation mediated by pain receptors. As we have seen, the same intense sensation can sometimes be viewed as painful and sometimes as pleasurable or simply intense. This definition is about the essence of the experience of pain.

By "aversion", I mean the opposite of affinity. Affinity is the willingness or desire to be in the same space as someone or something; it is an impulse toward closeness. Aversion is an unwillingness to be in the same space as someone or something, a desire to be distant from it or him. Aversion itself is not necessarily painful, if the object of the aversion is sufficiently distant. I dislike horseradish and cilantro, but if I don't have to taste them, I don't experience discomfort. But when these tastes are present in my experience, then I experience pain. I can't really understand why people can like these things, because to me they are painful and yucky respectively. Yet obviously the tastes of horseradish and cilantro aren't objectively painful or yucky. It is only my aversion to them that makes them so to me. (My problem is that I don't know how to overcome this aversion; eating lots of horseradish and cilantro probably wouldn't cause me eventually to like them by desensitizing me.) As George Bernard Shaw said, "Do not do unto others as you would have them do unto you. Their tastes may be different."

> *By "aversion", I mean the opposite of affinity. Affinity is the willingness or desire to be in the same space as someone or something; it is an impulse toward closeness.*

There is a fine line between pain and ecstasy sometimes. And the difference is acceptance of experience—whether we reach for experience with our attention or back away from it and try to avoid it. If you are able and willing to reach forward, to embrace and allow yourself to be fully aware of any experience, you will not experience it as traumatic. Some proponents of eastern religion advocate embracing all experience in the here-and-now, allowing oneself to experience it fully, not backing away from it or allowing oneself to be distracted from it by thoughts of the past or future. This would be an excellent idea, if it were possible.

Hamlet said, "To be or not to be: that is the question." But the real question is: "To confront or not to confront?" If you can and are willing to confront an experience, it becomes a challenge and a fruitful opportunity for personal growth. If you cannot or will not, it becomes a trauma, and it can become debilitating.

But that's an ideal. Some particularly sage or adept individuals may be able to succeed in confronting all experience. For most of us, though, that advice is not particularly helpful in practice. Things often move far too fast at the time of an intense experience. We simply cannot assimilate and process everything that is happening, and all its implications. We block out the fullness of the occasion in any way we can, so that in some way we can function and survive at the time. In this case, we regard the incident as a trauma instead of as a challenge, and if I don't go back later and view it fully, it can become debilitating. The act of repression that protects us from overload at the time actually amounts to an act of procrastination: we put off until later the awareness that could de-traumatize the incident. Then if later, when we do have the time, we never get around to confronting the incident in its fullness, it becomes a liability to us instead of a source of strength.

There are two ways in which an unconfronted incident becomes a liability:

1. We have only a certain finite amount of personal energy—or "intention units"—to spend on living our lives. Any procrastinated action, any unfinished business, ties up some of these intention units and diminishes the energy we have to spend on other things. That is especially true of intense experiences, because such incidents attract far more our attention than do routine, everyday occurrences. The reason why, at the end of a TIR session the viewer feels so energized is because she has reclaimed the lost intention units.

2. The effects of triggering or restimulation add to the liability an unresolved trauma. When we are triggered into a trauma, we experience the feelings, attitude and intentions we had at the time and confuse them with what is going on in the here-and-now. That leads to misperception and poor judgment, as well as acting out behavior that can be destructive or at best not constructive.

But the act of triggering is not really essentially a negative thing. It is really only a normal and useful instance of the power of association that inheres in each of us as a birthright. The fact that we can be being reminded of things based on similarity is, for instance, responsible for the fact that we can use language! A word is just a sound or a pattern that can trigger certain associations.

No doubt animals and young children learn the meanings of words by a process of unconscious association. A child comes to associate the word "mother" with (ideally) the presence of a warm, nourishing individual, "dog" with animals that wag their tails, etc. Later in life, we learn that we can control the action of associating and make it more precise by consciously using the process called "defining". A definition is really just an association that a person makes consciously.

We could regard what occurs at an end point in TIR as a conscious redefining or "undefining" of the experience: for a Vietnam combat vet, a tree line no longer carries the meaning that it carried before. In making this "undefinition", the viewer has broken the automatic association a link between the tree line and the concept of imminent sniper attack. A tree line no longer says, "Sniper attack!" to the viewer. Instead, it might say, "Orchard" or "Playground" or nothing at all.

When a past incident is triggered the result is uncomfortable, but it provides a golden opportunity to complete a viewing cycle! Again, we can confront or not confront. If, when restimulation occurs, we look away from what is coming into consciousness, the failure to confront the intense experience of being reminded converts the reminder itself into a trauma, whereas otherwise it would just be a challenge and an opportunity for growth. When someone is restimulated, and they have viewing accessible to them, it's an exciting time because at that time the incident is most accessible and most easily resolved.

In the action of viewing, I can complete the process of becoming aware of what was put on "hold" at the time of the original intense experience. I do this by running through the experience repeatedly, using TIR, until I have had time to fully assimilate and process it. When I do that, then what happens? The trauma longer traumatizes me. I have responded to the challenge the trauma represented, and have come out with the joy of experiencing personal growth. A trauma is just an intense experience that hasn't been fully viewed. When full viewing occurs—no matter when it occurs—the trauma becomes a source of personal growth.

A trauma is just an intense experience that hasn't been fully viewed. When full viewing occurs —no matter when it occurs—the trauma becomes a source of personal growth.

That is why I object to ways of handling trauma that do not involve actually contacting the incident and viewing it fully. That includes drug treatment, as well as methods for helping the client distract himself when triggering occurs. In the first place such non-anamnestic methods only aid the process of anesthesia by which the client can procrastinate the processing of the traumatic data. Even if the client is able to avoid the effects of triggering, she will end up somewhat deadened as individual, as the tied-up intention units have not been released. Secondly, non-anamnestic methods deprive the viewer of the opportunity for personal growth that addressing and mastering the trauma would provide. The net effect the trauma, then, remains negative when a thorough viewing could turn it into a net positive effect. [See Chapter 1 for definition of anamnestic method]

Intense experiences, even traumas, are actually necessary for personal growth. Historian Arnold J. Toynbee (1889-1975) pointed out that cultures that are not challenged by adversity of some kind eventually become decadent and weak. The same applies to people. We have a name for people who lead very sheltered lives, who are protected assiduously from any difficult experiences in life, who have all their needs met by others, and who need never face challenges. We call such people "institutional cases'". An institution is just a place that protects its inmates from the shocks of life. It has long been observed that people who live in institutions for long periods of time eventually turn out weaker for the experience. Their trauma threshold lowers, so that eventually just going out shopping might be experienced as traumatic. (I'm not talking about last-minute Christmas shopping. That *is* traumatic!). A normal person with a higher trauma threshold often regards shopping as a form of relaxation. Ideally, people should be exposed to some difficult situations in life. When they are, they begin to build up skills and self-confidence in dealing with life, and the result is accelerated personal growth, rather than personal degradation. Many Vietnam vets have told me that in a way their time spent in combat was the high point of their lives, perhaps because there they discovered a degree of inner strength and resourcefulness they had not had before. If they had never been put to the test, they might never have known what they were capable of.

People should ask themselves how big a game they want to play in life. And that means: how big a challenge are they willing to undertake? Now, let's look at the definition of happiness: happiness is the knowledge that one is making progress and overcoming barriers toward the fulfillment of an intention. The greater the intention and the more barriers one is overcoming, the happier one is. Happiness and intensity, the potential for pain, go hand in hand. If we never try anything because it might be painful, we lose our opportunity to be happy. Life becomes very insipid and dull. The fact is that going to meet challenges is a good idea, not a bad one. We should always be pushing the limits of what we can achieve; always seeking intense experiences that can challenge us better ourselves and our life-mastering skills. The alternative is stagnation and boredom.

A trauma is always a perceived, failure of some kind, a perceived severe frustration of some intention. It's a little death, because with every intention comes an identity whose job it is to carry out that intention. One is trying to be a husband, and then one's wife leaves; one is trying to be a successful businessman, and then financial disaster strikes. Part of "lifemanship" is having the willingness to move forward, to take chances, to assume an identity that might fail. This is the virtue we call "courage". Courage is the ability to "step forward" into—to assert—a new identity. If we are unwilling to confront the pain of failure, then we cannot bring ourselves to step forward we end up playing a smaller game and being restricted in life. Eventually, if we carry on this process indefinitely, we can become an institutional case (whether we are actually in an institution or not). Courage is not fearlessness. Courage is the willingness to continue to play out a role in spite of fear. When we have weathered and fully processed a series of losses, we become more courageous. We are willing to chances, because we know we can confront the pain of loss.

The complementary virtue to courage is humility. Humility is the ability to step back from an identity, to cease to assert it. In the absence of humility, we become stuck in certain identities and become inflexible in our approach to life. Both courage and humility are based on the same ability: the ability to confront loss. If you have humility, you can confront failing in a certain identity, because stepping back from things is part of your repertoire. You have enough self-confidence and self-esteem to know that you will be OK, regardless of what role you are playing. Since you can confront failure easily because of the humility, you will also be able to confront taking on responsibility better, because you don't see a great down-side potential. If it works and you survive as that identity, fine. If not, you can always step back and find another identity to take on. And all of this has to do with the ability to confront intensity of fear and confusion that attends starting a new activity and identity, and the intensity of pain and disappointment when you have to leave an activity and identity.

Often pain and ecstasy come as fully part of the same package. In the movie "Shadowlands" (1993), British writer C.S. Lewis falls in love with an American woman. She develops fatal bone cancer, and he then marries her. She has a remission, but it is a foregone conclusion that she will die within a year or so. They have a blissful time together, but Lewis's enjoyment is marred by the fact that her cancer is fatal. She explains to him what the deal is: the pleasure they are experiencing together is inextricably linked to the pain he will experience when she dies. The closer and more loving they become, the more painful will be the separation. But he takes a look at it and decides its well worth it. Looking at that movie, I realized that any relationship, if it is close and loving the way relationships are supposed to be, is going to end in pain and tragedy. There IS no way of avoiding that, short perhaps, of a mutual suicide. Either they are going to be estranged and separated some day or one or the other of them will die. To accept the closeness, you have also to be willing to accept the loss. It's all part of the same package. If you can't confront pain, you will not permit yourself to have relationship.

There is a popular and entirely inaccurate notion that great art and neurosis go hand in hand. Great artists who are neurotic are great despite their neuroses, not because of them. It helps to be sane in any activity, even that of a rock star! But the kernel of truth that belies this myth is that great artists generally have experienced life in one way or another. They taken chances and have had intense and traumatic experiences. It is not the traumas that have enriched their lives but the learning they were able to do by confronting those traumas, by allow themselves to experience the full intensity of life.

An aesthetic person, by definition, is one who does not indulge in anesthesia! [which is not to say that all aesthetes are teetotalers]

Maybe the reason why we are here on earth in physical bodies is that we can get a kind of learning here, an intensity of experience, that isn't available up where spirits float around and play harps, or whatever. (I'm not against floating around, though I would prefer to play lute or guitar....) There is a kind of nobility and strength that comes from confronting adversity. Why do we go to war movies, to adventure movies, to Shakespearean tragedies? Why does a movie like "Schindler's List" (1993) garner more Oscars than any other? "Schindler's List" is about the Holocaust, the torture and massacre of the Jews in Nazi Germany... and yet, somehow, it is uplifting! Why? Because the adversity, danger, pain, and deprivation the Jews had to face at that time provided an opportunity for extreme acts of valor and heroism. Experiential intensity brings out the best and the worst in people. If people cannot confront fullness of experience, they may engage in unspeakable acts of cowardice and cruelty; if they can, experience gives them a chance really show their mettle as spiritual beings. People that live only a protected, suburban, "Valley Girl" type of existence never have a chance to prove themselves in that way. When the most "awesome" thing they can envisage is a new sweater or a new car, they have really missed out on what life has to teach. What is truly awesome is when Anne Frank, in her tiny, secret room in Amsterdam, with more than ample reason to believe otherwise, was still able to hang onto the viewpoint that people at the core are basically good.

And that's another form of courage: being able to hold onto one's truth, despite the temptation to embrace the anesthetic of delusion. Courage is making mistakes that hurt others and continuing to take responsibility for one's actions despite the temptations to indulge in justifications that would help one feel less guilty. Courage is hanging onto the knowledge that you want to call up a certain girl and doing so despite the fact that you are terrified. It is not succumbing to the temptation (as I did on more than one occasion) to give yourself reasons why the girl probably isn't interested, telling yourself that she probably isn't home, that you don't really want to go out with her that much anyway, etc. As a youth, I sat in front of a phone for three hours with all this sort of mental activity was going on, and eventually I copped out. I seized on these delusory excuses as a reason not to call, when I really knew they weren't true.

Fear and truth are enemies. A courageous person doesn't allow fear to overcome truth.

Fortunately, certain necessary preconditions having been met, there is no such thing as an emotional trauma so severe that we cannot recover from it and come out better than we were before, provided we know what to do about it. Traumatic Incident Reduction and the other tools we bring to bear to complete the viewing of past traumas can transform traumatic experiences into sources of personal strength. If I know that, when something traumatic happens, I will be able de-traumatize it soon after the in a relatively short period of I will be more willing to try something that might be painful. In words, mere knowledge of the existence of viewing methodology helps provide courage and helps us be willing to get into things that might prove painful.

Nevertheless, despite the fact that we can obtain personal growth from being traumatized and then handling the trauma later in a session or two, that is not the ideal way to grow. To maximize personal growth, the ideal is to provide a correct gradient of challenge which lies just below the individual's trauma threshold. Hence, we don't applaud people who provide traumatic experiences for others. It's an inelegant way of learning. Any good teacher knows that you have to provide material to students on the right gradient. If you don't give them enough of a challenge they get bored; if you overwhelm them with new data, you actual give them a traumatic experience The ideal for maximum learning to expose individuals to experience of an intensity that falls just short the point of overwhelm—the trauma threshold—and so constitutes the maximum challenge the person can handle.

There are two basic kinds learning; both are necessary, and each has its appropriate gradient. Receptive learning involves collecting new information and data from the life and experience we contact outside our own mind. But once we have acquired the data, we must go through a process of assimilating them, of fitting them into our world views, of deciding what to accept and what to reject, and to discover what they mean—what implications they have for our life and how we are going to live it. Just acquiring a lot of facts does not really lead to any new abilities, except perhaps the ability to spew forth the facts. In order really to benefit from new learning, we must fully integrate it and bring it to a point where we can apply it to our lives. This is the process of integrative learning. If we attempted to engage only in integrative learning, it would be like trying to engage in digestion when one had an empty stomach—an unfruitful occupation. By the same token, if we only engaged in receptive learning, we would end up glutted with "indigestible knowledge stones"—with facts for which we had no use. We need, therefore, a proper balance of the two kinds of learning.

Life provides receptive learning. We can assist in this by providing schools and new experiences for people. And there are ways of structuring life so that it is more manageable and less overwhelming. One of the tools Metapsychology has to offer in this department is Steve Bisbey's Schema Program. That procedure enables you to look at your existing situation in life and past situations and goals, and then to examine your current goals and how you envisage these being realized, in concrete fashion; then to create an overall plan for implementing these, based on your current resources and on what aspects of your current situation need to be changed to create the ideal vision. You work on the policies and modus operandi [literally "methods of working"] that have either contributed or not contributed to the fulfillment of your dreams and corrects these. Then you work out a step-by-step program for moving toward your ideal situation, following appropriate gradient and using confrontable, do-able steps. [Ed. Note: The Schema Program is taught in a workshop format. See www.TIR.org/metapsy/calendar.htm]

Another "in-life" tool is what we call "the conditions". The conditions provide an organized means of letting you contemplate different activities in your life and decide what condition each of these activities is in—failure, danger, emergency, normal, success, or final success. The idea is that by knowing what condition you are in with respect particular sphere of activity, you can apply the strategy appropriate to that condition and thus into a higher condition, apply the next higher strategy—a different one—and so continue to move up until you reach success, and that bit of your vision has been accomplished. [Ed. Note: The Conditions are explained in Gerbode's *Beyond Psychology, 3rd Ed*, Chapter 9.]

Viewing, on the other hand, has entirely to do with integration of already-existing data. It, too, is a form of education—integrative education. And in viewing, it is necessary to use a proper gradient. As a first action, a facilitator doesn't necessarily throw the client into the worst incident she ever encountered. Fortunately, the viewer's mind provides its own form of protection. The viewer simply won't have her attention on something that is too deep or highly charged for her to deal with.

This gradient is incorporated the Metapsychology curriculum, a step by step program of actions that one can take with the aid of a facilitator in order to improve one's life. The first part of the Curriculum—Life Stress Reduction—consists of handling what the viewer's attention is already on, thus alleviating stress and allowing the viewer to be free to put his attention where he wants to put it. Stress reduction usually contains a remedial form of TIR, as well as a number of other techniques, used flexibly according to the needs of the viewer. When he has successfully completed Life Stress Reduction, the viewer feels revived and eager to play the game of life. In other words, he is willing to engage in more receptive learning!

The rest of the Curriculum consists of a methodical review, in a logical order, of all aspects of the viewer's experience. The Curriculum properly followed, will result in maximum rate of personal grow for the viewer. [See Appendix D for more detail on the Curriculum]

What is Science?
By Frank A. Gerbode, M.D.

Excerpted from the Fall 1995 issue of the Institute for Research in Metapsychology Newsletter

Richard Gist wrote:

> Science is about the veracity of opinions, not merely their articulation. "Ownership" of a position is a dangerous business, in that intuition is, more often than not, a misguiding beacon.... [T]he process of science stands, at least in principle, transcendent of the foibles of its mortal practitioners as an epistemological frame designed specifically to bite the hands which deed it.

So much has been said about science absent a good definition of the term that I thought I would assay one. Since my predilection is toward things person-centered for reasons that will become apparent, I would like to offer a person-centered definition of science. I would welcome comments or improvements on the definition.

First, of all, I think it is useful to distinguish between "a science" and science as an **activity**. Science, as an **activity**, is the art of non-coercive persuasion.

"Non-coercive persuasion" is the person-centered definition of "proof", since proving something to another person is simply the activity of persuading that person by legitimate means, i.e., without the use of any kind of force. Scientific activity, in fact, is any method of obtaining a consensus amongst a large number of individuals that does not use force: emotional, financial, or physical. It involves experiential demonstration and logical interpretation of what is demonstrated rather than threats, appeal to emotion, etc. Part of the activity of science is making hypotheses, trying to falsify [in the sense of "show to be untrue"] or verify them by experiments, etc., but science may proceed in other ways as well. Certain sciences, for instance, cannot use experiments to any significant degree to verify or falsify their findings. Astronomy and geology come to mind, in this respect, since the objects being studied in these fields cannot effectively be experimented upon. In this case, careful observation and reasoning are the persuasive elements. And every subdivision of the creative activity known as science is best served by its own set of means of proof (non-coercive persuasion). No one method or existing set of methods, therefore, can serve as a criterion for deciding what is, or is not, scientific activity. It depends on what one is studying. The inventiveness of the human mind is boundless, and undoubtedly new methods of engaging in the art of non-coercive persuasion will be added to our current repertoire.

A science is a body of data that follows a pattern that has been widely agreed upon, based on scientific activity.

As Kuhn pointed out, a science does not exist until a considerable consensus has been achieved—what he called a "paradigm". Up to that point, there is merely a proto-science, in which there may yet be a great deal of scientific *activity*. While at the leading edge of sciences like physics and chemistry, there may be controversies about points of theory and methodology, these sciences, like all sciences, have a considerable body of data that is so widely agreed upon that it can safely be written into textbooks. There is no disagreement, for instance, that the sodium ion has a valence of 1 or that force equals mass times acceleration.

The field of psychology, on the other hand, is a proto-science, not a science, because, although a great deal of scientific activity has taken and is taking place, such activity has not managed to forge any major consensus on fundamental beliefs about the nature of the mind or human behavior. In Kuhnian terms, the field is still "pre-paradigmatic". No theory of the mind and behavior has emerged that is so appealing and of such strong explanatory power that virtually everyone agrees on it.

Psychology **is** worthwhile as a form of scientific activity, even if it isn't a science. However, since we have been going along in this field for quite some time now without forging a consensus, perhaps it is time to look to see if we are thinking about the subject in the right way and using a kind of reasoning that can *lead* to a consensus.

A problem arises right at the outset, because there is no consensus about the **definition** of the activity called psychology. It used to be considered the study of the mind, but with the advent of Gilbert Ryle and the behaviorist / logical positivist revolution, the concept of mind fell into disrepute. With the decline of behaviorism came the idea that mind and brain are one, and psychology and neurology have recently tended to become confused with each other. Neurology buffs tend to reduce the concept of mind to that of the brain and nervous system, whilst New Age buffs tend to regard the brain and the rest of the physical universe as a kind of mental entity.

What happened to the idea of studying human experience in its own right? After all, if there are any universals in human experience, they ought to be the most accessible of data and the easiest to examine, and claims about them should be the easiest to verify or falsify.

If I make a claim that certain elements or patterns of elements of human experience are universal to all humans, regardless of age, gender, or culture, then each individual can look to his or her own experience to test my assertions. Moreover, human experience is the raw material from which we build our entire world-view, *including any notions we may have about the physical universe and causal and structural elements and relationships within it*. Epistemologically, experience is always prior.

What happened to the idea of studying human experience in its own right? After all, if there are any universals in human experience, they ought to be the most accessible of data and the easiest to examine...

We arrive at our concepts about the brain and neurology from our experience (largely from our education rather than from direct experience); we don't arrive at a knowledge of what we are experiencing from studying our brain. Husserl and other phenomenologists therefore sought to create a "strict science" of human experience that would serve as a basis for all other sciences, but the descriptions they have offered are (in my experience at least) very difficult to understand and curiously abstract for something that is meant to be experiential.

Since the original meaning of psychology as the study of the human mind and human experience has changed, largely, to the study of neurology and behavior, in my own work I have proposed a new name for the study of experience: "Metapsychology". Freud used this term in the late 19th century to describe the theory that lay behind the practice of psychoanalysis. In my usage, it describes the careful study, classification, and description of direct human experience that should underlie any cogent psychological theory. From such an experiential base could arise a consensus that could lead to a kind of psychology that could be a real science, in the Kuhnian sense.

One of the big problems in forging a consensus has been lack of an agreed-upon terminology. Suppose, however, that we could describe our experience clearly enough and with terminology sufficiently clearly defined that everyone would know exactly what we were talking about when we used terms like "mind", "concept", "phenomenon", "intention"? In my experience, many disagreements that don't resolve in a short period of discussion boil down to terminological problems and resolve when terminology is agreed upon.

Wittgenstein described philosophy as "a battle against the bewitchment of our intelligence by means of words". When we clearly define the words we use to describe experience, and when those words describe elements of human experience that *everyone* can experience for him- or herself, and if we avoid ill-defined and highly theory-laden terms like "id", "ego", "super-ego", "animus", etc., it then becomes possible to have a firm consensus from which to start talking about human nature and experience. Absent such clear definitions, we have the "Tower of Babel" with which the field of psychology is currently confronted.

With verbal and conceptual clarity about experiential entities, moreover, certain patterns in human experience become obvious which were muddied over before, and all this careful definition of terms begins to pay off. The technique of Traumatic Incident Reduction (TIR), for instance, is based entirely on Metapsychology, i.e., on carefully defined, experientially based concepts. The result is a technique that is simple, completely person-centered, and which makes a lot of sense intuitively, both to the therapist and to the client, and clients can understand completely what is going on in the procedure without having *any* kind of theoretical superstructure or interpretations of experience imposed on them. Many other useful helping techniques can be and have been derived from the metapsychological "infrastructure" that we have developed over the past ten years.

I am hoping that Metapsychology, i.e., a clear and careful examination of common experience, can lead to the consensus that the field of psychology needs in order to become a true science.

> *In TIR, clients can understand completely what is going on in the procedure without having any kind of theoretical super-structure or interpretations of experience imposed on them.*

Applied Metapsychology:
Therapy or Personal Growth?
By Frank A. Gerbode, M.D.

Excerpted from the Spring 1995 issue of the Institute for Research in Metapsychology Newsletter

Most work on personal change or improvement being done today falls into two camps: therapy, and what I will call "personal growth". As facilitators, some of us tend to characterize the work we do as a kind of therapy; others among us prefer to regard our work as the facilitation of personal growth.

Viewing as Therapy

There are a number of reasons why it is tempting to characterize our work as a form of therapy:

- It appears to follow the one-on-one format characteristic of therapies, rather than a workshop or training format.
- Like therapy, it may be aimed at improving the client's mental or emotional state.
- As therapists, we would fit an already well-defined and respected niche in society; as facilitators eschewing the therapeutic or medical model, we may render the task of identifying ourselves to the world at large a daunting one.
- If applied Metapsychology be regarded not as therapy but as a form of personal growth, its practitioners may tend to become identified with the New Age movement and thus tainted with the stigma of "flakiness" that that label carries in the eyes of many.
- As licensed therapists, we could accept third party payments for our work—always an advantage in the age we live in.
- Finally, the practice of "therapy" bestows a certain scientific panache on its practitioners. And we are, after all, beginning to see the validity of our work supported by significant clinical research including the different studies we will be hearing about this weekend at this conference.

Viewing as Personal Growth

On the other hand, there are also good reasons for us to perceive as well as label ourselves in a non-therapeutic way:

- If viewing—TIR, for instance—is identified as "therapy", or even as "counseling", we may not be able to establish the kind of grass-roots movement that much of our work is aiming to create. This is because in most areas (and increasingly so) one cannot legally call oneself a therapist or counselor without having had many years of training and higher education, and that automatically excludes the vast majority of the world's population from helping their fellows. Given the amount of help that needs to be done, in my view, this would be a tragic restriction on helping the world overcome its miseries.

- When it was first introduced some 200 years ago, the concept that therapy is what is needed to help people reduce the misery in their lives had some validity. It has since become counter-productive. 200 years ago, people who were disturbed or miserable were considered to be evil, lazy, possessed, or otherwise flawed, and were subjected to very inhumane treatment in the "snake pits" [mental asylums] of the time. The concept that they were suffering from a "mental illness" instead of moral turpitude led to a great reduction in cruelty and moral censure against people who were already miserable. Now, however, as writers like Thomas Szasz have pointed out, the label "mentally ill" has itself become a worse stigma than any moral censure could be, because in most people's eyes, mental illness is a *part* of you and not something you can cure and be over with, whereas moral turpitude is, by definition, something we think people can change about themselves (else what would be the point of continuing to preach to them about it?). Therefore, most people would not like themselves to be thought of as mentally ill, and most, therefore would resist "treatment" for such an illness. We have seen this particularly in Vietnam vets labeled as having "post-traumatic stress disorder" (PTSD). They would prefer to be doing something that isn't identified as therapy.

What is Applied Metapsychology Really?

The above are practical considerations that bear upon how we label our work, but the real answer to what we are doing should come from an honest examination of that work to see in what category it truly falls, not just what it might be convenient to call it.

To answer this question honestly, we must examine the core—even the *defining*—concept of Metapsychology: the person-centered viewpoint. Metapsychology is the study of human experience, *as seen from the point of view of the experiencer*. Built into the application of Metapsychology we call "viewing" is the concept that the client is the sole arbiter of what is real or unreal, good or bad, for herself. The client is respected as the ultimate authority on her own universe. Furthermore, the client is the sole judge of what constitutes improvement for herself. Hence, the client is entirely responsible for setting the goals of viewing.

Metapsychology vs. the Medical Model

The fundamental metapsychological viewpoint outlined above does not align well with the medical model on which the concept of psychotherapy is based. According to that model:

- There is a certain range of thought, behavior, and emotion that is considered "normal" and "healthy".
- One makes a diagnosis. That is, one determines how the "patient" has departed from the "normal" state.
- One then decides on a treatment to cause the patient to move forward to the state of normality, based on neurological, behavioral, or psychological models of mental illness and its causes.
- The therapist then "intervenes" to treat the patient and thereby to cause the patient to move into the "healthy" state he should be in.
- When the patient's behavior, thought, and emotion lie within the range thought of as "healthy", the treatment is adjudged to have been a success.

From the metapsychological viewpoint, this approach is entirely wrong-headed. The first problem is that the medical model on which psychotherapy is based places the locus of control squarely with the therapist. According to this model, the client is a "patient" and hence power-less. Although the client is expected to cooperate with the therapist, it is the *therapist* who is supposed to do the work. In Aristotelian terms, the therapist is "efficient cause", and the patient is merely a "material cause". In other words, the patient provides the raw materials out of which the therapist molds the cure. In viewing, it is the *viewer* who is the principal causative agent, the "efficient cause". The facilitator provides structure, and the viewer's mental and physical environment provides the content for the viewer to work on. In other words, the facilitator is merely a *material* cause in this case, along with the viewer's environment. This means that the whole ideology of viewing is structured to empower the client or viewer, whereas the ideology of therapy is structured to empower the therapist and, implicitly, to disempower the client.

The second problem lies with the concept of "normality". From the person-centered viewpoint, it is up to the client to decide what he wants to have in the way of behaviors, emotions, and thoughts. It is the facilitator's job to help the client achieve them. The facilitator does not "diagnose" from the outside, based on observation of the client, and there is no fixed state of "normality" to achieve.

Thirdly, the medical model is entirely a "negative gain" model. Its definition of "health" is "the absence of illness". There is no prescription or accounting for the possibility of a *positive* direction in which growth could occur, beyond normality. And that's a problem because—let's face it—the normal state of human affairs is none too good. The personal growth model is superior to the healing or therapeutic model, in this respect. It also allows for an indefinite amount of positive gain—how much depends entirely on how far the viewer is willing to go and how much he or she is willing to put into it.

Personal Improvement

What we are aiming for as facilitators is not a change into some *particular* state of being but simply a change for the better, "better" being defined by the client. That's why, in our work, although we do have a Curriculum (see Appendix D) with different sections that a viewer can go through in a certain order, we don't identify them as "levels" or "states". They are simply areas of life—potential stumbling blocks—a person can address systematically to gain an improvement, and when the viewer has attained an improvement he is satisfied with for the time being, he moves on to the next Section. The Sections of the Curriculum address (amongst other things) memory improvement, communication, problem resolution, alleviation of guilt and hostility, overcoming resistance to change, discharging past traumas, and moving out of fixed ideas. When one has completed a certain area, it doesn't mean that there is nothing more to handle in that area. The viewer can always revisit that Section of the Curriculum at a later time and make still more improvement in it. Thus, there are no status considerations of having completed a particular Curricular Section.

Personal improvement, then, is not the attainment of a fixed condition but betterment in one's current condition.

If we look at the progression of an individual's life from being in bad condition, through being in acceptable condition, to being in superb condition, what we see is simply a progression in personal improvement. We can adapt the concept of therapy to this model if, instead of referring to "normality", we refer to "acceptability" as its goal, and if we modify our thinking to regard the client as the means by which this improvement is being done, and the improvement being, not in the client, but in the client's mental and physical environment. In this modified sense of the term "therapeutic", we could say that any method used for human betterment may be therapeutic if it is used to help people whose lives are in bad condition to bring their lives into an acceptable condition. And the same technique may be a personal growth technique if it is used to bring a person up from having a merely acceptable life to having one that is truly superb—again, from that person's viewpoint—a type of life that is more desirable than most people would regard their life as being.

TIR, for instance, can be used either for therapy (in the modified sense given above) or for personal growth. For a person whose life is in bad condition because he is suffering from painful anxiety or the symptoms of PTSD, TIR can be used therapeutically to make life more acceptable to that person. The very same technique can be used later on in the viewer's Curriculum to help him become extremely resilient and stable, free from much in the way of the future possibility of triggering. Communication exercises done as part of the Communication Section of the Curriculum may be redone at any point to improve concentration, communication skills, and general ability to confront life and other people, or even to acquire skill as a facilitator. Viewing, in other words, is best perceived as neither inherently therapeutic in intent nor, primarily, as a means for personal growth beyond the normal. It is best seen as a way of achieving personal improvement in either the "therapeutic" range or the "personal growth" range.

Applied Metapsychology as Education

Viewing, in fact, is primarily educational in its intent, like various spiritual practices, martial arts, or athletic training. Meditation can be prescribed to help a very dissociated person control his attention; it can also be used by a stably happy person to attain high spiritual states. Viewing is also like weight training: while the latter may be used as part of a rehabilitation program for someone with a back injury, it can also be used to do major body building or as training for championship athletics. In other words, many improvement techniques, including *all* methods based on Metapsychology, are neither inherently personal-growth-oriented nor therapeutic—they may be used for either purpose.

All methods based on Metapsychology, are neither inherently personal-growth-oriented nor therapeutic—they may be used for either purpose

Training, viewing, and consultation—currently the three major applications of Metapsychology—are best viewed as the three principal forms of education. They represent, respectively:

1. Receptive education
2. Integrative education
3. Creative education.

Education falls naturally into these three stages. First we must have some kind of input of data. Secondly, we need to integrate the new data with old data that we have learned previously and with our whole world-view. Without this integration, the data is indigestible and unusable. Thirdly, we need to go out and apply that which we have learned to "real life". That is the creative phase—we must use our knowledge to create better conditions in life. In fact, a good test of whether one has integrated a certain set of data is to find out whether one can go ahead and use it creatively in life. Unintegrated data is not usable.

Thus, we offer training courses to teach important life skills (e.g., communication and empathy) as well as professional skills (principally facilitation).

Viewing is entirely integrative education. The facilitator never adds more data to what the viewer already has. She merely assists the viewer in achieving a better integration into his world view of the data he *already* has, so that he can achieve a world view that is more workable for him. She does this in a Socratic manner—by asking the right questions, rather than by attempting to provide the right answers.

Finally, we use consultation to help a client put into practice in life what he has learned in training and viewing. One form of consultation is the Schema Program, designed principally by Steve and Lori Beth Bisbey from England. We use the Schema Program to help clients to put order into their lives.

Sometimes people need a fair amount of integrative education (viewing) before they are ready to receive more data or apply data they already have. In school, from parents, from traumatic incidents, people have often received a great deal of data without having really had a chance to digest and integrate it all into a coherent world-view.

Summary

Applied Metapsychology cannot fully be encompassed under either the rubric of therapy or that of personal growth. It is a form of education that results in personal improvement—movement in a positive direction, whether from a bad condition to an acceptable or better one, or from an acceptable condition to a superb one. In fact, Applied Metapsychology can be used for either therapy or personal growth, but is not inherently either one.

Recordings of this lecture and several other conversations from this book are available on the *Beyond Trauma: Companion Disc.*

(A compilation of MP3 audio files playable on all computers)

Loving Healing Press

www.LovingHealing.com

Metapsychology: The Un-Belief System
by Frank A. Gerbode, M.D.

Transcript of 1990 IRM Conference Plenary Address

I want to talk today about the philosophical underpinnings of Metapsychology—what it's really based on, philosophically. I am sure you have been exposed to many different belief systems, and the last thing I want to do is inflict yet another one on you. Fortunately, Metapsychology is not a belief system at all but, rather, an *Un belief* System.

Let me explain what I mean by that. I'm going to bore you with a little personal history here. My life has consisted of a personal war on belief systems of all kinds. When I was a small child, my family, who were atheists, nevertheless went to church once a year because my grandmother had some sort of affiliation with a certain church in Piedmont. We went at Easter, when it was very pretty and there were a lot of flowers. We sang nice hymns. It was a lovely, aesthetic experience going to such a beautiful church. That was the extent of my religious upbringing.

In church, I could feel the good vibrations. Actually, we didn't have "good vibrations" in those days. That wasn't until the '60's. What we had was a feeling of sanctity and goodness and love. It was wonderful, and I thought, "Boy, I'd really like to believe in Christianity and God. The only trouble is: I don't know *how* to believe." I've never been able to believe in things I didn't believe in. I think it must be a genetic deficiency of some kind. No matter how much I *wanted* to believe in things because they were really good and nice, I couldn't. That has always been a problem with me; it has always gotten me in trouble; it has always made me unpopular. I remember when I was in school, I used to sneer at "school spirit". I thought school spirit was the stupidest thing in the world. I saw no reason why we should think we were in the best school in the world, when there were probably lots of schools in the world that were better. I also thought, "Well, my family's OK, but why think of it as the best family in the world? There are probably lots of families that are better than mine."

Patriotism also seemed really stupid to me. I remember when we had to recite the "Pledge of Allegiance". I always felt embarrassed standing there with my hand on my chest, and pledging allegiance...to a *flag*. And then, when I was about ten years old, they added "...under God" to the pledge. That made it even worse. What if you didn't believe in God? You had to pledge allegiance to a flag under something you didn't even believe in.

At any rate, I have always had a real problem with believing things. I'm just a very skeptical and disagreeable person. I doubt that I'm ever going to change in that respect.

It is said that everybody needs *some* sort of system to order his world, but when I looked for one, I really couldn't get excited about a *belief* system. I had to find something that was not based on faith or belief, but that I could look at from my own experience and *know*—and not have to believe something I didn't believe. True, we all have the task of building up a world view starting with whatever data we have been given and accepted without question. The challenge is to build up a world view based on the *fewest* assumptions; in other words, to construct the most parsimonious world view—a minimalist world view.

It has always intrigued me to wonder what would be the smallest set of assumptions you could start with and still derive a workable world view. The rule of the game was that there could only be a small number of assumptions, and they couldn't include things like "I go to the best school in the world, or "I belong to the best family in the world." When I went to college, I met philosophy student named Ed Becker—and our first real conversations were an attempt to answer the question: could you build up an entire philosophical system from the proposition, "A or not A"—that is, "either A is true, or A is not true." At the time, we thought perhaps you could. I've since been disillusioned about that.

> *I had to find something that was not based on faith or belief, but that I could look at from my own experience and know—and not have to believe something I didn't believe.*

There are a minimal number of things we need to believe, can't help but believe, and do believe. Because if we didn't believe these things, we couldn't live at all. Those are the things I'm interested in. Ordering my thoughts about these things has been a long process for me. It has been going on for at least twenty five or thirty years. But in the late 1980s, during the time when I was writing a book [*Beyond Psychology*] outlining the foundations of Metapsychology, the subject has really crystallized for me. I had to do some serious thinking about what I really did believe and what I didn't have to believe.

I figured that since I'm about the most skeptical person I've ever met, if I outlined the things *I* couldn't help believing, I might find that others couldn't help believing them either. Such ideas, I thought, might form a good basis for agreement amongst a wide group of people. And you wouldn't have to belong to some sort of organization that shared a particular belief system in order to agree with them. You wouldn't have to be a Buddhist, a Freudian, or a Moonie to apply Metapsychology. If I could boil the fundamental assumptions behind life down to a small number, then maybe it would be a very important accomplishment. Such, at any rate, was my dream of glory.

Well, I believe—and I'm going to be a bit dogmatic about this—that I was successful.

Of course, every one believes his own belief system is correct, so naturally I believe that I've been pretty successful in finding some of the fundamental truths that underlie experience. Not that these are necessarily going to prove unchangeable and that nobody will ever be able to find anything better. But I think I've done pretty well, and I certainly feel that one of my major contributions to the effort that we're all involved in has been to install beneath our practice a secure philosophical foundation—one that doesn't require actual belief. Encountering it, you can just look at your experience, and say, "Yes, I know that."

In fact, this has been a problem for me because what I have considered to be the most important thing that I wrote—and the best part of my book—is the philosophical part, the first 100-200 pages. This is the part that has all the boring definitions and tedious argumentation. This is the part everybody else seems to hate the most.

I find there are two categories of people who read my book. The first is those who just skim over it and don't really read it carefully. They don't have a problem with it. They just think it's sort of stupid for me to spend so much time with definitions and such, and they are waiting for me to get to the point. The other group is the ones who read it carefully. The problem with them is that they say, "Yeah, well, I knew that already. So what?" But actually I'm happy to get the latter response, because that's sort of the point of the exercise. We're trying to get at the foundations—the sorts of things you know already. So it's fine that careful readers have that reaction. The only problem is that it doesn't contribute to my glory as much. In order to be properly glorified, I would have to say things that sound very profound and mystical but that are actually not really comprehensible. Then people would feel they were dealing with a superior intellect who could obviously understand things they couldn't. *Sic transit gloria mundi*: literally "So the glory of this world passes away" (An exclamatory phrase used at the installations of the popes.)

> *There are a minimal number of things we need to believe, can't help but believe, and do believe. Because if we didn't believe these things, we couldn't live at all.*
>
> *Those are the things I'm interested in.*

This is an occupational hazard of trying to create an Un-belief System. I found that despite the fact that if you look at what I am saying from a certain viewpoint, it can appear pretty radical, I haven't had anyone actually disagree with me. Either they don't read it, or they read it and say, "So what?" But in any case, I have never gone through life caring too much what people thought, so I'm planning to present some of these ideas to you anyway. I'll try to do so concisely, and I'm going to cover a lot of ground. I'm going to violate the principle that in a lecture you're only supposed to say one thing. I'm going to try to paint in broad strokes the whole philosophical underpinning of Metapsychology.

The first thing to know about the subject is that it starts from ordinary consciousness. It is not a revealed truth. It is not something I obtained from either God or my Higher Self, so far as I know. Well, maybe I did. Who knows? But understanding the subject does not require that one be in an altered state of consciousness. As a matter of fact, my system relies entirely on a normal state of everyday, conscious experience. That's important for an Un-belief System. If you have a system that relies on some sort of special knowledge you get from having been in some special state of mind, then people who haven't experienced that particular state of mind have to take what you say on faith. If you want to create an Un-belief System, you'd better not have any particularly idiosyncratic special states of mind involved in it.

This requirement has gotten me in trouble sometimes. Just last weekend we did a seminar at a local community college, in which we talked about communication. We talked about the fact that in order to perceive something you have to be at a distance from it. And somebody in the audience piped up and said, "What about intuition? What about when you have oneness with the object of perception?" That really caught me off guard; I didn't know what to say. I did say, "Well, gee! My system really doesn't deal well with that because I'm talking about ordinary consciousness. So those of you who have experienced these mystical or intuitive states, please bear with me and accept the fact that in talking about Metapsychology I'm not coming from that viewpoint. You're probably going to have valid objections to some of the things I say, but what I'm saying is from a lower level of awareness. I'm sorry, but that's just the way it is." Or, rather, that's the way *I* am.

I have a pet peeve about the all-too-commonplace practice of Descartes bashing. In the last twenty years or so, a favorite pastime for those of a philosophical bent who have nothing better to do has been to say that Descartes—whose discovery of analytical geometry was only one of a long list of remarkable intellectual achievements—was an idiot because he said, "I think; therefore I am." But actually he wasn't an idiot. Our ordinary experience—though perhaps not mystical experience—fits very well with Descartes' ideas. In ordinary experience, we feel that we exist. We are not "One with the Universe", and we're not being a "Great Nothingness", or whatever. No. We actually feel that we exist. And not only that—we feel that there is a world around us. Naturally people with different belief systems have different viewpoints about the world and about the self.

In some belief systems, the self is an immortal soul; in others, the self is something else that has an immortal soul, and the soul goes off to heaven at some point ... and heaven knows what the *self* does when the soul goes away.

In another belief system, the self is just a body—a sophisticated computer made out of meat which does a lot of very interesting things and hasn't yet been duplicated in the field of artificial intelligence but will be one day.

Yet another belief system—what I call "New Age Pantheism"—says, "Yes, you are your body, but the whole physical universe, including your body, is part of a spiritual All-That-Is. All that is material is also spiritual, so you must be spiritual as well." In other words, the whole universe is God, and since you're part of the universe, you're part of God. Therefore it's all very spiritual and yet material at the same time.

These are belief systems. But what does the world look like from the viewpoint of an Un-belief System? What is the self and what is the world, according to this view? In other words, what is our personal everyday experience of ourselves and our personal everyday experience of the world?

I would like to propose that, in your ordinary experience, you are *that which is acting*. And your world *is that which you are acting upon*. I want to make one point clear here. When I talk about "ordinary experience," I'm inviting you to look at a tiny slice—an instant—of experience. I'm talking about what the world looks like to you at any particular time, from a particular viewpoint. Different people have different viewpoints at different times. And they're not always being the same person, the same identity. So from the viewpoint of a particular identity at a particular point in time, what does the world look like to you? From that viewpoint, those things you are acting on are *out there*, and that which is acting is *you*.

There are two basic kinds of actions that people can engage in. One type of action is an outflow from the self to the world. I call that "creative action", or "creation". Creation is making a change out in the world somewhere; it's making something different. That could mean putting something there that wasn't there before, changing something that is there, or destroying—getting rid of—something that was there. Something is actually different out in the world when you have performed a creative action.

The other kind of action is receptive action, or "reception". When you perform a receptive action, nothing changes in the world, but you are receiving some data. This is an inflow from the world to the self. Perception, for instance, is a receptive action. When I perceive that blackboard and the words written on it, the blackboard doesn't change just because I get data from it. It may be that at the level of sub-atomic particles, perception itself may change something. But in the world of ordinary experience, perception by itself does not change the world.

This brings up a common confusion, one that I had had until I started writing my book, and that is the confusion between *causation*, and *creation*. This confusion has resulted in a lot of philosophical problems. Causation and creation are two different things. It is possible to be causative both in your creative actions *and* in your receptive actions. You can cause inflow as well as outflow. There's no reason why perceiving something shouldn't be a causative act, even though it isn't creating a change out in the world. Various belief systems—such as Creativism and Constructivism—have failed to make that distinction, and so they say that we're creating our universe because we have various filters and whatnot that cause us to perceive it in a certain way. According to them, this means that we are actually creating it. But no. We don't experience the act of perceiving, however "filtered", as a creative action. When you are perceiving the world in a certain way, you don't conceive of yourself as actually *changing* it. It's just that you're getting an impression of what is *there*. That, I think, is an important distinction, and one that is usually not made. I hope I made it clearly. Because if you get embroiled in that confusion, you founder on the shoals of solipsism. You start thinking, "I'm creating everything because everything that I'm perceiving I'm perceiving in a certain way. Therefore I must be putting it there, because I'm contributing to the perception." No. That's not the way it is. No matter how I look at a star—whether I look at it with my naked eye or through a telescope, whether I turn upside down and look at it—it is still a star. It's still there. I'm just perceiving it in a different way. But I'm not changing the star.

At my age, it may take a fair amount of doing to stand on my head and look at a star that way, but despite the effort, I still don't feel I can take credit for creating the star. For what I am going to talk about next, I am going to use the word "entity" in a special sense. I'm not using the term as Stephen King uses it, but with the normal philosophical meaning: "an entity is something that exists." That's all—anything that exists. At any particular time, a person's world consists of all the entities that exist for him at that moment. An entity is just a part of a person's world.

Now, suppose we have an entity—a radio, say—and a person. What connects the person to the radio? It is an action that the person performs. In this case, perhaps, it is an act of perception, a receptive act. The act of perceiving the radio, like any action, does two things. First of all, it *joins* the person to an entity. It is through our receptive and creative actions that entities become a part of the world we're in. It's through perception that we see the things around us. We're thinking of things and we're aware of them. That's what *gives* us those things, so to speak. But our actions also *separate* us from the entities on which we act, because there is a distance across which the action takes place. The fact that you are able to be aware of something means that you are not that thing. It means that there is a distance of some kind between you and it. Again, we are talking here about ordinary consciousness, not a "oneness with the object of perception."

Now I would like to talk a little bit about identity—about what I *am*. I am capable of assuming various identities for various purposes. But what happens prior to my assuming an identity? Prior to assuming an identity, I have an intention. I want to do something—to create or receive something. What do I do when I form that intention? In order to fulfill the intention, I must assume an identity. So first I have an intention, and then I assume an identity to enable myself to fulfill that intention. Suppose, for instance, that I decide I want to make beautiful music. I do make music sometimes. I won't say "beautiful," but I do play a lute (Renaissance forerunner of the guitar) sometimes in my living room when nobody's listening. In order to do that, I must assume the identity of lute player. I have to get myself in the frame of mind in which I am being a lute player. Believe me, that's quite a different frame of mind from the frame of mind I have just now as a speaker. It's almost as though I'm a different person, but it's really just a different identity. An identity is a package of skills, abilities, ways of looking at things and—sometimes—actual physical tools that one assumes as part of oneself when one is trying to accomplish a task. So in order to be a lute player, I have to have a lute. And the lute becomes, as it were, an extension of my self. If I'm really being a lute player, I no longer perceive the instrument as something separate from me. I expand my self-definition to include the lute as well as all the data and skills I need to play it. My focus of attention moves outward, and what my attention is on is the sound of the music or perhaps my appreciative or unappreciative audience—or lack of audience, as is usually the case.

When I'm not being a lute player, I'm being something else, such as a father. I have a whole set of ideas and skills that go along with that identity as well. I'm not saying they're great skills, but at least they're skills.

In all this, the focus of attention is outward from the identity. At any particular time, you are never aware of what you *are*—of your own identity at that time. You always look outward from the identity you are being toward the world. As soon as you "step back" and start looking at that identity, you are no longer *being* that identity, which is an interesting thing. Say I'm being a lute player, and all of a sudden I start worrying about myself as a lute player, and I start thinking, "What kind of a lute player *am* I?" What has happened? All of a sudden I'm no longer being a lute player! I have stepped back and gotten some distance from it. I'm being a *critic* of myself as a lute player. Any identity or yours that you can *look* at, you are not *being* at the instant you are looking at it.

Sometimes, people get fixed in identities and can't get out of them—a really nasty type of trap. The usual reason why a person gets fixed in an identity is that he has found that identity to be safe and other identities to be unsafe. The reason identities can be safe or unsafe is that each identity has a ruling intention that the identity is trying to fulfill. Playing a lute, for instance, is ruled by the intention to make pretty, old-fashioned music. If I fail to make pretty music because I haven't practiced, then that identity has failed. In fact, every time you assume an identity, you risk failure of the intention that is ruling that identity. So some identities become unsafe because you have failed at them. And sometimes you get stuck in the ones you *haven't* failed at—the ones that are "safe".

I suppose one should not speak ill of one's parents, but my father provides a good illustration. He was a great heart surgeon. He had a wonderful bedside manner, and whenever he was being a surgeon, he was a winner. He got a great many awards and honors, and helped a lot of people. The only trouble was that he couldn't turn it off. When he came home in the evening, instead of having a nice dinner table atmosphere, we had "Grand Rounds". My siblings and I had to report on what we had done that day, and when we were finished, we got a consultation from him. *He could not turn it off.*

You can find many people being that way. Sometimes a great politician can't stop being a great politician—even when he goes home to talk to his three year old son—and it doesn't work very well. When we are successful in one identity and don't do as well in others, we tend to get stuck in the successful identity and find it difficult to step back from that identity because we feel insecure about doing so. Ideally, we should be able to step into or out of identities at will—to be versatile.

> **When we are successful in one identity and don't do as well in others, we tend to get stuck in the successful identity...**

Ideally, we can be whatever we need to be to handle whatever particular situation we are in without getting stuck in anything. Now that we've handled everything about the self, we are going to handle everything about the world. As I said, I'm painting very broad strokes here. The question is, "What is the world made of?" First of all, in Metapsychology, we're talking about the world of *experience* and not about the world of some belief system; we're talking about the world of the *Un*-belief System. That is the world we actually live in, the world we can't help living in.

One's world shifts with each identity that one assumes. When I assume the identity of a lute player, my world is filled with notes, finger positions, and various frustrations and victories that have to do with playing the lute. That's quite a different world from that of standing up in front of a group of people and lecturing. But there are certain qualities that are part of any world, regardless of what identity you are in. Any world contains certain types of things.

Now again, I'm not talking about a belief system about the world, though many such belief systems exist. There's a materialistic belief system that says the world is entirely made up of spinning and bubbling atoms and subatomic particles. There's another belief system that says the world is God, it's all spiritual, we're all part of it, and it's wonderful. Yet another belief system says the world is illusion and there really isn't any world. I'm not talking about any of that. I'm talking about how we experience the world—what it looks like from the point of view of the Un-belief System.

In ordinary consciousness, the world is partly objective—or physical, or whatever you want to call that stuff out there—and partly mental. Do mental pictures exist? (By mental picture, I mean any kind of mental image, whether visual, kinesthetic, tactile, olfactory, or whatever.) There's one person I know who refuses to admit he has mental pictures. He says, for instance, that he doesn't dream and that no one actually dreams. But I don't think he is really being honest. He is trying to prove a point rather than honestly reporting on his experience. Everybody else I've ever talked to about it has experienced mental pictures. They can see pictures or impressions of things that aren't out there in the physical universe, as when we dream. The Descartes bashers say Descartes made a big mistake in making the distinction between physical and mental. In so doing, they are ignoring something that is part of ordinary experience.

There are only three kinds of entities in the world of experience. This applies to everybody's world. No matter what identity you have assumed, you will only experience three kinds of entities while being that identity: phenomena, concepts, and facts.

1. **Phenomena**. These entities are the objects of sensory or non-sensory perception. By sensory perception, I mean perception via the physical senses. Things that you can touch, feel, see, hear, smell, or taste are phenomena perceived in this way. A table is a phenomenon; you can see one or feel one. A chalkboard is a phenomenon.

But phenomena also include the objects of non-sensory perception, by which I do not mean "extrasensory perception", or ESP. Non-sensory perception is part of ordinary consciousness; ESP is not. By "non-sensory perception", I mean what happens when you close your eyes and make a picture of a horse. You get a perception of something; that something is a mental picture and not a sensory perception. You are seeing with the "mind's eye", not with the body's eye. Similarly, if you're sitting in a plane and hearing the vibrations as a sort of white noise, you can sometimes imagine symphonies going on in your mind. Perhaps you have had an experience like that.

Parenthetically, I think that composers, even great ones, are just like us except that they have excellent memory, good concentration, and the ability to write down what they listen to in their minds. If I could keep my attention on the beautiful symphonies in my head, and if I only knew how to write music from memory, maybe I'd be able to compose great things too.

2. **Concepts**. The notion of a "concept" is somewhat more difficult to define. We sometimes call them "thoughts" or "ideas", and they are not the same as phenomena. I can have the concept of a horse without experiencing the phenomenon of a particular horse. When I think about horses, I may get impressions of different horses, sort of fleeting pictures of this one and that one. That is what I call the "penumbra" of the concept—the phenomena *around* the concept itself. But those phenomena are not the concept itself. The concept of the horse is something different. It's a little hard to get your hands on it, because it's not something you can touch or feel; it is something you can think, or conceptualize.

Consider the concept of motherhood. When I have that concept, I may get pictures of mothers cuddling babies, or maybe just sort of a warm fuzzy feeling, but these phenomena are not the concept itself. These are part of the phenomenal penumbra of the concept. What is the concept itself? The concept is a potential reality. A concept is something that *could* exist, but doesn't necessarily exist. The concept of a horse, for instance, is one that corresponds to an actual reality—there are still some horses around, in fact. On the other hand, the concept of Pegasus corresponds to a non-reality, because there aren't any winged horses around, yet we can still have the concept. So a concept is something that *could* be a reality in some universe, but might not be a reality currently.

3. **Facts**. A fact is not something you can perceive. A fact is something you can *know*. I *perceive* this podium. I don't *know* the podium. But a fact is something I know. I know, for instance, that women have babies. A fact is actually a concept to which one additional thing has been added. That is: "Yes!" In other words, I have the concept of certain creatures that gallop around, some of which are black, some brown, and one of which is Black Beauty. And then I say "Yes!" to that concept. I agree with it. I agree that it exists. That agreement creates a fact out of that concept. I have a concept to which I have said "Yes!", and, for me, it has become a fact.

I have the concept of Socrates' having been the teacher of Plato. That's not a phenomenon—Socrates and Plato are both long gone. But it *is* a fact that Socrates was the teacher of Plato. So, given the concept of Socrates' having been the teacher of Plato, what makes this concept into a fact in my experience is that I say to myself, "Socrates having been the teacher of Plato—Yes!" If I were to say, "Socrates having been the teacher of Plato—No!", that would mean it is not a fact but is only a concept—a fiction.

Those three things—facts, concepts, and phenomena—make up *any* world. Just those three things.

Now, I mentioned that every entity in a person's experience has an action that relates it to the self, and I have asserted that there are three kinds of entities. So it should come as no surprise that there are three kinds of actions corresponding to these different entities. Not only that, but, because any entity can be received or created, there are six kinds of actions altogether—three for receiving and three for creating. Let me go through those quickly.

1. **Perceptualizing**. Consider the actions that give us phenomena, the actions by which we "perceptualize". On the *creative* side we have *picturing*, which is making a mental picture. You can create phenomena. If I ask you to close your eyes and make a picture or get an impression of a horse, you can do it. That's a creative act. You're not creating something in your physical world, but you are certainly creating something in your mental world.

The receptive action that gives us phenomena is *perceiving*. And again, we have sensory and non-sensory perceptions.

2. **Conceptualizing**. The *creative* action that gives us concepts is *conceiving*. We don't create entirely new concepts very often, but we do do it sometimes. And when we do, it is usually pretty interesting.

The receptive action that gives us concepts is *interpreting*. When we see something—as when we look at the hills of California and notice that they're brown—that can give us several different ideas. We can interpret that brownness to mean that there has been insufficient water, that somebody sprayed herbicide on the hillside, or that it burned. There are a number of different ideas we can get by looking at and interpreting the data, and those ideas are concepts. So you get a concept by *interpreting* something. Now again, I'm talking about ordinary reality, because some people will say you can get concepts by intuition as well. Fine. But let's stick to ordinary reality.

3. **Cognizing**. You "cognize"—*create* a fact—by an action called "*postulating*". Postulating is the action of first conceiving a concept and then saying "Yes!" to it. You say, "My little finger raised in the next few seconds—Yes!" And by God, up it goes! This is a peculiar thing, because, experientially, we move our bodies by postulates. We do not experience ourselves as moving them by moving all those little muscles or by making the nerves do things. According to a certain materialistic belief system, all these things happen neurologically. That's fine, but in the *Un*-belief System, we move by postulates, and that is inescapable. If you decide to do something and it happens, that decision—that postulate—is what made it happen. That's how

you create a fact—you postulate. Whether the fact that you wind up having created is a body motion, or the possession of a million dollars, or whatever, that is how you created it.

How do we *receive* facts? By *understanding*. First we look at data—the California hills, for example—and then we interpret them, getting perhaps several different possible concepts or interpretations. The brown color might be due to lack of rain...to herbicide...to fires. And then we say "Yes!" to one of those interpretations—"Yes! It's lack of rain." At that point we have understanding. We have understood at that point that the brownness is caused by lack of rain. Now, people will object and say, "Well, look! This is crazy! Just saying 'Yes!' to something doesn't make it a fact. It's either a fact or it isn't. Come *on*, Gerbode!" Well, again, according to various belief systems, if *I* believe that the reason the grass is brown is because of herbicides, and somebody else thinks it's because of lack of water, then from the point of view of their belief system, what I have is not a fact. But from the point of view of the Un-belief System—from the point of view of *experience*—it is a fact for me. And that's the crucial distinction.

That doesn't mean that you can't change people's minds. You can. You can cause them to change their minds and cause things that are now facts for them *not* to be facts for them. That's fine. That can be a legitimate thing to do. But there are legitimate and illegitimate ways of changing people's minds. The legitimate ways are ways that are empowering to the individual, such as showing him things, demonstrating things, or educating him. I'm talking about "education" in the true sense of the word, which is *drawing out* knowledge ("*Educare*" means "to draw out of"). This means giving a person data in such a way that he can evaluate it for himself and decide *for himself* whether it's true or not.

A prime example of true education is the practice of Applied Metapsychology that we call "viewing"—a way of drawing out of a person the data that he knows. And it's an acceptable way to change people's minds. It is not taking power from them; it is empowering them. However, there are other ways of changing people's minds that are weakening to people. Being very authoritarian and speaking in a very dogmatic way, or saying things like: "You *must* believe this!" doesn't empower the other person to think for herself. Also, the use of authority, or force, or pain in order to enforce belief is not an empowering way of changing people's minds. So I don't recommend these methods.

Since I'm talking about empowerment, I want to get on to my next topic, which is: what *is* power, anyway? I'm talking about personal power, not the kind that is generated in power stations. My thoughts on this topic have really only appeared in the last year, because I've recently given it some close attention.

In order to understand the nature of power, it is first important to discuss the relationship between desire and intention. I first started looking at this topic after the first IRM Conference, during a conversation with Steve Bisbey about wishing and desiring. I was thinking about what the difference was between a wish and a desire. It occurred to me that you can wish for things that you know are impossible, and you can desire things you know are impossible, but you can't *intend* things that you know are impossible. [Ed Note: Stephen Bisbey passed away in late 2004 after a long illness.]

Desire is an impulse toward something's existing, an impulse toward having something exist for oneself in one's universe. At the age of fourteen, when I watched the movie, "Picnic", I formulated an intense carnal desire for Kim Novak. I knew for a fact that there was absolutely no possibility of my ever attaining this particular experience. Nonetheless, I wished to bring it into existence.

Desire, then, is the impulse toward bringing something into existence. It is really a form of positive regard toward the world or some part of it, an affinity for some entity. When you desire something, you have a very positive regard for it, such as I had then for the feeling—the phenomenon—of having Kim Novak making love to me.

So much for desire. Now we're sort of edging toward power, but the next concept we're going to look at is that of ability.

What is ability? Obviously, while I had the desire to have Kim Novak, I didn't have the *ability*. I didn't have the connections, the good looks, or whatever. Now, ability is the capacity to act in a certain way. And, as I mentioned, we all have certain basic abilities. We have the ability to *picture, perceive, conceive, interpret, postulate,* and *understand*. These are the basic abilities out of which every other ability we have is constructed. They are like the basic instruction set of a computer. By combining them in various ways and applying them to different entities, we build up everything else we are capable of doing.

Suppose you are a very able person. At any give time, there could be lots of things you are able to do that you're not doing. Why? Because you don't *desire* to do them. You could be the most brilliant and capable person in the world, but if you have no desire for things, no capacity to desire things—no drive—you are not going to make anything happen. People are going to look on you rightly as a weakling. So in order to be powerful, not only must you have ability, you must also have drive—the desire, the impetus to make things exist. If you don't have the impetus to make things exist, you are not going to bring anything into existence.

What is desire plus ability? *Desire plus ability is intention.* If you desire something and if you conceive yourself to be able to create or receive that thing, then you intend to create or receive that thing—again, from the point of view of the Un-belief System. We're not worried about what you're actually—by some external criteria—able to do or not. But in your own view, if you desire and are able, then you intend. So intention equals desire plus ability.

The capacity to intend is a person's personal power. It's the amount of intention a person can generate which constitutes his power. Intention is what makes things happen. It is the force which makes things happen. Anything you can intend very strongly is going to happen. Some people are capable of generating a stronger intention than others. You might say that a person has X number of intention "units" with which they do everything that they do, both creatively and receptively. The intention units that have to do with receiving are *attention* units, and those that have to do with creating are *volition* units. The total amount of intention (attention and volition) a person can generate is that person's power, and that power is composed of *understanding*, *control*, and *drive*. Or capacity to understand, capacity to control, and capacity to desire (drive).

I believe that if you don't desire anything, you also can't be happy—because happiness consists of making progress towards the fulfillment of an intention. If you didn't have any desires or intentions, you wouldn't be happy. You'd just be kind of "blah". I really don't think that not caring about anything is an ideal state to be in. I mean...life is meant to be *lived*, and part of being happy is having a lust for life. This is one of the main things we address in viewing, because, you see, a lust for life is just a positive regard for entities, for parts of the world. It's a positive feeling about their being there. It's not a bad thing, it's a positive feeling. The bad thing is not desire, but aversion—not *wanting* things, but *hating* things. That's what we've got to handle, not the positive side. And one way in which we handle that is by means of the technique called Traumatic Incident Reduction. TIR handles the negative feelings that cause people to have unwanted aversions to things. That is a very important part of what we do.

The total amount of intention a person can generate is that person's power, and that power is composed of *understanding*, *control*, and *drive*.

Corresponding to each of the components of power—which, again, are drive, understanding and control—there is a corresponding condition in the world that promotes each component, that empowers us, and that we seek. We seek a world that empowers us.

Corresponding to desire and drive, there are things in the world that we find pleasant or beautiful. We are attracted to—we have an impulse toward the existence of—things that are pleasant and beautiful. So we seek beauty, and we seek relief from pain.

What quality of the world would make it possible for us to understand things? Something about the world that gives it the quality of being a learning experience. I call that the "heuristic" quality of the world.

Thirdly, we seek a world that is orderly, because order is the objective element that corresponds to control. We can control things if they're in a certain order. And if we can perceive the order of things and put them into order, we can control them.

Basically, the type of world we want to live in—that people universally want to live in—is a world that strikes what each considers to be a proper balance between pleasure and beauty, learning, and order. And if any one of these overbalances the others, then the quality of life deteriorates.

If you're pursuing beauty but your life is going to hell in a handbasket, and you're not learning anything, then you won't really be happy. That's the trap drug abusers fall into.

If you're pursuing order but you're not having any fun, then life is a disagreeable grind, and you are bored.

If you're pursuing life as a learning experience, it can sometimes be very painful if it gets very disorderly and unpleasant. You can always chalk things up as learning experiences, though, no matter bad life is.

That has to do with entities of the world. Now I'd like to talk about other people, because we do have certain basic goals, relative to other people, which are different from those that relate to things. Power has to do with entities, but power is not the only thing we're after. I don't want to leave you with that impression. I think that what we seek even more than power is a state of relatedness to other people—what I call "communion".

> **I think that what we seek even more than power is a state of relatedness to other people...**

Communion is a combination of communication, comprehension and affection. Comprehension is a sharing of experience between people. If I am prehending something (having something in my grasp or awareness) and you are prehending the same thing, then we co-prehend—we comprehend—that thing. Affection is affinity or love for other people. These three elements—affection, communication, and comprehension—together constitute communion.

Communion with others is something we seek even more strongly than we seek power. In fact, I would venture to say that we seek power ultimately in order to have communion. I think any of us will find that the deepest points of satisfaction in our lives have been those times when we were in the deepest state of communication with another, when there was the deepest sharing of experience (comprehension), and where we had the strongest affection or love for other people.

These are the moments we live for. This is the point of the whole exercise.

So what can we do about it in the viewing and facilitation we do? The key to the answer to this question concerns the nature of help.

What is help? Some belief systems prescribe a specific ideal state that people ought to be in, and consider that help consists of moving them into that state. This is the basis of the medical model, and it gives us the concept of "therapy".

The physical body is an engine that runs at an ideal temperature; it has an ideal blood sugar; it has an ideal structure, etc. The object of a doctor is to get the body into that condition that is most nearly ideal. That works for the body. But what about the mind?

The concept of "therapy" has been carried over into psychiatry, which is considered to be a medical sub-specialty. According to the canons of psychiatry—such as they are—there is an ideal way in which the mind operates—a normal way to be, mentally. And the psychiatrist's job is to get a person from his current state of mind to that ideal, normal state—whether the person wants to go there or not. The patient's reluctance is sometimes a problem and is interpreted as "resistance". That's what you get if you look at help from the viewpoint of a belief system.

But if you work with an Un-belief System, you don't have a pre-conceived notion of how the person should be. Instead, help becomes the simple action of enabling him to get what he wants, whatever that happens to be. That's what help really is. And what people want most deeply, according to the Un-belief System, is this quality of communion with other people. So if we can help them get that, we're guaranteed to help them in getting what they in fact want, and not something we're imposing on them.

Viewing is therefore not a therapy; it's an un-therapy. It does not prescribe a specific desirable condition. It simply helps a person to get what he wants. And that is the best thing you can do for another person, since that's what he's trying to do for himself.

Rules of Facilitation

The Rules of Facilitation (condensed)
By Frank A. Gerbode, M.D

Much of the skill of a Traumatic Incident Reduction facilitator has nothing to do with one's knowledge of post-traumatic stress disorder or of the theory or technique of TIR. The facilitator's greatest challenge is to create an environment suitable for viewing and to conduct the session according to the rules governing the procedure.

The Rules of Facilitation were written to help the facilitator of a viewing session bring each session to a successful conclusion, that is, a successful conclusion according to the viewer.

The Rules of Facilitation empower the viewer to be independent, instead of dependent on the facilitator.

Considering how important these rules are in a session, think for a moment what life would be like if we adapted these rules to our day-to-day interactions with others.

1. **Ensure that the viewer is in optimum physical condition for the viewing session.** This means that a viewing session is not delivered to someone who is hungry, tired, physically ill, or under the influence of alcohol or psychoactive drugs (except when drugs are prescribed as a medical necessity). Sometimes viewing is delivered to a person who is not in optimum condition because that seems like the only way the person may ever get to an optimum condition. However, a viewer in a non-optimum condition has to work harder in session.

2. **Ensure that the session is being given in a suitable place and at a suitable time.** Ensure that the viewing environment is secure, private, clean, quiet, and environmentally comfortable. Also make sure that the time is safe, that is, enough session time is set aside for the viewer to reach a good end point for the session. Make sure all cell phones, pagers, and desk phones are turned off.

3. **Do not interpret for the viewer.** Do not tell the viewer anything about the material being viewed, including what it means or how to think or feel about it. Facilitators differ radically from therapists, who may offer interpretation and advice to the client. When a therapist is delivering a Metapsychology viewing session, he informs the client that he will be operating under a different set of rules.

4. **Do not evaluate for the viewer.** Avoid indicating, in any way, that what the viewer has said or done is right or wrong. Do not judge, criticize, disparage, or invalidate the viewer or her perceptions, assumptions, conclusions, values, reactions, thoughts, feelings, or actions. Also, do not validate the viewer because such praise may lead her to sense a judgmental atmosphere and to anticipate that the next judgment might not be so favorable.

5. **Control the session and take complete responsibility for it without dominating the viewer.** This makes it unnecessary for the viewer to be concerned about what comes next in the viewing procedure and allows total attention to be placed on the viewing.

6. **Be sure to comprehend what the viewer is saying.** A viewer knows right away when the facilitator does not comprehend and then feels alone and unsupported. The facilitator who does not comprehend must seek clarification and, at the same time, take responsibility for the need to do so. The facilitator might say, "I'm sorry. I didn't get what you said. Could you give it to me again", and would not say, "You are being unclear," or even, "Please clarify what you mean."

7. **Be interested in the viewer and in what the viewer is saying instead of being in teresting to the viewer.** A viewer generally knows immediately whether or not the facilitator is really interested. If the facilitator becomes interesting, the viewer's attention will be pulled away from the viewing itself. The facilitator's interest supports the viewer's willingness to view and report on the material being viewed.

8. **Act in a predictable way so as not to surprise or distract the viewer.** It is not appropriate for a facilitator to disclose personal feelings during a viewing session. The viewer has enough to do when confronting his personal issues without having to deal with extraneous actions, remarks, or displays of emotion on the part of the facilitator.

9. **Do not try to work with someone against that person's will or in the presence of any protest.** Sometimes a relative, friend or employer will succeed in persuading a person to do viewing when she does not really want to. In such a circumstance, viewing does not work well or at all. Accordingly, the facilitator must be guided only by the viewer's interest and priorities and must never try to coerce or manipulate the viewer into running a particular procedure when the viewer is not really interested in doing so. The facilitator must never rush the viewer. The viewer who senses that a quick response is being demanded will not take time to do the major beneficial action in viewing, the act of viewing itself.

10. **Carry each viewing action to a success for the viewer.** Be certain not to end a viewing procedure at a point of failure or incompleteness. This is the main reason sessions must not be fixed in length. One of the major functions of a facilitator is to help the viewer find the courage and confidence to confront difficult material that he has not been willing or able to confront alone. When viewing becomes painful, difficult, or embarrassing, the viewer may feel like ending the session. Should this occur, the facilitator's job is to encourage the viewer to stick with it and to confront and handle the difficulty to a point of resolution. Fortunately,

viewing procedures are sufficiently powerful and effective to warrant such confidence on the part of an experienced facilitator.

11. **Maintain a firm and primary intention to help the viewer.** As obvious as it may seem, a facilitator who is mainly interested in improving clinical skills or in making money, even if he also intends to help the viewer, will tend to lose a viewer's trust. In order to maintain the level of viewer/facilitator confidence required to preserve the viewer's sense of session security, the viewer's interests must be preserved at all times. The facilitator must agree not to reveal or use anything the viewer says for any purpose except to help the viewer and to enhance the process of viewing.

Although some of these Rules may seem obvious or simplistic, particularly to trained therapists, they need to be enumerated because they are essential to the overall method that supports the work of successful TIR related techniques.

B Frequently Asked Questions (FAQs)

This section should answer some questions for professional practitioners (clinical psychologists, social workers, counselors, therapists, ministers, etc.) interested in using TIR & related techniques. Others should consider reading the **FAQ for Those Interested in Receiving TIR & Related Techniques** beginning on p. 311.

FAQ for Practitioners Interested in Using TIR & Related Techniques

Contents:

1. What is TIR?
2. What is TIR Useful for?
3. How long has TIR been in use?
4. What is the anticipated outcome of TIR?
5. What are the contraindications and risks of TIR?
6. What are the historical antecedents of TIR?
7. How and why does TIR work?
8. How does TIR compare with other techniques for addressing traumatic stress?
9. What research exists to support the effectiveness of TIR?
10. How can I find out more about TIR?
11. How can one get trained in TIR?
12. What are the prerequisites for training?
13. How can I refer people to a TIR practitioner?

1. What is TIR?

TIR is a brief, one-on-one, non-hypnotic, person-centered, simple and highly structured method for permanently eliminating the negative effects of past traumas. It involves repeated viewing of a traumatic memory under conditions designed to enhance safety and minimize distractions. The client does the most important work in the session; the therapist or counselor offers no interpretations or negative or positive evaluations, but only gives appropriate instructions to the client to have him view a traumatic incident thoroughly from beginning to end. Hence, we use the term "viewer" to describe the client and "facilitator" to describe the person who is helping the client through the procedure by keeping the structure of the session intact and giving the viewer something definite to do at all times. The facilitator confines herself simply to giving a series of set instructions to the viewer; she offers no advice, interpretations, evaluations, or reassurances.

In what we call Basic TIR, which addresses known incidents, the viewer locates a specific trauma that he is interested in working on—one with a specific, finite duration. Then he treats the incident like a "videotape". First, he "rewinds" it to the beginning, then "plays" it through to the end—without talking about it while he is viewing it. *After* he has viewed it, the facilitator then asks him what happened, and he can then describe the event or his reactions to going through it.

After the viewer has completed one viewing (and one description), the facilitator has him "rewind the videotape" to the beginning and run through it again in the same fashion. The facilitator does not prescribe the degree of detail or content the viewer is to get on each run-through. The viewer will view as much as he is relatively comfortable viewing. After several run-throughs, most viewers will be able to contact the emotion and uncomfortable details in terms of the strengths of the emotion more thoroughly. Typically, the viewer will reach an emotional peak after a few run-throughs and then, on successive run-throughs, the amount of negative emotion will diminish, until the viewer reaches a point of having no negative emotion about the incident. Instead, he becomes rather thoughtful and contemplative, and usually comes up with one or more insights concerning the trauma, life, or himself. He displays positive emotion, often smiling or laughing, but at least manifesting calm and serenity. At this point, the viewer has reached an "end point" and the facilitator stops the TIR procedure.

In Thematic TIR, a specific feeling called a "theme" is used to discharge a sequence of related traumatic incidents.

A TIR session is not ended until the viewer reaches an end point and feels good. This may take anywhere from a few minutes to 3-4 hours. Average session time for a new viewer is about 90 minutes. Average total session hours to eliminate PTSD symptoms is 15 - 20 hours.

2. What is TIR useful for?

It is highly effective in eliminating the negative effects of past traumatic incidents. It is especially useful when:

a. A person has a specific trauma or set of traumas that she feels has adversely affected her, whether or not she has receiveda format diagnosis of "PTSD".

b. A person reacts inappropriately or overreacts in certain situations, and it is thought some past trauma might have something to do with it.

c. A person experiences unaccountable or inappropriate negative emotions, either chronically or in response to certain experiential triggers.

3. How long has TIR been in use?

TIR has been in use since 1984 in something similar to its current form. It has undergone minor modifications over the years, mostly in the interests of greater simplicity and teachability.

4. What is the anticipated outcome of TIR?

In the great majority of cases, TIR correctly applied results in the complete and permanent elimination of most PTSD symptomatology. It also provides valuable insights, which the viewer arrives at quite spontaneously, without any prompting from the facilitator and hence can "own" entirely as his own.

By providing a means for completely confronting a painful incident, TIR can and does deliver the mastery of the situation a person would have had if he had been able to fully confront the trauma at the time it occurred.

5. What are the contraindications and risks of TIR?

TIR is contraindicated for use with clients who:

a. Are psychotic or nearly so. TIR is most definitely an exposure or uncovering technique and hence is not appropriate for such clients.

b. Are *currently* abusing drugs or alcohol. Clients should avoid taking painkillers, sleeping pills, tranquilizers or drugs which may impair their physical or mental abilities for at least 24 hours prior to a viewing session. Some substances require a longer abstinence before viewing can take place.

   c.   Are not making a self-determined choice to do TIR. For TIR to work, the client has to want to do it. If the client is there under duress (e.g., on court order) or trying to please someone, TIR will not work. It may be possible, however, to explain to a reluctant client what TIR is. The client must be motivated to do the work before starting.

   d.   Are in life situations that are too painful or threatening to permit them to concentrate on anything else. If the client is afraid of being murdered or engaged in violent fighting with his spouse, for instance, such issues/situations would have to be addressed first by consultation to develop a plan to handle the current life situation before the client will be ready to do TIR.

   e.   Have no interest in or attention on past traumas. A general rule is to follow the interest of the client. The larger subject of Applied Metapsychology includes a large array of techniques that help a viewer to bring greater order and certainty to her mental environment.

Since the TIR technique is completely client-centered and non-forceful, clients will protect themselves if they are getting in too deeply by simply discontinuing the procedure. Hence there are no negative effects from properly facilitated TIR. If the facilitator were to try to *force* the client to run an incident, TIR could cause a considerable (though temporary) upset. But one of the cardinal Rules of Facilitation (see Appendix A) is never to force the client and always to follow the client's interest. Since we follow the client's interest at all times, we don't encounter resistance. If the client resists, we consider that we are not addressing the material the client should be looking at, at present.

6. What are the historical antecedents of TIR?

TIR grew mainly out of the work of Carl Rogers and Sigmund Freud. In *Two Short Accounts of Psycho Analysis*, Freud describes a method to resolve sequences of similar traumas:

> "What left the symptom behind was not always a *single* experience. On the contrary, the result was usually brought about by the convergence of several traumas, and often by the repetition of a great number of similar ones. Thus it was necessary to reproduce the whole chain of pathogenic memories in chronological order, or rather in reversed order, the latest ones first and the earliest ones last; and it was quite impossible to jump over the later traumas in order to get back more quickly to the first, which was often the most potent one."

Freud later abandoned this technique in favor of free-association. It seems likely that (in retrospect) the reason it didn't work well was the degree of interference the analyst introduced by interpretations and by forcing the analysand [client] in various ways, and the lack of a systematic, repetitive approach to achieving the desired anamnesis.

The work of Carl Rogers was invaluable in providing rules – such as a proscription against interpretations and evaluations – and an overall viewpoint of respect for the authority of the client, both of which we use to help create a safe environment for running TIR.

Although Rogers first described his work as "non-directive" and later as "person-centered", it seems obvious that "non-directive" doesn't mean the same thing as "person-centered". "Person-centered" describes the attitude of respect for the superior authority of the client and the concomitant rules for not stepping on the client's reality. "Non-directive" means the client gives structure to the session. These two are actually separate dimensions (see Fig. 1). For instance, classical, free-associative psychoanalysis is non-directive, but not person-centered. Cognitive and behavioral therapies are non-person-centered (because the therapist disputes the reality of the client) and directive (the therapist determines the agenda). Rogers is non-directive and person-centered. TIR falls into the fourth category: person-centered *and* directive, as the TIR facilitator provides structure for the client to be able to do the work of the session.

	Non-person centered	Person-centered
Directive	Cognitive and Behavioral Therapies	TIR and Applied Metapsychology
Non-Directive	Classical, free-associative psychoanalysis	Pure Rogerian

Dimensions of Direction and Person-Centeredness (Fig. 1)

7. How and why does TIR work?

Freud based his work on the theory that in order to recover from past traumas, it is necessary to achieve a full anamnesis (recovery of lost memory). He never adequately explained *why* anamnesis was necessary; however let's consider a person centered explanation.

A trauma, by definition, is an incident that is so painful, emotionally or physically, that one tends to flinch away from it, not to let oneself be aware of it, or, in Freud's terms, to repress it. It is the *flinch* and not the objective content of the incident that makes it a trauma. An event that is challenging and exciting for one individual may be traumatic for another. The one for whom it is a mere challenge is able to "stay with it" and master it; the one who experiences it as a trauma is usually not.

By definition, then, a trauma contains repressed material. Contained in a trauma, too, is one or more intentions. At the very least, there is the intention to push it away, to blot it out, to repress it. And there are usually other intentions as well, such as the intention to fight back, to get revenge, to run away, or (quite commonly) the intention to make sure that nothing like this incident ever happens again.

> *By definition, then, a trauma contains repressed material.*

An activity continues so long, and only so long, as the corresponding intention exists. That means that for each ongoing intention, there is an activity (at least a mental one) that continues as part of the here and now.

People subjectively define time in terms of the activity they are engaged in. Objectively, time is a featureless continuum. But subjectively, time is divided up into chunks—periods of time. For every given activity (and for every given intention) there is a corresponding period of time, and so long as you have an intention, you remain in the period of time defined by that intention (and activity). Holding onto an intention holds you in the period of time that commenced with the formulation of that intention. There are only two ways of ending an intention:

1. Fulfilling the intention, whereupon it ends spontaneously. You can't keep intending to win a race after you have won it.

2. Unmaking it. Even if you don't fulfill an intention, you can decide not to have that intention anymore and cause it to end. This, however, requires a conscious decision. You have to be aware of the intention and why you formed it.

But what if the intention is buried in the middle of a repressed trauma? In this case, neither condition (1) nor (2) can be satisfied, and the intention persists indefinitely. The person remains in the period of time defined by that intention, i.e., *the person remains in the traumatic incident.* The incident floats on as part of present time and is easily triggered (i.e., the person is easily reminded of it, consciously or unconsciously).

The only way a person can exit from that period of time (and from the intentions, feelings and behaviors engendered by the trauma) at which point the following becomes clear:

a. What intentions were formulated at the time of the incident.

b. Why they were formulated at that time.

Then, and only then, one can satisfy condition (2), above, for ending an intention, and one can let go of the intention. Without a thorough anamnesis, condition (2) cannot be satisfied.

8. How does TIR compare with other techniques for addressing traumatic stress?

Please see Chapter 10.

9. What research exists to support the effectiveness of TIR?

Charles Figley and Joyce Carbonell have studied four different approaches to trauma resolution: TIR, EMDR, V/KD, and TFT. In their view, all are very effective. However, also as noted above, their study was not designed as an outcome study.

The largest controlled study to date (57 subjects), completed in February, 1995, compares TIR to DTE and waiting list controls, using a variety of test instruments, on crime victims with PTSD. Waiting list controls showed no significant improvement over time; DTE showed significant improvement over controls ($P < .01$) on test instruments relating to PTSD; TIR performed significantly better than DTE ($P < .01$) on most test instruments. This study was part of a Ph.D. thesis by Lori Beth Bisbey and was done under the auspices of the California School of Professional Psychology, San Diego, CA.

Another doctoral study was done by Wendy Coughlin (St. Petersburg, FL) on the effects of TIR on Panic Disorder. That study showed TIR producing significant improvement on test scores.

See also the list of research projects on p. 322 as well as Chapter 8.

10. How can I find out more about TIR?

Visit www.TIR.org

11. How can one get trained in TIR?

You can learn TIR by taking the basic TIR Workshop (see Appendix C) from a certified TIR trainer. Consult the Traumatic Incident Reduction Association website as above in order to find the nearest certified trainer.

12. What are the prerequisites for training?

A willingness and intention to help others and a reasonable degree of intelligence.

13. How can I refer people to a TIR practitioner?

Visit www.TIR.org

FAQ for Those Interested in Receiving TIR & Related Techniques

Q: I have heard the terms facilitator and viewer. What do they mean and why don't you use therapist and client or patient?

A: We have chosen the neutral term, *facilitator* rather than "therapist" or "counselor" for the reason that "therapy" can imply that there is something wrong with the person who is coming for help, and "to counsel" means "to advise". Neither of these fits well with the concept of person-centered work. In addition to this, some TIR practitioners are licensed therapists while others come from different backgrounds. The word facilitator as we use it was coined by Carl Rogers.

We use the word *viewer* because it is the client, the viewer, who is doing the most important work in the session, that of viewing his or her own mental world. The facilitator assists in this process.

In this book you at times see *practitioner, therapist,* and *facilitator* being used interchangeably depending on the viewpoint of the speaker/writer. Likewise you will see *client* and *viewer* used interchangeably. We do avoid the use of the word *patient* and the medical model in general as we do not find it empowering for the people who come to us.

Q: I know that I've had traumatic incidents in my life. How do I know that TIR will be useful for me?

A: The best way to find that out is to work with a trained practitioner. Probably you will have at least a few sessions before starting into TIR depending on the issues you want to work on and the judgment of your facilitator. TIR addresses one specific incident or one specific feeling at a time, and that incident or feeling is taken to an end point. An *end point* is a new concept in one-on-one person-centered work. Rather than ending sessions according to an arbitrary time period, the session is completed on a point of success for the client. Each piece of work is ideally taken to an end point within one session, meaning that that particular piece is completed to the satisfaction of the viewer.

Q: Do I need to qualify for a diagnosis of post traumatic stress disorder (PTSD) in order to benefit form TIR?

A: Not at all. While almost everyone has some traumatic experiences that can be relieved and resolved with TIR, not everyone has PTSD.

Q: What should I do to prepare myself for this work in order to get the best results?

A: First of all you need to be getting good food and adequate rest. This can be difficult if traumatic incidents are in restimulation and are claiming attention. If this is the case, do the best you can and consult with your facilitator about it.

Sometimes life can be too chaotic to allow a person to do the work of viewing (whether using TIR or other techniques) effectively. If that is the case, your facilitator can work with you to devise a plan to get life flowing more smoothly before embarking upon viewing sessions.

Some drugs and medicines interfere with viewing. Antidepressants (SSRI's) and mild pain killers are fine. Drugs that inhibit consciousness such as tranquilizers and heavier pain killers do interfere. Consult with your facilitator about this.

Q: How can I find someone who delivers TIR?

A: A list of certified facilitators can be found on www.TIR.org. There are also many more trained facilitators who are delivering TIR but who are not yet certified.

Q: How long does TIR take?

A: Resolution of an unwanted condition can sometimes be achieved in as short a time as one or two sessions. However a condition that has been in existence for some time or has many aspects usually takes longer to completely resolve. A single incident such as a car accident, operation, loss of a loved one, etc., is commonly complete for the viewer in a matter of a few hours or even less. Larger issues such as a lack of self-esteem or self-confidence, or on-going relationship problems, which may have a number of roots, require several sessions to resolve. Life Stress Reduction (see p. 325), which consists of a case plan tailored for the individual client's goals and which usually makes use of a number of techniques beside TIR, typically takes 15 – 20 hours.

Q: What if I'm not ready for TIR because it's too challenging for me to look directly at my traumas?

A: Often people find it is easier to face the memory of these events in the safe time and space of a TIR session than it is to haul the weight of the traumatic memories around with them while trying to keep those memories from resurfacing. Some people are not ready for TIR right away. The larger subject of Applied Metapsychology contains a large array of techniques useful of reducing stress (see Life Stress Reduction, p. 325) and building confidence. These other techniques are not just to prepare a client to be able to do TIR, but are productive of significant progress in themselves.

Q: How much does TIR cost?

A: Fees vary in different parts of the world. They are set by the facilitator in private practice or by organizations employing TIR facilitators. A few grant subsidized providers such as

Victim Services Center of Miami, Florida and Victim Services Lambeth (London, UK) provide free services for qualifying individuals.

Q: I understand that TIR is not done in a "50 minute hour". How long does a TIR session last?

A: Both the facilitator and the viewer need to schedule sufficient time for TIR to be taken to an end point. One and half to two hours is about average, though the sessions can be much longer or shorter than that. After you have done some of this work together, you and your facilitator will often have a better idea what is a normal session length for you, though session length also depends upon the severity or complexity of what is being addressed.

Q: Will I be able to have my TIR session billed to my insurance provider?

A: Contact your nearest facilitator to find out. Some practitioners who are licensed therapists accept insurance. The open-ended session length required by TIR does not fit the standard model, but some therapists have worked out arrangements with insurance companies in their areas.

Q: How does TIR work? How is it different from other methods?

Although certain discrete elements of the Traumatic Incident Reduction (TIR) procedure can be found in other methods, the procedure, when taken as a whole, is unique in distinctive ways:

- TIR is highly directive, yet not interpretive.
- TIR is based on the creation of a safe space by a precise division of labor between facilitator and viewer, stringent rules prohibiting evaluation or invalidation, and a powerful and precise communication technique.
- TIR sessions have no fixed length; you stop the procedure when the viewer reaches an appropriate end point.
- TIR handles emotional charge resulting not only from what has been done to the client, but also from what he has done to others, observed others doing to others, and what he has done to himself.
- TIR uses repetition as a powerful tool to reduce charge after the source of the charge has been located.
- TIR is systematic, cut-and-dried, and requires a minimum of special ability on the part of the facilitator other than:
  - The ability to manage and control communication.
  - Willingness to observe strictly the Rules of Facilitation.
  - An honest desire to help.

TIR can easily be learned and used by both professionals and lay practitioners, with supervision, to help others.

Q: I've hardly had any traumatic events in my life and I am not sure that they are having any bad effect on me. Does that mean that I am "in denial"? What do you have for people like me?

A: If you have areas of your life that you would like to improve or develop, there is a great adventure waiting for you in Life Stress Reduction (see above) and the Metapsychology Viewing Curriculum. Traumatic experiences are not the only things that make people feel limited or less able than they'd like to be. There are also things like upsets, worries, confusions, uncertainty, and just plain not feeling that they are living up to their potential.

One of the many nice things about person-centered work is that you will never be accused of being in denial. If you show up with issues, concerns or goals, a well-trained facilitator will be able to make up a case plan tailored specifically for you, a sort of road map from where you are to where you'd like to be.

This also applies to the person who comes in very interested in relieving the pain of past traumas but who one day wakes up and realizes that those events are no longer casting a shadow over life. New goals are possible.

Appendix		
C	# Training and Resources	

The TIR Workshop (TIRW): TIR Training – Level One

This workshop covers the nature of trauma, the consequences of traumatic incidents, and the Traumatic Incident Reduction (TIR) technique, a one-on-one, highly structured, yet person-centered approach to resolving the emotional charge contained in traumas and permanently eliminating their negative aftereffects in a brief amount of time. It also contains data on how past traumas may be triggered and how unwanted feelings, emotions, sensations, attitudes, and pains (FESAPs or "themes") arising from past trauma may be traced back to their origins and eliminated. The workshop also teaches Unblocking, a technique that is highly useful in preparing a client for TIR and for handling issues that are not directly trauma-related. Unblocking can be applied to broad areas of life (e.g. "your marriage", "your job", etc.).

Prerequisites:
Time: *3 4 days*
Objectives:

- Comprehend the nature of restimulation and destimulation

- Comprehend the mechanics of a conditioned response chain

- Define the Traumatic Incident Network

- Distinguish between primary and secondary traumatic incidents

- Identify cases that are appropriate for resolution with Traumatic Incident Reduction (TIR)

- Describe the procedural logic of Basic and Thematic TIR

- State the session prerequisites for TIR

- Assess client readiness for TIR

- Define the roles of viewer and facilitator in TIR

- Create a "safe space" for the client in which traumatic incidents can be reviewed to resolution

- Be comfortably and unwaveringly present with the client, regardless of the content of the traumatic material

- Correctly identify the proper end point of any TIR procedure

- Employ TIR successfully in the rapid resolution of trauma-related conditions in both formal and informal settings.

- Deliver TIR and Unblocking instructions smoothly and clearly

- Handle the communication cycle and use acknowledgments to encourage or complete communication

- Handle a variety of client concerns that may arise within a session so that TIR can be successfully completed

Outline:

I.   Conditioned Response Phenomena
    a.   Post-traumatic stress disorder (PTSD) with obvious flashbacks
        i.   The nature of trauma
        ii. Pavlovian theory of trauma and trauma resolution using TIR.
    b.   Related conditioned response disorders with absent flashback
        i.   Conditioned response chains
        ii. Primary and secondary trauma
        iii. The Traumatic Incident Network
        iv. The mechanics of restimulation
II. Theory of Traumatic Incident Reduction
    a.   How TIR works
    b.   Basic TIR
    c.   Thematic TIR
    d.   Facilitation and Viewing
III. Establishing a Safe Environment
    a.   Rules of Facilitation (see Appendix A)
    b.   Communication Exercises (CE's)
    c.   Facilitator exercises
IV. Unblocking – an adaptable TIR-related technique
V.   TIR Procedure
    a.   Steps of the procedure
    b.   TIR exercises
VI. Experiential – supervised facilitation
    a.   Giving one or more TIR sessions
    b.   Receiving one or more TIR sessions

TIR Expanded Applications Workshop (TIR-EA)

This workshop was designed to complement and expand upon the TIR Workshop. It was developed after extensive interviews with graduates of the TIR Workshop, their trainers, and their viewers.

The TIR – Expanded Applications workshop consolidates knowledge and skills gained in the first workshop and goes on from there to add an array of new tools to the facilitator's repertoire. New methods taught this workshop will benefit a wide range of clients, from clients who may be fragile and overwhelmed up to clients who are very high-functioning people.

The new techniques presented can be used to prepare a client for TIR, building up ego strength (ability to face life) and developing the client's capacity to successfully address specific areas of life. These techniques also provide the tools for a case plan that is more varied and interesting to any viewer than one containing only TIR and Unblocking. In addition to providing new tools, the TIR-EA Workshop expands the use of TIR itself to fit more situations. Sometimes life problems and distractions make it hard for the client to settle comfortably into the role of a viewer. In this workshop, the student learns to differentiate between facilitation – applying the techniques of TIR and Metapsychology for the benefit of a viewer, and consultation – addressing practical problems and handling them in real life to remain within the person-centered context while doing either.

TIR – Expanded Applications serves as an ideal preparation for the Case Planning for TIR and Life Stress Reduction Workshop.

The TIR – Expanded Applications Workshop results in greatly increased confidence and certainty in using TIR and related techniques and provides for the facilitator the ability to address and resolve a much wider range of human difficulties and preoccupations.

Co-facilitation (students exchanging sessions) allows workshop participants to gain subjective insight into the value of these new techniques.

Prerequisites: *TIR Workshop*
Time: *3 4 days*
Objectives: Please see www.TIR.org and click on Practitioner Training for full details

Case Planning for TIR and Life Stress Reduction (CP-LSR)

The TIR workshop teaches TIR and Unblocking only. This workshop introduces participants to a much broader range of metapsychological techniques and also has an extensive section on Case Planning. With these new tools at their disposal, facilitators can precisely address a great many more situations and conditions than they could using only TIR and Unblocking.

Case planning makes use of extensive intake interviews that serve not only to gather data but also to provide case improvement for the client. Properly conducted, they will:

- Be recognized by the client as beneficial in themselves.

- Give the client an understanding of the scope of work possible.

One goal of this workshop is to provide participants with skills and data that will enable them to conduct such interviews.

Depending on the needs and interests of the client, case plans may incorporate both TIR and other techniques taught in this workshop. In competent hands, a full case plan is capable of addressing and resolving an enormous number of issues, including a host of unwanted mental and emotional conditions.

Life Stress Reduction (LSR) often provides stable relief from conditions that clients have for years attempted unsuccessfully to resolve. And while LSR enables clients to reduce or eliminate current negative emotional charge, it also contributes to their achieving enduring positive states of mind, and can clear the way for increased awareness and self-realization. Like the TIR workshop, this workshop is intimate, participatory and may be intensely rewarding..

Prerequisites: *TIR Workshop*
Time: *4 days*
Objectives: Please see www.TIR.org and click on Practitioner Training for full details

Exploration and Enhanced Rapport Workshop (E&ER)

Better, faster, and more rewarding results with clients are guaranteed after this intensive 2-day workshop. In this workshop, facilitators gain a whole new perspective on communication. The vital elements necessary for full success as practitioners of any helping method, including TIR, are demonstrated in a series of exercises.

Facilitators and other members of the helping professions tend to be communicative people, or they wouldn't have been attracted to this line of work. While recognizing and validating your existing ability to have good rapport with clients and to communicate well, this workshop will show you how to make further improvements in your level of communication and rapport, leading to better and faster results.

In the second half of the workshop we take a detailed look at the art of Exploration, a technique that, unlike TIR, has no predetermined questions. You will learn how to remain person-centered while using this relatively unstructured technique. Your mastery of Exploration in all its various applications ensures smoother progress for your clients and greater satisfaction for both client and facilitator.

During the course of the workshop you will have the opportunity to try out this material by co-facilitating (exchanging sessions) with another student.

Prerequisite: *TIR Workshop*
Time: *2 days*
Objectives:

- Understand the basis of all rapport and how to put this understanding to good use.

- Understand the effects of presence, intention, and interest on the quality of communication.

- Understand each part of the communication cycle in depth, leading to greater quality of communication, both in session and in life.

- Understand and be able to apply the differences between social communication and session communication.

- Understand and be able to accurately observe and repair the factors that cause communication to fail.

- Use the method of Exploration in all of its applications to deepen rapport and to increase the effective use of session time.

Other Workshops (availability varies)

For a complete list of other workshops available, please see www.TIR.org and click on Practitioner Training for full details

Effective Communication Workshop (ECW)

This workshop uses simple but powerful communication exercises that magnify and clarify the components of communication. While practicing these exercises, students discover the means to improve their ability to communicate effectively and achieve more satisfying relationships. This workshop is the Communication Exercises for use in life.

Prerequisite: None. **Time:** Two days.

Enhanced Rapport In Life Workshop (ERLW)

This one day builds upon the ECW (see above) and takes the participant's abilities to build rapport to a new level. Guaranteed enhanced quality of communication and hence of relationships from this workshop!

Prerequisite: The Effective Communication Workshop. **Time:** One day.

Empathy Workshop (EWS)

This workshop based on the methods of Marshall Rosenberg provides a definition of empathy, then teaches the students the communication skills they will need to become effective and empathic in life.

Prerequisite: None. **Time:** 2 days.

Internships

A newly trained TIR facilitator goes into session with the steps of the procedure, the Rules of Facilitation (see Appendix A), improved communication skills, and a basic understanding of how and why TIR works, but she is still a novice. She lacks the extensive experience with the technique, and the increased knowledge that supervision can supply.

With some supervision by a TIR trainer, some technical direction, and a fair amount of experience, the novice TIR facilitator begins to use overall strategies instead of just rules. For example, he may become good at assessing ego strength, environmental distractions, and knowing when to get more data before proceeding with a viewing program. At this level, a TIR facilitator delivers consistently successful TIR and Unblocking sessions.

Internships are a good way for a TIR facilitator to quickly advance from novice to advanced beginner, and then, with further experience, to become competent, proficient, and, finally, expert. Compassion fatigue is not an issue for an expert facilitator, because she can deliver consistently successful sessions.

Internships are offered by most certified trainers.

Certification

Certification occurs upon completion of a TIR internship. Certified facilitators enjoy the following benefits:

- Recognition for TIR and Metapsychology skills

- TIR website listing as a Certified TIR Facilitator

- Authorization to use the TIRA and AMI logo in promoting TIR-related services

- Eligibility to enroll on a TIR Instructor Program

Research on or Involving TIR

Research papers available from Dissertation Express are indicated with Order Numbers in the list below.

- Bisbey, L., (January, 1995). "No Longer a Victim: a Treatment Outcome Study of Crime Victims with Post-Traumatic Stress Disorder." (Doctoral Dissertation, California School of Professional Psychology, San Diego, CA.)
  [Ed. Note: Her dissertation compared TIR and Imaginal Flooding with a control group with 57 subjects]
  Specify Order Number 9522269
- Coughlin, W., (May, 1995). "Traumatic Incident Reduction: Efficacy in Reducing Anxiety Symptomatology." (Doctoral Dissertation, Union Institute, Cincinnati, OH.)
  Specify Order Number 9537919
- Figley, C. and Carbonell, J. "Active Ingredient" Series at Florida State University, 1994-95. http://www.fsu.edu/~trauma/art2v2i2.html
- Odio, Francine (2003) "Traumatic Incident Reduction (TIR) Program for Children." (Doctoral Dissertation, Carlos Albizu University.)
  Publication Number AAT 3100829 from Digital Disserations
- Valentine, Pamela V. (1997) "Traumatic Incident Reduction: Brief Treatment of Trauma-Related Symptoms in Incarcerated Females." (Doctoral Dissertation, Florida State University. Advisor: Smith, Thomas E.)
  Specify Order Number 9725020

DISSERTATION *express*

Students, faculty, staff and researchers can now order their own unbound copies of dissertations and theses with express delivery to their home, school or office. Select from over one million titles available from UMI.

Go to **http://wwwlib.umi.com/dxweb/**

Metapsychology/TIR-Related Literature

In order of publication date:

Gerbode, F.A. (1989). *Beyond Psychology: an Introduction to Metapsychology*, 3rd Ed. (1995) Menlo Park, CA: IRM Press

Moore, R.H. (1992). "Cognitive-Emotive Treatment of the Post-Traumatic Stress Disorder". In W. Dryden and L. Hill (Eds.) *Innovations in Rational Emotive Therapy*. Newbury Park, CA: Sage Publications

Moore, R.H. (1993). "Innovative Techniques for Practitioners". *The RET Resource Book for Practitioners*. New York, NY: Institute for Rational-Emotive Therapy.

Gerbode, F.A. & Moore, R.H. (1994). Beliefs and Intentions in RET. *Journal of Rational Emotive & Cognitive Behavior Therapy*, Vol. 12, No. 1., Albert Ellis Institute

French, Gerald D., MA, CTS and Harris, Chrys, Ph.D., CTS (1998), *Traumatic Incident Reduction (TIR)*. CRC Press

Bisbey, L., MA, CTS and Bisbey, S. (1999) *Brief Therapy for Post Traumatic Stress Disorder: Traumatic Incident Reduction and Related Technique*. John Wiley & Sons.

Descilo, Teresa (1999) "Relieving the Traumatic Aspects of Death with Traumatic Incident Reduction and EMDR". In: pp. 153-182; Figley, Charles R [ed.]; *Traumatology of Grieving: Conceptual, Theoretical, and Treatment Foundations*; Philadelphia: Brunner/Mazel,

Gerbode, F.A. (2005). "Traumatic Incident Reduction" in Garrick and Williams [ed.] *Trauma Treatment Techniques: Innovative trends*. New York, NY: Haworth Press.

Volkman, Marian (2005) *Life Skills: Applying Metapsychology to Daily Life*. Ann Arbor, MI. Loving Healing Press.

Volkman, Victor (2005) *Beyond Trauma: Conversations on Traumatic Incident Reduction*, 2nd Ed. Ann Arbor, MI. Loving Healing Press.

Selected Journal Articles about TIR

Commons, Michael L. "The Power Therapies: a Proposed Mechanism for their Action and Suggestions for Future Empirical Validation" .*Traumatology*, 6(2): pp. 119-138, August 2000, ISSN: 1534-7656

Dietrich, Anne M; Baranowsky, Anna B; Devich-Navarro, Mona; Gentry, J Eric; Harris, Chrys Jay; Figley, Charles R   "A review of alternative approaches to the treatment of post traumatic sequelae." *Traumatology*, 6(4): pp. 251-271, December 2000, ISSN: 1534-7656

Figley, Charles R; Carbonnell, Joyce L; Boscarino, Joseph A; Chang, Jeani. "A Clinical Demonstration Model for Assessing the Effectiveness of Therapeutic Interventions: an Expanded Clinical Trials Methodology." *International Journal of Emergency Mental Health*, 1(3): pp. 155-164, Summer 1999

Gallo, Fred P. "Reflections on active ingredients in efficient treatments of PTSD, part 2." *Traumatology*, 2(2): pp. [Article 2], 1996 ISSN: 1534-7656

Mitchels, B. (2003). "Healing the wounds of war and more: an integrative approach to peace-- the work of Adam Curle and others with Mir I. Dobro in Upanja, Croatia". *British Journal of Guidance and Counselling*, 31(4), 403-416.

Valentine, P. and Smith, Thomas E. "Evaluating Traumatic Incident Reduction Therapy with Female Inmates: a Randomized Controlled Clinical Trial." *Research on Social Work Practice*, v. 11, no. 1, pp. 40-52, January 2001, ISSN: 1049-7315

Valentine, P. "Traumatic Incident Reduction I: Traumatized Women Inmates: Particulars of Practice and Research", *Journal of Offender Rehabilitation* Vol. 31(3-4): 1-15, 2000

Valentine, P. and Smith, Thomas E. "A Qualitative Study of Client Perceptions of Traumatic Incident Reduction (TIR): a Brief Trauma Treatment." *Crisis Intervention and Time Limited Treatment*, v. 4, no. 1, pp. 1-12, 1998, ISSN: 1064-5136

Valentine, P. "Traumatic Incident Reduction: A Review of a New Intervention." *Journal of Family Psychotherapy*, 6, (2), 79-85, 1995.

Wylie, M. S. "Researching PTSD: Going for the Cure." *Family Therapy Networker*, 20(4), pp. 20-37, July/Aug. 1996.

Appendix D
Metapsychology Viewing Curriculum

Practitioners delivering TIR and related techniques offer a comprehensive approach to self-actualization called viewing. Viewing is a person-centered method in which one person, a facilitator, provides a safe space and a structure that helps another, called a viewer, to closely examine his world in order to gain insight and ability. The viewing curriculum, is a step by step approach to inspecting the structure of the mind. The Curriculum is divided into sections that address broad sweeping areas of life such as communication, problem resolution, and tolerance of change.

When viewers are given the means to inspect the long-term patterns that determine the structure of their lives, they often experience revelatory breakthroughs as they release emotional "charge" (repressed, unfulfilled intention).

Before starting the Curriculum program, the viewer engages in a Life Stress Reduction plan, tailored to his or her individual needs.

Life Stress Reduction

The journey of self-discovery begins by addressing the concerns and issues on which the viewer is currently focused, clearing away the mental debris that is creating unhappiness and inhibiting progress in life. This form of work may include resolving the effects of past traumas using Traumatic Incident Reduction, but other techniques are typically used as well.

After Life Stress Reduction, the viewer can expect to have renewed hope, general good feelings, revitalization in life, and a readiness to address issues that are universally a part of the human condition.

The Metapsychology Viewing Curriculum

Each section of the Curriculum addresses a broad area of life common to everyone. By examining these areas, one by one, in a logical sequence, the viewer can reduce accumulated charge and develop greater ability in those areas. We all have the ability to communicate, for instance, and to resolve problems, at least enough to survive. Significantly improving these abilities has a profound impact on the quality of life.

Help Section

After the Life Stress Reduction, the viewer first addresses issues of help and control. Relieving charge on these subjects can produce major positive changes, especially in relationships. Help and control are also important because every viewing technique involves both. The viewer needs to be able to both give and accept help and control to gain the best depth and insight from the rest of the Curriculum. This section contains a number of objective and subjective techniques, the result of which is a viewer who is comfortable with help and control and with her present-time viewing environment.

Memory Section

The purpose of the Memory Section is to help the viewer recover the ability to contact his past easily. In this section, the facilitator directs the viewer to locate pleasant moments in the past. Finding non-traumatic incidents helps to separate out areas of past trauma from non-traumatic areas of the past. Viewers can then see that the rough spots are contained in discrete moments of time and not strung together in one lifelong traumatic episode. The result of this section is a viewer who can contact the past easily.

Communication Section

Once a viewer has improved contact (in the Help Section) with her present, and (in the Memory Section) with her past, she is ready to work on improving her contact with other people by addressing charge on the subject of communication. Quality of communication is a significant factor in the quality of relationships.

Improving the viewer's ability to communicate to the facilitator can even improve the speed and effectiveness of viewing.

On completing this section the viewer will have significantly improved her ability to give and receive communication.

Resolution Section

Communication is a prerequisite to the resolution of problems. Most problems are best resolved by effective and thorough communication. Hence we address problems after addressing communication.

The activity of living consists of resolving problems, so this section also has a direct impact on the quality of life. When a problem remains unsolved, one becomes preoccupied or worried about it. It is then hard to move on and pay attention to other things in life.

As a result of doing this section, the viewer can have more interesting and enjoyable problems, can resolve them more easily, and can live life more effectively.

Reconciliation Section

A person commits a misdeed when he has been unable to resolve a problem in a more constructive fashion. Unwanted situations, when encountered, must be handled in some way or other. Ideally, they are handled by confronting, understanding, and communicating, leading to a resolution of the problems contained therein. Thus it is best to address communication and problems before addressing misdeeds.

Guilt and hostility mainly spring from one's own misdeeds, which may be hidden, or from charge connected with others' misdeeds. Being basically good, a person will naturally act in the best way he can for the good of all, but if he is weak in his ability to solve problems, he will feel "forced" to commit misdeeds.

Completing this section results in reconciliation with, and forgiveness of, both self and others and consequent relief from guilt and hostility.

Resilience Section

Committing misdeeds leads to upsets for oneself and others. Once misdeeds are cleared up, the viewer can fruitfully address upsets. Handling major upsets is therefore best addressed after misdeeds, guilt, and hostility have been handled.

Upsets also occur as a result of unwanted, often unexpected, changes. They produce emotional pain and can make life miserable.

When a person has handled major upsets and unwanted changes in life, she becomes more resilient: more able to handle upsets and to tolerate change. Life becomes freer and more enjoyable.

General TIR Section

At this point in the Curriculum, the viewer has become much more aware. Now he has the opportunity to address with TIR any remaining traumas, unwanted feelings, emotions, attitudes, sensations, or pains that were not accessible earlier.

Rightness Section

Up to this point, the viewer has been mainly dealing with negative feelings, past traumas, and other types of charge, all of which exert a compelling influence on her thinking and behavior. When these influences have been reduced, she is better able to change her habits of thinking and behaving.

The Rightness Section consists of addressing misconceptions, false information, and fixed ideas, since these affect our ability to be right.

An odd fact about human beings is that we always think our current beliefs are right. Otherwise we wouldn't believe them! Our urge to be right and to justify our actions results in a certain rigidity of thinking and behavior that does not serve us well. At this point in the Curriculum, the viewer has eliminated much of the compelling emotional charge that holds these fixed ideas in place. He can now make use of the techniques of the Rightness Section to examine those ideas and to choose whether to accept or change them.

The result of this section is a viewer who has determined for himself what is right, but feels less of a need to assert his rightness.

Index

9

TIR AND METAPSYCHOLOGY LECTURE SERIES:

MP3 format CDs containing <u>4 to 10 hours</u> of audio
Including lectures, workshops, interviews, and roundtables.

- MP3 Audio CDs play on **all computers**
- Also works with DVD and CD players marked "**MP3 Compatible**".
- Includes a license to burn one complete set of CDs for personal use (in case you want to use a conventional CD player.)

Vol. M1: Gerbode on TIR and Metapsychology
Vol. M2: Critical Issues in Trauma Resolution (5 hours)
Vol. M3: Beyond Vietnam—Soldiers in their Own Words
Vol. M4: Beyond Trauma—Companion Disc
Vol. M5: Moore on TIR and Metapsychology
Vol. S1: David B. Cheek, M.D. and Near Birth Experiences.

Visit our website to order today!

Loving Healing Press
www.LovingHealing.com

Life Skills:
Improve the Quality of Your Life with Metapsychology.

Life Skills, by Marian K. Volkman, is the first ever self-help book based on Metapsychology techniques. Based on the work of Frank A. Gerbode, M.D

• Learn handy and usually quite fast techniques to assist another person after a shock, injury or other distress.

• Learn simple methods for expanding your awareness on a daily basis.

• Gain a deeper understanding of what a relationship is, and how to strengthen and nurture it.

• Learn the components of successful communication, what causes communication to break down, and how to repair breakdowns.

• Gain vital keys to understanding those behaviors of other people that have previously been inexplicable to you.

• Learn an effective tool for making important life decisions.

"The chapter on the importance of relationships is worth the price of the book alone" —James W. Clifton, Ph.D.

Praise *for Life Skills*

"Life Skills is replete with examples, exercises, episodes from the author's life, and tips   this is a must for facilitators, clients, and anyone who seeks heightened emotional welfare — or merely to recover from a trauma."
—Sam Vaknin, PhD, author of *Malignant Self Love: Narcissism Revisited*

"Life Skills is a serious, impressive, and thoughtful work with one objective in mind: teaching how to reach one's full potential in practical, pragmatic, easy to follow steps that will literally change one's life."   —James W. Clifton, M.S., Ph.D., LCSW

"Life Skills by Marian Volkman is not to be read once and then put away. It is a guide to living a full, satisfactory life, a philosophy, a challenge. If you take the trouble to do the exercises the way the author suggests, they will change your life."
—Robert Rich, M.Sc., Ph.D., M.A.P.S., A.A.S.H.

Loving Healing Press
5145 Pontiac Trail
Ann Arbor, MI 48105
(734)662 6864
info@LovingHealing.com
Dist.: Baker & Taylor

Pub. April 2005 — 180 pp trade/paper — 7"x9"
ISBN 13 978 1 932690 05 7— $16.95 Retail
Includes biblio., resources, and index.
For general and academic libraries.
http:/www.LifeSkillsBook.com

Exclusive offer for readers of Beyond Trauma

Loving Healing Press

Share the experience of
*Beyond Trauma: Conversations on
TIR* with a colleague, friend,
or loved one.

Order direct from the publisher
with this form and save!

Got Parts?	**An Insider's Guide to Managing Life Successfully with Dissociative Identity Disorder**

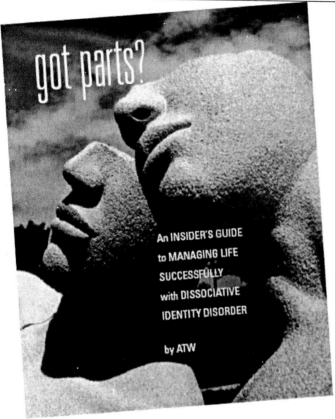

Dissociative Identity Disorder (DID) (a.k.a Multiple Personality Disorder) is now understood to be a fairly common outcome of severe trauma in children below seven years of age: most typically extreme and repeated physical, sexual, and/or emotional abuse.

Got Parts was written by a survivor of DID in conjunction with her therapist and therapy group. Got Parts is filled with successful strategies, coping techniques, and helpful ways to increase the day to day functioning of adult survivors of DID in relationships, work, parenting, self confidence, and self care.

Praise for *Got Parts?*

"Got Parts is an excellent book: it is wonderfully clear, concise and compassionate. I have worked full time with MPD clients for 15 years and this book would be the first required reading." —Karen Hutchins, MA LPC, Cicada Recovery Services

"I think Got Parts is an excellent resource for helping people bring order out of internal chaos. It is reassuring, clear, direct, and hopeful." —Pat Sherman, LCSW

"Got Parts represents a systematic, structured program geared towards positive results for those labeled DID." —James Walter Clifton, M.S., Ph.D. LCSW, LMHC

"Got Parts is firmly grounded in state of the art knowledge about this disorder. Recommended." —Sam Vaknin, Ph.D.

Pub. Jan. 2005 • 136 pp trade/paper • 6"x9" • ISBN-10 1-932690-03-4 • $16.95 Retail
http://www.GotParts.org

Traumatic Incident Reduction, 2ⁿᵈ Edition

By Gerald French and Chrys J. Harris

Traumatic Incident Reduction (TIR) explores a powerful regressive, repetitive, desensitization procedure becoming known in the therapeutic community as an extremely effective tool for use in the rapid resolution of virtually all trauma-related conditions. Replete with case histories and accounts of actual TIR sessions, this book provides a "camera-level" view of TIR by describing the experience of performing TIR.

"TIR emphasizes empowerment of the client; it is an excellent technique for viewing one's old trauma and processing them. This book is a superb description of the technique. It is a considerable contribution to the field of trauma therapy, and I have been enriched by this book."

Shabtai Noy, Ph.D, Senior clinical and school psychologist, Jerusalem, ISRAEL

"Wonderful ... French & Harris provide a wealth of information not only on handling clients suffering from known traumata and their sequellae, but also on ways and means of effectively addressing feelings, emotions, sensations, attitudes, beliefs and pains that have their roots in frequently forgotten incidents from the past."

Alex D Frater, M.A.H.A., C.T.S.,
Former Vice President, Australian Hypnotherapy Assoc.
Campbelltown NSW, AUSTRALIA

"Not just another technique for 'management' or 'assimilation' of intrusive trauma symptoms, TIR actually pulls PTSD, anxiety and panic disorders out by their roots, once and for all! In 30+ years of clinical practice, I've never known or used a more remarkably efficient and effective procedure."

Robert H. Moore, Ph.D., Clearwater, FL

"Recommended for the lay counselor, as well as, for the professional therapist as an insight into how trauma is integrated into current and past experiences."

Bonnie Griffith, Valparaiso, IN

Pub. May 2005 • 200 pp trade/paper • 6"x9" • ISBN-10 1-932690-06-9 • $29.95 Retail

Loving Healing Press
www.LovingHealing.com

Printed in the United Kingdom
by Lightning Source UK Ltd.
111657UKS00001B/1-6

9 781932 690040